Creating a New "Great Divide": The Exoticization of Ancient Culture in Some Recent Applications of Orality Studies to the Bible

PAUL S. EVANS
pevans@mcmaster.ca
McMaster Divinity College, McMaster University, Hamilton, ON L8S 4K1, Canada

One of the main contributions of orality studies in Old Testament/Hebrew Bible studies has been to reject the thesis of the "great divide," which posited a gulf between oral and written cultures of the ancient world. While critique of the thesis is to be welcomed, some of the criticisms have set up an artificial great divide of their own. This new divide exoticizes ancient culture by exaggerating the differences between modern and ancient cultures. I caution against this trend and show that this exoticizing of ancient culture can be seen in the perceived function of ancient and modern texts and the perceived differences between the mind-set of ancient literates and modern literates. I suggest that a balanced approach needs to take into account the complexity of both orality and literacy in reconstructing the function of scribes and their texts in ancient Israelite circles.

In recent years there has been a resurgence in orality studies as applied to the study of the Old Testament/Hebrew Bible.[1] This focus on oral dimensions of biblical texts has drawn on the burgeoning field of orality and literacy studies,

The nucleus of this essay was presented at the Annual Congress of the Canadian Society of Biblical Studies, which met in Ottawa, Canada, in June 2015. I would like to thank Mark Leuchter (Temple University) and Ehud Ben Zvi (University of Alberta) for their helpful comments.

[1] I have called this a resurgence since a focus on the oral characteristics of biblical books is not really new at all. In the past scholars have uncovered vestiges of an oral past in the Old Testament/Hebrew Bible texts. These endeavors spawned classical form-critical approaches, which focused on the (preliterary) oral dimensions of biblical texts. Form critics often began with a study of the form and then turned to look for analogies in both ancient and modern cultures (e.g., Hermann Gunkel, *The Legends of Genesis* [New York: Schocken, 1966; German original, 1901]). Similarly, the recent resurgence of interest in the oral dimensions of biblical texts shares similar concerns in looking for analogous cultural models to help make sense of the biblical material.

749

the foundations of which were laid by the seminal work of Milman Parry and Albert Lord, along with the scholars of the so-called Toronto school, namely, Harold Innis, Marshall McLuhan, Eric Havelock, and Walter J. Ong.[2] A theory owing to the legacy of these pioneering scholars has been that of the "great divide" that contrasts oral cultures and literate ones to the extent that a chasm between them is envisioned. That is, the orality affected only preliterary traditions and had no effect on traditions once they reached written form. This great-divide theory has triggered significant debate over the years, particularly regarding theories of the development of cultures and civilization.[3] The writings of the Toronto school led to the dominance of this theory, even though among these pioneering scholars there was no unanimity regarding its existence or its putative "greatness."

Some revisionist work in the area of orality and literacy has contested the great-divide theory. One area in which this has been vigorously argued is in the area of compositional styles, with many emphasizing continuity between oral and literate cultures and suggesting that oral traditions continued to exist alongside and to interact with literate traditions.[4] Another contested claim concerns the assertion that oral and written cultures were almost universally different, implying not only cultural differences but the psychological superiority of the latter.[5] In this vein, some

---

[2] Milman Parry, *L'épithète traditionnelle dans Homère: Essai sur un problème de style homérique* (Paris: Les Belles Lettres, 1928); Albert Bates Lord, *The Singer of Tales*, Harvard Studies in Comparative Literature 24 (Cambridge: Harvard University Press, 1960); Harold Adams Innis, *The Bias of Communication* (Toronto: University of Toronto Press, 1951); Eric Alfred Havelock, *The Muse Learns to Write: Reflections on Orality and Literacy from Antiquity to the Present* (New Haven: Yale University Press, 1986); Marshall McLuhan and Bruce R. Powers, *The Global Village: Transformations in World Life and Media in the 21st Century* (New York: Oxford University Press, 1989); Walter J. Ong, *Orality and Literacy: The Technologizing of the Word* (London: Methuen, 1982). Running parallel to these theorists was the work of anthropologist Jack Goody, whose fieldwork seemed to confirm the foundational theoretical work. See Goody, *The Domestication of the Savage Mind*, Themes in the Social Sciences (Cambridge: Cambridge University Press, 1977); Goody, *The Interface between the Written and the Oral*, Studies in Literacy, Family, Culture, and the State (Cambridge: Cambridge University Press, 1987); Goody, *The Power of the Written Tradition*, Smithsonian Series in Ethnographic Inquiry (Washington, DC: Smithsonian Institution Press, 2000).

[3] J. J. Blom refers to the great-divide theory as "primitivism" (review of *Orality and Literacy: The Technologizing of the Word*, by Walter J. Ong, *English Studies* 64 [1983]: 182–85).

[4] Twyla Gibson, "The Philosopher's Art: Ring Composition and Classification in Plato's Sophist and Hipparchus," in *Orality and Literacy: Reflections across Disciplines*, ed. Keith Thor Carlson, Kristina Fagan, and Natalia Khanenko-Frieson (Toronto: University of Toronto Press, 2011), 73–109, here 74.

[5] E.g., Marshall McLuhan, *The Gutenberg Galaxy: The Making of Typographic Man* (Toronto: University of Toronto Press, 1962); Eric Alfred Havelock, *Preface to Plato* (Oxford: Blackwell, 1963); Claude Lévi-Strauss, *The Savage Mind* (Chicago: University of Chicago Press, 1966). See the critiques by Ruth Finnegan, *Literacy and Orality: Studies in the Technology of Communication* (Oxford: Blackwell, 1988). See also the essays in Carlson, Fagan, and Khanenko-Frieson, *Orality and Literacy: Reflections across Disciplines*.

have denigrated the great-divide theory as "primitivism"[6] insofar as it discriminates against nonliterates by underscoring the achievements of literate cultures.[7] Furthermore, the writings of the Toronto school have sometimes been criticized for their technological determinism, assumptions of evolutionary normativism, and the coherence of their work with ideas of Western European exceptionalism.[8] Some proponents of the great divide can be read as suggesting that the development of writing was essential for the development of civilization and for the higher evolution of human consciousness.[9] In order to counter this bias, some studies have underscored the achievements of nonliterate societies (e.g., the Inca civilization) in order to offset the evolutionary aspects of the theory.[10] Most, however, have stayed away from the extremes, and many recent studies have pointed out that these implications are not inherent in the work of the Toronto school.[11]

Within the last twenty or so years, explicitly biblical studies have also criticized the great-divide hypothesis on several fronts and have underscored the intensely oral character of the culture of ancient Israel.[12] Such studies maintain that recognizing this pervasive orality is essential for the interpretation of the biblical text and is a corrective to the assumption that orality was relevant only to a preliterary stage.[13] Against the view that such a gulf separates oral and literate cultures, it has been suggested that the relation of orality and literacy be understood as a continuum of sorts, rather than a line in the sand.[14] Along this continuum, oral and

[6] Blom, review of *Orality and Literacy*, 183; similarly, Finnegan, *Literacy and Orality*, 12–14.

[7] R. J. Connors counters this view as "narrow and discriminatory" (review of *The Muse Learns to Write: Reflections on Orality and Literacy from Antiquity to the Present*, by Eric A. Havelock, *Quarterly Journal of Speech* 73 [1988]: 380). Cf. Brian V. Street, *Literacy in Theory and Practice*, CSOLC 9 (Cambridge: Cambridge University Press, 1984), 183; Paul A. Soukup, "Orality and Literacy 25 Years Later," *Communication Research Trends* 26 (2007): 2–32, here 8.

[8] Keith Thor Carlson, Kristina Fagan, and Natalia Khanenko-Frieson, "Introduction: Reading and Listening at Batoche," in Carlson, Fagan, and Khanenko-Frieson, *Orality and Literacy*, 7–8.

[9] Ibid., 7.

[10] E.g., Finnegan, *Literacy and Orality*.

[11] E.g., Thomas J. Farrell, *Walter Ong's Contributions to Cultural Studies: The Phenomenology of the Word and I–Thou Communication*, Hampton Press Communication Series (Cresskill, NJ: Hampton, 2000), 16–26, 156–63; R. L. Enos, review of *The Muse Learns to Write: Reflections on Orality and Literacy from Antiquity to the Present*, by Eric A. Havelock, *Rhetoric Society Quarterly* 17 (1987): 209–12, here 209–10; Deborah Tannen, "The Commingling of Orality and Literacy in Giving a Paper at a Scholarly Conference," *American Speech* 63 (1988): 34–43, here 40–42; Soukup, "Orality and Literacy," 8.

[12] E.g., Susan Niditch, *Oral World and Written Word: Israelite Literature*, LAI (Louisville: Westminster John Knox, 1996); Raymond F. Person, "The Ancient Israelite Scribe as Performer," *JBL* 117 (1998): 601–9, https://doi.org/10.2307/3266629; David M. Carr, *Writing on the Tablet of the Heart: Origins of Scripture and Literature* (Oxford: Oxford University Press, 2005).

[13] Niditch, *Oral World*, 3.

[14] Ibid., 108–30. Similarly, Carr critiques the great-divide theory and places his study in a

literate cultures interacted and influenced each other on a sliding scale. That is, the influence of orality was felt even when texts were being composed, and literacy and orality existed side by side, each influencing the other.

Studies following this lead posit the influence of orality even on late Israelite literature, given the largely oral context of postexilic Israelite culture. Even when texts were being written and copied, they largely *functioned* orally. Texts were used as aids in oral performance, rather than as repositories of information or texts actually meant to be read. Similarly, due to these needs and priorities, scribes largely functioned as "performers" rather than copyists, and the texts they produced are best seen as scribal "performances." Oral culture was so influential that the scribes who composed and copied biblical books, though literate, had an "oral mind-set" that would not have perceived the idea of variation and change in the same way as would a modern literate person.[15] This putative oral mind-set may not only account for what we perceive as textual variants in the manuscript evidence for biblical books but may even explain divergences in the MT itself between, for example, Chronicles and its putative *Vorlage*, the Deuteronomic History.

In my judgment, this area of research has pushed Hebrew Bible scholarship in the right direction: a reassessment of the so-called great-divide thesis is warranted. Some of the assertions and conclusions offered in place of a great divide, however, also merit critical attention. In this essay, I will show not only that some of these latter claims are based on a failure to take into account the full range of relevant historical data in ancient Israel but also that some of what has been said in denigration of a great-divide thesis has in fact set up another artificial great divide of its own: between ancient and modern cultures. This new divide exoticizes ancient culture in a way that exaggerates the differences between modern and ancient cultures.[16] This outcome is evident especially in assertions regarding the differing functions of ancient and modern texts and in the differing mind-sets of ancient literates and modern literates.

Through detailed examination of these positions and consideration of ancient historical evidence as well as modern analogues, this study will demonstrate the artificial nature of this new construction of the relationship between orality and

---

"stream of scholarship that emphasizes ways societies with writing often have an intricate interplay of orality and textuality, where written texts are intensely oral, while even exclusively oral texts are deeply affected by written culture" (*Writing on the Tablet of the Heart*, 7).

[15] Person, "Ancient Israelite Scribe," 601–9; Person, "The Role of Memory in the Tradition Represented by the Deuteronomic History and the Book of Chronicles," *Oral Tradition* 26 (2011): 537–50; Person, *The Deuteronomic History and the Book of Chronicles: Scribal Works in an Oral World*, AIL 6 (Atlanta: Society of Biblical Literature, 2010), 41–51.

[16] Larry W. Hurtado, "Oral Fixation and New Testament Studies? 'Orality,' 'Performance' and Reading Texts in Early Christianity," *NTS* 60 (2014): 321–40, here 324. Werner Kelber similarly speculates that "orality-literacy studies could likewise arouse the suspicion of reinventing a romanticized past" ("In the Beginning Were the Words: The Apotheosis and Narrative Displacement of the Logos," *JAAR* 58 [1990]: 69–98, here 70).

literacy. I will suggest that any approach to these issues needs to take into account the complexity of both orality and literacy in reconstructing the function of scribes and their texts in ancient Israelite circles.

I. The New Great Divide: Differing Functions of Ancient and Modern Texts

Texts to Be Performed—Not Read

Several Hebrew Bible scholars who reject the great-divide theory have accentuated the differences between how texts functioned in the ancient world and how they function today. It has been suggested that, rather than function as repositories of information, ancient texts had as their main purpose to aid memorization or oral performance.[17] In this vein, it is further asserted that, unlike modern texts, ancient texts were *not* designed actually to be read.[18] This position is often defended by pointing to the material form of ancient texts, such as:

1. Scrolls were difficult to navigate, requiring unrolling and rerolling.[19]
2. Many texts had no spaces between words (e.g., Greek uncial texts were written in all capitals with no spaces).
3. Ancient Semitic texts lacked vowel markers (with only consonants represented in the script).
4. Texts written using the Sumero-Akkadian cuneiform system required the memorization of thousands of syllabic images or forms in order to read.

These perceived limitations of the physical presentation of texts have led some to conclude that ancient readers must have already memorized these texts in order to read them.[20] Ironically, while such studies attempt to counter anachronistic models of ancient texts and ancient reading based on our own experiences in a print culture, these perceived difficulties in reading ancient scrolls are themselves anachronistic.[21] The fact that we moderns might have difficulty in reading these ancient scrolls does not mean that ancient users did so. To a modern reader (like myself), who is accustomed to reading a modern book, the use of a scroll would seem

---

[17] E.g., David M. Carr, "Torah on the Heart: Literary Jewish Textuality within Its Ancient Near Eastern Context," *Oral Tradition* 25 (2010): 17–39, here 19.

[18] E.g., Carr, *Writing on the Tablet of the Heart*, 4, 6.

[19] E.g., ibid., 98.

[20] Carr writes, "The visual presentation of such texts presupposed that the reader already knew the given text and had probably memorized it to some extent" (ibid., 5). Carr allows that "some masters of the tradition could sight-read such texts," but most could not (ibid., 4).

[21] Ibid., 14.

awkward indeed. Even when the codex was invented, however, most people continued to prefer the scroll over the codex for quite some time.[22] This point suggests that they did not find reading scrolls as difficult as we might today.[23]

Regarding the uncial form or *scriptio continua* instead of word separation, there is evidence that in Greek and Latin manuscripts this form was actually preferred by readers, who considered its format elegant.[24] Furthermore, Greek uncials did make accommodations to readers by making columns of narrow lines (ca. fifteen to twenty letters), beginning each subsequent sentence/verse in a column slightly to the left of where the first letter on the previous line began, in order to help the reader more quickly find the next unit (prose texts), or setting out poetic texts to reflect their poetic structure.[25] Furthermore, ancient Aramaic and Hebrew epigraphic texts clearly use word dividers to accommodate readers (see Tel Dan Stela; Mesha Stela).[26]

Regarding the lack of marked vowels in ancient Semitic texts, this is clearly projecting the concerns of a modern reader of texts written in a Latin alphabet, which contains distinct letters for vowels, onto the ancient reader. In fact, Semitic languages do not share this concern. Modern Hebrew and Arabic do not print vowels despite the sophistication of modern printing, which is quite capable of doing so. This is perhaps not as much an anachronistic concern as an ethnocentric one.

Regarding the impediment of the requirements of readers to memorize thousands of syllabic images, forms, or phrases and words in order to read a text, this is, again, placing modern perceptions of this difficulty on the ancient reader. In fact, the situation is no different today, despite our texts being much more "reader friendly." Whether we realize it or not, modern readers do exactly this. No competent reader "sounds" out words in a text but instead recognizes words and phrases automatically. This is what is known as automaticity of word recognition, without which reading any text would be tedious.[27] All this is to say that the physical form of scrolls does *not* actually appear to demonstrate that these texts were not really meant to be read but only used by those who had already memorized them or that they only functioned to aid memorization.

---

[22] Hurtado, "Oral Fixation?," 324.

[23] Ibid., 330.

[24] Ibid., 328.

[25] Ibid., 329. See, e.g., E. G. Turner, *Greek Manuscripts of the Ancient World*, 2nd rev. and enl. ed., ed. P. J. Parsons (London: University of London, Institute of Classical Studies, 1987), pl. 84 (Phaedrus) and pl. 31 (Euripides). See also Hurtado, "Oral Fixation?," 329.

[26] Contra Carr, who incorrectly asserts that it is not until the Hellenistic period that we find "texts with word-separation" (*Writing on the Tablet of the Heart*, 4).

[27] G. Brian Thompson, William E. Tunmer, and Tom Nicholson, eds., *Reading Acquisition Processes*, Language and Education Library (Clevedon, UK: Multilingual Matters, 1993).

II. The New Great Divide: Differences between Ancient and Modern Scribes

Ancient Scribes Were Performers

One of the differences between ancient and modern cultures asserted by some scholars drawing on orality studies has been that ancient scribes were not copyists but "performers" and that each textual manuscript was a scribal "performance."[28] By *performance* scholars seem to mean something like ancient oral delivery (rather than the reading of these texts) with texts being recited from memory and presuming interaction with their audiences.[29] Several studies on Hebrew Bible texts have been published employing so-called performance criticism and reflect the assumptions and conclusions of this line of research.[30] Raymond F. Person has summed up the concept in this way:

> The ancient Israelite scribes were literate members of a primarily oral society.... When they copied their texts, the ancient Israelite scribes did not slavishly write the texts word by word, but preserved the texts' meaning for the ongoing life of their communities in much the same way that performers of oral epic re-present the stable, yet dynamic, tradition to their communities. In this sense, the ancient Israelite scribes were not mere copyists but were also performers.[31]

Despite their potential for stimulating new perspectives on old questions, such assertions regarding ancient scribes as performers and texts as scribal performances lack clarity. Performance requires an audience, and it is not clear who that perceived audience is thought to be. David M. Carr seems to suggest that the

---

[28] Carr, *Writing on the Tablet of the Heart*, 44; Person, "Ancient Israelite Scribe," 602; Niditch, *Oral World*, 117–25.

[29] Carr, *Writing on the Tablet of the Heart*, 292; Person, "Ancient Israelite Scribe," 602.

[30] See Robert D. Miller II, "Orality and Performance in Ancient Israel," *RSR* 86 (2012): 183–94; Miller, "Oral Performance in Ancient Israel," in *"My Spirit at Rest in the North Country" (Zechariah 6.8): Collected Communications to the XXth Congress of the International Organization for the Study of the Old Testament, Helsinki 2010*, ed. Hermann Michael Niemann and Matthias Augustin, BEATAJ 57 (Frankfurt am Main: Lang, 2011), 229–40; Miller, *Oral Tradition in Ancient Israel*, Biblical Performance Criticism 1 (Eugene, OR: Cascade, 2011); Galen L. Goldsmith, "The Cutting Edge of Prophetic Imagery," *JBPR* 3 (2011): 3–18; Terry Giles and William Doan, *Twice Used Songs: Performance Criticism of the Songs of Ancient Israel* (Peabody, MA: Hendrickson, 2009); Giles and Doan, "Performance Criticism of the Hebrew Bible," *Religion Compass* 2 (2008): 273–86; Giles and Doan, "The Song of Asaph: A Performance-Critical Analysis of 1 Chronicles 16:8–36," *CBQ* 70 (2008): 29–43; Giles and Doan, *Prophets, Performance, and Power: Performance Criticism of the Hebrew Bible* (New York: T&T Clark, 2005); Carole R. Fontaine, "The Proof of the Pudding: Proverbs and Gender in the Performance Arena," *JSOT* 29 (2005): 179–204.

[31] Person, "Ancient Israelite Scribe," 602.

audience consisted largely of other scribes: "Scribal performances of traditions would have been corrected as often from parallel performances within a network of scribal masters as from consultation of a written version of a tradition."[32] This seems to posit that the reading or recitation of traditions by a scribal master would have corrected other "readings" or recitations of tradition rather than refer to a text. In other words, literate scribes would "perform" a text in such a way that other literate scribes might "correct" their performance in light of a master scribe. Susan Niditch also underscores the role of oral performance but appears to envision a wider audience than does Carr. She suggests that biblical traditions "were performed to audiences, *taking basic shape in content and theme in response* to the audiences who hear the performances."[33] Similarly, Person appears to have in mind the broader community as audience in that he compares their role to "performers of oral epic" who "re-present the stable, yet dynamic, tradition to their communities."[34]

New Testament scholars have made similar claims regarding New Testament texts as "performance literature," suggesting that in communicating Scripture, often no written text was employed (or perhaps one was present but not consulted) as the texts "were originally composed and experienced orally."[35] The situation with the composition and transmission of the New Testament, however, is quite different from that concerning the Hebrew Bible. The New Testament was written in Koine Greek, that is, the Greek of the common people. Postexilic Hebrew Bible books (the ones in view in most of this scholarly discussion) were written in Hebrew at a time when Aramaic had virtually replaced Hebrew as the language of the common person. This may not be as problematic for the model posited by Niditch, as the texts she has in mind ("stories about the patriarchs and matriarchs; portions of the exodus story; some of the tales of the judges") for this model are classically thought to be preexilic.[36] Yet discussions of the oral performance of postexilic texts such as Chronicles (or Samuel–Kings in Person's view) are more problematic.[37] Suggestions that postexilic texts were primarily for performance does not take into account the fact that Hebrew as a living language died in this period. This loss of the Hebrew language is reflected in the book of Nehemiah, wherein the Levites and Ezra have to translate the Torah into Aramaic in order for the people to understand (Neh 8:7–8). The extent to which Hebrew was replaced by Aramaic among Jews living in

---

[32] Carr, *Writing on the Tablet of the Heart*, 292.

[33] Niditch, *Oral World*, 120 (emphasis added).

[34] Person, "Ancient Israelite Scribe," 602.

[35] David Roads, "Biblical Performance Criticism: Performance as Research," *Oral Tradition* 25 (2010): 157–98, here 157.

[36] Niditch, *Oral World*, 120. Of course, not all scholars today would agree that these portions of Genesis, Exodus, and Judges were written before the exile.

[37] Person views both the Deuteronomic History and Chronicles as contemporaneous, postexilic, competing histories (*Deuteronomic History and the Book of Chronicles*, 1–2).

Palestine during the Persian and Hellenistic period has been debated in scholarship, but there is a general consensus that Aramaic replaced Hebrew in the Persian period (thus the need for targumim).[38] In light of this language reality, it is difficult to envision how texts written in Standard Biblical Hebrew (or Classical Hebrew) were "performances" to the community. How, then, can the transmission or composition of Hebrew texts be explained as performance when there is no audience?

Ancient Scribes Had an Oral Mind-Set

Another area in which differences between ancient and modern cultures have been exaggerated is in the area of their putative mind-sets. Person has championed the view that the mind-set of ancient literate scribes would be quite different from a modern literate mind-set due to the effect of the largely oral culture of which the ancient Israelite scribe was a part.[39] In other words, he posits something like an "illiterate scribe" who, though literate, had an oral mind-set.

In his work, Person has relied heavily on the early twentieth-century work of Lord and Parry, who, in interviews with illiterate Serbo-Croatian poets, found that a poet may consider a *phrase* to be a single *word* and that the phrase when repeated, even though it contained variation from the first phrase, was considered to be the same word.[40] For clarity's sake I will quote part of the interview.

> NIKOLA: Let's consider this: "Vino pije licki Mustajbeze" ("Mustajbeg of Lika was drinking wine"). Is this a single word?
> MUJO: Yes.
> N: But how? It can't be *one*: "Vino pije licki Mustajbeze."
> M: In writing it can't be one.
> N: There are four words here.

---

[38] See William M. Schniedewind, "Aramaic, the Death of Written Hebrew, and Language Shift in the Persian Period," in *Margins of Writing, Origins of Cultures*, ed. Seth L. Sanders, University of Chicago Oriental Institute Seminars 2 (Chicago: University of Chicago Press, 2006), 137–47; Joachim Schaper, "Hebrew and Its Study in the Persian Period," in *Hebrew Study from Ezra to Ben-Yehuda*, ed. William Horbury (Edinburgh: T&T Clark, 1999), 15–26; Angel Sáenz-Badillos, *A History of the Hebrew Language* (Cambridge: Cambridge University Press, 1993), 112–13; Chaim Rabin, "The Historical Background of Qumran Hebrew," in *Aspects of the Dead Sea Scrolls*, ed. Chaim Rabin and Yigael Yadin, ScrHier 4 (Jerusalem: Magnes, 1958), 144–61.

[39] For example, Person has asserted this first in his essay "Ancient Israelite Scribe," which was reprinted as chapter 4 of *The Deuteronomic School: History, Social Setting, and Literature*, StBibLit 2 (Atlanta: Society of Biblical Literature, 2002), 83–97. Person once again restates (and partially republished verbatim) these ideas in *Deuteronomic History and the Book of Chronicles*, 43–51.

[40] Niditch's model of oral performance (*Oral World*, 120) also partially relies on Lord and Parry, though, contra Lord and Parry, she emphasizes the continual interplay of orality and literacy (119).

> M: It can't be one in writing. But here, let's say we're at my house and I pick up the *gusle* [a traditional single-stringed instrument]—"Pije vino licki Mus-tajbeze"—that's a single word on the *gusle* for me.
> N: And the second word?
> M: And the second word—"Na Ribniku u pjanoj mehani" ("At Ribnik in a drinking tavern")—there.⁴¹

From this evidence Person has underscored the importance of realizing that oral societies do not understand the lexeme *word* in the same way as do modern societies.⁴² In fact, to an oral mind-set "one word" can mean a phrase or larger discourse. Person writes, "In this interview, we can see a clash of cultures as the literate Yugoslav insists that [four literal words] is not one word but four, while the oral poet insists that it is only one word."⁴³

Person further points out that the Hebrew term דבר has a similar flexibility in its semantic range, as it can mean a word, a commandment, a happening, an affair, and so on. Thus, he cautions:

> We must keep in mind, however, that the ancient Israelite unit of meaning or "word" may not correspond to our own highly literate understanding of "word" as we struggle to understand more about the primarily oral culture in which the ancient Israelite scribes lived and worked.⁴⁴

While I do not wish to dispute the flexibility of the semantic range of דבר, it must be pointed out that the same flexibility exists in the English lexeme *word*. The following examples should suffice: "he sent word he would be late"; "she kept her word"; "he is a man of his word"; "we just received word of her return"; "spread the word that she is leaving"; "word on the street is …" "put in a good word for me"; "word is that they are hiring"; "wait till I give the word"; or "I would like to have a word with you."

Given the similar semantic flexibility in the English lemma *word* and in the Hebrew דבר, there seems to be little rationale to suggest that this flexibility is indicative of Hebrew scribes possessing an ancient oral mind-set that was more comfortable with variation and less concerned with exact detail than is the case with a literate mind-set.⁴⁵

---

⁴¹ Cited in Person, "Ancient Israelite Scribe," 603; Person, *Deuteronomic School*, 90; Person, *Deuteronomic History and the Book of Chronicles*, 48.

⁴² Person, *Deuteronomic History and the Book of Chronicles*, 49.

⁴³ Person, "Ancient Israelite Scribe," 604; Person, *Deuteronomic School*, 90; Person, *Deuteronomic History and the Book of Chronicles*, 48.

⁴⁴ Person, "Ancient Israelite Scribe," 604; Person, *Deuteronomic School*, 90; Person, *Deuteronomic History and the Book of Chronicles*, 48.

⁴⁵ While this interview with the Serbian musician/poet is interesting and suggestive to an extent, in my judgment all this interview really shows is that, in this *somewhat* modern interview, one musician/poet [guslar-ist] has considered a "word" to be *not* literally a word and that a change in a sentence really was "no change." Furthermore, it is clear that the musician/poet says this is so

Regarding the oral mind-set of literate scribes, the same fieldwork by Parry and Lord on which Person relies actually denied the possibility of what I have called an illiterate scribe.[46] Lord clearly concluded:

> The written technique ... is not compatible with the oral technique, and the two could not possibly combine, to form another, a third, a "transitional" technique. It is conceivable that a man might be an oral poet in his younger years and a written poet later in life, but it is not possible that he be both an oral and a written poet at any given time in his career. The two by their very nature are mutually exclusive.[47]

In fact, Lord held that the advent of writing in society had an inexorably adverse effect on oral tradition.[48] Thus, according to the Parry–Lord school, an illiterate scribe is not only an oxymoron but an impossibility.

Walter Ong has examined the effect of the onset of literacy on the oral mind-set, taking into account a broad range of fieldwork with literate and illiterate subjects.[49] Ong shows that this fieldwork has actually underscored the differences between a completely illiterate person and someone with even slight literacy.[50] This is evident in the differences between nonliterate and even slightly literate subjects in terms of abstract thinking, categorization, logic, defining terms, and articulating self-analysis.[51]

The fieldwork of Aleksandr Romanovich Luria, for example, found that nonliterate persons strongly resisted requests for word defnitions. An illiterate peasant is asked, "Try to explain to me what a tree is," and the response is, "Why should I? Everyone knows what a tree is; they don't need me telling them."[52] Another illiterate person is asked to define a car: "Say you go to a place where there are no cars.

---

only when he is composing or singing—for he says "but here, [when] I pick up my [instrument] ... that's a single word on the [instrument] for me" (Person, "Ancient Israelite Scribe," 603; Person, *Deuteronomic School*, 90; Person, *Deuteronomic History and the Book of Chronicles*, 48.) This *extremely limited example* and such outdated research cannot bear the weight of the argument based on it. In fact, this overreliance on Parry and Lord has been noted by Carr, who writes, "Person remains remarkably dependent on the Parry–Lord hypothesis of oral composition and 'oral mentality,' while much recent scholarship on the oral–written interface has moved beyond" (review of *The Deuteronomic School: History, Social Setting, and Literature*, by Raymond F. Person, *JNES* 63 [2004]: 301–3, here 303).

[46] Parry, *L'épithète traditionnelle*; Lord, *Singer of Tales*.
[47] Lord, *Singer of Tales*, 129.
[48] Ibid., 124–38.
[49] Ong, *Orality and Literacy*, 31–73.
[50] Ibid., 50. Cf. Aleksandr Romanovich Luria, *Cognitive Development: Its Cultural and Social Foundations*, trans. Martin Lopez-Morillas and Lynn Solotaroff (Cambridge: Harvard University Press, 1976); J. C. Carothers, "Culture, Psychiatry, and the Written Word," *Psychiatry* 22 (1959): 307–20.
[51] Ong, *Orality and Literacy*, 50–54.
[52] Ibid., 52; Luria, *Cognitive Development*, 86.

What will you tell people [a car is]?" The response was basically, "when you get right down to it, I'd say: 'If you get in a car and go for a drive, you'll find out.'"[53] When the slightly literate subject is asked the same question, however, he responded, "It's made in a factory. In one trip it can cover the distance it would take a horse ten days to make—it moves that fast. It uses fire and steam. We first have to set the fire going so the water gets steaming hot—the steam gives the machine its power.... I don't know whether there is water in a car, must be. But water isn't enough, it also needs fire."[54]

Luria also offers an example in which an illiterate peasant is given a syllogism and asked to respond. "In the Far North, where there is snow, all bears are white. Novaya Zembla is in the Far North and there is always snow there. What color are the bears there?"[55] The response: "I don't know; I've seen a black bear. I've never seen any others.... Each locality has its own animals."[56] When the syllogism is asked of a young farmer who was "barely literate," however, he responded, "You say that it's cold there [in Novaya Zembla] and there's snow, so the bears there are white."[57] Similarly, a middle-aged, barely literate farmer responds, "To go by your words, they should all be white."[58] All this is to say that a move toward literacy does appear to have a significant effect on thinking and reasoning.[59]

Ong is not alone in attributing a tremendous cognitive change in an illiterate who becomes literate. The work of anthropologist Jack Goody, who collected evidence from African tribal communities, also found a lack of logical/syllogistic reasoning among illiterate individuals.[60] The same conclusion has been drawn by ethnographers and communication theorists.[61] If, in fact, there is a great difference between a nonliterate and a slightly literate mind-set, caution must be taken in attributing a nonliterate mind-set to a highly literate individual such as, for example, the author(s) of Chronicles.

It is also true, however, that the ascendancy of literacy does not remove all residue of orality. In other words, the results of this fieldwork or Ong's conclusions

---

[53] Luria, *Cognitive Development*, 87; cf. Ong, *Orality and Literacy*, 53.

[54] Luria, *Cognitive Development*, 90; cf. Ong, *Orality and Literacy*, 53.

[55] Luria, *Cognitive Development*, 108.

[56] Ibid., 109. As Ong comments, in the illiterate peasant's view, "You find what color bears are by looking at them. Who ever heard of reasoning out in practical life the color of a polar bear?" (*Orality and Literacy*, 52).

[57] Luria, *Cognitive Development*, 113; cf. Ong, *Orality and Literacy*, 52.

[58] Luria, *Cognitive Development*, 114.

[59] As Ong puts it, "A little literacy goes a long way" (*Orality and Literacy*, 52).

[60] Goody, *Interface between the Written and the Oral*, 205; cf. Goody, *Power of the Written Word*; Goody, *Domestication of the Savage Mind*.

[61] Gibson, "Philosopher's Art," 43. For another study that has underscored the effects literacy has on nonliterates, see David R. Olson and Nancy Torrance, *Literacy and Orality* (Cambridge: Cambridge University Press, 1991).

should not be overstretched to support or prove the great-divide theory.[62] Ong himself emphasized the ongoing effects of orality and talked about cultures carrying "an overwhelmingly massive oral residue,"[63] even going so far as to state that "primary orality lingered in residue ... centuries after the invention of writing and even of print."[64] More recent work has underscored the complexity of orality and literacy and has argued against viewing them as mutually exclusive; instead, scholars recognize them as interwoven dimensions of language.[65]

Oral Mind-Sets Were Not Concerned with Exact Repetition

Given that orality has continuing residual effects on literate cultures, to what extent can we posit aspects of an oral mind-set on an ancient Israelite scribe? According to Person, scribes with an oral mind-set preserved tradition in a way that generated variety and fluidity in their texts since, as "performers," scribes allowed variations if the "performance" required. As already noted, drawing on the

---

[62] Some have critiqued Ong's work and suggested that it supports the great-divide theory, e.g., Jonathan Boyarin, "Voices around the Text: The Ethnography of Reading at Mesivta Tifereth Jerusalem," in *The Ethnography of Reading*, ed. Jonathan Boyarin (Berkeley: University of California Press, 1993), 212–38; and, in the same volume, Daniel Boyarin, "Placing Reading: Ancient Israel and Medieval Europe," 10–37. Many have pointed out, however, that Ong in fact did *not* support the great-divide theory. See, e.g., Farrell, *Walter Ong's Contributions*, 16–26, 156–63; Tannen, "Commingling of Orality and Literacy," 40–42. Soukup, *"Orality and Literacy,"* 8. As Enos observes, "So enticing are [Ong's] insights that [they] tempt the reader to over-extend, and over-estimate, the impact of literacy. Perhaps, however, that is a fault resting with the reader rather than with [Ong]. In our eagerness to (at last) offer the scholarly world a clearly stated concept that makes speaking and writing relationships apparent, we have taken the observations of [Ong] more as definitive claims rather than cogently articulated descriptive frameworks waiting for research that will sharpen understanding further" (review of Havelock, *Muse Learns to Write*, 209–10).

[63] Ong himself emphasized the ongoing effects of orality (*Orality and Literacy*, 35; cf. 36, 38, 40) and talked about cultures carrying "an overwhelmingly massive oral residue" (35) and about "early literate culture" having a "massive oral residue" (68). For example, he writes, "Early written texts, through the Middle Ages and the Renaissance, are often bloated with 'amplification,' annoyingly redundant by modern standards. Concern with *copia* remains intense in western culture so long as the culture sustains massive oral residue" (40).

[64] Ibid., 74. Cf. Myron C. Tuman, "Words, Tools, and Technology (review of Walter Ong's *Orality and Literacy: The Technology of the Word*)," *College English* 45 (1983): 769–79. Despite the changes that literacy brings to the oral mind-set, Ong asserts that orality does not disappear since it is natural to humans (while writing is not) (*Orality and Literacy*, 109–12). Cf. Soukup, *"Orality and Literacy,"* 5.

[65] Tannen, "Commingling of Orality and Literacy," 42. Cf. D. L. Rubin et al., "Reading and Listening to Oral-Based Versus Literate-Based Discourse," *Communication Education* 49 (2000): 121–33; Soukup, *"Orality and Literacy,"* 9. These scholars also do not read Ong as holding to a great-divide theory. In their own work, however, Tannen and Rubin have moved away from using terminology like "orality-literacy" to avoid the confusion that they might be ascribing to a great-divide theory.

fieldwork of Lord, which found that the songs of Serbian poets were never sung the same way twice, Person suggested that this comfort with variation in the repetition of tradition is one aspect of an oral mind-set that affected ancient literati such as the Chronicler.[66] The fieldwork on which this argument relies, however, is insufficient to support it.

First, the presence of variation in the repeated poems of oral poets does not mean that oral poets did not strive for exact repetition. After all, Lord noted that these illiterate singers actually lived in a widely literate culture and admired literacy.[67] In fact, they believed (incorrectly) "that a literate person can do even better what they do, namely, recreate a lengthy song after hearing it only once."[68]

Second, other fieldwork has shown that many nonliterates actually *do* strive for verbatim repetition. For example, among the nonliterate people of LoDagaa in Ghana, the "Invocation to the Bagre" was something that everyone knew, yet recordings of the invocation show that the wording varied significantly from recitation to recitation. Researchers found, however, that when *they* recited the invocation among them the LoDagaa would often stop and *correct the researchers' version* if it failed to correspond to what the LoDagaa thought the correct version was.[69] In some communities, concern with verbatim repetition actually varies with different types of oral texts. It has often been observed that longer oral narratives and stories were fairly flexible in their wording, while shorter, poetic (often ritualistic) oral texts were quite fixed. For example, Joel Sherzer found considerable flexibility in the telling of oral narratives and stories among the Kuna of Panama.[70] Similarly, Donald Bahr found that, in Pima oral tradition, long narrative oral texts always included certain facts but allowed variation in their actual wording.[71] Regarding shorter ritual texts, however, Sherzer found that, among the Kuna in magical chants

---

[66] E.g., Person, "Ancient Israelite Scribe," 606. Similarly, Carr has suggested that oral performers "do not aim for absolute verbatim accuracy" or "word-for-word ... reproduction" and suggests that this characteristic may explain textual variants (which he calls "memory variants") in various manuscripts of the Hebrew Bible ("Torah on the Heart," 26).

[67] Lord, *Singer of Tales*, 28.

[68] Ong, *Orality and Literacy*, 60. As Ong notes ironically, "As literates attribute literate kinds of achievement to oral performers, so oral performers attribute oral kinds of achievement to literates" (ibid).

[69] Goody, *Domestication of the Savage Mind*, 118–19.

[70] Joel Sherzer, *Verbal Art in San Blas: Kuna Culture through Its Discourse*, CSOLC 21 (Cambridge: Cambridge University Press, 1990); Sherzer, "Poetic Structuring of Kuna Discourse: The Line," in *Native American Discourse: Poetics and Rhetoric*, ed. Joel Sherzer and Anthony C. Woodbury, CSOLC 13 (Cambridge: Cambridge University Press, 1987). See also Anthony K. Webster, "Keeping the Word: On Orality and Literacy (with a Sideways Glance at Navajo)," *Oral Tradition* 21 (2006): 295–324, here 299.

[71] Donald Bahr, Lloyd Paul, and Vincent Joseph, *Ants and Orioles: Showing the Art of Pima Poetry* (Salt Lake City: University of Utah Press, 1997), 175. The Pima are North American natives who traditionally lived in Arizona along the Salt and Gila Rivers.

or oral puberty rite texts, "not the slightest linguistic variation is tolerated."[72] Similarly, Gary Witherspoon has found that the Navajo strove for verbatim repetition in their prayers.[73] It is possible that with *both* types of oral texts, nonliterates *are* concerned with fixity but that verbatim fixity is achievable only in shorter, poetic texts and not in longer, narrative stories. For example, Ruth Finnegan observed that Fijian oral historians are deeply concerned with maintaining fixed oral narratives and preserving them from change throughout the transmission process.[74] The extent to which they are successful at verbatim repetition of long oral narratives is another issue.

On the basis of these ethnographic studies, it is clear that comfort with variation in the repetition of tradition is *not* indicative of an oral mind-set, as oral peoples may also strive for exact repetition.[75] (This is not to say that verbatim repetition is actually achieved among oral peoples.) Furthermore, these studies have implications for the question of whether ancient biblical writers like the Chronicler had an oral mind-set. If nonliterate people (or those we could say had an oral mind-set) did in fact care about correct repetition—even verbatim repetition—we should be cautious in ascribing to literate scribes a mind-set that was *not* concerned with verbatim repetition. If nonliterates admire literates' ability to repeat things exactly, it must be allowed that a literate scribe may have valued verbatim repetition as well. If the allowance for variation in longer oral narratives (as opposed to shorter ritual texts) was due to the difficulty of maintaining verbatim repetition in lengthy texts, a literate scribe (unlike an oral narrator), working from written traditions, could conceivably have achieved verbatim repetition. Thus, variation in written tradition is not so easily explained as being due to an oral mind-set.

III. Conclusion

I do not intend to be dismissive of orality studies but instead to offer a cautionary corrective regarding their application to biblical studies. The recent resurgence of interest in orality in biblical studies is to be welcomed. Perhaps the pendulum has swung back to concerns Gunkel brought to the fore long ago. The texts we are dealing with reflect living communities that once existed. We should not be

---

[72] Sherzer, "Poetic Structuring," 103; Sherzer, *Verbal Art*, 240 n. 1.

[73] Gary Witherspoon, *Language and Art in the Navajo Universe* (Ann Arbor: University of Michigan Press, 1977); Webster, "Keeping the Word," 298.

[74] Finnegan, *Literacy and Orality*, 86–109. Cf. Gibson, "Philosopher's Art," 8.

[75] Ong, *Orality and Literacy*, 60. Cf. Jeffrey Opland, "Imbongi Nezibongo: The Xhosa Tribal Poet and the Contemporary Poetic Tradition," *PMLA* 90 (1975): 185–208; Opland, "Discussion Following the Paper 'Oral Poetry: Some Linguistic and Typological Considerations,' by Paul Kiparsky," in *Oral Literature and the Formula*, ed. Benjamin A. Stoltz and Richard S. Shannon (Ann Arbor, MI: Center for the Coordination of Ancient and Modern Studies, 1976), 107–25.

surprised, therefore, to see some characteristics of oral origins in the texts themselves. While the theory of a great divide between oral and literate cultures has rightly been questioned, we must be cautious not to put in its place a new great divide that exoticizes ancient cultures and exaggerates differences between ancient and modern literate cultures. In my judgment, recognizing some differences between oral and literate cultures does *not* make one a proponent of the great divide. As fieldwork has shown, literacy does have a powerful effect on nonliterates; therefore, caution needs to be exercised before an oral mind-set is ascribed to a literate scribe. Furthermore, once an oral tradition becomes written tradition, there is at least some difference. After all, even in antiquity the difference between oral and written was acknowledged, as seen in how Socrates (as recorded by Plato) in his dialogue with Phaedrus claimed that "written words go on telling you just the same thing forever" (Plato, *Phaedr.* 275e).

On the other hand, orality surely continued to affect literate cultures (and still does today). The work of Niditch has shown that oral characteristics vary with different types of biblical texts that are located at different places or stages on the orality–literacy continuum. In my judgment, her approach is by and large compatible with the present study, which has exposed extensive variation in oral literature and cautions future studies against treating orality homogeneously.[76] As fieldwork has shown, there is no homogeneity in orality, and neither should we assume homogeneity in literacy.

[76] As Webster notes, treating oral literature homogeneously "would be to miss the subtle ways that oral literature is circulated, replicated, and perpetuated" ("Keeping the Word," 300).

The Date of the Shema (Deuteronomy 6:4–5)

NATHAN MACDONALD
nm10011@cam.ac.uk
St John's College, Cambridge CB2 1TP, United Kingdom

In 1992, Timo Veijola argued that the love commandment in Deut 6:5 was an interpolation into the Shema. On the basis of its vocabulary, he showed it to be consistent with a late Deuteronomistic stratum in Deuteronomy, which he labeled the *Bundestheologische Redaktion* (DtrB). In this essay I argue that Veijola's argument about the integrity of Deut 6:4–5 was based on a misunderstanding of Joüon's Hebrew grammar. Veijola's central insight, however, about the date of Deut 6:5 was sound and can be correlated with further evidence from the vocabulary and reception history of Deut 6:4. Thus, the widely held assumption that Deut 6:4 stood at the head of a Josianic book of Deuteronomy and was the slogan of the Josianic reformation is shown to rest upon precarious foundations.

In 1805, W. M. L. de Wette argued that the book of Deuteronomy was not only the ספר התורה, "the book of the law," discovered in Josiah's reign but also a pious fraud. The original book of Deuteronomy, *Urdeuteronomium*, was essentially a version of the Covenant Code (Exod 21–23) thoroughly revised in light of the principle of cult centralization.[1] From the perspective of the drafters of the

---

The research for this essay was undertaken as part of the Sofja-Kovalevskaja project on early Jewish monotheisms supported by the Alexander von Humboldt Stiftung and the German Federal Ministry of Education and Research. Earlier versions of the paper were given in Göttingen, at King's College London, at the International Organization for the Study of the Old Testament in Munich, and at the Annual Meeting of the Society of Biblical Literature in San Diego, California. I am grateful to everyone who asked questions or made suggestions on those occasions.

[1] W. M. L. de Wette, "Dissertatio critico-exegetica qua Deuteronomium a prioribus Pentateuchi Libris diversum, alius cuiusdam recentioris auctoris opus esse monstratur" (University of Jena, 1805). For the Latin text, German translation, and discussion, see Hans-Peter Mathys, "Wilhelm Martin Leberecht de Wettes 'Dissertatio critico-exegetica' von 1805," in *Biblische Theologie und historisches Denken: Wissenschaftsgeschichtliche Studien aus Anlass der 50. Wiederkehr der Basler Promotion von Rudolf Smend*, ed. Michael Kessler and Martin Wallraff, Studien zur Wissenschaften in Basel 5 (Basel: Schwabe, 2008), 171–211; and for an English translation and discussion, see Paul B. Harvey Jr. and Baruch Halpern, "W. M. L. de Wette's '*Dissertatio*

Deuteronomic Code, sacrifice and other cultic service to YHWH were to take place at only one sanctuary, which, though never explicitly named, was the Jerusalem temple. De Wette's identification was to have significant implications for the scholarly understanding of *Urdeuteronomium*'s literary integrity, not just its date of composition. It is apparent that much of the book's framework is superfluous to the aspirations of the seventh-century reformers. This recognition, together with other indications of the framework's composite nature, has led to industrious attempts to distinguish *Urdeuteronomium* and its various redactional layers. This has proved to be one of the most demanding tasks in critical scholarship and continues to call forth fresh and interesting proposals—though none has secured a broad consensus.[2]

In the early twentieth century, the influential argument was made that *Urdeuteronomium* began with Deut 6:4: "Hear O Israel, YHWH our God YHWH one." The theological affirmation grounded the reform agenda of cultic centralization. As there was to be but one God for Israel, so also there was to be one cultic place.[3] Earlier scholarship was convinced that it was possible to reconstruct an original paraenesis from Deut 6–11, particularly through attention to the presence of *Numeruswechsel*. In more recent redaction criticism, confidence has diminished, and it is increasingly recognized that a very large part of Deut 6–11 does not come from the hands of the seventh-century reformers.[4] In a number of recent proposals the only traces of *Urdeuteronomium* prior to Deut 12 are found in Deut 6:4(–5).[5]

Critica ...': Context and Translation," *ZABR* 14 (2008): 47–85. See also Reinhard G. Kratz, *The Composition of the Narrative Books of the Old Testament*, trans. John Bowden (London: T&T Clark, 2005), 118; Bernard M. Levinson, *Deuteronomy and the Hermeneutics of Legal Innovation* (New York: Oxford University Press, 1997).

[2] See Norbert Lohfink, "Deuteronomium," *NBL* 1:414–18, here 416: "Daß das Dtn eine komplizierte Entstehungsgeschichte hat, ist offensichtlich. Doch gibt es darüber keine Theorie, die sich durchgesetzt hätte." For an account of contemporary scholarship, see Eckart Otto, *Deuteronomium 1–11*, 2 vols., HThKAT (Freiburg im Breisgau: Herder, 2012), 1:62–230.

[3] Horst Dietrich Preuss provides a summary of earlier scholarship and numerous bibliographical references. He states, "Da nach Meinung mehrerer Forscher Dtn 6,4-9 sich als alter Text erweisen lassen, wäre in 6,4 der mögliche Anfang des 'Urdtn.s' zu sehen, der mit der Betonung der 'Einheit' Jahwes gut auf die älteste Schicht von Dtn 12 hingeführt und somit die Forderung nach Kultzentralisation an nur 'einem' Kultort gut von der 'Einheit' Jahwes her begründet haben könnte" (*Deuteronomium*, EdF 164 [Darmstadt: Wissenschaftliche Buchgesellschaft, 1982], 100).

[4] See, e.g., A. D. H. Mayes, *The Story of Israel between Settlement and Exile: A Redactional Study of the Deuteronomistic History* (London: SCM, 1983), 22–39; Reinhard Achenbach, *Israel zwischen Verheissung und Gebot: Literarkritische Untersuchungen zu Deuteronomium 5–11*, EHS.T 422 (Frankfurt am Main: Lang, 1991); Eduard Nielsen, *Deuteronomium*, HAT 1.6 (Tübingen: Mohr Siebeck, 1995), 69–130; Timo Veijola, *Das fünfte Buch Mose: Deuteronomium*, ATD 8 (Göttingen: Vandenhoeck & Ruprecht, 2004).

[5] Eckart Otto, *Das Deuteronomium: Politische Theologie und Rechtsreform in Juda und Assyrien*, BZAW 284 (Berlin: de Gruyter, 1999), 361–62; Thomas C. Römer, *The So-Called Deuteronomistic History: A Sociological, Historical and Literary Introduction* (London: T&T Clark, 2005), 59–60, 75; cf. Kratz, *Composition of the Narrative Books*, 126–33.

When so many aspects of pentateuchal scholarship have been in flux in recent years, the ascription of the Shema to the *Urdeuteronomium* is a striking point of stability. Nevertheless, I want to examine just how secure the evidence for this consensus is.[6]

My investigation will proceed in four stages. First, I will examine the important arguments made by Timo Veijola that the love commandment in Deut 6:5 was an interpolation into the Shema belonging to a late redactional stratum. I will contend that Veijola's argument about the integrity of Deut 6:4–5 was based on a misunderstanding of Paul Joüon's Hebrew grammar. Second, I will consider the attempt by Eckart Otto to argue that covenant ideas are integral to the Josianic book of Deuteronomy. I will propose that his arguments that 612 BCE marks the *terminus ad quem* for *Urdeuteronomium* are not secure. In contrast, Veijola's observations about the striking distribution of the love commandment within the book of Deuteronomy demand an explanation. Third, drawing on my assessment of the arguments by Veijola and Otto, I will demonstrate that there are grounds for doubting the widespread view that Deut 6:4–5 opened *Urdeuteronomium*. The lack of a verbal connection with the centralization commandment and the absence of literary resonances in the earliest levels of Deuteronomy suggest that Deut 6:4–5 was introduced after the book's initial composition. Fourth, I will offer some preliminary proposals about how Deut 5–11 may have developed, if Deut 6:4 was not its original core.

---

[6] It is to the credit of Raik Heckl that his recent article on the subject does not assume that *Urdeuteronomium* began with Deut 6:4 but seeks to provide arguments for the position ("Der ursprüngliche Anfang des Deuteronomiums und seine literarische Transformation," *ZABR* 20 [2014]: 71–96). But the case is not compelling. The weakness of the arguments is hard to disguise, for Heckl begins with the reception of Deut 6:4–9 in the Jewish daily practice of reciting the Shema. "Die Dominanz und die Anfangsstellung von Dtn 6,4ff. (bzw. der Deuteronomiumtexte) bereits in der Antike lassen erkennen, dass die Praxis mit dem Deuteronomium und wahrscheinlich auch mit Dtn 6,4 begonnen hat" (84). But the texts that constitute the Shema were chosen because of their reference to recitation and prove nothing about the original beginning of *Urdeuteronomium*, as Heckl admits: "Ein Beweis dafür, dass Dtn 6,4 am Anfang des Deuteronomiums stand, ist dies zwar nicht, doch eine besondere Bedeutung von Dtn 6,4ff. ist unverkennbar" (ibid.). Second, Heckl argues that the superscription in Deut 5:1, שמע ישראל את־החקים ואת־המשפטים, took up and manipulated the original opening in 6:4. But this assumes the relationship between 5:1 and 6:4. Even if one were to accept that 5:1 is later than 6:4, this does not prove that 6:4 was the original beginning of *Urdeuteronomium*. Third, Heckl points to the similarity of 6:4–5 to 26:16–17, which he understands to be the conclusion of *Urdeuteronomium*. But this relies on the equally unproven hypothesis that 26:16–19 concluded *Urdeuteronomium*, and that is far from undisputed (see A. D. H. Mayes, *Deuteronomy*, NCBC [Grand Rapids: Eerdmans, 1981], 337–39; Nielsen, *Deuteronomium*, 235–42). Fourth, Heckl notes the reception of Deut 6:4–5 in the Deuteronomistic History (Josh 22:5; 1 Kgs 8:48; 2 Kgs 23:3, 25). Yet none of these texts belongs to the earliest layer of the Deuteronomistic History: on this point advocates of the Harvard school (attributing them to Dtr²) and the Göttingen school (attributing them to DtrN) could agree.

I. Timo Veijola's Interpretation of the Shema

In 1992, Timo Veijola published two essays in which he examined the redaction, the theology, and the background of the Shema.[7] In a careful discussion of its translation and interpretation, Veijola rejects the view that Deut 6:4 is a statement of mono-Yahwism. The mono-Yahwistic interpretation, which has many supporters, views Deut 6:4 as a rejection of the worship of local manifestations of YHWH at different shrines. Veijola insists that, "although this view cannot in principle be dismissed out of hand … it is unlikely in view of the fact that nowhere in Deuteronomy is cult centralization grounded in the nature of 'one YHWH' and that this aspect does not emerge anywhere in the biblical reception of Deut 6:4b."[8] Instead, he argues that Deut 6:4 should be translated "Hear, O Israel: YHWH is our God, YHWH is unique," declaring "the commitment to the only true God, which is obligatory for Israel."[9]

With most scholars since Antti Filemon Puukko, Veijola views Deut 6:4 as the theological statement that opens *Urdeuteronomium*, but building on the analysis of Felix García López he argues that it needs an introduction, which can be found in 4:45*, 5:1aα*:

> 4:45These are the statutes and ordinances, which Moses spoke to the Israelites when they came out of Egypt. 5:1Moses assembled all Israel, and he said to them: Hear O Israel, 6:4YHWH is our God, YHWH is unique.

This is then followed by Deut 6:6–9* and the earliest layer of the law of centralization: Deut 12:13–14, 17–18, 21.[10]

Perhaps the most original contribution of these essays was Veijola's attribution of 6:5 to a late Deuteronomistic redactor.[11] He offered two arguments. First, verse 5

---

[7] Timo Veijola, "Höre Israel! Der Sinn und Hintergrund von Deuteronomium VI 4–9," *VT* 42 (1992): 528–41; Veijola, "Das Bekenntnis Israels: Beobachtungen zur Geschichte und Theologie von Dtn 6,4–9," *TZ* 48 (1992): 369–81. These essays were published together as Timo Veijola, "Das Bekenntnis Israels: Beobachtungen zu Geschichte und Aussage von Dtn 6,4–9," in Veijola, *Moses Erben: Studien zum Dekalog, zum Deuteronomismus und zum Schriftgelehrtentum*, BWANT 149 (Stuttgart: Kohlhammer, 2000), 76–93.

[8] Veijola, "Das Bekenntnis Israels" [2000], 83: "Obwohl diese Sicht grundsätzlich nicht von der Hand zu weisen ist, … ist sie doch unwahrscheinlich angesichts dessen, daß im Deuteronomium die Kultzentralisation nirgendwo mit dem Wesen des 'einen Jahwe' begründet wird und daß dieser Aspekt in den biblischen Wirkungsgeschichte von Dtn 6,4b überhaupt nicht in Erscheinung tritt."

[9] Veijola, *Das fünfte Buch Mose*, 178–79: "Höre Israel: Jahwe ist unser Gott, Jahwe ist einzig … die Bindung an den einzigen wahren Gott, die für Israel verpflichtend ist."

[10] Antti Filemon Puukko, *Das Deuteronomium: Eine literarkritische Untersuchung*, BWANT 5 (Leipzig: Hinrichs, 1910); Felix García López, "Analyse littéraire de Deutéronomie V–XI," *RB* 84 (1977): 481–522.

[11] See also Udo Rüterswörden, *Das Buch Deuteronomium*, NSKAT 4 (Stuttgart: Katholisches Bibelwerk, 2006), 51–52.

is closely bound to verse 4b thematically, and together these verses make a distinct unit. At the same time, verse 5 does not belong syntactically to verse 4b. Veijola observes:

> It is entirely possible for a perf. cons. to follow a nominal sentence, but in such cases it is usually a statement about the future, in which the perf. cons. presupposes and continues, both chronologically and logically, the participle (normally introduced with a הנה). A grammatical connection of this sort is lacking between v. 4b and v. 5, which would justify the consecutio part. plus perf. cons. Verse 4b contains a timeless statement, which on a syntactic level cannot be continued by the following perf. cons. ואהבת "and you shall love."[12]

Rather, verse 5 belongs to the series of perfect consecutives that continue the imperative שמע of verse 4a. Further confirmation of this conclusion is provided by the second-person singular, which is appropriate since Israel is the subject of verse 4a. Therefore, verse 5 belongs syntactically to the series of perfect consecutives in verses 6–9 and not to verse 4b. This results in a problematic situation according to which verse 5 is both an element of the instructions for practice *and* part of the content to be remembered. Thus, the instructions in verses 6–9 about "these words" (v. 6) cannot originally have included verse 5 but only verse 4b. Second, Veijola observed that the demand to love YHWH and the expression "with all your heart and all your soul" occurred only in Deuteronomistic texts. Were Deut 6:5 to be attributed to *Urdeuteronomium*, it is rather puzzling that it shows no discernible impact anywhere else in Deuteronomic material. "In light of this finding, the question arises as to whether Deut 6:5 would not have left earlier verbal traces in the Deuteronomistic literature, if the demand to love YHWH with all your heart, all your soul and all your strength had constituted the solemn overture of the original Deuteronomy."[13] In further support of Veijola's contention, it could be argued that, if anything, the threefold form makes more sense as an emphatic development of the twofold form, "all your heart and all your soul." It would be more logical if this were the end point, rather than the source of development.

Veijola named the Deuteronomistic redaction, to which he attributed verse 5, the covenant theology redaction (*Bundestheologische Redaktion*, or DtrB). In a number of studies, and finally in his regrettably unfinished commentary, he

---

[12] Veijola, "Das Bekenntnis Israels" [2000], 80: "Es ist zwar durchaus möglich, daß einem Nominalsatz ein Perf. cons. folgt, aber in dem Fall handelt es sich in der Regel um eine futurische Aussage, wobei das Perf. cons. das—gewöhnlich durch הנה eingeleitete—Partizip in zeitlicher und logischer Hinsicht voraussetzt und fortsetzt. Zwischen V. 4b und V. 5 fehlt jedoch eine grammatische Verbindung dieser Art, die die consecutio Part. + Perf. cons. rechtfertigen würde. Vers 4b enthält eine zeitlose Aussage, die auf der syntaktischen Ebene nicht von dem nachfolgenden Perf. cons. ואהבת 'und du sollst lieben' fortgesetzt wird."

[13] Ibid., 81: "Angesichts dieses Befundes stellt sich die Frage, ob Dtn 6,5 nicht schon früher wörtliche Spuren in der dtr Literatur hinterlassen hätte, wenn die Forderung, Jahwe mit ganzen Herzen, ganzer Seele und ganzer Kraft zu lieben, die feierliche Ouvertüre des ursprünglichen Deuteronomiums gebildet hätte."

developed his understanding of this redaction.[14] This redactional level has a distinctive theology that emphasizes Israel's relationship with YHWH as covenantal. The possession of the land promised to the patriarchs depends on obedience to the commandments, most especially the prohibition of following other deities. The exclusive relationship to the covenantal overlord is to be both internalized and policed externally. Thus, the individual heart and intention must be oriented to YHWH alone, and rebellion against YHWH must be violently suppressed.

Veijola's interpretation of the Shema makes a significant contribution to our understanding of Deut 6:4. Most particularly, his analysis of this *Bundestheologische Redaktion* raises significant questions for how deeply embedded covenant conceptuality is in the book of Deuteronomy, even if his proposal about a distinctive redactional level is not followed. Despite its significance, Veijola's argument has a number of critical flaws.

First, it proves difficult to distinguish between Veijola's interpretation of Deut 6:4 and later covenant theology. According to Veijola, "Of course, the nominal sentence 'YHWH is unique' should not be understood in the sense of an absolute monotheism, but in light of the preceding parallel statement ('YHWH is our God') it simply means that YHWH is to be *our* only God."[15] But it is precisely this exclusive relationship that underlies the later *Bundestheologische Redaktion* and justifies its intolerance toward any rebellion (Deut 13; 28). It is comparable to statements found in Assyrian treaty documents that insist on the loyalty of subjects to the Assyrian king; for example, "from this day on [for as long as we live we will be subjects of Assurbanipal, king of Assyria], (that) Assurbanipal, king of Assyria [shall be our king and lord, and (that) we will be totally devoted] to Assurbanipal, king of Assyria, our lord."[16] The difficulties are apparent when Veijola admits what many others have observed: that there is a close conceptual relationship between verses 4 and 5.[17] Veijola speaks of an "undeniable connection that exists on the

---

[14] See the following articles by Veijola in his collection *Moses Erben*: "'Der Mensch lebt nicht vom Brot allein': Zur literarischen Schichtung und theologischen Aussage von Deuteronomium 8," 153–75; "Wahrheit und Intoleranz nach Deuteronomium 13," 109–30; "Bundestheologische Redaktion im Deuteronomium," 153–75. See also Veijola, "Bundestheologie in Dtn 10,12–11,30," in *Liebe und Gebot: Studien zum Deuteronomium*, ed. Reinhard G. Kratz and Hermann Spieckermann, FRLANT 190 (Göttingen: Vandenhoeck & Ruprecht, 2000), 206–21; and Veijola, *Das fünfte Buch Mose*, passim.

[15] Veijola, "Das Bekenntnis Israel" [2000], 85: "Der Nominalsatz 'Jahwe ist einzig' will natürlich nicht im Sinne des absoluten Monotheismus verstanden werden, sondern im Horizont der vorangehenden, parallelen Aussage ('Jahwe ist unser Gott') schlicht besagen, daß Jahwe *unser* einziger Gott sei."

[16] SAA 2:64, 9.3′–5′; see also SAA 2:36 and 41, 6.195 and 301; 2:66, 9.32′–33′.

[17] See, inter alios, Eduard Nielsen, "'Weil Jahwe unser Gott ein Jahwe ist' (Dtn 6,4f.)," in *Beiträge zur alttestamentlichen Theologie: Festschrift für Walther Zimmerli zum 70. Geburtstag*, ed. Herbert Donner, Robert Hanhart, and Rudolf Smend (Göttingen: Vandenhoeck & Ruprecht,

conceptual level."[18] But the main criterion for identifying the *Bundestheologische Redaktion* is its conceptual distinctiveness. On what basis, then, should Deut 6:4 be excluded from the *Bundestheologische Redaktion*?

Second, the purpose served by Deut 6:4 in opening *Urdeuteronomium* is unclear. Veijola juxtaposes Deut 6:4, 6–9* with 12:13–21* but severs the link between the Shema and cult centralization. In earlier critical scholarship it was the assumed link between the uniqueness of YHWH and the uniqueness of the sanctuary (one God, one cultic place) that made the Shema so convincing as the proposed opening of *Urdeuteronomium*. As classically understood, the principal theme of *Urdeuteronomium*, which colors every part of the book, is cult centralization, and the pithy formula of the Shema provided the ideal summary of the book's key idea. For Veijola, the Shema no longer has this role, and its appearance in *Urdeuteronomium* is rendered inexplicable.

Third, a crucial part of Veijola's case for attributing verse 5 to a later hand is fundamentally flawed. For Veijola, almost the only nominal sentences that are followed by the perfect consecutive are statements about the future with a participle. He appeals to Joüon §119n at this point,[19] but in this paragraph Joüon addresses only cases of the participle followed by *wəqataltí*. Other types of nominal sentences followed by *wəqataltí* are not discussed, but Joüon should not be read to imply that other examples do not exist—not least because many do. Bruce Waltke and M. O'Connor draw attention to a number of different nominal sentences followed by the perfect consecutive. "The *wəqataltí* form after nominal clauses shows the same range of meanings as after suffix-conjugation forms: it is found in the apodosis after a conditional clause; in a consequent situation, which may be volitional; or with an imperfective sense."[20] A comparable example to Deut 6:4–5 would be Ruth 3:9: ותאמר אנכי רות אמתך ופרשת כנפך על־אמתך, "And she answered, 'I am Ruth, your servant; spread your cloak over your servant'" (NRSV). Here, as in the Shema, a

---

1977), 288–301; W. Herrmann, "Jahwe und des Menschen Liebe zu ihm zu Dtn. VI 4," *VT* 50 (2000): 47–54.

[18] Veijola, "Das Bekenntnis Israels" [2000], 80: "Unbestreitbaren Verbindung, die auf der gedanklichen Ebene besteht." Veijola also writes, "Der Zusammenhang wird auf der gedanklichen Ebene gesehen: Dem einen bzw. einzigartigen Jahwe entspreche eine umfassende Liebe, die emphatisch durch die dreifache Wiederholung von כל zum Ausdruck gebracht werde" (ibid.).

[19] Ibid.

[20] *IBHS* §32.2.4a. Veijola's misstatement is all the more surprising given that he had read P. A. H. de Boer's article on Deut 6:4–5. De Boer asks precisely the same question as Veijola: "Can verses 4b and 5 belong together in line with known Hebrew syntax?" But De Boer rightly answers, "If we take verse 4b as a nominal sentence, the answer is in the affirmative, for it is not unusual to continue such a sentence with *waw perfect*" ("Some Observations on Deuteronomy vi 4 and 5," in *Von Kanaan bis Kerala: Festschrift für Prof. Mag. Dr. Dr. J. P. M. van der Ploeg zur Vollendung des siebzigsten Lebensjahres am 4. Juli 1979*, ed. W. C. Delsman et al., AOAT 211 [Neukirchen-Vluyn: Neukirchener Verlag, 1982], 45–52, here 48).

nominal sentence of identification is followed by a perfect consecutive with a volitional meaning and a different subject.

Without the syntactic argument, the other features Veijola points to in order to substantiate his position lack persuasive force. The shift from first-person plural to second-person singular, for example, can be explained in a number of ways. It has often been taken as an indication that we have the incorporation of an existing slogan in verse 4b.[21] It could be no more than a formal feature, distinguishing the creedal form in verse 4b from the commandment in verse 5. A similar pattern can be observed in 26:1–11, where the Israelite farmer's confession is in the first-person plural (vv. 5–9) and the instructions about the offering are in the second-person singular (vv. 1–4, 10–11).

Fourth, Veijola is inconsistent in identifying later elements. He rightly observes that the demand to love YHWH is found in late additions to *Urdeuteronomium* or in the frame of the book, but he failed to observe that the same could also be said of the elements of Deut 6:4. This is a matter to which we will return.

II. THE SHEMA AND COVENANT THEOLOGY

Veijola's identification of the love commandment as a relatively late element in the book of Deuteronomy is, in my view, correct. Nevertheless, this position has been criticized by others. Veijola's conclusions about the command to love YHWH and the centrality of covenant theology to the book of Deuteronomy stand in sharp contrast to the position taken by Eckart Otto. In Otto's view, *Urdeuteronomium* is to be found in Deut 13* and 28* and was composed as a subversion of the Neo-Assyrian loyalty oath. Elements of the loyalty oath to Esarhaddon were transformed into a pledge of loyalty to YHWH. The composition of Esarhaddon's loyalty oath and the end of Neo-Assyrian hegemony in the Near East mark respectively the *terminus a quo* and the *terminus ad quem* for *Urdeuteronomium*. Against Veijola, Otto defends the integrity of Deut 6:4–5 and sees the command to love as a

---

[21] For Deut 6:4b as a preexistent formula, see Erik Aurelius, "Der Ursprung des Ersten Gebots," *ZTK* 100 (2003): 1–21, here 7; Christoph Levin, "Über den 'Color Hieremianus' des Deuteronomiums," in *Das Deuteronomium und seine Querbeziehungen*, ed. Timo Veijola, SESJ 62 (Göttingen: Vandenhoeck & Ruprecht, 1996), 117. I will not consider the murky question of the prehistory of Deut 6:4. Oswald Loretz (*Des Gottes Einzigkeit: Ein altorientalisches Argumentationsmodell zum "Schma Jisrael"* [Darmstadt: Wissenschaftliche Buchgesellschaft, 1997]; Loretz, "Die Einzigkeit eines Gottes im Polytheismus von Ugarit: Zur Levante als Ursprungsort des biblischen Monotheismus," in *Polytheismus und Monotheismus in den Religionen des Vorderen Orients*, ed. Manfred Krebernik and Jürgen van Oorschot, AOAT 298 [Münster: Ugarit-Verlag, 2002], 71–89) and Mark S. Smith (*God in Translation: Deities in Cross-Cultural Discourse in the Biblical World*, FAT 57 [Tübingen: Mohr Siebeck, 2008], 143–46) argue that its background is to be sought in the kingship of one God above the other deities. My argument places all such proposals in doubt.

characteristic motif of the Neo-Assyrian loyalty oath.[22] For Otto, then, the love commandment is a significant constituent of the Josianic book of Deuteronomy. "As the opening of the Deuteronomic reform program, Deut 6:4–5 tightly dovetails with the fundamental commandment about cult centralization (Deut 12:13–27*) and the demand for loyalty (Deut 13:2–12*)."[23] Literarily, the insistence on Israel's loyalty forms a bracket around the characteristic commandment of the earliest version of Deuteronomy, the command for cult centralization. As a result, the love commandment cannot have originated in any later layer of the book of Deuteronomy.

Otto's insistence on a seventh-century date for Deuteronomy's covenant theology has itself been criticized. Crucial to Otto's argument is his view that the loyalty oath died out with the collapse of the Neo-Assyrian Empire. But the lack of extant Neo-Babylonian treaties cannot be taken as evidence that they did not exist or that Neo-Assyrian exemplars were not part of the Mesopotamian scribal curriculum in later periods.[24] Kazuko Watanabe lists 230 appearances of *adê* in cuneiform, forty-one of which come from the Neo-Babylonian and Persian periods.[25] In addition, David B. Weisberg notes a number of similarities between the loyalty oaths binding craftsmen in early Achaemenid Babylonia and earlier Neo-Assyrian loyalty oaths.[26] The recent discovery of Esarhaddon's loyalty oath at Tell Tayinat provides new insight into the Assyrian employment of loyalty oaths in Syria-Palestine[27] and

---

[22] Otto argues that "die von T. Veijola beobachtete Besonderheit in der Anknüpfung an V.5 erklärt sich ausreichend damit, daß V.4b eine vorgeformte Bekenntnisformel ist, grammatisch sich V.5 durchaus auf V.4a bezieht und ein Sollen ausdrückt, inhaltlich aber V.5 direkt an V.4b anknüpft" (*Das Deuteronomium: Politische Theologie*, 361–62). Because Otto does not attribute verses 6–9 to *Urdeuteronomium*, he does not have the same problem as Veijola does that verse 5 belongs syntactically to verses 6–9 but, in terms of its content, belongs to what precedes.

[23] Ibid., 362: "Dtn 6,4–5 ist als Eröffnung des dtn Reformprogramms eng mit dem Hauptgesetz der Kultzentralisation (Dtn 12,13–27*) und der Loyalitätsforderung (Dtn 13,2–12*) verzahnt."

[24] Steven W. Holloway, review of *Das Deuteronomium: Politische Theologie und Rechtsreform in Juda und Assyrien*, by Eckart Otto, *JNES* 66 (2007): 205–8. The perdurance of the treaty form from the second into the first millennium and its geographical spread point to its political utility for ancient Near Eastern states, and it seems unlikely that it would have fallen into disuse after 612 BCE.

[25] Kazuko Watanabe, *Die adê-Vereidigung anlässlich der Thronfolgeregelung Asarhaddons*, BaM.B 3 (Berlin: Gebr. Mann, 1987), 9–23. I have not included places where *adê* occurs in personal names or in a fragmentary context.

[26] David B. Weisberg, *Guild Structure and Political Allegiance in Early Achaemenid Mesopotamia*, YNER 1 (New Haven: Yale University Press, 1967), 32–42. According to Ezek 17:13, Nebuchadnezzar made a covenant with Zedekiah after the removal of his father, Jehoiachin (v. 12).

[27] For the text and discussion, see Jacob Lauinger, "Esarhaddon's Succession Treaty at Tell Tayinat: Text and Commentary," *JCS* 64 (2012): 87–123; Hans U. Steymans, "Deuteronomy 28 and Tell Tayinat," *VeEc* 34 (2013), https://doi.org/10.4102/ve.v34i2.870.

increases the likelihood that a loyalty oath was imposed on Manasseh.[28] Nevertheless, the similarities of Deut 13 and 28 to Esarhaddon's loyalty oath provide no more than a *terminus a quo*; we have almost no evidence of how the loyalty oath may have been transmitted or appropriated in the Syro-Palestinian region.

If arguments for 612 BCE as a *terminus ad quem* for *Urdeuteronomium* are rather vulnerable, the same is less true of Veijola's examination of the love commandment. Veijola's arguments are based on the striking distribution of the love commandment within the book of Deuteronomy. The command to love YHWH is otherwise found only in Deut 10:12; 11:1, 13, 22; 19:9; 30:6, 16, 20, while the expression "heart and soul" is restricted to Deut 4:29; 10:12; 11:13, 18; 13:4; 26:16; 30:2, 6, 10. None of these texts belongs to *Urdeuteronomium*, and there is considerable agreement that they belong to some of the latest levels within Deuteronomy.[29] The

---

[28] Christoph Koch, on the other hand, suggests that the similarities between Deuteronomy and Esarhaddon's loyalty oath may be the result of a Northwest Semitic treaty tradition rather than evidence that one specific set of Neo-Assyrian treaties formed the exclusive model for *Urdeuteronomium* (*Vertrag, Treueid und Bund: Studien zur Rezeption des altorientalischen Vertragsrechts im Deuteronomium und zur Ausbildung der Bundestheologie im Alten Testament*, BZAW 383 [Berlin: de Gruyter, 2008]). He draws attention to Aramean treaties such as Sefire and suggests that these might have been the means by which the treaty traditions were mediated to Israel rather than through encounter with the loyalty oath of Esarhaddon He rejects the arguments of those who see particularly strong parallels between Esarhaddon's loyalty oath and Deut 13 and 28 (e.g., Hans Ulrich Steymans, *Deuteronomium 28 und die adê zur Thronfolgeregelung Asarhaddons: Segen und Fluch im Alten Orient und in Israel*, OBO 145 [Fribourg: Universitätsverlag, 1995]; Otto, *Das Deuteronomium: Politische Theologie*, 15–90; Bernard M. Levinson and Jeffrey Stackert, "Between the Covenant Code and Esarhaddon's Succession Treaty: Deuteronomy 13 and the Composition of Deuteronomy," *JAJ* 3 [2012]: 123–40).

[29] As we have already seen, Veijola would attribute these occurrences to his DtrB. There is some overlap, however, between his DtrB and Mayes's "late deuteronomistic author" (Mayes, *Deuteronomy*; Veijola, *Das fünfte Buch Mose*). Deuteronomy 4:1–40 and 29:1–30:10 are closely related and usually attributed to the same hand. Deuteronomy 4 concludes the first Mosaic speech and is dependent on—and usually considered later than—Deut 1–3. Chapters 1–3 are themselves part of a late framing of the book, either as the introduction to a Deuteronomistic History (so Noth) or as a bridge to the Tetrateuch (so Otto). For the late Deuteronomistic date of these chapters, see, inter alios, Eckart Otto, *Das Deuteronomium im Pentateuch und Hexateuch: Studien zur Literaturgeschichte von Pentateuch und Hexateuch im Lichte des Deuteronomiumsrahmens*, FAT 30 (Tübingen: Mohr Siebeck, 2000); Jon D. Levenson, "Who Inserted the Book of the Torah?," *HTR* 68 (1975): 203–33; Georg Braulik, *Die Mittel deuteronomischer Rhetorik: Erhoben aus Deuteronomium 4,1–40*, AnBib 68 (Rome: Biblical Institute Press, 1978); Braulik, "Literarkritik und die Einrahmung von Gemälden: Zur literarkritischen und redaktionsgeschichtlichen Analyse von Dtn 4,1–6,3 und 29,1–30,10 durch D. Knapp," *RB* 96 (1989): 266–88; A. D. H. Mayes, "Deuteronomy 4 and the Literary Criticism of Deuteronomy," *JBL* 100 (1981): 23–51, https://doi.org/10.2307/3265533. Deuteronomy 10:12–11:32 concludes the paraenesis of chapters 5–11 and appears to be something of a pastiche including material from early chapters. For these chapters, see, inter alios, Veijola, "Bundestheologie in Dtn 10,12–11,30"; Mayes, *Deuteronomy*, 207–19; Eckart Otto, "Deuteronomistische und postdeuteronomistische Perspektiven in der Literaturgeschichte von Deuteronomium 5–11," *ZABR* 15 (2009): 65–215, here 210–13. The love

earliest reference to loving YHWH in Deuteronomy is probably to be found in the Decalogue, where its meaning is clearly explicated as entailing obedience: "those who love me and keep my commandments" (5:10; cf. 7:9). Thus, despite the widespread assumption that 6:5 was part of the programmatic introduction to *Urdeuteronomium*, there is no evidence that the verse had an influence upon either *Urdeuteronomium* or even the earliest redactional layers. Thus, Veijola's contention that Deut 6:5 was not part of *Urdeuteronomium*, but a relatively late arrival, has some justification.

III. The Shema and *Urdeuteronomium*

To this point I have demonstrated two things. First, Veijola was correct to attribute the love commandment to relatively late Deuteronomistic strata. Second, there are insufficient grounds for detaching Deut 6:5 from the surrounding verses. The only reasonable conclusion to draw from these two observations is that 6:4–5 is a relatively late addition to the book of Deuteronomy. Yet, as we have seen, this pushes against the consensus within Old Testament scholarship that 6:4 was an integral part of *Urdeuteronomium* and a theological slogan of the Deuteronomic agenda.

The main argument in favor of the Shema as part of *Urdeuteronomium* is the apparent congruence between the affirmation of YHWH as one and the program

---

commandment in Deut 13:4 occurs in a plural section (13:4b–5), which would ordinarily exclude it from *Urdeuteronomium*. Although Paul-Eugène Dion ("Deuteronomy 13: The Suppression of Alien Religious Propaganda in Israel during the Late Monarchic Era," in *Law and Ideology in Monarchic Israel*, ed. Baruch Halpern and D. W. Hobson, JSOTSup 124 [Sheffield: JSOT Press, 1991], 147–216) and Veijola ("Wahrheit und Intoleranz") have argued that no part of chapter 13 is as early as *Urdeuteronomium*, the place of chapter 13 in *Urdeuteronomium* is greatly disputed in contemporary scholarship (see, e.g., Levinson and Stackert, "Between the Covenant Code"; Otto, *Das Deuteronomium: Politische Theologie*, 15–90). Nevertheless, those who argue that chapter 13 is Deuteronomic exclude verses 4b–5 as a later addition (Otto, *Das Deuteronomium: Politische Theologie*, 39–40; cf. Bernard M. Levinson, "Textual Criticism, Assyriology, and the History of Interpretation: Deuteronomy 13:7a as a Test Case in Method," *JBL* 120 [2001]: 211–43, here 239, https://doi.org/10.2307/3268293), and Dion's detailed arguments for the Deuteronomistic origins of verses 4b–5 are compelling ("Deuteronomy 13," 168–72, 177–88; see also Koch, *Vertrag, Treueid und Bund*, 116–20). Deuteronomy 19:8–10 contains Deuteronomistic ideas such as the gift of the land to the fathers, and the idea of the additional three cities of refuge presupposes the conquest of Transjordan described in chapters 1–3. For these verses, see, inter alios, Mayes, *Deuteronomy*, 287; Eckart Otto, "Aspects of Legal Reforms and Reformulations," in *Theory and Method in Biblical and Cuneiform Law: Revision, Interpretation and Development*, ed. Bernard Levinson, JSOTSup 181 (Sheffield: Sheffield Academic, 1994), 160–96, here 195; Nielsen, *Deuteronomium*, 187–90. Deuteronomy 26:16 provides a transition between the end of the Deuteronomic law and the covenant formula (26:17–19). Its vocabulary and ideas have been identified as Deuteronomistic; see, inter alios, Mayes, *Deuteronomy*, 338.

of centralization. The oneness of God provided the theological basis for cult centralization: one God worshiped in one sanctuary. In some recent reconstructions of *Urdeuteronomium*, the Shema immediately precedes the command to centralize worship (12:13–27*). Otto draws attention to the close literary connection.

> The threefold בְּכָל־ in Deut 6:5 functions as a prelude to the numerous appearances of בְּכָל־ in the commandment about cult centralization (Deut 12:3, 15[2x], 18, 20, 21). בְּכָל־נַפְשְׁךָ in Deut 6:5 is resumed by בְּכָל־אַוַּת נַפְשְׁךָ in Deut 12:15, 20. Above all, however, Deut 6:4–5 and Deut 12:13–27* are connected by the common theme of one God and the one cult place: *YHWH, so says the creed, is unique, and he has chosen, so says the centralization commandment, one unique cult place.*[30]

Thus, the Josianic book of Deuteronomy opened in the following manner:

> Hear, O Israel, YHWH, our god, YHWH is one [אחד]. So you shall love YHWH your god with all [בכל] your heart, with all [בכל] your soul and with all [בכל] your might. Take care that you do not offer your burnt offerings at any [בכל] place you happen to see. But only at the place that YHWH will choose in one [באחד] of your tribes. There you shall offer your burnt offerings and there you shall do all [כל] that I command you.[31]

The critical problem, as Veijola noted, is that אחד is not used as a slogan in the book of Deuteronomy.[32] This point is not diminished by the juxtaposition of Deut 6:4–5 and 12:13–27*, for the resulting catchwords—כל and אחד—do not make a compelling argument for a close literary relationship. First, בכל is far too common an expression—occurring no fewer than sixty-three times in Deuteronomy alone—to claim a deliberate, close relationship between 6:4–5 and 12:13–14. In addition, the expression is used in contrasting ways in the two passages. It describes the wholehearted commitment of the Israelites and the numerous cultic sites that they are *not* to frequent. Second, אחד in 12:14 is not in a rhetorically prominent position, nor is the expression "one of your tribes" found anywhere else in Deuteronomy. If 6:4 were the slogan of the Deuteronomic theological vision, it would be difficult to

---

[30] Otto, *Das Deuteronomium: Politische Theologie*, 363–64 (emphasis original): "Das dreimalige בְּכָל־ in Dtn 6,5 präludiert das mehrfache בְּכָל־ in den Zentralisationsgesetzen (Dtn 12,3.15[2x].18.20.21). בְּכָל־נַפְשְׁךָ in Dtn 6,5 wird durch בְּכָל־אַוַּת נַפְשְׁךָ in Dtn 12,15.20 wieder aufgenommen. Vor allem aber sind Dtn 6,4f. und Dtn 12, 13–27* durch das gemeinsame Thema des einen Gottes und des einen Kultortes miteinander verbunden: *JHWH, so sagt es das Bekenntnis, ist einzig, und, so sagen die Zentralisierungsgesetze, einen einzigen Kultort hat er erwählt.*"

[31] This translation and reconstruction of the text are taken from Thomas Römer, "Cult Centralization in Deuteronomy 12: Between Deuteronomistic History and Pentateuch," in *Das Deuteronomium zwischen Pentateuch und Deuteronomistischem Geschichtswerk*, ed. Eckart Otto and Reinhard Achenbach, FRLANT 206 (Göttingen: Vandenhoeck & Ruprecht, 2004), 168–80, here 170.

[32] It might be suspected that the political slogans of modern Europe, for example, *ein Volk, ein Reich, ein Gott* or *un roi, une loi, une foi* have inadvertently been introduced into the interpretation of Deuteronomy.

explain the lack of prominence given to אחד in *Urdeuteronomium*. Instead, Deuteronomy insists not that people and sanctuary are "one" but that they are "chosen" (בחר).³³

An examination of the distribution of lexemes in Deuteronomy provides further confirmation that 6:4–9 was not part of *Urdeuteronomium*. As we have already seen, Veijola demonstrated that the command to love YHWH and the expression "heart and soul" are to be found only in Deuteronomistic layers. But the same is true also of elements that are characteristic of verse 4. The term *Israel* (ישראל) is not found in any of the laws that concern centralization and are definitively associated with *Urdeuteronomium*,³⁴ and ישראל as a form of address is otherwise found only in Deut 5:1, 6:3, 9:1, 10:12, 20:3, and 27:9. There are grounds for thinking that all of these texts are at least Deuteronomistic.³⁵ Similarly, Moses's identification with the people by means of the first-person plural or the use of the first-person plural in creedal statements is common in Deut 1–4, 5, 6, and 29.³⁶ These are mostly,

---

³³ Thus, if there is any relationship to the affirmation that "YHWH is one," it is one of contrast. "Chosen" suggests a dependent relationship on YHWH, to whom alone the predication "one" is applied. Similarly, Nathan MacDonald, *Deuteronomy and the Meaning of "Monotheism,"* FAT 2/1 (Tübingen: Mohr Siebeck, 2003), 216.

³⁴ In the Deuteronomic law code ישראל occurs in 13:12; 17:4, 12, 20; 18:1, 6; 19:13; 20:3; 21:8, 21; 22:19, 21; 23:18; 24:7; 25:6.

³⁵ Deuteronomy 5:1aβ–b is an addition that is indebted to the late Deuteronomistic chapter 4. It focuses attention on the statutes and ordinances that follow in chapter 12 rather than on the immediate concern with the Decalogue (Mayes, *Deuteronomy*, 165; Lothar Perlitt, *Deuteronomium*, BKAT 5 [Neukirchen-Vluyn: Neukirchener Verlag, 2013], 414; Otto attributes it to his DtrD [*Deuteronomium 1–11*, 2:667–84]). Deuteronomy 6:3 is part of the transition between the Decalogue and the Shema and is not to be dated earlier than either. The phraseology in 6:2–3 is again indebted to Deut 4 (Mayes, *Deuteronomy*, 174; Perlitt, *Deuteronomium*, 442–44). Deuteronomy 9:1 is part of a repurposing of the golden calf story and is no earlier than that narrative. The small pericope, verses 1–3, is indebted to the Deuteronomistic narrative in chapters 1–3, in particular, 1:28 (Achenbach, *Israel zwischen Verheissung und Gebot*, 335–44; Norbert Lohfink, *Das Hauptgebot: Eine Untersuchung literarischer Einleitungsfragen zu Dtn 5–11*, AnBib 20 [Rome: Pontifical Biblical Institute, 1963], 200–206). Deuteronomy 10:12 is part of the extended paraenesis attached to the story of the golden calf, which is widely identified as a late Deuteronomistic insertion with a close relationship to chapter 4 (Mayes, *Deuteronomy*, 207–8; Timo Veijola, "Bundestheologie in Dtn 10,12–11,30," in Kratz and Spieckermann, *Liebe und Gebot*, 206–21. Deuteronomy 20:3 is usually identified as part of a secondary intrusion (vv. 2–4) into a law concerning warfare (20:1–9). Its secondary nature is indicated by the second-person plural, the reference to priests rather than officials, and its apparent contradiction and partial duplication of verse 8 (Mayes, *Deuteronomy*, 292–93). Deuteronomy 27:9 is part of a chapter that is widely recognized as disruptive. It is possible that verses 9–10 were part of the original core of the chapter and followed immediately after 26:16–19, with which they are closely linked as a secondary extension (Richard Nelson, *Deuteronomy: A Commentary*, OTL [Louisville: Westminster John Knox, 2002], 315).

³⁶ Deut 1:6, 19–20, 22, 25, 27–28, 41; 2:1, 8, 13–14, 29–30, 32–37; 3:1, 3–4, 6–8, 12, 29; 4:7; 5:2–3, 24–27; 6:4, 20–25; 9:28; 12:8; 26:3, 7–8, 15; 29:7–8, 14, 16, 29.

if not entirely, Deuteronomistic.[37] Though it can be argued that 6:4b was a preexisting formula, this does not explain the lack of influence of the first-person plural in the earliest revisions of *Urdeuteronomium*.

The picture from elsewhere in the Hebrew Bible is consistent with a later appearance of the Shema, even if the evidence is only circumstantial. Thus, despite the view that the Shema opened *Urdeuteronomium* and was a popular slogan for the seventh-century reform movement,[38] the expression "YHWH is one" never appears in the history from Joshua to 2 Kings. As Norbert Lohfink observes, "there are many keywords in the Deuteronomic/Deuteronomistic vocabulary which are often repeated in this material, but *yhvh 'elohenu yhvh 'echadh*, 'Yahweh our God, Yahweh is unique,' is not one of these."[39] The preferred form of monotheistic affirmation is "YHWH is God [האלהים]" or something similar.[40] It might be argued

---

[37] Since Martin Noth it has been recognized that Deut 1–3 are Deuteronomistic (Noth, *The Deuteronomistic History*, JSOTSup 15 [Sheffield: JSOT Press, 1981]). Deuteronomy 4 was composed no earlier, and possibly later, than chapters 1–3 (Eckart Otto, "Deuteronomium 4: Die Pentateuchredaktion im Deuteronomiumsrahmen," in Veijola, *Das Deuteronomium und seine Querbeziehungen*, 196–222; Dietrich Knapp, *Deuteronomium 4: Literarische Analyse und theologische Interpretation*, GTA 35 [Göttingen: Vandenhoeck & Ruprecht, 1987]). Deuteronomy 5:2–3, 24–27 are part of the narrative account of the giving of the Decalogue, which is itself later than *Urdeuteronomium*, as has already been observed. It is possible that 5:2–3 is an addition to the chapter (Mayes, *Deuteronomy*, 165), though this is disputed (Otto, *Deuteronomium 1–11*, 2:667–84). Deuteronomy 5:24–27 is not straightforward and has probably been expanded in a process of *Fortschreibung* (see Mayes, *Deuteronomy*, 172–73). Deuteronomy 9:28 belongs to the rehearsal of the golden calf story. The original calf story is probably to be found in 9:9–21, and the intercession in 9:26–29 is a secondary expansion (Otto, *Deuteronomium 1–11*, 2:943–69). Deuteronomy 12:8 belongs to what is usually identified as a Deuteronomistic expansion of the centralization commandment (12:8–12) (Römer, *So-Called Deuteronomistic History*, 61–63). Though the "creed" that accompanies the presentation of the firstfruits in 26:5–9 was long considered an early statement of Israelite faith, recent scholarship has shown that it is a late construction that presupposes many parts of the pentateuchal narrative (Jan Christian Gertz, "Die Stellung des kleinen geschichtlichen Credos in der Redaktionsgeschichte von Deuteronomium und Pentateuch," in Kratz and Spieckermann, *Liebe und Gebot*, 30–45). The ceremony for the offering of the triennial tithe in 26:12–15 takes up themes from 26:1–11 and shows other evidence of Deuteronomistic editing (Mayes, *Deuteronomy*, 335–37). Deuteronomy 29:1–30:10 is in a close relationship to chapters 1–3 (4) and should likewise be attributed to a Deuteronomistic writer (Otto, *Das Deuteronomium im Pentateuch*, 138–55).

[38] Rainer Albertz, for example, argues "'Hear, Israel, Yahweh, our God, Yahweh is one' (Deut 6.4) was the reform slogan which was hammered home to the population time and again in public pronouncement (cf. 20.2)" (*A History of Israelite Religion in the Old Testament Period*, OTL [Louisville: Westminster John Knox, 1994], 206). It is very difficult to see how the assertion that it was "hammered home ... time and again" is derived from the historical evidence available.

[39] Norbert Lohfink and J. Bergmann, "אֶחָד 'echādh," *TDOT* 1:193–201, here 196.

[40] Deut 4:35, 39; 7:9; 2 Sam 7:28; 1 Kgs 8:60; 18:37, 39; 2 Kgs 19:15, 19 (cf. Josh 2:11; 2 Kgs 5:15). For a discussion of the monotheistic statements in the Deuteronomistic History, see Juha Pakkala, *Intolerant Monolatry in the Deuteronomistic History*, Publications of the

that we find "YHWH is God" only because it was a more adequate statement of monotheism than Deut 6:4, which is no more than a monolatrous affirmation. Not only does this credit the ancient writers with the subtlety of our modern distinctions, but it also does not explain why the statement "YHWH is one" was retained in Deut 6 and not elsewhere. Echoes of the Shema begin to appear in texts only from a much later period. In Zech 14:9 the realization of the Shema is projected into the eschatological future: "YHWH will be one" (יהיה יהוה אחד), while Malachi justifies his position on marriage by appeal to the "one God who created us" (הלא אל אחד בראנו; 2:10). The growing significance of the Shema in late biblical texts highlights its absence in earlier Israelite literature.[41]

It is here in the *Wirkungsgeschichte* of Deuteronomy that a theology of the "one" first clearly begins to be developed, but it is only in the later Second Temple period that a connection between one God and one temple is explicitly articulated. Philo writes, "Since God is one, there should be also only one temple" (*Spec.* 1.67; Colson, LCL). In the *Antiquities*, Josephus rephrases the beginning of the Deuteronomic law in the following manner:

> Let there be, in the fairest part of the land of the Chananaians, one holy city [ἱερὰ πόλις ἔστω μία] that is renowned for its excellence, whichever God selects for Himself through prophecy; and let there be one Temple [νεὼς εἷς] in it and one altar of stones [βωμὸς εἷς ἐκ λίθων] that are not hewn but chosen and joined together, which, smeared with whitewash, will be appealing and clean to view. Let the access to this be not by steps but by a sloping ramp. In another city let there be neither an altar nor a temple, for God is one and the stock of the Hebrews one [θεὸς γὰρ εἷς καὶ τὸ Ἑβραίων γένος ἕν]." (*A.J.* 4.8.5 §§200–201)[42]

Its appearance at this point may owe something to the Greco-Roman environment. As Anthony J. Guerra observes, this kind of theology provided Jewish apologists with "a bridge between their religion and the growing theological consensus of the contemporary educated gentile of the Hellenistic period."[43] In summary, the reception history is consistent with the Shema's relatively late appearance, and it undermines the significance that scholars have argued the Shema had in the preexilic period. The importance of the Shema emerged only during the Second Temple period.

Finnish Exegetical Society 76 (Göttingen: Vandenhoeck & Ruprecht, 1999); Pakkala, "The Monotheism of the Deuteronomistic History," *SJOT* 21 (2007): 159–78.

[41] See Nathan MacDonald, "The Beginnings of One-ness Theology in Late Israelite Prophetic Literature," in *Monotheism in Late Prophetic and Early Apocalyptic Literature*, ed. Nathan MacDonald and Ken Brown, FAT 2/72 (Tübingen: Mohr Siebeck, 2014), 103–23.

[42] Translation according to Louis H. Feldman, *Flavius Josephus, Judean Antiquities 1–4*, FJTC 3 (Leiden: Brill, 2000), 398–400.

[43] Anthony J. Guerra, *Romans and the Apologetic Tradition: The Purpose, Genre, and Audience of Paul's Letter*, SNTSMS 81 (Cambridge: Cambridge University Press, 1995), 94.

IV. The Growth of Deuteronomy 5–11

To this point I have argued that the Shema should be seen not as the earliest introduction to *Urdeuteronomium* but as a relatively late entrant into the book of Deuteronomy. Clearly this conclusion has significant implications for understanding the development of chapters 5–11. Scholars have long seen 6:4–5 as the seed from which the paraenetic framework grows. Deuteronomy 5–11 is an exegetical exposition of *das Hauptgebot*.[44] Christoph Levin puts the matter elegantly: "Without Deut 6:4–5, everything else hangs in the air."[45] My proposal would clearly require extensive analysis beyond what is possible in this article; what I hope to show, however, is that Levin's comment is unduly dramatic.

Levin's claim does point to the fact that some passages in Deut 5–11 are dependent on 6:4–5. The clearest example is probably the instructions about repeating and displaying the words of Moses in 11:18–20. These echo the instructions in 6:6–9, which are themselves logically dependent on 6:4–5. Two observations suggest that 11:18–20 is later.[46] First, while the expression "these words" probably refers to 6:4 or 6:4–5,[47] which could feasibly be written on amulets and on gates, the phrase "these words of mine" in 11:18 has no obvious referent and may refer to the whole of the Deuteronomic law.[48] It would appear, then, that the concrete instructions in 6:6–9 have been given a metaphorical sense in chapter 11 in a process of secondary development. Second, while the instructions in 6:6–9 are almost identical to 11:18–20, we find the rare verb שנן in 6:7, while 11:19 has the common למד. The most likely explanation is that the familiar term has replaced the unusual one. If 11:18–20 is later than 6:4–5, then this is likely true of most, perhaps even all, of 10:12–11:32. This passage is a loosely structured sermon that repeats ideas and phrases from elsewhere in chapters 5–11. Regular *Numeruswechsel* in this passage is probably not evidence of a complex compositional history but is a late imitative style. The passage provides a paraenetic bridge between the story of the golden calf and the opening of the Deuteronomic law. Another passage that is certainly later than 6:4–5 is 6:10–19. This text is also characterized by regular *Numeruswechsel* and clearly breaks the connection between 6:6–9 and 6:20–25, both of which use the second-person singular and concern the teaching of

---

[44] Lohfink, *Das Hauptgebot*.

[45] Levin, "Über den 'Color Hieremianus,'" 117: "Ohne Dtn 6,4–5 hinge alles weitere in der Luft."

[46] See Karin Finsterbusch, *Deuteronomium: Eine Einführung*, UTB 3626 (Göttingen: Vandenhoeck & Ruprecht, 2012), 98–99.

[47] For the difficulty in determining the referent of "these words," see Georg Braulik, "Die Ausdrücke für 'Gesetz' im Buch Deuteronomium," *Bib* 51 (1970): 39–66; MacDonald, *Deuteronomy*, 125–28.

[48] Otto, "Deuteronomistische und postdeuteronomistische Perspektiven," 183.

children.⁴⁹ The passage can be seen as an extended exposition on the commandment in 6:5 to love YHWH.

But if 6:4–5 does not belong to the latest layer of Deuteronomy, we do not need to conclude that it belongs to the earliest. A helpful starting point is Otto's proposal for the development of Deuteronomy. He identifies three main stages in redactional growth distinguished by the way they provide the book with a narratival location. The reform program of *Urdeuteronomium* has no narrative setting and is not attributed to Moses. DtrD, the main Deuteronomistic redaction of Deuteronomy, locates the promulgation of Deuteronomy through Moses on Mount Horeb.⁵⁰ This perspective is later revised by a DtrL, which maps a relationship to the Tetrateuch by distinguishing a Horeb and a Moab covenant and identifying Deuteronomy with the latter.⁵¹ Otto's proposal for DtrD highlights the way that the narratives about the giving of the Decalogue (chapter 5) and the golden calf (chapters 9–10) belong together. Their close relationship is indicated by their consistent use of the plural, even if the laws these narratives incorporate—the Decalogue and *Urdeuteronomium*—are expressed in the singular. The story of the giving of the Decalogue ends in 5:28–31 with Moses being commanded to go up on Mount Horeb to receive the commandments. The story of the golden calf begins in 9:9 with Moses ascending the mountain. In its present form, the narrative link between the Decalogue and the golden calf has been disrupted by the paraenetic material in chapters 6–8. Much of this paraenetic material is judged to be quite late—and certainly later than DtrD. Thus, Otto views 6:10–19; 7:3b–16, 25–26; and 8:1–9:6 as post-Deuteronomistic *Fortschreibungen* and attributes 6:22–23 and 7:1–3a, 17–24 to DtrL. The earliest texts incorporated in DtrD are to be found only in chapter 6, specifically 6:4–9*, 20–25.⁵²

---

⁴⁹ Gottfried Seitz, *Redaktionsgeschichtliche Studien zum Deuteronomium*, BWANT 93 (Stuttgart: Kohlhammer, 1971), 70–74.

⁵⁰ Otto, *Das Deuteronomium im Pentateuch*, 4: "Das Siglum steht für die dtr Hauptredaktion des Deuteronomiums und leitet sich von ihrer dekalogischen Strukturierung des Gesetzes im Deuteronomium (Dtn 12–25) ab." Otto discusses this redaction in ibid., 111–29.

⁵¹ Ibid., 4: "Das Siglum DtrL leitet sich aus der dtr Verbindung des Deuteronomiums mit der Landnahmeüberlieferung des Josuabuches." Otto discusses this redaction in ibid., 129–38. The idea of a Deuteronomistic redaction that linked Deuteronomy and Joshua originated with Norbert Lohfink, "Darstellungkunst und Theologie in Dtr 1,6–3,29," *Bib* 41 (1960): 105–34. For some serious criticisms of the theory of a DtrL, see Christophe Nihan, "The Literary Relationship between Deuteronomy and Joshua: A Reassessment," in *Deuteronomy in the Pentateuch, Hexateuch, and the Deuteronomistic History*, ed. Konrad Schmid and Raymond F. Person, FAT 2/56 (Tübingen: Mohr Siebeck, 2012), 79–114. For my argument I will retain the abbreviation DtrL for the purposes of distinguishing the different narrative reframings of the Deuteronomic law code, with no assumptions to be drawn about the nature of the relationship between Deuteronomy and Joshua.

⁵² For detailed discussion of Deut 1–11 by Otto, see now the two-volume *Deuteronomium 1–11*.

In many respects Otto's proposal provides both a compelling explanation of the shifting narrative perspective in Deut 1–11 and a persuasive account of the main lines in the development of chapters 1–11. One detail that is not explained in a satisfactory manner is the decision by DtrD to incorporate 6:4–9*, 20–25 between chapter 5 and chapters 9–10. Not only does this break the narrative rehearsal of the events on Mount Horeb, but it also detaches the law concerning centralization from its putative theological justification. Why was the entire narrative not placed before *Urdeuteronomium*? It is easier to explain the present state of the text as the result of the insertion of paraenetic material between chapter 5 and chapters 9–10. The problem with Otto's proposal may be combined with the observation that there is nothing in the story of the Decalogue and the golden calf that depends on 6:4–5. There is no part that is left "hanging in the air," as Levin has it, if the Shema is not present. The purpose of DtrD's narrative is to attribute the Deuteronomic law code to Moses, who received it from YHWH at Horeb, to distinguish it from the Ten Commandments that the people themselves heard, and to emphasize the importance of obeying the prohibition of idolatry. While DtrD's narrative is not the earliest introduction to *Urdeuteronomium*, it is arguably the earliest introduction that can be recovered with any certainty.

V. Conclusion

In this article I have sought to displace the Shema from the place attributed to it by some scholars, as the introduction to *Urdeuteronomium* and the motto of the Josianic reform movement. As all interpreters agree, Deut 6:4–5 is a carefully crafted creed, but I have argued that its honing took place somewhat later in the growth of Deuteronomy than is usually thought to be the case. As Braulik suggested, YHWH is one in the same way that the beloved in Songs 6:9 is one: the only one worthy of devotion from Israel. This is what the book of Deuteronomy will come to describe as a covenant relationship. It is rightly understood, as many interpreters have suggested before, as a positive restatement of the first commandment. It should not be understood as William F. Bade first suggested as an expression of mono-Yahwism aimed at the diffusion of YHWH into many local forms.[53]

Although Veijola's arguments that the love commandment in 6:5 was a late addition to the book of Deuteronomy cannot be upheld, his essential conclusion is sound. He failed, however, to appreciate the potentially radical consequences of his argument. The importance of his argument can be seen only when it is shown that verse 5 was not a late interpolation but an integral part of verses 4–5, or perhaps even verses 4–9. Veijola continued to hold that verse 4 was the earliest introduction to *Urdeuteronomium*, despite the fact that he took most of the steps needed to undermine this assumption.

---

[53] W. F. Bade, "Der Monojahwismus des Deuteronomiums," *ZAW* 30 (1910): 81–90.

The Lists of Levitical Cities (Joshua 21, 1 Chronicles 6) and the Propagandistic Map for the Hasmonean Territorial Expansion

YITZHAK LEE-SAK
leeyitzhak@gmail.com
Building # 9, Bar-Kochva, French-Hill, Jerusalem, Israel

The dates of the lists of Levitical cities (Josh 21 and 1 Chr 6) remain controversial. The same is true for their apparent status as units distinct from the surrounding texts. Many scholars have cast doubt on the historical reliability of the lists and have suggested a variety of alternative dates for their composition. Some European scholars have argued that the lists pertain to part of the final redaction of the Hexateuch or Chronicles. This proposed redaction would have been produced as late as the mid-Hellenistic period. An early third-century date for the Greek translations of the Hexateuch or Chronicles or the earliest attestation of these texts in the Qumran documents would support the late-redaction hypothesis. Reevaluating all of the above claims in this article, I will demonstrate that the lists could have been a historical reality only during the Hasmonean period. This claim is built on recent archaeological data from the town sites mentioned in the lists. To this end, I will investigate the distribution of the lists between the Iron Ages and the Hellenistic/Hasmonean period. Based on these two independent studies, I will propose that these lists functioned as a propagandistic map for the Hasmonean state during the territorial expansion of Hyrcanus and that they were later delivered to his successors. A subsequent study will examine Josh 21 and 1 Chr 6 in their MT and LXX forms, as well as several relevant canonical and extracanonical witnesses, and will propose that these two chapters may have been composed and become part of their respective biblical books in the mid- to late second century BCE.

Biblical scholars have generally accepted the view that the two lists of the distribution of the Levitical cities (Josh 21 and 1 Chr 6) share almost identical

I owe a profound debt of gratitude to all those who have instructed me, reviewed the earlier manuscripts of this work, and provided valuable suggestions: my two PhD supervisors, Prof. Oded Lipschits and Prof. Israel Finkelstein; my mentors, Prof. Thomas Römer, Dr. Jaeyoung Jeon, Prof. Koog-Pyoung Hong, and Dr. Frank Clancy; and my friends in the Department of Archaeology and Ancient Near Eastern Cultures in Tel Aviv University. All dates mentioned across this article are BCE unless otherwise indicated.

content and are distinctly isolated from their respective surrounding contexts.[1] Joshua 21 in particular can be construed not only as the abbreviated form of the contents of the conquest of the land and its distribution to each tribe (Josh 1–19) but also as the opening to Joshua's farewell sermon (Josh 23) and the covenant of Shechem (Josh 24).[2]

Joshua 21, however, is not connected with the preceding and subsequent contexts; rather, it can be considered an independent literary unit. Similarly, 1 Chr 6 is quite distinct from the rest of 1 Chr 1–9, because other chapters in this section following the genealogy of the ancestors and David refer to the tribal allotments.[3] Sara Japhet has argued that the "similarity between this pericope (1 Chr 6) and other genealogies in regard to their components only serves to emphasize the essential difference."[4] It is appropriate, therefore, to examine these texts independently.

Given the uniqueness of the lists, a number of scholars have discussed whether they could reflect a specific political reality during the biblical period of ancient Israel. Some researchers have refuted the historicity of the lists because of conflicting archaeological and historical data for each city on the lists from the Iron Age (henceforth IA) through the Persian or Hellenistic period. Moreover, although some scholars have concluded that the lists could not function as an administrative map,[5] others have favored the theory that the lists indeed reflect the reality of ancient Israel in a particular period.[6] Rejecting both opinions, Menaḥem Haran has adopted a mediating position, arguing that the lists include historically realistic data (dispersion of the Levites), on the one hand, and a utopian picture of the preexilic period (the identical size of the pasture of each city), on the other.[7]

---

[1] The lists are very similar to each other, except for some disparities in the names of cities. See table 1 below.

[2] Götz Schmitt, "Levitenstädte," ZDPV 111 (1995): 28–48; Ralph W. Klein, 1 Chronicles: A Commentary, Hermeneia (Minneapolis: Fortress, 2006), 191.

[3] Ehud Ben Zvi, "The List of the Levitical Cities," JSOT 54 (1992): 77–106, here 77–78. Gary N. Knoppers, I Chronicles 1–9: A New Translation with Introduction and Commentary, AB 12A (Garden City, NY: Doubleday, 2004), 444. Note peculiar Priestly expressions of 1 Chr 6 (Post-P), גורל, נתן ערים, בני מטה + PN (6:39, 40, 42, 46, 48–50, 52), which are absent in other surrounding chapters. They are extraneous to the style of other chapters.

[4] Sara Japhet, I & II Chronicles: A Commentary, OTL (Louisville: Westminster John Knox, 1993), 145.

[5] See A. Graeme Auld, "The Levitical Cities: Text and History," ZAW 91 (1979): 194–206; Manfred Oeming, Das wahre Israel: Die "genealogische Vorhalle" 1 Chronik 1–9, BWANT 128 (Stuttgart: Kohlhammer, 1990), 154–55; Ben Zvi, "List of the Levitical Cities," 77–106; Richard D. Nelson, Joshua: A Commentary, OTL (Louisville: Westminster John Knox, 1997), 236–37; Ernst Axel Knauf, Josua, ZBK.AT 6 (Zurich: TVZ, 2008), 172–79; Hartmut N. Rösel, Joshua, HCOT (Leuven: Peeters, 2011), 328–41.

[6] See nn. 8, 11, and 12 below.

[7] Menaḥem Haran, "Studies in the Account of the Levitical Cities: I. Preliminary Considerations," JBL 80 (1961): 45–54, https://doi.org/10.2307/3264565; and Haran, "Studies in the

A number of scholars have applied diverse dates to Josh 21 and 1 Chr 6, some arguing prior to the 1990s CE that such lists were originally produced by royal scribes of the united monarchy.[8] These studies, however, have not escaped severe criticism.[9] Biblical historians and archaeologists cannot demonstrate any credible scribal activities of the royal court or any evidence of a powerfully centralized polity in the central highlands before the mid-ninth century.[10] Given the results of the above observations about tenth-century historical realia, therefore, the conclusions of previous studies are unwarranted. Other researchers have attributed the lists to a number of different periods, such as the mid- to late monarchic, the Persian, or even the Hellenistic period. Focusing on archaeological data as a foundation for their interpretation, John L. Peterson and Robert G. Boling have maintained that the material culture of the cities in the lists suggests a date of composition during the reign of Jeroboam II or Uzziah.[11] Other scholars such as Albrecht Alt and Nadav Na'aman have claimed that the lists echo a blueprint of Judah under Josiah's authority.[12] In contrast, A. Graeme Auld, Ehud Ben Zvi, Ernst Axel Knauf, and

---

Account of the Levitical Cities: II. Utopia and Historical Reality," *JBL* 80 (1961): 156–65, https://doi.org/10.2307/3264206.

[8] William F. Albright, "The List of Levitic Cities," in *Louis Ginsberg Jubilee Volume on the Occasion of His Seventieth Birthday* (New York: American Academy for Jewish Research, 1945), 49–73; Tryggve N. D. Mettinger, *Solomonic State Officials: A Study of the Civil Government Officials of the Israelite Monarchy*, ConBOT 5 (Lund: Gleerup, 1971), 98–101; Yohanan Aharoni, *The Land of the Bible: A Historical Geography*, rev. and enl. ed. (Philadelphia: Westminster, 1979), 301–5; Zechariah Kallai, *Historical Geography of the Bible: The Tribal Territories of Israel* (Jerusalem: Magnes, 1986), 447–76.

[9] See, in particular, the criticism by the Copenhagen school: Thomas L. Thompson, *Early History of the Israelite People: From the Written and the Archaeological Sources*, SHANE 4 (Leiden: Brill, 1992); Niels P. Lemche, "On Doing Sociology with 'Solomon,'" in *The Age of Solomon: Scholarship at the Turn of the Millennium*, ed. Lowell K. Handy, SHCANE 11 (Leiden: Brill, 1997), 312–35.

[10] Israel Finkelstein and Benjamin Sass, "The West Semitic Alphabetic Inscriptions, Late Bronze II to Iron IIA: Archeological Context, Distribution and Chronology," *HBAI* 2 (2013): 149–220; Nadav Na'aman, "The Kingdom of Judah in the 9th Century BCE: Text Analysis versus Archaeological Research," *TA* 40 (2013): 247–76; Omer Sergi, "Judah's Expansion in Historical Context," *TA* 40 (2013): 226–46.

[11] John L. Peterson, "A Topographical Surface Survey of the Levitical 'Cities' of Joshua 21 and I Chronicles 6: Studies on the Levites in Israelite Life and Religion" (PhD diss., Seabury-Western Theological Seminary, 1977); Robert G. Boling, *Joshua: A New Translation with Introduction and Commentary*, AB 6 (Garden City, NY: Doubleday, 1982), 477–97.

[12] Albrecht Alt, "Bemerkungen zu einigen judäischen Ortslisten des Alten Testaments," in *Kleine Schriften zur Geschichte des Volkes Israel*, 3 vols. (Munich: Beck, 1953), 3.2:289–305; Nadav Na'aman, "A New Look at the System of Levitical Cities," in *Borders and Districts in Biblical Historiography: Seven Studies in Biblical Geographic Lists*, JBS 4 (Jerusalem: Simor, 1986), 203–36; Na'aman suggested that nine of thirteen Aaronide cities in Judah and Simeon were a possible reflection of the Josianic political situation, while the remaining cities mirror the utopian feature of the tribal allotments of Josh 13–19.

Gary N. Knoppers have insisted that the contents of the lists might reflect the utopian picture of Yehud during the Achaemenid period.[13] According to these scholars, the dating of the lists cannot reflect an actual historical period at all, since the Israelites or Judeans did not control the boundary depicted in the lists during any period between the tenth century and the fourth century. This opinion has been dominant in recent scholarly circles.

A question that must be asked, however, is why the dating of the lists has been limited to the tenth through fourth centuries. In order to evaluate the credibility of the previous scholarly conclusions, I will consider the updated archaeological, historical, and textual data pertaining to the lists.

I. Archaeological Data

Archaeological Observations Concerning the Listed Cities

In this section, I will review the archaeological information related to each listed site. These data lead to the conclusion that a number of places can be identified with sufficient certainty. Information can be extracted from excavation expeditions and surface surveys of the properly identified sites, as the table below shows.[14] One may then recapitulate the archaeological results of the cities in terms of the activity intensity of the settlement from the Iron IA–IIA through the Hellenistic/Hasmonean periods.

Tables 1 and 2 indicate that only eighteen identified cities mentioned in the lists were certainly occupied during the Persian period; nine other cities were scarcely inhabited, and the remainder (eighteen cities) were not settled then. Additionally, it is noteworthy that merely two cities (V*) that were well excavated and surveyed are ascribed to the IA IIA–early IA IIB period. Moreover, two sites do not reveal IA IIB–C material culture. In contrast to these cases, other sites do clearly display IA IIB and Hellenistic/Hasmonean remains. If one accepts the lists' historical reliability, it would seem that IA IIB and the Hellenistic/Hasmonean periods are more viable options.

This result derives from archaeological information based on the geographical scope of the lists, which include "definitely and probably identified" cities. If one then limits this observation of the cities that are not only "excavated" but also "definitely identified," what conclusions can be drawn?

---

[13] Ben Zvi, "List of the Levitical Cities," 77–106; Knauf, *Josua*, 172–79; Knoppers, *I Chronicles*, 443–44.

[14] The exact information for several sites is not available, as appropriate surveys or excavations have not been or cannot be undertaken due to external conditions.

TABLE 1. Levitical Cities Listed in Joshua 21 and 1 Chronicles 6
(Only definite and probable identifications)

Josh 21	1 Chr 6 (Eng. vv. 54–81)	Modern Arabic Name	Condition of Excavation or Identification	IA II[15]	Persian Period	Hellenistic/ Hasmonean Period
Hebron[16] (21:11, 13/6:55, 57)		Tell er-Rumeideh	(E), (DI)	V**	V	V Strong
Libnah[17] (21:13/6:57)		Tell Bornât	(E), (PI)	V	–	–
		Tell Zeitah		V	V	V
		Tell el-Judeideh		V	–	V
Yattir[18] (21:14/6:57)		Khirbet ʿAttîr	(S), (DI)	V**	Weak	V

Abbreviations
(E)   Excavated
(S)   Surveyed
(DI)   Definitely Identified
(PI)   Probably Identified
(V)   Settlement Activity
(V*)   Settlement Activity only during the IA IIA–the early IA IIB
(V**) Settlement Activity only during the mid-IA IIB–IA IIC

[15] Since the archaeological data of the so-called united monarchy are so meager, the time span of Iron Age I (IA I) is not included here. See Israel Finkelstein and Eli Piasetzky, "Radiocarbon Dating the Iron Age in the Levant: A Bayesian Model for Six Ceramic Phases and Six Transitions," *Antiquity* 84 (2010): 374–85, https://doi.org/10.1017/S0003598X00066643.

[16] Moshe Kochavi, "The Land of Judah," in *Judaea, Samaria and the Golan: Archaeological Survey 1967–1968*, ed. Moshe Kochavi [in Hebrew] (Jerusalem: Carta, 1972), 17–89, here 61–62; Avi Ofer, "Hebron," *NEAEHL* 2:606–9; Emanuel Eisenberg and Alla Nagorski, "Tel Hevron," *Hadashot Arkheologiyot: Excavations and Surveys in Israel* 114 (2002): 112–13.

[17] Christopher McKinny and Amit Dagan, "The Explorations of Tel Burna," *PEQ* 145 (2013): 294–305, https://doi.org/10.1179/0031032813Z.00000000067; Itzhaq Shai and Joe Uziel, "All for Archaeology and Archaeology for All: The Tel Burna Archaeology Project's Approach to Community Archaeology," *Journal of Community Archaeology* 3 (2016): 57–69, here 58–60, https://dx.doi.org/10.1080/20518196.2015.1123887. Tel Burna (Tell Bornât), however, cannot be absolutely identified with Libnah. Other candidates can be suggested: Tel Zayit (Tell Zeitah) (see Ron E. Tappy, "The 1998 Preliminary Survey of Khirbet Zeitah el-Kharab [Tel Zayit] in the Shephelah of Judah," *BASOR* 319 [2000]: 27–31), and Tel Goded (Tell el-Judeideh) (see Nachum Sagiv, Boaz Zissu, and David Amit, "Tel Goded," *ESI* 18 [1998]: 149–51, here 149). In my opinion, Tel Zayit is a convincing candidate for the identification of Libnah.

[18] Hanan Eshel, Jodi Magness, and Eli Shenhav, "Khirbet Yattir, 1995–1999: Preliminary Report," *IEJ* 50 (2000): 153–68.

Josh 21	1 Chr 6 (Eng. vv. 54–81)	Modern Arabic Name	Condition of Excavation or Identification	IA II	Persian Period	Hellenistic/ Hasmonean Period
Eshtemoa[19] (21:14/6:57)		es-Samûʿ	(S), (DI)	V	–	V
Holon[20] (v. 15)	Hillen? (v. 58)	Khirbet ʿAlîn	(S), (PI)	V Strong	V	V
Debir[21] (21:15/6:58)		Khirbet Rabûd	(E), (DI)	V Strong	Weak	V
Ain[22] (v. 16)	Ashan? (v. 59)	Khirbet ʿAin	(S), (PI)	V	–	V
Beth-Shemesh[23] (21:16/6:59)		Tell el-Rumeileh	(E), (DI)	V*	–	Weak
Gibeon[24] (v. 17)	–	el-Jîb	(E), (DI)	V**	–	V
Geba[25] (21:17/6:60)		Jabaʿ	(S), (DI)	V**	Weak	V

[19] Zeʾev Yeivin, "Eshtemoa," *NEAEHL* 2:423–24; Israel Finkelstein, "The Historical Reality behind the Genealogical Lists in 1 Chronicles," *JBL* 131 (2012): 65–83, here 68, https://doi.org/10.2307/23488212.

[20] Ofer's survey offers the following percentages for each biblical period of the total of pottery sherds: IA II 72%, Persian 6%, Hellenistic 3%, Early Roman 1%, Late Roman 1%, Byzantine 10%, Medieval 1%, Later 6%. See Avi Ofer, *The Highland of Judah during the Biblical Period* [in Hebrew] (PhD diss., Tel Aviv University, 1993), chapter 3.47, and table no. 45 sub-no. ד (320/36/1).

[21] Moshe Kochavi, "Khirbet Rabud," *NEAEHL* 4:1252; Peterson, *Topographical Surface Survey*, 536. Kochavi and Peterson did not mention the archaeological remains of the Persian period. Despite the scanty remains available, however, Persian and Hellenistic material culture has recently been identified. See Raphael Greenberg and Adi Keinan, *Israeli Archaeological Activity in the West Bank 1967–2007: A Sourcebook* (Jerusalem: Ostracon, 2009), 135 no. 935.

[22] John L. Peterson, "Ain," *ABD* 1:132. Another candidate for this site identification, Khirbet Asan, is inaccessible.

[23] Shlomo Bunimovitz and Zevi Lederman, "Beth-Shemesh," *NEAEHL* 1:249–53; 5:1644–48; Bunimovitz and Lederman, *Tel Beth-Shemesh, A Border Community in Judah: Renewed Excavations 1990–2000; The Iron Age*, 2 vols., Tel Aviv University Sonia and Marco Nadler Institute of Archaeology Monograph Series 34 (Winona Lake, IN: Eisenbrauns, 2016), 419–69.

[24] Finkelstein, "Genealogical Lists," 69.

[25] Amir Feldstein et al., "Southern Part of the Maps of Ramallah and el-Bireh and Northern Part of the Map of ʿEin Kerem," in *Archaeological Survey of the Hill Country of Benjamin*, ed. Israel Finkelstein and Yitzhak Magen [in Hebrew] (Jerusalem: Israel Antiquities Authority, 1993), 177–79. Persian-period pottery is reported only in Zechariah Kallai, "The Land of Benjamin and Mt. Ephraim," in Kochavi, *Judaea, Samaria and the Golan*, 153–93, here 183.

Josh 21	1 Chr 6 (Eng. vv. 54–81)	Modern Arabic Name	Condition of Excavation or Identification	IA II	Persian Period	Hellenistic/ Hasmonean Period
Anathoth[26] (21:18/6:60)		Râs el-Kharûbeh		V**	V	V
		Khirbet Deir es-Sidd	(S), (PI)	V	Weak	V
		Anata		V Strong	Weak	V Strong
Almon[27] (v. 18)	Alemeth (v. 60)	Khirbet ʿAlmît	(S), (DI)	V	V	V
Shechem[28] (21:21/6:67)		Tell Balâṭah	(E), (DI)	V Strong	Weak	V Strong
Gezer[29] (21:21/6:67)		Tell el-Jazari	(E), (DI)	V Strong	V	V
Beth-Horon[30] (21:22/6:68)		Beit ʿÛr el-Fauqa (upper)	(S), (DI)	V Strong	Weak	V
		Beit ʿÛr el-Taḥtā (lower)		V Strong	Weak	V Strong

[26] For Râs el-Kharûbeh, see Uri Dinur and Nurit Feig, "Eastern Part of the Map of Jerusalem," in Finkelstein and Magen, *Archaeological Survey*, 341–427, here 359–60. For Khirbet Deir res-Sidd, see ibid., 393; Yonathan Nadelman, "The Identification of Anathoth and the Soundings at Khirbet Deir es-Sidd," *IEJ* 44 (1994): 62–74, here 74. For Anata, see Abraham Bergman, "On the Identification of Anathoth" [in Hebrew], *ErIsr* 18 (1985): 209–11; and Dinur and Feig, "Eastern Part," 359–60.

[27] Dinur and Feig, "Eastern Part," 380–81; Greenberg and Keinan, *Israeli Archaeological Activity*, 77 no. 408.

[28] Arye Borstein, "Shechem," in *The Oxford Encyclopedia of the Bible and Archaeology*, ed. Daniel M. Master (Oxford: Oxford University Press, 2013), 2:348–57.

[29] Steven Ortiz, Samuel Wolff, and Gary Arbino, "Tel Gezer," *Hadashot Arkheologiyot: Excavations and Surveys in Israel* 123 (2011), http://www.hadashot-esi.org.il/report_detail_eng.aspx?id=1820&mag_id=118; Steven Ortiz and Samuel Wolff, "Guarding the Border to Jerusalem: The Iron Age City of Gezer," *NEA* 75 (2012): 4–19.

[30] Israel Finkelstein, Zvi Lederman, and Shlomo Bunimovitz, *Highlands of Many Cultures: The Southern Samaria Survey; The Sites*, 2 vols., Monograph Series 14 (Tel Aviv: Institute of Archaeology, 1997), 1:161–64. (Beit ʿÛr et Taḥtā: // IA II 20.9%; IA II/Per 2.0; Per 2.7; Per/Hell 13.5%; Hell 15.5%); ibid., 303–5. (Beit ʿÛr el-Fauqa: IAIII 56.1%; IA II/Per 1.3%; Per 3.2%; Per/Hell 3.9%; Hell 6.5%). The percentages are for the pottery sherds surveyed in the two sites of Beth-Horon (the upper and lower Beth-Horon) for the specific biblical periods.

Josh 21	1 Chr 6 (Eng. vv. 54–81)	Modern Arabic Name	Condition of Excavation or Identification	IA II	Persian Period	Hellenistic/ Hasmonean Period
Elteke[31] (v. 23)	–	Tell es-Shallâf	(S), (PI)	V**	V	V
Gibbe-thon[32] (v. 23)	–	Tell el-Melat	(S), (DI)	V Strong	V	V
Aijalon[33] (21:24/6:69)		Yālô	(S), (DI)	V	V	V
Gath-Rimmon[34] (21:24/6:69)		Tell Jerîsheh	(E), (PI)	V*	–	V
		Tell Abu Zeitin		V	–	V
Taʿanach (v. 25)[35]	Aner ? (v. 70)	Tell Taʿannek	(E), (DI)	V Strong	V	V Strong
Gath-Rimmon (v. 25)[36]	Bileam? (v. 70)[37]	Khirbet Belʿameh	(E), (PI)	V	–	V

[31] John L. Peterson, "Elteke," *ABD* 2:483–84.

[32] Oren Shmueli, "Iron Age Tombs North of Tel Maloṯ" [in Hebrew], *ʿAtiqot* 65 (2011): 41–46.

[33] Ram Gophna and Yoseph Porat, "The Land of Ephraim and Manasseh," in Kochavi, *Judaea, Samaria and the Golan*, 196–241, here 236.

[34] John L. Peterson, "Gath-Rimmon," *ABD* 2:910–11.

[35] During the Hellenistic/Hasmonean period, the village of Taʿanach was located on the northeastern side of the tell. See Albert E. Glock, "Taanach," *ABD* 6:287–90; Siegfried Kreuzer, "Taanak," *EDB*, 1268–69.

[36] Peterson, *Topographical Surface Survey*, 219. The identification of Gath-Rimmon is not yet decided, while that of Bileam (Ibleam) can be suggested, despite the textual corruption between Josh 21 and 1 Chr 6.

[37] Ibid.; Eveline J. van der Steen, "Putting Khirbet Balamah on the Archaeological Map," *PEQ* 133 (2001): 111–29.

Josh 21	1 Chr 6 (Eng. vv. 54–81)	Modern Arabic Name	Condition of Excavation or Identification	IA II	Persian Period	Hellenistic/ Hasmonean Period
Kishion (v. 28)[38]	Gedesh? (v. 72)	Tell el-ʿAjjul	(S), (PI)	V	V	V
		Tell el-Muqarqash		V	–	–
		Khirbet Qasyûn		V	–	V
Daberath[39] (21:28/6:72)		Khirbet Dabûriyeh	(S), (PI)	–	V	V
Avdon (v. 30)[40]	Avdon (v. 74)	Khirbet ʿAbda	(S), (PI)	V	V	V
Helkath (v. 31)[41]	Hukok (v. 75)	Khirbet Huqoq	(E), (DI)	V**	V	V
Rehob[42] (21:31/6:75)		Tell el-Gharbi (Tell Birwe)	(S), (PI)	V	Weak	V
Kedesh[43] (21:32/6:76)		**Tell Qudish**	(E), (DI)	V**	V	V
Jokneam[44] (v. 34)	–	Tell Qeimûn	(E), (DI)	V (except for IA IIC)	V	V

[38] Tell el-ʿAjjul (IA I, IA II, Hellenistic, Roman/Byzantine, and medieval periods), Tell el-Muqarqash (IA I, IA II, and Byzantine periods), and Khirbet Qasyûn (EB, MB, LB, IA I, IA II, Hellenistic, Roman and Byzantine periods). See John L. Peterson, "Kishion," *ABD* 4:88–89.

[39] John L. Peterson, "Daberath," *ABD* 2:1.

[40] Yoab Lerer, "Tel ʾAvdon," *Hadashot Arkheologiyot: Excavations and Surveys in Israel* 123 (2011), http://www.hadashot-esi.org.il/report_detail_eng.aspx?id=1706&mag_id=118.

[41] Jodi Magness et al., "Huqoq – 2013," *Hadashot Arkheologiyot: Excavations and Surveys in Israel* 126 (2014), http://www.hadashot-esi.org.il/Report_Detail_Eng.aspx?id=12648.

[42] Moshe W. Prausnitz, "Notes and News," *IEJ* 12 (1962): 143; John L. Peterson, "Rehob," *ABD* 5:660–61. Pottery sherds can be dated to MB, IA I–II, Persian, and Hellenistic periods.

[43] Yohanan Aharoni, "Kedesh," *NEAEHL* 3:855–56; Andrea M. Berlin and Sharon C. Herbert, "Tel Kedesh," in Master, *Oxford Encyclopedia of the Bible and Archaeology*, 2:373–81.

[44] Amnon Ben-Tor, "Jokneam," *NEAEHL* 3:805–11. Jokneam in the Hellenistic/Hasmonean period was likely a small settlement.

Josh 21	1 Chr 6 (Eng. vv. 54–81)	Modern Arabic Name	Condition of Excavation or Identification	IA II	Persian Period	Hellenistic/ Hasmonean Period
Jahaz[45] (21:36/6:78)		Khirbet el-Medeiniyeh eth-Themed	(E), (DI)	V Strong	–	V (Nabatean period)
Mephaath[46] (21:37/6:79)		Tell Jâwah	(S), (PI)	V	–	–
		Umm er-Rasas				
Ramoth[47] (v. 38)	Ramoth of Gilead (v. 80)	Tell er-Rumeith	(E), (PI)	V (except for IA IIC)	–	V
		er-Ramtha	(S), (PI)	V	–	–
Mahanaim[48] (21:38/6:80)		Tell ed-Dhahab	(S), (PI)	V	–	V
		Tell Hajjaj		–	V	V
Heshbon[49] (21:39/6:81)		Tell Ḥesbân	(E), (DI)	V Strong	V	V Strong
Jazer[50] (21:39/6:81)		Khirbet Aṣṣār	(S), (PI)	V	–	V

[45] Robert Chadwick, P. M. Michèle Daviau, and Magareet Steiner, "Four Seasons of Excavations at Khirbat al-Mudayna on the Wadi ath-Thamad, 1996–1999," *ADAJ* 44 (2000): 257–70; P. M. Michèle Daviau, "Hirbet el-Mudeyine in Its Landscape: Iron Age Towns, Forts, and Shrines," *ZDPV* 122 (2006): 14–30, pls. 4–9.

[46] Khirbet Nefa'ah is one of the candidates for the biblical Mephaath. Two other locations have been suggested such as Tell Jâwah and Umm er-Rasas.

[47] Nelson Glueck, "Ramoth-Gilead," *BASOR* 92 (1943): 10–16, https://doi.org/10.2307/1355267; Israel Finkelstein, Oded Lipschits, and Omer Sergi, "Tell er-Rumeith in Northern Jordan: Some Archaeological and Historical Observations," *Semitica* 55 (2013): 7–23.

[48] Israel Finkelstein, Ido Koch, and Oded Lipschits, "Biblical Gilead," *UF* 43 (2011): 131–59, here 146–48. Tell-Hajjaj was occupied only during IA I.

[49] Remains of the whole period can be excavated; http://www.madabaplains.org/hisban/overview-excavations.htm.

[50] Finkelstein, Koch, and Lipschits, "Biblical Gilead," 140–41.

TABLE 2. Summary of Table 1
(45 candidates applicable to 34 cities out of 48 cities)

DI+PI	Strong	Medium		Weak	No Activity
IA IIA– the early IA IIB	11	See V* 2	22 (two sites do not have IA–IIC remains)	0	2
Mid-IA IIB– IA IIC		See V** 8			
Persian	0	18		9	18
Hellenistic/ Hasmonean	6	33		1	5

TABLE 3. Table of Sites "Definitely Identified and Excavated" in the Lists

DI/E	Strong	Weak	Medium	No Evidence
IA II	5	0	5	0
Persian	0	4	2	4
Hellenistic/ Hasmonean	2	1	7	0

Ten cities (in bold type in table 1) are clearly identified and sufficiently excavated: Hebron, Debir, Beth-Shemesh, Gibeon, Geba, Shechem, Gezer, Tel Kedesh, and Jahaz, as well as Heshbon.[51] The information in table 1 matches that of table 3. In this respect, two options, the IA IIB and the Hellenistic/Hasmonean periods can be suggested for an archaeological dating of the lists' historical period.

The present study, however, is limited by a lack of archaeological evidence: First, fourteen towns among all the listed cities (about 29% of the total) cannot be properly observed because their locations remain unidentified.[52] Second, two problematic candidates relate to a settlement hiatus in the IA II (Tell Hajjaj and Khirbet Dabûriyeh), and five date to the Hellenistic/Hasmonean periods (Tell

---

[51] See the footnotes above for more specific archaeological information on these cities.
[52] These sites are not securely identified (in the following list, when there are two references in parentheses, the first is to Joshua and the second to 1 Chronicles): Juttah (Josh 21:16); Kibzaim/Jokmeam (21:22/6:68); Golan (21:27/6:71); Beeshterah/Ashtaroth (21:27/6:71); Jarmuth/Ramoth (21:29/6:73); Ein Gannim/Anem (21:29/6:73); Mishal/Mashal (21:30/6:74); Hammoth-Dor/Hammon (21:32/6:76); Kartan/Kiriathaim (21:32/6:76); Kartah/Tabor (21:34/6:77); Dimnah/Rimmono (21:35/6:77); Nahalal (21:35); Bezer (21:36/6:78); Kedemoth (21:37/6:79).

Bornât, Tell el Muqarqash, Tell Jâwah, Um er-Rasas, and er-Ramtha). From among the forty-five candidates, these seven cases cannot be presented as evidence of actual settlement. To be sure, four candidates may be replaced by others that can be regarded as relevant for the identification of towns, excluding Khirbet Dabûriyeh (Daberah), and Tell Jâwah plus Um er-Rasas (Mephaath). But these three potential candidates for the two sites, Daberah and Mephaath, have not yet been properly investigated and therefore should be excluded from historical consideration.

Thus, the results are not unambiguous and should lead readers to reconsider whether the lists are historical or whether they should be viewed as utopian. If Josh 21 and 1 Chr 6 reflect the historical situation of a specific period, the tables above offer the IA IIB and the Hellenistic/Hasmonean period as likely candidates for a historical setting. But if the lists are not historical but rather mirror an ideal situation, the Persian period can also be offered as a possible setting. The following section will assess which period would most likely be reflected in the lists.

II. Historical Data

Can an IA IIA–Early IA IIB Reality Be the Background for the Lists?

Since a tenth-century date for the present lists is improbable, it is necessary to turn to the ninth and eighth centuries. The latter is problematic, because prior to the early ninth century, the northern kingdom had not yet captured the geographical territories represented by the lists. Afterwards, Omri and his son Ahab ruled the Ayalon Valley, the Sharon coastal plain, most parts of Galilee, the Gilead, the northern part of Moab, and most parts of Benjamin.[53] In the south, the kingdom of Judah no doubt remained a small kingdom located in the core of the Judean highlands before the days of Jehoshaphat or Jehoram. The kingdom of Judah expanded toward the Shephelah and the Arad Valley beginning in the mid-ninth century.[54] In view of this summary of the tenth through eighth centuries, can the extent of the territory of both kingdoms after the mid-ninth century be used to date the lists? This approach should be rejected for four reasons. First, table 1 shows that more than ten sites were not consistently settled at the time.[55] Second, the areas that encompass Golan and Ashtaroth were never returned to the Omride dynasty after Aram-Damascus subjugated them (ca. 895–850 BCE).[56] Third, the regions in which Abdon, Rehob, and Mishal were located belonged to the territory of

---

[53] Israel Finkelstein, *The Forgotten Kingdom: The Archaeology and History of Northern Israel*, ANEM 5 (Atlanta: Society of Biblical Literature, 2013), 105–9.

[54] Na'aman, "Kingdom of Judah," 247–76; Sergi, "Judah's Expansion," 226–46.

[55] See the cities marked V**, whose settlement ranges from IA mid-IIB to IIC.

[56] Anson F. Rainey and R. Steven Notley, *The Sacred Bridge: Carta's Atlas of the Biblical World* (Jerusalem: Carta, 2006), 197–209.

Phoenicia.⁵⁷ Finally, the lists seem to echo a unified political entity, whereas the political situation of the ninth century confirms the existence of two different kingdoms.

Can one then argue that the lists represent the territorial reality of the eighth century, as Peterson and Boling suggest?⁵⁸ The supposition that the lists represent the territory of Israel under Jeroboam II and Judah under Uzziah cannot be supported for three reasons. First, most cities of the northwestern Mediterranean coast were not annexed to the territory of the Israelites at that time.⁵⁹ Second, the cities allocated to the tribe of Reuben belonged to the territory of Moab during that time. The northern border of the kingdom of Moab (as the line beyond Heshbon, from Abel ṣittim to Minnit) may have been retained during the eighth–seventh centuries.⁶⁰ Third, the fact that lists suggest a unified administrative system flatly contradicts the idea that Israel and Judah already constituted distinct political entities. To summarize, the IA IIA–early IIB period cannot be the historical setting behind the lists.

Do the Lists Fit the Political Situation of the Josianic Period?

Several scholarly attempts noted earlier have suggested that the lists represent the historical reality of the Josianic period.⁶¹ The results of these studies, however, are not conclusive. First, the extent of the kingdom of Judah during Josiah's reign is not comparable to that of the lists.⁶² Second, Na'aman's attempt to date part of the list to the Josianic period is unconvincing. Na'aman intriguingly suggests that only thirteen cities of Judah, Simeon, and Benjamin match the territory of Josiah's days. The rest of the cities are likely to be Josiah's ideal propaganda for territorial expansion, while other parts are nonhistorical or utopian.⁶³ Yet Na'aman offers no clear criteria by which to judge part of the lists to be historically authentic. Third, Josiah could not achieve his political ambition under the umbrella of the Saite dynasty; hence, this propaganda would have to be explained away as being "a delusion."⁶⁴ Fourth, as Israel Finkelstein has noted, the lists do not mention

---

⁵⁷ Ibid., 198–99.

⁵⁸ Peterson, *Topographical Surface Survey*; Boling, *Joshua*, 494.

⁵⁹ Rainey and Notley, *Sacred Bridge*, 217; and see the map on 219.

⁶⁰ Nadav Na'aman, "Rezin of Aram and the Land of Gilead," *ZDPV* 111 (1995): 105–17.

⁶¹ Alt, "Einigien judäischen Ortslisten," 289–305; Na'aman, "System of Levitical Cities," 203–36.

⁶² Ido Koch and Oded Lipschits, "The Rosette Stamped Jar Handle System and the Kingdom of Judah at the End of the First Temple Period," *ZDPV* 129 (2013): 55–78, here 58.

⁶³ Na'aman, "System of Levitical Cities," 203–36.

⁶⁴ Josiah was killed by the Egyptians at the site of Meggido in 609 BCE. The Egyptian influence filled the power vacuum in Syria-Palestine after the retreat of the Assyrians in the 630s BCE until the rise of Nebuchadnezzar II.

Beersheba and Lachish, whose city status was so important in the Josianic period.[65] Fifth, pottery sherds dating to the Josianic period have not been found in any of the excavated portions of Beth-Shemesh, except for a small number inside a water reservoir, most of which were found under the shaft used for drawing water.[66] Beth-Shemesh may have been deserted during the Josianic period, but the reservoir continued to be utilized by several inhabitants who lived nearby. Sixth, the lists encompass Gezer and Aijalon, both places that were never part of the Judean kingdom.[67] A Josianic dating of the lists therefore seems unlikely.

Can the Lists Reflect a Utopian Image of the Persian Period?

Some scholars who date the lists to the Persian period have argued that the geographical extent of the lists does not reflect the utopian reality of the province of Yehud, because its territory was too small. Consequently, they understand the lists as a model of "the ideal rationale of the Great Israel" during the Persian period. Following Ben Zvi's article in 1992, this argument has been widely accepted.[68] Recent investigations of the boundaries of the province of Yehud have been carried out to sketch its borders, based not only on the geographical lists (Ezra 2; Neh 2, 3, 11, 12) but also on the distribution of Yehud seal impressions.[69] According to Oded Lipschits, Neh 3 may play a key role in depicting the geographical extent of Yehud.[70] First, the northern demarcation is represented by the line of Beth-Horon–Gibeon and beyond Bethel. Second, the western boundary would be the line of Eshtaol–Beth-Shemesh–Jarmuth–Azekah, not reaching Timnah, Gath, and Libnah. Third, the southern border would be the line of Qeilah and Beth-Zur, except for Hebron and Mareshah. These data show that many sites (Hebron, Juttah, Eshtemoa, Yattir, Debir, Libnah, Elteke, Gezer, Beth-Horon, and the areas beyond Gibeon) did not belong to the province of Yehud, but some cities were under the hegemony of the province of Idumea.

Likewise, archaeology stands in contrast to the utopian picture of Yehud. Finkelstein mentioned two missing elements: En-Gedi and Ramat-Raḥel are strikingly absent from the lists, yet the great number of Yehud stamp impressions

---

[65] Finkelstein, "Genealogical Lists," 74.

[66] Bunimovitz and Lederman, "Beth-Shemesh," 1644–48; Bunimovitz and Lederman, *Tel Beth-Shemesh*, 419–69.

[67] Finkelstein, "Genealogical Lists," 74.

[68] Ben Zvi, "List of the Levitical Cities"; Oeming, *Das wahre Israel*, 154–55; Schmitt, "Levitenstädte"; Nelson, *Joshua*, 236–37; Ludwig Schmidt, "Leviten- und Asylstädte in Num XXXV und Jos. XX; XXI 1–42," *VT* 52 (2002): 103–21; Rösel, *Joshua*, 328–41.

[69] Oded Lipschits, *The Fall and Rise of Jerusalem: Judah under Babylonian Rule* (Winona Lake, IN: Eisenbrauns, 2005), 168–74; Lipschits and David S. Vanderhooft, *The Yehud Stamp Impressions: A Corpus of Inscribed Impressions from the Persian and Hellenistic Periods in Judah* (Winona Lake, IN: Eisenbrauns, 2011).

[70] Lipschits, *Fall and Rise*, 168–74.

unearthed from the sites demonstrates their importance during the period. Moreover, neither typical Yehud impressions nor standard Persian remains can be found in Gibeon and Beth-Zur.[71]

Accordingly, one must consider whether the author could regard Josh 21 and 1 Chr 6 as a utopian map for the Yehud community. Methodologically, viewing the lists as a sort of idealized map is not impossible if they were part of genealogies in 1 Chr 2–9. Genealogies are not history per se, but they do clearly have a multigenerational dimension, which may reflect corporate memories, present realities, future hopes, and authorial idealization. The lists, however, differ from the genealogies in 1 Chr 2–9, insofar as they deal with the territorial distribution of the Levites, covering almost the entire territory of Israel. Most scholars before the 1990s, therefore, understood the lists as a kind of political map of ancient Israel, in contrast to recent scholars' views of the lists as a mapping of the idealized territory of Persian Yehud.

Moreover, no significant towns of Persian Yehud appear in the lists, and most cities listed in the territories of Judah and Simeon sat in the province of Idumea, which was Edomite territory. To be sure, some Judeans lived within the boundary of Idumea; the demographic realities were in fact quite complicated.[72] Is it likely that the Judean author(s) of that time would have referred to the cities of the harsh enemy, the Edomites, while omitting the essential cities of Yehud, in order to argue that these areas would be "our original land"? If the author(s) did indeed aim to draw the idealistic map for the community of Persian Yehud, this suggestion would not be reasonable. The Levitical town distribution clearly is not consistent with such an ideal picture of the Persian Yehud territory.

Are the Lists Congruent with the Situation in the Hellenistic Period?

Textual evidence for the geography of Judea in the Hellenistic period is lacking. According to Finkelstein, only the Zenon papyri describe Mareshah and Adoraim as belonging to the territory of Idumea.[73] Yehud stamp impression types 13–15 unearthed from Jerusalem, Ramat Raḥel, Jericho, En-Gedi, Mizpah, and Nabi Samuel cannot be used as evidence since the lists lack any reference to these cities.[74] Additionally, only 5 to 10 percent of all of the Yehud stamp impressions unearthed from the sites mentioned in the list can be described as

---

[71] Finkelstein, "Genealogical Lists," 74–77.

[72] Amos Kloner, "The Introduction of the Greek Language and Culture in the Third Century BCE according to the Archaeological Evidence in Idumaea," in *Judah between East and West: The Transition from Persian to Greek Rule (ca. 400–200 BCE)*, ed. Lester L. Grabbe and Oded Lipschits, LSTS 75 (London: T&T Clark, 2011), 158–62.

[73] Finkelstein, "Genealogical Lists," 77.

[74] Oded Lipschits and David S. Vanderhooft, "A New Typology of the Yehud Stamp Impressions," *TA* 34 (2007): 12–37.

representing these pottery types.[75] The delineation of the geographical situation of the Hellenistic period is limited, therefore, by the lack of relevant data.

Is the Hasmonean Political Reality Relevant to That of the Lists?

In contrast to the dearth of information in the early Hellenistic documents, several literary materials from the Hasmonean period describe the scope of Judea after the first half of the second century BCE.[76] According to 1 Maccabees, the main expansion of the Hasmonean state began after the reigns of Jonathan and Simon Maccabeus (152–135 BCE) and continued until Alexander Jannaeus's rule (103–76 BCE). During the lifetime of Judas Maccabeus (d. 160 BCE), Simon had already conducted his campaign to Arbata and Ptolemais (Acco) and supported the Jews beyond the mountains of Carmel, and even in Tyre and Sidon (1 Macc 5:14–23). Jonathan was confirmed to be the high priest and governor ruling "the four nomes," whereas Simon was appointed governor of the coastal plain, from "the ladder of Tyre" to the brook of Egypt (1 Macc 10:57–65; Josephus, *Ant.* 13.2.3 §§46–57, 13.4.5 §§103–105, 13.5.2–5 §§133–153). Jonathan successively annexed the wilderness of Judea, Ekron, Joppa, and Ashkelon via the battle of Jamnia and the area north of Judea such as Lod, Ephraim, and Ramathaim. He managed the region of Perea in Transjordan, as well as the valley of Hazor and beyond it, including Tel Kedesh in the lists (1 Macc 9:28–33, 10:57–11:74; 12:24–38; *Ant.* 13.1.1–5.10 §§5–180). The western areas of the Shephelah, Gezer, and Joppa were annexed after Simon's campaign (1 Macc 13:42–48; 14:5; *Ant.* 13.6.7 §215).

During the reign of John Hyrcanus (135/134–104 BCE), Judea's expansion was accelerated by a series of military campaigns.[77] Hyrcanus conquered Madaba in the Transjordan, Shechem, the temple of Mount Gerizim, Samaria, and the province of Idumea, including Hebron and Mareshah up to Beer-Sheba—and perhaps along the line of the Jezreel Valley (*Ant.* 13.9.1–10.3 §§255–283; *J.W.* 1.2.6–7 §§63–66; Jdt 1:8–9; 2:28; 3:1–6, 10; 4:4, 6; 7:4). Inheriting his father's penchant for exploits, Aristobulus conquered Galilee including Gischla (*Ant.* 13.11.3 §319; *J.W.* 1.3.3 §76). His brother Alexander Jannaeus established the span of the territory of the so-called united monarchy of David and Solomon (*Ant.* 13.15.3–5 §§395–404; *J.W.* 1.4.8 §106). After overcoming his terrible defeat by Obadas I's ambush attack in the Golan in 93 BCE, Jannaeus gained part of Tyre and Sidon and occupied the area of the modern Golan highlands, as well as the rest of the Transjordan area including the Nabatean towns of Moab and Gilead in 83–80 BCE.

After Hyrcanus's rule, propaganda was designed for political expansion through military campaigns. The successive rulers of Hasmonean royal family may have

---

[75] Ibid.

[76] Rainey and Notley, *Sacred Bridge*, 308–33.

[77] Jonathan Bourgel, "The Destruction of the Samaritan Temple by John Hyrcanus: A Reconsideration," *JBL* 135 (2016): 505–23.

been influenced by the slogan "restoration of the glory of the united monarchy" (1 Macc 15:33: "We have taken over ... the inheritance of our fathers").[78]

It is noteworthy that the entire area that the Hasmonean rulers captured and over which they reigned (the final picture of Jannaeus's territory at his political zenith [about 83–80 BCE]) matches the range of the lists suggested by the archaeological and historical data. This yields two possibilities for the exact dating of the lists. First, the lists might reflect the propagandistic map on the basis of the existent cities that induced the Hasmonean leaders to acquire new territory and to invoke the restoration of the previous glory. Alternatively, the lists might depict the territorial expansion of the Hasmonean state at its zenith during Jannaeus's reign.

In order to determine which of these options is more likely, one must consider why the lists do not mention the north-central highlands, the Samaria regions, but instead refer only to the city of Shechem. John Hyrcanus undertook hostile action against the Samaritans, destroyed the temple of Mount Gerizim (128 BCE and/or 108/107 BCE), captured Samaria, and finally demolished Shechem (108/107 BCE). Perhaps the absence of the highland cities and the appearance of the name "Shechem" in the lists reflect the historical situation between the 120s BCE and 108 BCE.

In view of the data presented above, the former possibility is more likely. The lists probably functioned as a map for territorial restoration. As a strategic outline for the military campaigns, the lists continued to influence Hyrcanus's successors. They received the propagandistic mandate and dutifully extended the demarcations of their state in accordance with it. This ideal territory, presented as Hyrcanus's cherished goal, would eventually be established by his son Alexander Jannaeus about 83–80 BCE.[79]

III. Conclusion

Archaeological and historical facts concerning the lists in Josh 21 and 1 Chr 6 demonstrate that the geographical picture during the Hasmonean era is the most appropriate setting for these lists. I challenged the assumption that the lists could have been written during an earlier period. In addition, I have shown that the

---

[78] Jonathan A. Goldstein, *I Maccabees: A New Translation with Introduction and Commentary*, AB 41 (Garden City, NY: Doubleday, 1976), 62–64; Seth Schwartz, "Israel and the Nations Roundabout: 1 Maccabees and Hasmonean Expansion," *JJS* 42 (1991): 16–38, https://doi.org/10.18647/1577/JJS-1991. The redaction of 1 Macc 15:33 is probably to be dated to the last days of Hyrcanus.

[79] Ze'ev Safrai, "The Gentile Cities of Judea: Between the Hasmonean Occupation and the Roman Liberation," in *Studies in Historical Geography and Biblical Historiography Presented to Zecharia Kallai*, ed. Gershon Galil and Moshe Weinfeld, VTSup 81 (Leiden: Brill, 2000), 63–90, here 77.

inclusion of enemy cities and the exclusion of Judean cities of the Persian period indicate that the lists do not represent a utopian vision of the Yehud community.

Of course, this does not settle the matter; there is also textual evidence to consider. A subsequent study will examine Josh 21 and 1 Chr 6 in their MT and LXX forms, as well as several relevant canonical and extracanonical witnesses, all with a view to determining when these two chapters may have been composed and become part of their respective biblical books. If, as seems to be the case, Josh 21 and 1 Chr 6 must not necessarily be dated before the mid-second century, it will only strengthen my proposal that these lists served as the propagandistic map for the Hasmonean territorial expansion during Hyrcanus's reign and were inherited by his successors.

Hands, Heads, and Feet: Body Parts as Poetic Device in Judges 4–5

KAROLIEN VERMEULEN
karolien.vermeulen@uantwerpen.be
University of Antwerp, 2000 Antwerp, Belgium

Scholars have identified lists of body parts as a compositional device in Biblical Hebrew poetry and as a way to highlight key themes in the biblical text or uncover hidden meanings. In addition, body parts have been given metaphorical and euphemistic senses. In this article I propose that body parts can form a poetic device *an sich*. This device is characterized by its willful exploitation of space: bodily space (with oppositions such as up–down and left–right), interpersonal space (connecting different characters), and literal space occupied by words in verses and phrases (with the opposition first–last). I will address each of these types of space and illustrate them with examples from Judg 4–5. In addition, I will examine the effect of the device, in terms of both story building and story decoding. A comparison between the prosaic and poetic accounts of the story of Jael and Sisera will show that the use of body parts, like other poetic devices, generates different reading experiences.

In his *Classical Hebrew Poetry*, Wilfred Watson argues that lists of body parts can function as a compositional device in Biblical Hebrew poetry. He deems the technique "secondary," discussing it in his book after the section on poetic devices, which features key words and irony, among others. Body parts in lists typically appear top-to-toe or, less commonly, toe-to-top.[1] The best-known examples in the Hebrew Bible are the portrayals of the lovers in the Song of Songs (4:1–7, 5:11–16,

---

This research was supported by a grant from the Belgian American Educational Foundation (BAEF) and the Research Foundation Flanders (FWO). I wish to thank Scott Noegel, Elizabeth Hayes, and Vivian Liska, as well as the anonymous reviewers, for their comments on previous drafts of this article.

[1] Wilfred G. E. Watson, *Classical Hebrew Poetry: A Guide to Its Techniques*, rev. ed., T&T Clark Biblical Languages (London: T&T Clark, 2005), 353–56. Scholars consider these descriptive lists of body parts a key feature of the *waṣf*, a descriptive love poem named after later Arabic love poems with this form but found much earlier in various ancient Near Eastern literary texts. See Wolfram Hermann, "Gedanken zur Geschichten des altorientalischen Beschreibungsliedes," *ZAW* 75 (1963): 176–96.

6:4–7, 7:2–10).² The practice of listing body parts stems from descriptions of divine statues, such as the one of the idols in Ps 115:4–7. Other ancient Near Eastern writings offer similar examples, for instance, the description of the Ugaritic Baal or that of the Akkadian Ninurta.³ Recently, Scott Noegel has noted that lists of body parts often occur together with idiomatic uses of these parts and wordplay on them. Taking into account the symbolic meaning of body parts, Noegel argues that the parts enhance the themes of the biblical texts both in poetry and in prose. He further states that concentrations of body parts often (but not exclusively) occur in prophetic or mantic texts, where they express a wish to reveal hidden meanings related to Israel and Israelite history.⁴

Building on these studies, I propose that body parts in the Hebrew Bible can function as a poetic device *on their own* (i.e., not as a list or metaphor). They achieve effects different from compositional, emphatic, and revelatory functions. As a poetic device, body parts exploit the inherent spatiality of the parts, directing readers in their understanding of the dynamics of the story. The narrative of Jael and Sisera in Judg 4–5, which features a high number of body parts in both versions, provides a case study of this process. After brief comments on the definition of a poetic device, I will discuss the characteristics of the body part as poetic device by means of examples from Judg 4–5. I will also address the effects of the device on readers and the generic difference between the two versions of the story of Jael and Sisera.

I. Body Parts as Poetic Device

In general, a poetic device can be described as a language tool that the composer of a text, oral or written, employs to achieve a certain effect on his or her

---

²Other full or partial lists occur, e.g., in Pss 115:5–7; 135:16–17; Prov 6:12–15, 17; Isa 30:27–28a; 32:3–6; Dan 2:32–33; and Ezek 1:5–13, 26–28. See Watson, *Classical Hebrew Poetry*, 353–55. Further examples can be found in Scott Noegel, "Bodily Features as Literary Devices in the Hebrew Bible," in *Studies in Bible and Exegesis Presented to Samuel Vargon* [in Hebrew], ed. Moshe Garsiel et al., Studies in Bible and Exegesis 10 (Ramat Gan: Bar-Ilan University Press, 2011), 509–31. Most of these lists, especially those of metaphorical body parts, have been discussed in the various commentaries.

³Marvin H. Pope and Jeffrey H. Tigay, "A Description of Baal," *UF* 3 (1971): 117–30, here 119–20; Franz Köcher, "Der babylonische Göttertypentext," *MIOF* 1 (1953): 57–107. Both Watson and Noegel connect these descriptions of divine statues with the lists of human body parts found in biblical and other ancient Near Eastern literature (Watson, *Classical Hebrew Poetry*, 353–56; Noegel, "Bodily Features," 512–14). The popularity of the lists lives on in later literature as well, especially in love poetry (see, e.g., Peter Cole, *The Dream of the Poem: Hebrew Poetry from Muslim and Christian Spain, 950–1492*, Lockert Library of Poetry in Translation [Princeton: Princeton University Press, 2007]).

⁴Noegel, "Bodily Features," 509–31, esp. 530–31.

readership. The device is poetic when the composer and (preferably) also the reader perceive it as rendering the saying different, unfamiliar, and thus foregrounded. Poetry in general, and biblical poetry in particular, is characterized by unusual ways of using language.[5] The adjective *poetic* in the label "poetic device" by no means limits the occurrence and efficacy of the feature to poetry or to the realm of literature in general. Rather, the label should be understood as conventional, referring to a feature that typically will occur more frequently in poetry. This will be the case for Judg 4–5.[6]

In order to speak of body parts as a device different from lists or metaphor, however, the several occurrences of the device must share one or more formal characteristics and a consistent set of functions. For the device under study, the formal characteristic is evident: the presence of body parts. These can be used in the text in their literal sense, for example, the feet of Sisera in Judg 4:15 (וירד סיסרא מעל המרכבה וינס ברגליו, "and Sisera came down from his chariot and fled on his feet"), but also in a metaphorical, euphemistic, or lexicalized (or idiomatic) sense.[7]

---

[5] Katie Wales, *A Dictionary of Stylistics*, 3rd ed. (London: Routledge, 2014), 323. Most major works on Biblical Hebrew poetry lack a formal definition of "poetic device." Watson defines each of the separate devices but not the general notion of "poetic device" (*Classical Hebrew Poetry*, 55–62, 273–348). Similarly, Robert Alter, *The Art of Biblical Poetry*, new and rev. ed. (New York: Basic Books, 2011); Jan P. Fokkelman, *Reading Biblical Poetry: An Introductory Guide* (Louisville: Westminster John Knox, 2001). Fokkelman's definition of a poem, however, reflects his understanding of poetic devices indirectly: "A poem is the result of (on the one hand) an artistic handling of language, style and structure, and (on the other hand) applying prescribed proportions to all levels of the text" (35). In other works, the notion of "device" is identified as a misnomer, at odds with the nature of Hebrew poetry (James L. Kugel, *The Idea of Biblical Poetry: Parallelism and Its History* [New Haven: Yale University Press, 1981; repr., Baltimore: Johns Hopkins University Press, 1998], 73, 86).

[6] Watson uses the term *poetic* for the body-part device in the context of Biblical Hebrew poetry but also pertaining to other ancient Near Eastern poetry (*Classical Hebrew Poetry*, 273–74, 348, 353–56). Noegel calls it a "literary" device, most likely because he discusses both poetic and prosaic texts ("Bodily Features," 509).

[7] I do not here include allusions to body parts through wordplay, which Noegel discusses along with metaphorical and literal uses ("Bodily Features"). First, the text does not support a body-part reading for such examples, since it does not retain a double meaning for many polysemous words. Second, the allusions are not body parts of characters and are therefore not spatially embedded in the narrative world. This embedding and the accompanying embodiment (as in the effect of the human body on cognition; see n. 22) should not be confused with the notion that in the ancient Near East the essence of a thing was present, "embodied," if you will, in the word referring to the thing (see Isaac Rabinowitz, *A Witness Forever: Ancient Israel's Perception of Literature and the Resultant Hebrew Bible*, ed. Ross Brann and David I. Owen, Occasional Publications of the Department of Near Eastern Studies and the Program of Jewish Studies, Cornell University, 1 [Bethesda, MD: CDL, 1993], 6–14; Scott B. Noegel, *Nocturnal Ciphers: The Allusive Language of Dreams in the Ancient Near East*, AOS 89 [New Haven: American Oriental Society, 2007], 37–38). To illustrate this, a metaphorical hand is still connected to a person in a space, and an idiomatic face remains connected to the narrative space and the characters acting

In Judg 4:9, the hand metaphorically stands for power: ביד אשה ימכר יהוה את סיסרא, "The LORD will deliver Sisera into the hand of a woman."⁸ Judges 5:26–27 describes the murder of Sisera using many body parts that can be understood as sexual euphemisms, for example, the feet/legs of Jael.⁹ An example of a lexicalized use of a body part occurs in Judg 4:23 with the expression לפני, literally, "before the face of," thus "before."¹⁰

In addition to the formal feature, the body parts should fulfill a particular function or a combination of functions in order to qualify as poetic device. Although the combination of device and function should not be seen as exclusive, unique, or rigid—one can use most stylistic devices in an emphatic way—many poetic devices do have a particular function that distinguishes them from others.¹¹ For example, onomatopoeia "serves to convey the meaning of a word by sound."¹² This function is not present in metaphor, chiasmus, or any other poetic device but is distinctive of onomatopoeia. Contrary to formal features, functions are not readily available and require the analysis of the feature in context.

Previous researchers have paid attention to the role of some of the body parts in the story of Jael and Sisera. The hands of Jael and Deborah have been deemed images of power by which female characters overshadow the male characters in the narrative.¹³ Although some scholars see little warrant for a sexual interpretation of

---

within. On the contrary, the "eye" (עין) in a conjugated form of the verb ענה ("answer") does not carry such a connotation (see, e.g., Jonah 2:3 [Eng. 2:2], an example discussed by Noegel, "Bodily Features," 525). Would it be the eye of the speaker, the addressee, or the one about whom one is talking in the answer? In spite of this, the allusion to the eye foregrounds the other, spatially embedded, body parts in the text and, as such, serves the overall purpose of the body-part device as discussed in this article.

⁸In many of Noegel's examples, the hand features prominently as a symbol of power ("Bodily Features," passim). For the hand in Judg 4, see also Elie Assis, "'The Hand of a Woman': Deborah and Yael (Judges 4)," *JHebS* 5 (2005): 1–12, here 3–7, https://doi.org/10.5508/jhs.2005.v5.a19.

⁹Danna Nolan Fewell and David Gunn, "Controlling Perspectives: Women, Men, and the Authority of Violence in Judges 4 and 5," *JAAR* 58 (1990): 389–411, esp. 394; Victor H. Matthews, *Judges and Ruth*, NCBiC (Cambridge: Cambridge University Press, 2004), 73; Barnabas Lindars, *Judges 1–5: A New Translation and Commentary* (Edinburgh: T&T Clark, 1995), 279; Susan Niditch, *Judges: A Commentary*, OTL (Louisville: Westminster John Knox, 2008), 81. Another example is the wombs mentioned in Judg 5, referring to the captured women who will be serving as concubines. See Pamela Tamarkin Reis, "Uncovering Jael and Sisera: A New Reading," *SJOT* 19 (2005): 24–47, here 28; Nicole Wilkinson Duran, "Having Men for Dinner: Deathly Banquets and Biblical Women," *BTB* 35 (2005): 117–24, here 123; Alter, *Art of Biblical Poetry*, 54.

¹⁰This type of body-part reference is included also in Noegel's analysis ("Bodily Features," passim). See also *IBHS*, 220–21, §11.3.

¹¹Watson, *Classical Hebrew Poetry*, 32.

¹²Ibid.

¹³Assis, "'Hand of a Woman,'" 6–7, 9. On female dominance, see also Robert B. Chisholm, "What's Wrong with This Picture? Stylistic Variation as a Rhetorical Technique in Judges," *JSOT*

the overall story based on word choices, others have argued in favor of such a reading.[14] Danna Nolan Fewell and David Gunn suggest that the story presents a reversed rape in which the female hand violates the male mouth, the meaning they attribute to the word רקה.[15] In a more recent article, Pamela Tamarkin Reis gives a similar sexual reading of the story, strengthening her argument by relying on the euphemistic use of body parts in the story.[16]

II. Body Parts in Judges 4–5: A Case Study

Following the formal characteristic as defined above, one can compile a list with twenty-eight occurrences of body parts in Judg 4–5.[17] In the narrative account (4:1–24), body parts occur sixteen times in twenty-four verses: one pair of eyes (v. 1), six hands (vv. 2, 7, 9, 14, 21, 24), three pairs of feet (vv. 10, 15, 17), three faces (vv. 14, 15, 23), two temples (vv. 21, 22), and two mouths (vv. 15, 16). The poetic account of the story in Judg 5:24–30 has eleven occurrences in seven verses: two hands—one of which is specified as the right hand (v. 26, twice), two pairs of feet

---

34 (2009): 171–82, here 176; Fewell and Gunn, "Controlling Perspectives," 391, 394; Reis, "Uncovering Jael and Sisera," 30; Donald F. Murray, "Narrative Structure and Technique in the Deborah–Barak story (Judges IV 4–22)," in *Studies in the Historical Books of the Old Testament*, ed. J. A. Emerton, VTSup 30 (Leiden: Brill, 1979), 155–89, here 183; James W. Watts, *Psalm and Story: Inset Hymns in Hebrew Narrative*, JSOTSup 139 (Sheffield: JSOT Press, 1992), 88; Matthews, *Judges and Ruth*, 66; Elie Assis, "The Choice to Serve God and Assist His People: Rahab and Jael," *Bib* 85 (2004): 82–90, here 85.

[14] Assis disagrees mainly with how the sexual allusions have been interpreted, not with the acknowledgment of them in scholarship ("'Hand of a Woman,'" 10). In addition, he nuances the role the allusions play, noting that they occur in relation to Jael but not in the passages with Deborah, whom he views as the main character of the narrative (11). For a stronger emphasis on the sexual undertones of the story, see Yair Zakovitch, "Sisseras Tod," *ZAW* 93 (1981): 364–74; Susan Niditch, "Eroticism and Death in the Tale of Jael," in *Gender and Difference in Ancient Israel*, ed. Peggy L. Day (Minneapolis: Fortress, 1989), 43–47; Niditch, *War in the Bible: A Study in the Ethics of Violence* (New York: Oxford University Press, 1993), 113–17; Mieke Bal, *Death and Dissymmetry: The Politics of Coherence in the Book of Judges*, CSHJ (Chicago: University of Chicago Press, 1988), 213; Duran, "Having Men for Dinner," 119.

[15] Fewell and Gunn, "Controlling Perspectives," 389–411.

[16] Reis, "Uncovering Jael and Sisera," 28, 41–43.

[17] I thank Scott Noegel for pointing out the example of פעמי in Judg 5:28. Two more examples (also suggested by Noegel) are פה and אף in Judg 4:20 and 5:28, respectively. Whereas both (the former if revocalized as פֶּה) may be considered body-part references on the lexical level, this does not hold true for their use in the text. In other words, the (consonantal) forms may be polysemous, but they do not generate a polysemous reading once put in the text. Rather, they function as the eye (עין) in answer (ענה), alluding to and emphasizing the other "real" body parts, that is, those that are lexically and textually references to the body of characters.

(v. 27, twice), more feet (v. 28), one temple (v. 26), two heads (vv. 26, 30), two wombs (v. 30, twice), and one neck (v. 30).[18]

TABLE 1. Body Parts in Judges 4 and 5

	Judges 4	Judges 5
ראש		26, 30
פנים	14, 15, 23	
רקה	21, 22	26
עין	1	
פה	15, 16	
צואר		30
יד	2, 7, 9, 14, 21, 24	26
ימין		26
רחם		30 (twice)
רגל	10, 15, 17	27 (twice)
פעם		28

A closer look at these body parts reveals that they share another remarkable characteristic: they willfully exploit space.[19] Body parts have a spatial connotation by definition, as cognitive studies have shown. Michiel van Elk and Olaf Blanke illustrate this with the following example:

> Show a four-year-old boy the picture of an airplane and ask him to indicate the position of the eyes and arms of the plane. Probably without problems he will point to respectively the cockpit and the wings. As the example illustrates, young children already have a clear representation of the spatial relation between different body parts and the words referring to these body parts.[20]

The writers of the stories of Judg 4 and 5 seem to have emphasized this spatial connotation of body parts rather than letting it be a side effect of embodied cognition.

---

[18] Reis notices that the combined stories feature the hand seven times. The number seven had a special value of "supernatural power" insofar as "in 5.26 … when only one more 'hand' is needed to complete the seven count, Jael takes the peg in her hand but takes the hammer in her 'right'. In Hebrew this word signifies the right hand, but it avoids the use of the actual word 'hand'" ("Uncovering Jael and Sisera," 45). Noegel, too, points out the importance of the number seven but in another passage, Prov 6:1–35 ("Bodily Features," 526–27).

[19] Noegel mentions space once in his discussion of the destruction of the statue of Dagon next to the ark of God. The movement of falling down is understood as a symbol of complete humiliation. Just as the upper body parts of Dagon end up on the ground, so the Ashdodites will suffer lesions below the waist ("Bodily Features," 523–24).

[20] Michiel van Elk and Olaf Blanke, "The Relation between Body Semantics and Spatial Body Representations," *Acta Psychologica* 138 (2011): 347–58, here 347.

They play out the spatial connotations of the body parts in the tales and may even have added more body parts exactly because of their potential for storytelling. In order to show this, and for reasons of clarity, I will subdivide space into three categories in my further discussion, namely, bodily space, interpersonal space, and literal space.

Bodily Space: Oppositions Vertical–Horizontal and To–From

Bodily space is the spatial position connected to the specific body part and the place it occupies in real-life human bodies. Typically, this position is mentally mapped onto the three dimensions of space: a vertical axis for positions and movements upward and downward and two horizontal axes for positions and movements left or right and backward or forward.[21] Body parts are situated at an intersection of the three axes. Especially in the horizontal plane, movements are often perceived in terms of center–periphery. Thus, when Sisera flees to Jael's tent (Judg 4:17), his feet (position "down" on the vertical axis) move in the horizontal plane away from the battlefield, considered the center. And when he falls down at Jael's feet (4:27), his head (position "up" on the vertical axis) describes a vertical movement downward toward the feet of Jael (position "down" on the vertical axis). In addition to moving vehicles, the body parts can also be the point of reference themselves, remaining immobile amid the movement around them, such as in 4:22, where Sisera's temple is not going anywhere.[22]

Authors can use bodily space to situate the places, events, and characters of a story in space. Relying on the readers' experience as human beings in space, they can, for example, evoke positive connotations by consistently exploring upper spatial terms and movements upward.[23] Bodily space, in this particular case body parts, then becomes a tool to affect and direct the readers of a text and their ultimate

---

[21] Nicolas Wyatt, *Space and Time in the Religious Life of the Near East*, BibSem 85 (Sheffield: Sheffield Academic, 2001), 35–40. Wyatt identifies the left–right axis as the spatial/moral one and forward–backward axis as the time axis. For the current analysis, this distinction does not prove very useful. What seems to matter for the movement of body parts in the horizontal plane is their position toward the perceived center.

[22] For a similar discussion of directionality in relation to metaphors, see George Lakoff and Mark Johnson, *Metaphors We Live By* (Chicago: University of Chicago Press, 1980), 14–21 (chapter on orientational metaphors). In their later work this leads to the notion of conceptual embodiment: "the idea that the properties of certain categories are a consequence of the nature of human biological capacities and of the experience of functioning in a physical and social environment" (George Lakoff, *Women, Fire, and Dangerous Things: What Categories Reveal about the Mind* [Chicago: University of Chicago Press, 1987], 12). This notion is fully explored in George Lakoff and Mark Johnson, *Philosophy in the Flesh: The Embodied Mind and Its Challenges to Western Thought* (New York: Basic Books, 1999).

[23] Lakoff and Johnson, *Metaphors We Live By*, 14–21.

understanding of that text.²⁴ The following analysis of Judg 4 and 5 shows how such a process works.

The prose story of Jael and Sisera explores the bodily space repeatedly, as table 2 reveals (translations are from the NRSV). Six of the seventeen references to body parts are located in the middle area where the hand is, three are down (the feet), and the remaining eight are up.²⁵ Especially interesting is the middle of the story (vv. 14–17), where the body parts from upper and lower space are alternated, contrasting the position of Barak and Sisera and creating a hierarchy between them.²⁶

TABLE 2. Movement in Judges 4

	Hebrew Text	Position	Movement
Judg 4:1	ויספו בני ישראל לעשות הרע בעיני יהוה The Israelites again did what was evil <u>in the sight of</u> the LORD	up	horizontal to
Judg 4:2	וימכרם יהוה ביד יבין מלך כנען So the LORD sold them <u>into the hand of</u> King Jabin of Canaan	middle	horizontal to
Judg 4:7	ונתתיהו בידך I will give him <u>into your hand</u>	middle	horizontal to
Judg 4:9	כי ביד אשה ימכר יהוה את סיסרא for the LORD will sell Sisera <u>into the hand of</u> a woman	middle	horizontal to²⁷
Judg 4:10	ויעל ברגליו אשרת אלפי איש and ten thousand warriors went up <u>behind him</u>	down	horizontal to

---

²⁴ The three levels of space as identified in critical-spatial theory are present here: the physical place of events as Firstspace; the connotations of directions as good or bad as a crossover between physical and symbolic space, thus Firstspace and Secondspace; and, finally, the use of both Firstspace and Secondspace by the author when producing the story world and by the reader when reproducing the space as Thirdspace. For the theoretical underpinnings, see Henri Lefebvre, *La production de l'espace*, Société et urbanisme (Paris: Anthropos, 1974); Edward W. Soja, *Postmetropolis: Critical Studies of Cities and Regions* (Malden, MA: Blackwell, 2000).

²⁵ Upper body parts consist of the head and its parts as well as the neck and throat. The legs and feet are lower body parts. I consider all other body parts, roughly parts of the torso and the arms, middle body parts. This division is based on the lists of body parts elsewhere in the Hebrew Bible, where the body parts appear from top to toe (or vice versa). These lists include parts of the three sections I distinguish with hands and belly in the middle of the enumeration (contrary to Noegel, who regards the hands of Dagon in 1 Sam 5:1–6 as an upper body part ["Bodily Features," 523–24]). In addition, this distinction is based on the appearance of the human body itself.

²⁶ Murray, "Narrative Structure and Technique," 171.

²⁷ The text leaves it open whether it is Deborah, as it seems at first, or Jael who is the referent. See, among others, Assis, "'Hand of a Woman,'" 4; Murray, "Narrative Structure and Technique," 177; Matthews, *Judges and Ruth*, 65.

Judg 4:14	קום כי זה היום אשר נתן יהוה את סיסרא בְּיָדֶךָ Up! For this is the day on which the LORD has given Sisera into your hand.	middle	horizontal to
Judg 4:14	הלא יהוה יצא לְפָנֶיךָ The LORD is indeed going out before you.	up	horizontal to
Judg 4:15	ויהם יהוה את סיסרא ואת כל הרכב ואת כל המחנה לְפִי חרב לפני ברק And the LORD threw Sisera and all his chariots and all his army by the sword into a panic before Barak.	up[28]	horizontal to
Judg 4:15	ויהם יהוה את סיסרא ואת כל הרכב ואת כל המחנה לפי חרב לִפְנֵי ברק And the LORD threw Sisera and all his chariots and all his army by the sword into a panic before Barak.	up	horizontal to
Judg 4:15	וירד סיסרא מעל המרכבה וינס בְּרַגְלָיו Sisera got down from his chariot and fled away on foot.	down	horizontal away
Judg 4:16	ויפל כל מחנה סיסרא לְפִי חרב All the army of Sisera fell by the sword.	up	horizontal to
Judg 4:17	וסיסרא נס בְּרַגְלָיו אל אהל יעל And Sisera had fled on foot to the tent of Jael.	down	horizontal away
Judg 4:21	ותשם את המקבת בְּיָדָהּ and she took a hammer in her hand	middle	horizontal to
Judg 4:21	ותתקע את היתד בְּרַקָּתוֹ and drove the tent peg into his temple	up	vertical to
Judg 4:22	והנה סיסרא נפל מת והיתד בְּרַקָּתוֹ and there was Sisera lying dead with the tent peg in his temple.	up	no movement
Judg 4:23	ויכנע אלהים ביום ההוא את יבין מלך כנען לִפְנֵי בני ישראל So on that day God subdued King Jabin of Canaan before the Israelites.	up	horizontal to
Judg 4:24	ותלך יַד בני ישראל הלוך וקשה על יבין מלך כנען Then the hand of the Israelites bore harder and harder on King Jabin of Canaan	middle	horizontal to

[28] The body part פה places the sword in the upper part of the vertical axis (similarly, v. 16), even though the hand holding the sword is not an upper body part. Note that neither in verse 15 nor in verse 16 is the hand itself mentioned. Full attention is drawn to the attacking sword, representing power.

Whereas the different body parts cover all the areas on the vertical axis in terms of location, the movement that is connected to them in the story is predominantly horizontal. People are brought *toward* others or are fleeing *from* them. Two exceptions can be found in verses 21 and 22. When Jael kills Sisera with the tent peg (v. 21), the movement is vertical, driving the weapon into the head of the sleeping Sisera. In the following verse, spatial movement is lacking: the tent peg already sticks in Sisera's temple when Barak reenters the scene. The reference thus is stative. The majority of body parts indicate a movement toward. Only the feet of Sisera are moving away from the scene (vv. 15, 17).[29] Additionally, the body parts are, except for the hand in verse 24, the point of reference of the movement.

In the account of the story in chapter 5, a different picture emerges. Of the eleven body parts, four refer to the middle, four to spaces up, and three to positions down. The distribution is similar to the one in the prosaic account but with a strong contrast between up and down. In 5:26 the head of Sisera is mentioned twice, followed by a double reference to the feet of Jael.[30] The head falls all the way down to the feet, traveling along the vertical axis. Compare this to the prose account, where the hand of Jael goes down to Sisera, only covering a space from middle to down.

Table 3. Movement in Judges 5

	Hebrew Text	Position	Movement
Judg 5:26	ידה ליתד תשלחנה She put her hand to the tent peg	middle	horizontal / vertical to
Judg 5:26	וימינה להלמות עמלים and her right hand to the workmen's mallet	middle	horizontal / vertical to
Judg 5:26	והלמה סיסרא מחקה ראשו she struck Sisera a blow, she crushed his head	up	vertical to
Judg 5:26	ומחצה וחלפה רקתו she shattered and pierced his temple	up	horizontal to
Judg 5:27	בין רגליה כרע נפל שכב He sank, he fell, he lay still at her feet.	down	vertical to

---

[29] Susanne Gillmayr-Bucher pays attention to the movement in the story but not in terms of body parts. She considers the movement more important for the creation of space in the narrative than for the mentioning of places (*Erzählte Welten im Richterbuch: Narratologische Aspekte eines polyfonen Diskurses*, BibInt 116 [Leiden: Brill, 2013], 88). So also Ellen van Wolde, who looks at the use of verbs of motion ("Yaʿel in Judges 4," *ZAW* 107 [1995]: 240–46). This brings her to a different conclusion in that Sisera's movement is downward vertical rather than horizontal as described above (ibid., 243).

[30] Gillmayr-Bucher discusses the contrast between head and feet spatially as well (*Erzählte Welten*, 89). See also Alter, *Art of Biblical Poetry*, 52–53.

Judg 5:27	בין רגליה כרע נפל at her feet he sank, he fell	down	vertical to
Judg 5:28	מדוע אחרו פַעֲמֵי מרכבותיו Why tarry the hoofbeats of his chariots?	down	horizontal to
Judg 5:30	רחם רחמתים a girl or two	middle	horizontal to
Judg 5:30	רחם רחמתים a girl or two	middle	horizontal to
Judg 5:30	לראש גבר for every man	up	horizontal to
Judg 5:30	צבע רקמתים לצוארי שלל two pieces of dyed work embroidered for my neck as spoil	up	horizontal to

In terms of movement, the space in the poetic story seems to be used in a more balanced way, playing out the different spatial movements against each other. The account opens with two notions that may refer to horizontal and vertical movement simultaneously (v. 26). The exact nature of the actions depends on whether Jael is thought to be standing or sitting when she reaches for the tent peg and the hammer.[31] This is followed by a vertical and a horizontal movement, as if to affirm the ambiguity of the previous two lines with regard to their spatiality. The killing of Sisera is a vertical action, as in the prose version, but more prominently present this time through repetition.[32] The afterthought featuring the mother of Sisera, which is lacking in the narrative account, concludes without vertical movement (the feet/steps are not coming near) but with horizontal movements in contrast to the vertical movements of Jael defeating Sisera.[33]

---

[31] Commentators describe Sisera as standing in this passage, which is one of the notable differences from the prose account in chapter 4 (see, e.g., J. Clinton McCann, *Judges*, IBC [Louisville: John Knox, 2002], 57; Gillmayr-Bucher, *Erzählte Welten*, 89). Jack M. Sasson includes other suggestions (such as squatting or sitting) to conclude: "The poet seems less concerned with choreographing the attack than with displaying its savagery" (*Judges 1–12: A New Translation with Introduction and Commentary*, AYB 6D [New Haven: Yale University Press, 2014], 307).

[32] Gillis Gerleman, "The Song of Deborah in the Light of Stylistics," *VT* 1 (1951): 168–80, here 177; McCann, *Judges*, 57; Alter, *Art of Biblical Poetry*, 52–53.

[33] According to some, the counterpart of this passage in chapter 4 is Barak coming into the tent and seeing the dead Sisera (e.g., Robert S. Kawashima, "From Song to Story: The Genesis of Narrative in Judges 4 and 5," *Proof* 21 [2001]: 151–78, here 161). Others do not see a counterpart for Sisera's mother (e.g., Heinz-Dieter Neef, "Deboraerzählung und Deboralied: Beobachtungen zum Verhältnis von Jdc. IV und V," *VT* 44 [1994]: 47–59, here 54). Within the song, the mother of Sisera is generally contrasted with Deborah, the mother of Israel, and with Jael, who acts like a mother to Sisera. See, e.g., Lillian R. Klein, *The Triumph of Irony in the Book of Judges*, JSOTSup 68 (Sheffield: Almond, 1988), 45; Reis, "Uncovering Jael and Sisera," 43; Niditch, *Judges*, 81.

In both chapters, the body parts function as an interpretive tool for the reader. The bodily space that is evoked is mainly horizontal in the narrative account and centripetal toward the body parts. For the poetic account, the space is full of contrast between up and down as well as between horizontal and vertical movement. These observations will become more meaningful when interpreted in light of the two other types of space explored by the body-part device.

Interpersonal Space: Connecting Characters

In addition to bodily space, body parts also define the spatial position between characters in a story. Ellen van Wolde has analyzed the spatial movement of the characters in Judg 4, especially Jael's, based on the use of verbs of motion, such as קום, ירד, and נפל. She notes a contrast between a vertical upward movement of Jael, and also Deborah, and an opposite movement for Barak and Sisera.[34] Susanne Gillmayr-Bucher also considers Jael's movement and Sisera's lack of movement as essential to building the space of the story. According to Gillmayr-Bucher, in the poetic account the bodies of both characters determine the space.[35] The following discussion complements these studies, examining the connection of characters to body parts.

In the poetic account, the majority of body parts mentioned belong to either one of the main characters, Jael or Sisera. In addition, body parts are used in reference to unnamed women and men (5:30).[36] The "feet" of Sisera's chariots (5:28) seem to fulfill an intermediary function here, still connected to Sisera but in a more distanced way. In verses 26 and 27, Jael's body parts envelop those of Sisera. They also outnumber Sisera's four to two. This still leads to a balanced pattern of 2–2–2, but Jael is clearly and literally given more space than her antagonist Sisera. In terms of spatial movement, the hands of Jael force Sisera's head onto her feet. She is the leading figure, whereas Sisera is only following. The spatial disturbance of a head ending up at the ground indicates the defeat of Sisera.[37] All of this happens in a

---

[34] Van Wolde, "Yaʿel in Judges 4," 244.

[35] Gillmayr-Bucher, *Erzählte Welten*, 88–89.

[36] Various scholars have noted the elimination of other characters in Judg 5:24–27, with only Jael and Sisera remaining (e.g., Fewell and Gunn, "Controlling Perspectives," 400, 403–5; Gerleman, "Song of Deborah," 171).

[37] Alan J. Hauser, "Judges 5: Parataxis in Hebrew Poetry," *JBL* 99 (1980): 23–41, here 34–35, https://doi.org/10.2307/3265698. Others understand the scene as referring to a birth or a sexual encounter. For the former, see Duran, "Having Men for Dinner," 118; Don Seeman, "The Watcher at the Window: Cultural Poetics of a Biblical Motif," *Proof* 24 (2004): 1–50, here 19; Mieke Bal, *Murder and Difference: Gender, Genre, and Scholarship on Sisera's Death*, ISBL (Bloomington: Indiana University Press, 1988), 131. For the latter, see Fewell and Gunn, "Controlling Perspectives," 403–5; Reis, "Uncovering Jael and Sisera," 39–42. The spatial contrast plays on an up–down orientation, connected to a good–bad distinction by Lakoff and Johnson. This association draws an even sharper contrast between the two protagonists (*Metaphors We Live By*, 14–21).

very stylized and parallel way: the hands match the heads and the heads match the feet. Pushing Sisera down makes Jael stand on top of the vertical axis. The interpersonal space in which the events play out is vertical only (in contrast to the narratological space created by the body parts described before, which uses both directions more or less equally).

At the end of the poetic version, the speech of Sisera's mother in verse 30 is uplifting indeed. Following upon a strong up–down contrast in verses 26–27, her words attempt to undo the vertical movement that ended with Sisera's head on the floor. The "feet" of the chariots (פעמי מרכבותיו; v. 28) evoke the idea that Sisera is still on his feet rather than at the feet of somebody else. Furthermore, the wombs of the presumed booty (רחם רחמתים; v. 30) are residing in the middle of the vertical axis, as if an attempt to bridge the gap between up, where Sisera's head initially was, and down, where his head is after his encounter with Jael. The restoration continues when the head of a man (לראש גבר; v. 30) is mentioned. The male is put on top of the female, moving from a middle position, evoked by the wombs, to a top position, suggested by the head and neck.[38] Yet the words are only comfort; they cannot undo the powerful act of Jael. The words do express in a very effective way the hopes of the mother of Sisera.[39]

Also in Judg 4, the interpersonal space between Jael and Sisera is clearly oriented in one direction, in this case the horizontal one.[40] Deborah predicts in verse 9 that Sisera will be overpowered by Jael's hand. Initially Sisera tries to flee, away from the battle scene and into the tent of Jael, more horizontal movements (vv. 15–17).

---

[38] This analysis follows the parallelism in verse 30 (צבע רקמתים לצוארי שלל with רחם רחמתים לראש גבר) and assumes that the neck (צוארי) around which the cloths are put is that of a male, unspecified character. Another possibility is that the phrase should be paralleled with שלל צבעים לסיסרא (here the similarity seems to be lexically rather than syntactically motivated); then the neck is Sisera's (Lindars, *Judges 1–5*, 286; Sasson, *Judges 1–12*, 310). It seems that the text allows for both identifications. Other readings have been suggested in which the neck is female, either of the Canaanite women, who would then, ironically, describe their own future as booty, or of Sisera's mother (Matthews, *Judges and Ruth*, 75).

[39] Niditch, *Judges*, 82; Sasson, *Judges 1–12*, 309. Fewell and Gunn offer a different interpretation of the passage: "Instead of capturing a womb, a womb captured him. And thus the singers celebrate poetic justice.... By forcing the Canaanite women to approve unconsciously their own imminent rape, the singer victors can end their recital in mocking triumph" ("Controlling Perspectives," 408). See also Robert B. Chisholm, *A Commentary on Judges and Ruth* (Grand Rapids: Kregel, 2013), 243: "At first we may feel some sympathy for this concerned other, but sympathy quickly turns to utter disdain as we discover that she was as greedy for plunder and as insensitive to Israelite suffering as the oppressive Canaanite kings."

[40] This observation derived from the body parts differs from that of van Wolde, who describes the movement in the story as a contrast of vertical movements based on the verbs: Deborah and the men of Zebulun and Naphtali go up, whereas Barak and Sisera go down. Further, Jael is mentioned in the first group of those going up—but through the association of her name with the verb עלה, not through the occurrence of a verb expressing upward motion. As van Wolde herself notes, קום in relation to Jael is lacking ("Yaʿel in Judges 4," 243–44).

Jael then drives a tent peg into his head while he is asleep (v. 21). This action is vertical, as one may assume that Sisera was lying down and Jael was at least half standing if not standing fully.[41] As noted before, except for the actual killing, the interpersonal space between Jael and Sisera mainly covers a horizontal space in which the characters move. Sisera moves *away from* the battle scene (presented as לפי חרב, "to the mouth of the sword") to *move toward* Jael (ברגליו, "on his feet"). In other words, Sisera is not the center of attention nor a reference point in the narrative, yet Jael clearly is. Other elements in the text, such as the use of motion verbs, confirm this pattern of movement of the two main characters.[42]

Judges 4 features additional players: God, the Israelites, Jabin, Barak, and also the inanimate sword, to be connected with Barak.[43] At the beginning of the story, the Israelites do wrong in the eyes of God (4:1) and are therefore given into the hand of Jabin (4:2); at the end the roles are reversed: God makes Jabin bow down before (the face of) the Israelites (4:23), while it is the hand of the Israelites that is now upon Jabin (4:24).[44] The movements are mostly horizontal in nature.

As for Barak, he is a third party in the encounter between Jael and Sisera; that is, the battle Barak was supposed to fight with Sisera is fought by Jael. When that battle is over, she delivers Sisera, dead at that moment, to Barak (4:22). Deborah promises that Sisera will come into Barak's power (hand) with God's help (4:7), a movement toward him. In her follow-up announcement, Sisera will be brought in the hand of a woman, but God will still go in front of Barak (4:9, 14) and his people behind him (4:10). Three times the army of Sisera, including Sisera, is running into the sword of Barak and his army (4:15–16). All seems to go as predicted, but then Sisera flees (4:16), which results in a spatial scene without Barak. When he recurs

---

[41] According to Reis, the vertical movement may have started even before the murder, as she reads the word שמיכה as Jael's body as cover. Jael would then have been literally on top of Sisera ("Uncovering Jael and Sisera," 29). Reis furthermore argues that the subject of the verb צנח is not the tent peg but Jael (32–34). She concludes, "How delicious for the Israelite readers or auditors to take the point that Jael, from her position astraddle the enemy commander, also dismounts from an animal" (34).

[42] Gillmayr-Bucher, *Erzählte Welten*, 87; Murray, "Narrative Structure and Technique," 183; Jan P. Fokkelman, "The Song of Deborah and Barak: Its Prosodic Levels and Structure," in *Pomegranates and Golden Bells: Studies in Biblical, Jewish, and Near Eastern Ritual, Law, and Literature in Honor of Jacob Milgrom*, ed. David P. Wright, David Noel Freedman, and Avi Hurvitz (Winona Lake, IN: Eisenbrauns, 1995), 595–628, here 620; Hauser, "Judges 5," 35–37; Yairah Amit, "Judges 4: Its Contents and Form," *JSOT* 39 (1987): 89–111.

[43] Amit, "Judges 4," 102. Amit notes that all players in the story move a lot. She interprets this as a way to obscure their role and prevent one of them from being foregrounded all the time. All of this, according to Amit, is aimed at focusing on the main hero in the narrative: God (ibid.; see also Amit, *The Book of Judges: The Art of Editing*, BibInt 38 [Leiden: Brill, 1999], 216–17). I agree with Amit that there is indeed a lot of movement; however, this movement is not a "hustle-bustle" but consistent.

[44] Van Wolde, "Yaʿel in Judges 4," 241; Barry G. Webb, *The Book of Judges*, NICOT (Grand Rapids: Eerdmans, 2012), 179.

there are no body parts mentioned referring to him, indicating that he has become superfluous to the narrative development.⁴⁵ The interpersonal space between Barak and Sisera is horizontal only. Barak is not able to bring Sisera down permanently (he forces him off his chariot, but this is when Sisera is fleeing).⁴⁶ Taking into account all the players in Judg 4, one finds that the interpersonal spaces are mainly horizontal.

As with the bodily spaces, the interpersonal spaces created by the body parts in the texts reveal a different pattern for the two accounts of the story of Jael and Sisera. Whereas bodily space mainly draws on the embodied cognition of writer and reader and thus projects a text-external mental map onto the story world, the interpersonal space is a text-internal creation of space. By playing out the spatial position of the characters through the use of body parts, the writer creates a hierarchy between the characters: Jael brings Sisera down, but his mother tries to reverse this movement by depicting males bringing back female booty (Judg 5). Likewise, Jael and Sisera battle in a way similar to Barak and Sisera in chapter 4, up until the actual killing of Sisera, which changes the direction from horizontal to vertical and from an undifferentiated to a hierarchical position.⁴⁷

Literal Space: Place in the Verse and the Text

Finally, one can consider the literal space of body parts in the story. Where do they occur in the text as a whole and where do they appear in particular phrases? This use of space draws on the notion of foregrounding and on word order. It is not uniquely reserved for body parts but nevertheless adds to the exploitation of space by this particular device. Literal space engages with the material level of the text. It interacts with and influences the textual space constructed by the writer and the

---

⁴⁵ Amit considers Barak to be secondary from the beginning, interpreting the preposition לפני as follows: "it appears to stress Barak's secondary, perhaps even passive, role at the start of the war" ("Judges 4," 94–95). Athalya Brenner, too, thinks of Barak as passive in the story ("A Triangle and a Rhombus in Narrative Structure: A Proposed Integrative Reading of Judges IV and V," in *A Feminist Companion to Judges*, ed. Athalya Brenner, FCB 4 [Sheffield: JSOT Press, 1993], 98–109, here 100).

⁴⁶ Based on the feet of Barak mentioned in verse 10 and the chariots of Sisera in verse 13, Lindars (after Malbim) mentions a contrast between the two ways of movement (*Judges 1–5*, 190–91). This contrast, however, is not expressed by means of body parts. According to van Wolde, both Barak and Sisera are going down: the former is depicted as coming from Mount Tabor; the latter, as coming down from his chariot, lying down to sleep, and staying there when dead ("Yaᶜel in Judges 4," 243). An analysis of the body parts shows that Barak and Sisera are indeed moving in the same spatial field: Barak may come down from the mountain, but he does not kill Sisera, while Sisera goes so far down that there is no possibility of return. Yet these actions are surrounded by many horizontal actions, evoked by the body parts but also by other verbs.

⁴⁷ Wyatt has described the vertical axis as addressing the transcendent and infernal dimension (*Space and Time*, 40). Applied to the story, this means not only that Sisera dies and would go to the underworld but also that Jael is associated with the upper realms where God resides.

reader. In addition, it helps to shape the space of the story world in which the characters act. Of the three types of space discussed—bodily space, interpersonal space, and literal space—literal space is most easily identified with poetic devices.

A nice example occurs in the text of Judg 4, which opens with an eyes–hand sequence and closes with a face–hand arrangement. This similar combination envelops the larger narrative.[48] In between, hands initially take a leading role with four of them in a row, only to be left for an upper position when the persecution of Sisera and his army is related—they are up against the mouth of the sword (4:15–16). This action is twice contrasted with the fleeing feet of Sisera (4:15 and 17). The contrast subtly indicates that Barak may win the battle with Sisera. When the story shifts to the tent of Jael and her encounter with Sisera, the fleeing feet (down) run into the hand of Jael (middle), who hits him at the temple (up, twice). At the end of the narrative, the winning position of Jael is taken over by the Israelites, who subdue King Jabin (up), and the story ends with the middle position of the hand in which this king now rests.

Note that the majority of the body parts occur in the encounters of Sisera with Barak and Jael respectively. Both passages make use of the upper space of the body yet in a very different way. Barak's sword (up) is contrasted with the feet of Sisera (down), playing out a spatial contrast of up and down, while Jael's hand starts in the relative lower position to bring down Sisera's head, which, narratologically speaking, he had laid down himself already, to sleep. The exploration of the upper space here coincides with two high points in the story.[49]

If a clear overall pattern is lacking in Judg 4, except for the outer *inclusio*, the opposite is true of the poetic account. After an opening without body parts (5:24–25), the text features two hands matching with two heads (v. 26) that are consequently matched with two feet (v. 27).[50] Both the pileup of body parts and the pattern of matching are repeated in the afterthought of verse 30. The hands of Jael are replaced by wombs, and the head of Sisera is now the head of any man. At the seam of the two passages (v. 28), more "feet" transform the overall 2–2 pattern into a 2–2–3–2–2 sequence, centering on the downfall of Sisera. Despite the formal recurrence of pairs of body parts, the passage with Sisera's mother stresses a lack: although it speaks of male heads and necks, it does not explicitly attribute these to Sisera. As many scholars have noted, the reader knows what the mother seems to deny, that is, that the head of the dead Sisera is not going to return.[51]

---

[48] Amit, *Book of Judges*, 200. According to Kawashima, the narratological *inclusio* consists in opening and ending the story with Barak ("From Song to Story," 161). This would be an *inclusio* within the one described above.

[49] Lindars, *Judges 1–5*, 200; Robert H. O'Connell, *The Rhetoric of the Book of Judges*, VTSup 63 (Leiden: Brill, 1996), 111, 120.

[50] Alter, *Art of Biblical Poetry*, 52–53.

[51] Reis, "Uncovering Jael and Sisera," 43; Seeman, "Watcher at the Window," 15, 20; Matthews, *Judges and Ruth*, 78; Gillmayr-Bucher, *Erzählte Welten*, 101.

As a final point, one can take into account the position of the body parts on the sentence level. In chapter 4, the body parts occur nearly always in the last position of either the sentence or a part of the sentence. Two major exceptions to this pattern are in verses 9 and 24. In the former, the ‎כִּי‎-phrase opens with a body part—the hand of a woman. Although it is not impossible in Biblical Hebrew to move a prepositional phrase like this to the front of a sentence, it is quite remarkable in this narrative.[52] All other examples in chapter 4 occur in sentences with similar prepositional constructions, but these appear at the end of the sentence (e.g., "in the eyes of God" in v. 1, or "to the mouth of the sword" in v. 15). In the phrase in verse 9, the word order emphasizes the ambiguous ‎אִשָּׁה‎, and the body-part feature is foregrounded as well.[53] In verse 24, the last sentence of the narrative, the hand is prominent again; that is, it does not occur at the end of the sentence, which is the regular pattern. This time the sentence structure is unmarked.[54] The prolepsis of the body part is the result of its role as subject of the sentence, something that is unique in this account of the story. All other body parts are used in prepositional constructions. The literal space taken up by the body parts in verses 9 and 24 draws the audience's gaze to (1) the hand of a woman—as commentators have suggested many times, a rather unusual event; and (2) to the reversal of fates, a recurring motif in the book of Judges, here with additional emphasis on the happy ending for the Israelites.[55]

---

[52] Although this issue is debated, the more common opinion on word order is that Biblical Hebrew is a verb–subject–object language (Adina M. Moshavi, *Word Order in the Biblical Hebrew Finite Clause: A Syntactic and Pragmatic Analysis of Preposing* [Winona Lake, IN: Eisenbrauns, 2010], 7, 10–17). See also, e.g., T. Muraoka, *Emphatic Words and Structures in Biblical Hebrew* (Jerusalem: Magnes, 1985), 53; *IBHS*, 128–30, §8.3. Chisholm remarks on the syntax in this passage: "He alters a syntactical or literary structural pattern to highlight an element of irony in the event being narrated" ("What's Wrong," 172).

[53] Emphasis forms the common explanation for marked word order (Moshavi, *Word Order*, 18; also Muraoka, *Emphatic Words*, 1–46). This can be further specified as contrast, juxtaposition, anteriority/circumstantiality, or narrative-unit demarcation. Of these the first option, contrast, seems to be the most fitting. Just as putting the prepositional construction at the beginning of the sentence is rather unusual, the giving of an enemy into the hands of a woman is exceptional as well.

[54] Moshavi, *Word Order*, 7. The word order in Judg 4 suggests that the unmarked order is indeed verb–subject–object, whereas deviations from this pattern form the marked order. See also Tal Goldfajn, who argues for a contextual interpretation of word order and its meaning: "SV word order that interrupts a previous VS sequence may thus express a range of important temporal indications" (*Word Order and Time in Biblical Hebrew Narrative* [Oxford: Clarendon, 1998], 97).

[55] For the first point, see Elie Assis, "Man, Woman, and God in Judg 4," *SJOT* 20 (2006): 110–24, here 119: "The focus on God, and the desire to avoid depiction of yet another charismatic military leader may also motivate the emphasis on Deborah's gender.... The fact that she is a woman removes her from the arena of war." For the second point, see Chisholm, "What's Wrong," 176; Duran, "Having Men for Dinner," 117; Bal, *Murder and Difference*, 86.

In Judg 5, the body parts and their literal space are notably different: the contrast, present in terms of bodily and interpersonal space, is also played out in the literal space occupied by the text. In 5:26 the hands of Jael are mentioned first in the phrases. The head of Sisera, in the parallel phrases, occurs in last position. Jael and Sisera thus could not have been farther apart. This creates an additional spatial distance between the two characters and emphasizes the head position of Jael, both grammatically and narratologically. Consequently, the feet of Jael are again placed up front in 5:27, creating the effect that Jael is all over Sisera and is taking up all the space.[56] The afterthought in verses 28–30 mentions the feet of Sisera's chariots last in the phrase, the wombs in the first position, and the head of the man in the last position. This is analogous to the situation between Jael and Sisera and seems to function as affirmation. Whereas Sisera's mother and her ladies on some level may try to manipulate the reality of the son's death, by changing the spatial pattern the literal space in the text confirms that the son has lost the battle anyway.[57]

The literal space occupied by the body parts confirms some of the earlier tendencies: the clash of characters (and their bodies) and the hand of Jael bringing Sisera's head down in chapter 4, the contrast between Jael and Sisera expressed by means of literal distance, and the pairing of spatially opposite body parts in chapter 5. In addition, a spatial enveloping of the story of chapter 4 foregrounds God, as expected at the top of the vertical axis and confirmed by the body part "eye" (4:1). Moreover, God is behind the reversal of fates that turns the initial hand of Jabin upon the Israelites into the hand of the Israelites upon Jabin. It even forces Jabin to bow down before the same Israelites, who now spatially side with God (4:23–24).[58] In the poetic account, literal space helps to further understanding of the afterthought in 5:28–30. Formal recurrence of body parts, suggesting an ongoing battle, goes hand in hand with a prolepsis of the female body parts and a postponing of the male ones, implying that the battle has ended in Jael's favor.

---

[56] Alter, *Art of Biblical Poetry*, 52–53. Interestingly, the head positions in the poetic account are taken up by body parts of the female characters. In comparison, in 4:9, another deviating construction, a female character and her body part are moved up front as well.

[57] Gerleman, "Song of Deborah," 170. See also Fewell and Gunn, "Controlling Perspectives," 407: "The singers, however, are merely setting us up. Having inveigled our sympathies for the Canaanite mother, they proceed to turn us against her. We fall prey to the singers' device designed to ensure our disgust." Manipulation is here to be understood as metanarratological. It is not the reality that is played but the audience in the reality.

[58] This is one of the few occasions in the story where Noegel's conclusion seems to apply—that a pileup of body parts can form a metanarrative on divine order and its impact on Israelite history ("Bodily Features," 530–31).

III. Conclusion

In this article, I have argued that body parts can function as a separate poetic device that is characterized by an exploration as well as an exploitation of the bodily, interpersonal, and literal space created by them. The story of Jael and Sisera as told in Judg 4 and 5 has served as a case study of the device. An analysis of the "body-part spaces" reveals that the mainly horizontal movements in chapter 4 contrast with the horizontal and vertical movements in chapter 5. Translating the space to that of characters, the contrast is more prominent: horizontal in the narrative, vertical in the song. The latter incorporates an internal opposition of a downward movement (Sisera) and an upward one (Jael). This is once more contrasted with the literal spatial pattern that presents both Jael's passage and that of Sisera's mother as analogous, with female body parts distanced from male ones. While this pattern is used consistently in chapter 5, chapter 4 exploits the literal textual space only twice, fronting the hand of the woman (4:9) as well as the hand of the Israelites (4:24). Based on the present analysis, one can conclude that the narrative account of the story *shows* the potential of the body-part device, whereas the song *fully realizes* that potential—that is, the potential to use space as a rubric in both story building and story decoding.[59] Further research will reveal whether this feature recurs in other stories and, if so, if they have anything in common with Judg 4 and 5. Even if the present case study is unique, the way in which both accounts play with the spatial connotations of body parts brings to mind the sophisticated use of various other poetic devices applied elsewhere in the biblical text.

---

[59] This concurs with the idea that the prose account and the song are complementary and are to be read together. See Terry Giles, *Twice Used Songs: Performance Criticism of the Songs of Ancient Israel* (Peabody, MA: Hendrickson, 2009), 135; Reis, "Uncovering Jael and Sisera," 46; Rachel C. Rasmussen, "Deborah the Woman Warrior," in *Anti-covenant: Counter-reading Women's Lives in the Hebrew Bible*, ed. Mieke Bal, JSOTSup 81 (Sheffield: Almond, 1989), 79–93, here 83; O'Connell, *Rhetoric of the Book of Judges*, 101.

New and Recent Titles

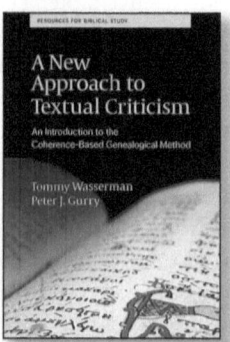

A NEW APPROACH TO TEXTUAL CRITICISM
An Introduction to the Coherence-Based Genealogical Method
Tommy Wasserman and Peter J. Gurry
Paperback $19.95, 978-1-62837-199-4   162 pages, 2017   Code: 060399
Hardcover $34.95, 978-0-88414-267-6 E-book $19.95, 978-0-88414-266-9
Resources for Biblical Study 80

TOWARD A LATINO/A BIBLICAL INTERPRETATION
Francisco Lozada Jr.
Paperback $36.95, 978-1-62837-200-7   148 pages, 2017   Code: 060385
Hardcover $51.95, 978-0-88414-270-6 E-book $36.95, 978-0-88414-269-0
Resources for Biblical Study 91

A SAMOAN READING OF DISCIPLESHIP IN MATTHEW
Vaitusi Nofoaiga
Paperback $29.95, 978-1-62837-197-0   156 pages, 2017   Code: 063808
Hardcover $44.95, 978-0-88414-263-8 E-book $29.95, 978-0-88414-262-1
International Voices in Biblical Studies 8

GOSPEL JESUSES AND OTHER NONHUMANS
Biblical Criticism Post-poststructuralism
Stephen D. Moore
Paperback $24.95, 978-1-62837-190-1   164 pages, 2017   Code 060691
Hardcover $39.95, 978-0-88414-252-2 E-book $24.95, 978-0-88414-251-5
Semeia Studies 89

MIXED FEELINGS AND VEXED PASSIONS
Exploring Emotions in Biblical Literature
F. Scott Spencer, editor
Paperback $49.95, 978-1-62837-194-9   418 pages, 2017   Code: 060396
Hardcover $64.95, 978-0-88414-257-7 E-book $49.95, 978-0-88414-256-0
Resources for Biblical Study 90

EARLY JEWISH WRITINGS
Eileen Schuller and Marie-Theres Wacker, editors
Paperback $44.95, 978-1-62837-183-3   316 pages, 2017   Code 066006
Hardcover $59.95, 978-0-88414-233-1 E-book $44.95, 978-0-88414-232-4
The Bible and Women 3.1

SBL Press • P.O. Box 2243 • Williston, VT 05495-2243
Phone: 877-725-3334 (toll-free) or 802-864-6185 • Fax: 802-864-7626
Order online at www.sbl-site.org/publications

"He Will Take the Best of Your Fields": Royal Feasts and Rural Extraction

GALE A. YEE
gale.yee@gmail.com
Episcopal Divinity School, New York, NY 10027

In 1 Sam 8:10–18, the judge Samuel warns the people who demand a king to rule over them that, among other things, he will conscript their sons into his armies; compel them to work on his plantations and reap his harvests; take their daughters to be perfumers, cooks, and bakers; and take the best of their grain and vineyards and redistribute them among his courtiers. In this article I focus on the virtually invisible laborers who produced, processed, and prepared food for feasts on the king's plantations and in his kitchens rather than on their royal consumers. I give special attention to female millers and bakers. This work interlinks Jack Goody's study of elite feasting with other societal structures of class and the distributions of power and authority. I examine the toll that this extraction of material resources and labor took on agrarians in the lavish feasts that kings held to reinforce social and political ties with domestic and foreign elites (see 1 Kgs 4:20–28, 18:19, Neh 5:16–18).

The primary focus of the literature on the subject of feasting in the Hebrew Bible and in the ancient Near East has been on elite feasts.[1] This focus makes sense

[1] Stefania Ermidoro, *Commensality and Ceremonial Meals in the Neo-Assyrian Period*, Antichistica 8 (Venice: Ca' Foscari–Digital Publishing, 2015); Deirdre N. Fulton et al., "Feasting in Paradise: Feast Remains from the Iron Age Palace of Ramat Raḥel and Their Implications," *BASOR* 374 (2015): 29–48. See the following articles from *Feasting in the Archaeology and Texts of the Bible and the Ancient Near East*, ed. Peter Altmann and Janling Fu (Winona Lake, IN: Eisenbrauns, 2014); Jodi Magness, "Conspicuous Consumption: Dining on Meat in the Ancient Mediterranean World and Near East," 33–59; Steve Renette, "Feasts on Many Occasions: Diversity in Mesopotamian Banquet Scenes during the Early Dynastic Period," 61–86; and Carol Meyers, "Menu: Royal Repasts and Social Class in Biblical Israel," 129–47. See also Nathan MacDonald, "Feasting Fit for a King," in *Not Bread Alone: The Uses of Food in the Old Testament* (Oxford: Oxford University Press, 2008), 134–65; John L. McLaughlin, *The Marzēaḥ in the Prophetic Literature: References and Allusions in Light of the Extra-biblical Evidence*, VTSup 86 (Leiden: Brill, 2001); Jacob L. Wright, "Commensal Politics in Ancient Western Asia: The Background to Nehemiah's Feasting (Part I and Part II)," *ZAW* 122 (2010): 212–33, 333–52; Jean Bottéro, *The*

given that feasts served to reinforce social, political, and economic ties with other elites, as well as to underscore and strengthen their dominance over subordinates.[2] The primary sources about ancient royal feasts were themselves the products of elites. They informed us of the 450 foreign prophets who dined at Jezebel's table (1 Kgs 18:19), the extravagant banquet that Ahasuerus threw for his nobles, ministers, and officials in Susa for 187 days (Esth 1:1–9), and the exotic menu for Assurnasirpal II's ten-day festival for 69,574 people to commemorate his new city.[3] Yet, except for the detailed ration lists that recorded the food doled out to low-level laborers,[4] the primary sources ignored those who carried the economic burden for these lavish royal banquets in agrarian societies: the people who produced, processed, prepared, and served the food and cleaned up afterwards.

There were two exceptions in the Hebrew Bible to the invisibility of these producers, preparers, and servers. Samuel the judge warned the people who demanded a king to rule over them that, among other things, the king would conscript their sons into his armies, compel them to work on his plantations and reap his harvests, take their daughters to be flavorers,[5] cooks, and bakers, and take the best of their grain and vineyards and redistribute them among his courtiers (1 Sam 8:10–18). The second exception, 1 Kgs 4:7–19, lists the twelve officials governing

---

Oldest Cuisine in the World: Cooking in Mesopotamia (Chicago: University of Chicago Press, 2004); Denise Schmandt-Besserat, "Feasting in the Ancient Near East," in *Feasts: Archaeological and Ethnographic Perspectives on Food, Politics, and Power*, ed. Michael Dietler and Brian Hayden (Tuscaloosa: University of Alabama Press, 2010), 391–403; Sharon Zuckerman, "'… Slaying Oxen and Killing Sheep, Eating Flesh and Drinking Wine …': Feasting in Late Bronze Age Hazor," *PEQ* 139 (2007): 186–204; and the essays in Tamara L. Bray, ed., *The Archaeology and Politics of Food and Feasting in Early States and Empires* (New York: Kluwer Academic/Plenum, 2003).

[2] Michael Dietler and Brian Hayden, "Digesting the Feast: Good to Eat, Good to Drink, Good to Think," in Dietler and Hayden, *Feasts*, 7–17; Janling Fu and Peter Altmann, "Feasting: Backgrounds, Theoretical Perspectives, and Introduction," in Altmann and Fu, *Feasting in the Archaeology and Texts of the Bible and the Ancient Near East*, 9–23.

[3] D. J. Wiseman, "A New Stela of Aššur-Naṣir-Pal II," *Iraq* 14 (1952): 24–44.

[4] Michael Jursa, "Labor in Babylonia in the First Millennium BC," in *Labor in the Ancient World*, ed. Piotr Steinkeller and Michael Hudson, International Scholars Conference on Ancient Near Eastern Economics 5 (Dresden: ISLET, 2015), 345–96, esp. 355–64; Wolfgang Heimpel, *Workers and Construction Work at Garšana*, CUSAS 5 (Bethesda, MD: CDL, 2009), 90–122; Michael Jursa, "The Remuneration of Institutional Labourers in an Urban Context in Babylonia in the First Millennium BC," in *L'archive des fortifications de Persépolis: État des questions et perspectives de recherches; Actes du colloque organisé au Collège de France par la "Chaire d'histoire et civilisation du monde achéménide et de l'empire d'Alexandre" et le "Réseau international d'étude et de recherches achéménide" (GDR 2538 CNRS), 3–4 novembre 2006*, ed. Pierre Briant, Wouter F. M. Henkelman, and Matthew W. Stolper, Persika 12 (Paris: de Boccard, 2008), 387–427; I. J. Gelb, "The Ancient Mesopotamian Ration System," *JNES* 24 (1965): 230–43.

[5] MacDonald argues that רקחות should be translated as "flavorers," consistent with the women's other culinary occupations for the king's table in 1 Sam 8:13 ("Feasting Fit for a King," 164). Although רקחות is used in the Hebrew Bible of those who prepare spices for ointments and incense, it has been used for adding spices to food or drink (see Ezek 24:10; Song 8:2).

the newly reorganized regions of northern Israel that were responsible for providing food for the royal court one month out of the year. Their extraction from these districts was evidently quite extensive, especially in the large quota and variety of meats, which were rarities in the nonelite Israelite diet.[6] According to 1 Kgs 4:22–23 (MT 5:2–3), the daily provision for Solomon's court was thirty cors of choice flour (סלת) and sixty cors of meal (קמח), ten fat oxen, twenty pasture-fed cattle, one hundred sheep, besides deer, gazelles, roebucks, and fatted fowl.[7] Using these exceptions as starting points, I will examine the toll that this extraction of labor and goods took on agrarians in the feasting of kings.

The classic study by Jack Goody provides an excellent theoretical base for this investigation. For Goody, the discussion of elite feasting must be interlinked with other societal structures of class and the distribution of power and authority.[8] A class of elites did not exist in isolation but within a larger system of relationships. These relationships existed on different continua of exploiter/exploited and dominance/subjection, both vertical and horizontal.[9] Research on feasting must therefore involve the rest of society of which it is a part. The nonproducers demanding food for feasts in an agrarian society cannot be understood without discussion of the food's producers. Goody provides a comprehensive grid (below) that lays out the four main processes involved in providing and transforming food for consumption: growing, allocating/storing, cooking, and eating.[10] These processes include phases in which particular economic class relations are embedded: production, distribution, preparation, and consumption. Most research on feasting in the Hebrew Bible seems to be focused on the fourth phase, consumption, during which

---

[6] Nathan MacDonald, *What Did the Ancient Israelites Eat? Diet in Biblical Times* (Grand Rapids: Eerdmans, 2008), 78–79.

[7] In addition, the districts had a monthly quota of barley and straw for Solomon's forty thousand horses (1 Kgs 4:26–28). In light of the following discussion, one may speculate whether his horses ate better than the majority of the population, which lived at the level of subsistence but had to provide for these horses from their surplus. Certainly Ahab was more concerned about water and pastureland for his horses and mules than about sustenance for his people, who were starving during famine (1 Kgs 18:5).

[8] Jack Goody, *Cooking, Cuisine and Class: A Study in Comparative Sociology*, Themes in the Social Sciences (Cambridge: Cambridge University Press, 1982), 37. This was also the concern of Susan Pollock, "Towards an Archaeology of Commensal Spaces: An Introduction," special volume, *eTopoi: Journal for Ancient Studies* 2 (2012): 1–20, here 13: A "focus on commensality should not lead to the neglect of the production and distribution of food and drink as well as the raw materials out of which they are made. What we eat and drink, with whom, and under what circumstances all presuppose that someone procures, prepares, and serves food." See also Jason R. Kennedy, "Commensality and Labor in Terminal Ubaid Northern Mesopotamia," special volume *eTopoi: Journal for Ancient Studies* 2 (2012): 125–56, who argued that many studies focusing on consumption have failed to take into account Karl Marx's emphasis on the dialectical unity of production, consumption, distribution, and exchange (128).

[9] Eric Hobsbawm, *On History* (New York: New Press, 1997), 87.

[10] Goody, *Cooking, Cuisine and Class*, 37–48.

"the identity and differentiation of the group is brought out in the practice of eating together or separately, as well as in the content of what is eaten by different collectivities."[11] This study, however, is more concerned with the first three phases of these processes, in which, according to Goody, economic factors dominate, namely, the production, distribution, and preparation of food involved in holding a banquet. These are the domains of those invisible producers, processors, preparers, and servers of food in the biblical text and their social-economic relations with the consumers of that food.

TABLE 1. The Four Main Processes in Providing and Transforming Food for Consumption (Goody, *Cooking, Cuisine and Class*, 37).

Processes	Phases	Locus
Growing	Production	Farm
Allocating/storing	Distribution	Granary/market
Cooking	Preparation	Kitchen
Eating	Consumption	Table
Cleaning up	Disposal	Scullery

I. "Anyone Unwilling to Work Should Not Eat" (2 Thessalonians 3:10): Production and Distribution

Roland Boer's recent book *The Sacred Economy of Ancient Israel* facilitates the discussion of Goody's phases of the economic production and distribution of food in ancient Israel. According to Boer, Israel's economy was composed of five institutional forms: subsistence survival, kinship-household, patronage, the (e)states, and tribute exchange. Subsistence survival and the kinship-household were allocative, economically dependent on distribution and reallocation of labor and goods. The (e)states and tribute exchange were extractive: products and labor were expropriated for those who did not produce food, namely, the upper classes. Patronage could be allocative or extractive depending on which of the other forms were dominant. These five forms oscillated in relations of dominance and subordination under the three regimes in which one of them held sway: the allocative subsistence regime and the extractive palatine and tribute-exchange regimes.[12]

The Levant and ancient Israel were agrarian societies with important smaller pastoral economies, growing crops and shepherding flocks. Their economies were

---

[11] Ibid., 38.
[12] Roland Boer, *The Sacred Economy of Ancient Israel*, LAI (Louisville: Westminster John Knox, 2015). Boer conflates the estate and state. Estates were first a feature of temples and later, in the formation of states, were under the palace (110–11).

deeply rooted in social relations that were both closely united with and dependent on the natural environment. The subsistence regime was the most prominent and stable economic feature of southern Levant, including Israel, for most of its history. Its institutional form, subsistence survival, embraced risk-reducing policies that ensured continued survival during adverse times. Crop and livestock surpluses were kept not for profit but for survival during times of hardship.[13] Furthermore, it was labor, not land, that was of primary concern. Without bodies to work the land to make it productive, that land would have been useless by itself. Given the high maternal and infant mortality rate and lower life expectancy in antiquity,[14] securing labor was a much greater concern than owning real estate.[15]

According to Boer, the estate system under the palatine regime was the main extractive institutional form in the Levant from the third millennium until the sustained economic crisis at the end of the second millennium.[16] The palatine regimes of the early Israelite monarchies resembled the Bronze Age urban-based polities ("city-states"), in which a tiny aristocracy was served by an assortment of townspeople and supported by surrounding sectors inhabited by agrarians and pastoralists. Although these polities declined in Palestine during the transition from Late Bronze to Iron I, they reappeared with the Iron II monarchies.[17] Estates operated at a low level in the early kingdoms of Israel until they were subsumed by the tribute-exchange regime under the Neo-Assyrians.[18] Land could be seized for estates by the upper classes either through illegitimate means (see 1 Kgs 21) or through debt resulting from economic exploitation (Isa 5:8, Mic 2:1–2).[19] During these monarchies, agriculture was divided between two different economic

---

[13] David C. Hopkins, "Life on the Land: The Subsistence Struggles of Early Israel," *BA* 50 (1987): 178–91; I. M. Diakonov, "The Commune in the Ancient East as Treated in the Works of Soviet Researchers," in *Introduction to Soviet Ethnography*, ed. Stephen P. Dunn and Ethel Dunn, 2 vols. (Berkeley: Highgate Road Social Science Research Station, 1974), 519–48, here 522–23.

[14] Carol L. Meyers, *Rediscovering Eve: Ancient Israelite Women in Context* (New York: Oxford University Press, 2013), 97–102.

[15] Boer, *Sacred Economy of Ancient Israel*, 70, 228–29; Hopkins, "Life on the Land," 189; Gershon Galil, *The Lower Stratum Families in the Neo-Assyrian Period*, CHANE 27 (Leiden: Brill, 2007), 348–50; Mario Liverani, "The Near East: The Bronze Age," in *The Ancient Economy: Evidence and Models*, ed. J. G. Manning and Ian Morris, Social Science History (Stanford, CA: Stanford University Press, 2005), 47–57, here 50–51.

[16] Boer, *Sacred Economy of Ancient Israel*, 112.

[17] David C. Hopkins, "The Weight of the Bronze Could Not Be Calculated: Solomon and Economic Reconstruction," in *The Age of Solomon: Scholarship at the Turn of the Millennium*, ed. Lowell K. Handy, SHCANE 11 (Leiden: Brill, 1997), 304–5.

[18] Boer, *Sacred Economy of Ancient Israel*, 114, 131.

[19] D. N. Premnath, "Loan Practices in the Hebrew Bible," in *To Break Every Yoke: Essays in Honor of Marvin L. Chaney*, ed. Robert B. Coote and Norman K. Gottwald, SWBA 2/3 (Sheffield: Sheffield Phoenix, 2007), 173–85; Matthew J. M. Coomber, "Prophets to Profits: Ancient Judah and Corporate Globalization," in *Bible and Justice: Ancient Texts, Modern Challenges*, ed. Matthew J. M. Coomber, BWo (London: Equinox, 2011), 212–37.

structures that often conflicted with each other: those of the allocative village communes and those of the extractive state.[20] The following chart expresses visually the processes of state extraction.[21]

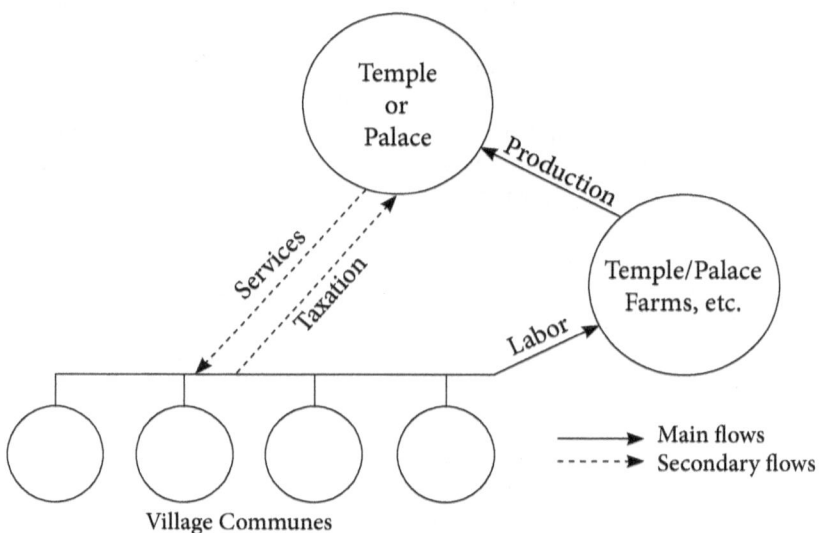

FIGURE 1. The Process of State Extraction. Adapted from Liverani, "The Near East: The Bronze Age," 52.

Because the surpluses of subsistence survival were inadequate to provide the expensive items desired by the upper classes, grants of cultivable land were given out as estates to nonproducers, depicted in the chart as "Temple/Palace Farms" (see 1 Sam 22:7, 2 Sam 9:6–10, 1 Chr 27:25–31; cf. 1 Sam 27:6–12). The class division was between those who lived solely by their own labor in the village communes

---

[20] Boer, *Sacred Economy of Ancient Israel*, 110–13; David C. Hopkins, "Bare Bones: Putting Flesh on the Economics of Ancient Israel," in *The Origins of the Ancient Israelite States*, ed. Volkmar Fritz and Philip R. Davies, JSOTSup 128 (Sheffield: Sheffield Academic, 1996), 124–25. Cf. Mario Liverani, "Land Tenure and Inheritance in the Ancient Near East: The Interaction between 'Palace' and 'Family' Sectors," in *Land Tenure and Social Transformation in the Middle East*, ed. Tarif Khalidi (Beirut: American University of Beirut, 1984), 33–44, here 34–35; and Igor M. Diakonoff, "Socio-economic Classes in Babylonia and the Babylonian Concept of Social Stratification," in *Gesellschaftsklassen im alten Zweistromland und in den angrenzenden Gebieten: XVIII. Recontre assyriologique internationale, München, 29. Juni bis 3. Juli 1970*, ed. D. O. Edzard, Bayerische Akademie der Wissenschaften, Philosophisch-historische Klasse NS 75 (Munich: Bayerischen Akademie der Wissenschaften, 1972), 41–52, here 43.

[21] See Daniel M. Master, "Economy and Exchange in the Iron Age Kingdoms of the Southern Levant," *BASOR* 372 (2014): 81–97, here 83–86.

and those in the temple/palace, who regularly drew on the uncompensated labor product of others by means of taxation, labor conscription, tribute, debt foreclosures, and so forth.[22] The estates produced the surpluses needed for luxury items and the expansion of state activities, such as building projects, military expansion, and, for our purposes, lavish banquets. The economics of the state would be based, first, on *the extraction of agricultural goods and flocks* from both the estates (in the chart, "production") and the village communes (in the chart, "taxation").[23] These goods were then redistributed upward in this stratified society to the court, army, and other royal authorities (see 1 Sam 8:16–17, 2 Chr 31:4–5). The tenants, indentured servants, prisoners of war, and debt slaves who farmed the family estates and villas were expected to supply a significant portion of their produce, between one-third and one-half, to the palace and to be able to survive on what was left over.[24] Moreover, studies of ancient Near Eastern iconography and texts reveal that the vast accumulation and redistribution of agricultural and animal goods gained from military victories, along with prisoners of war, were also significant parts of feasting itself.[25] Although not secured through military conquests, Solomon's taxation and feasting evoked similar means of surplus extraction and hierarchical redistribution (1 Kgs 4:7–28).

Second, and very interconnected with the first point, state economics would be based on *the extraction of labor* from the village communes to farm the agricultural estates, work on the building projects, make weapons for or fight in military campaigns, process and prepare food, and participate in other ventures of the court. The biblical text provides a number of examples of royal demands for corvée labor (1 Kgs 5:13–18; 9:15, 20–22; 12:18; 2 Chr 8:8–10; 10:18; cf. Exod 1:11; Esth 10:1).[26] With respect to Assyrian feasts and building projects, the majority of the 69,574 "happy guests" attending the opening feast of Assurnasirpal II's new palace were

[22] Norman K. Gottwald, "The Expropriated and the Expropriators in Nehemiah 5," in *Concepts of Class in Ancient Israel*, ed. Mark R. Sneed, SFSHJ 201 (Atlanta: Scholars Press, 1999), 1–19, here 10–11.

[23] See Michael Heltzer, "Labour in Ugarit," in *Labor in the Ancient Near East*, ed. Marvin A. Powell, AOS 68 (New Haven: American Oriental Society, 1987), 237–50, here 237.

[24] Boer, *Sacred Economy of Ancient Israel*, 116–17.

[25] Schmandt-Besserat, "Feasting in the Ancient Near East," 391–403; Wright, "Commensal Politics in Ancient Western Asia (Part I)," 223–32.

[26] J. Alberto Soggin, "Compulsory Labor under David and Solomon," in *Studies in the Period of David and Solomon and Other Essays: Papers Read at the International Symposium for Biblical Studies, Tokyo, 5–7 December, 1979*, ed. Tomoo Ishida (Winona Lake, IN: Eisenbrauns, 1982), 259–67; Isaac Mendelsohn, "On Corvée Labor in Ancient Canaan and Israel," *BASOR* 167 (1962): 31–35; A. F. Rainey, "Compulsory Labour Gangs in Ancient Israel," *IEJ* 20 (1970): 191–202; cf. Diakonoff, "Socio-economic Classes in Babylonia," 43–45; Heltzer, "Labour in Ugarit," 237–39. See Shemaryahu Talmon, "The New Hebrew Letter from Seventh Century B.C. in Historical Perspective," *BASOR* 176 (1964): 30–31, regarding a complaint of a corvée laborer against his supervisor after he finished his harvesting quota.

undoubtedly the 47,074 male and female prisoners of war who had been forced to work on the construction of the new city, according to D. J. Wiseman (cf. Deut 20:10–14).[27]

Along with the natural hazards of farming, such as blight, insect infestation, and drought, the diversion of labor from the subsistence farming communities to the agricultural estates, building projects, and military significantly burdened the rural sectors of the Israelite state. Because labor shortage was a persistent issue, the primary tax on the village communities was the levy of human bodies rather than their quota of crops or flocks. It was economically advantageous for the elites to transfer as many subsistence workers as possible into the estate system and keep them there as indentured servants, corvée or hired laborers, debt slaves, and so forth.[28] The state's need for cheap and unpaid labor put an intense strain on the agriculture of the villages, which operated according to reliable subsistence survival strategies, thus threatening the viability of the system on which the elite depended.[29] Conflicts occurred when the ruling classes wanted more labor from the villages that resisted these efforts. These conflicts became exacerbated under the tribute-exchange regime when the Assyrians imposed their own demands for tribute on the Israelite and Judean royal courts, which passed them on to the villages.[30]

Other biblical texts provide evidence for this material and labor extraction from the villages during the monarchic period. We begin first with 1 Sam 8:11–18, cited at the start of this essay. Samuel warns the people that a king will take the best of their lands (fields, vineyards, and olive orchards) and distribute them to his royal officers (v. 14). He will also hand over to his courtiers tithes of their grain and vineyards (v. 15). He will appropriate one-tenth of their flocks (v. 17). With respect to labor resources, a king will draft their sons into various aspects of military service, as charioteers, horsemen, commanders, and chariot and weapons manufacturers. He will have them plow and harvest on his plantations (vv. 11–12). He will take their daughters to work in the royal kitchens and bakeries (v. 13). He will carry off the best of their male and female slaves and their work animals, putting them to his own use (v. 16).

First Samuel 8:11–18 has been the subject of much scholarly scrutiny, particularly with regard to its dating.[31] Isaac Mendelsohn argues against late

---

[27] Wiseman, "New Stela of Aššur-Naṣir-Pal II," 28.

[28] For a discussion of the tax and debt cycles the populace endured, see Norman K. Gottwald, "Sociology (Ancient Israel)," ABD 6:79–89, here 84. For an extended study, see Gregory C. Chirichigno, *Debt-Slavery in Israel and the Ancient Near East*, JSOTSup 141 (Sheffield: JSOT Press, 1993).

[29] Gottwald, "Expropriated and the Expropriators," 11.

[30] Boer, *Sacred Economy of Ancient Israel*, 118–21, 149–55, 158–63. Cf. Peter R. Bedford, "The Economy of the Near East in the First Millennium BC," in Manning and Morris, *Ancient Economy*, 58–83, here 76.

[31] For a review of the literature, see Jonathan Kaplan, "1 Samuel 8:11–18 as 'A Mirror for Princes,'" *JBL* 131 (2012): 625–42, here 626–30, https://doi.org/10.2307/23488259.

authorship condemning the monarchy by correlating 1 Sam 8 with relevant Akkadian texts from Ugarit.[32] On the other hand, Mark Leuchter thinks that 1 Sam 8 reflects Israel's experience with Assyria during the ninth–eighth centuries BCE and links the text to the seventh-century Josianic period in Judah.[33] Jonathan Kaplan convincingly argues that 1 Sam 8 belongs to a genre of discourse found in eighth- to seventh-century Babylonian and Assyrian circles that sought to limit kingly power, lest it bring ruin on cult and country. By drawing on existing catalogs of monarchic excess circulating in the Judean court, 1 Sam 8 also sought to restrict such abuses of royal extraction and outline the proper responsibilities of the king *via negativa*.[34] These studies indicate that these economic abuses by monarchs persisted throughout the ancient Near East and that there was "push back" against them.

As already noted by a number of scholars, the eighth-century prophets in particular were critical of royal extraction.[35] Amos consistently lambasts officials who "trample on the poor and take from them levies of grain" (5:11–12, 2:6–8, 4:1, 8:4–6) for their conspicuous consumption at the price of the nation's ruin (6:1–7, 5:11). Isaiah and Micah both condemn the confiscation of lands by royals (Isa 3:13–15; 5:8–10; Mic 2:1–2, 9; 3:1–3).[36] Amos denounced the practice of debt slavery to fulfill the demands for labor (Amos 2:6–8, 8:6),[37] and Micah and Jeremiah both censured the corvée (Mic 3:10, Jer 22:13–19).

---

[32] Isaac Mendelsohn, "Samuel's Denunciation of Kingship in Light of the Akkadian Documents from Ugarit," *BASOR* 143 (1956): 17–22.

[33] Mark Leuchter, "A King Like All the Nations: The Composition of 1 Sam 8,11–18," *ZAW* 117 (2005): 543–58.

[34] Kaplan, "1 Samuel 8:11–18 as 'A Mirror for Princes,'" 625–42.

[35] Marvin L. Chaney, "The Political Economy of Peasant Poverty: What the Eighth-Century Prophets Presumed but Did Not State," *Journal of Religion and Society* 10 (2014): 34–60; Matthew J. M. Coomber, *Re-reading the Prophets through Corporate Globalization: A Cultural-Evolutionary Approach to Economic Injustice in the Hebrew Bible* (Piscataway, NJ: Gorgias, 2010); D. N. Premnath, *Eighth Century Prophets: A Social Analysis* (St. Louis: Chalice, 2003); Walter J. Houston, *Contending for Justice: Ideologies and Theologies of Social Justice in the Old Testament*, LHBOTS 428 (London: T&T Clark, 2008), 18–98; Houston, "Was There a Social Crisis in the Eighth Century?," in *In Search of Pre-exilic Israel: Proceedings of the Oxford Old Testament Seminar*, ed. John Day, JSOTSup 406 (London: T&T Clark, 2004), 130–49; Hemchand Gossai, *Justice, Righteousness, and the Social Critique of the Eighth-Century Prophets*, AmUStTR 141 (New York: Lang, 1993).

[36] Hans Walter Wolff refers to the elite robbery and exploitation of the people in Mic 3:1–3 as "economic cannibalism" (*Micah: A Commentary*, trans. Gary Stansell [Minneapolis: Fortress, 1990], 100).

[37] Marvin L. Chaney, "Producing Peasant Poverty: Debt Instruments in Amos 2.6–8, 13–16," in *Reading a Tendentious Bible: Essays in Honor of Robert B. Coote*, ed. Marvin L. Chaney, Uriah Y. Kim, and Annette Schellenberg, HBM 66 (Sheffield: Sheffield Phoenix, 2014), 19–34; Roland Boer, "Biting the Poor: On the Difference between Credit and Debt in Ancient Israel and Southwest Asia," *Journal of Religion and Society* 16 (2014): 1–21; Chirichigno, *Debt-Slavery in Israel and the Ancient Near East*.

Nehemiah 5 is especially relevant for this study, not only because economic abuses by elites toward their Jewish kin evidently continued in fifth-century Yehud but also because it details the customary extraction for feasts held by its governors.[38] According to Neh 5:1–4, there was an outcry of the men and their wives against their wealthier Jewish kin, protesting the extraction of property and persons to pay for defaulted loans incurred because of famine.[39] The people were starving; in order to survive, they were forced to sell not only their lands but their sons and daughters as debt slaves. Besides these burdens, the people had to borrow on their fields and vineyards to pay the king's tax.[40] The sexual exploitation of daughters by their unscrupulous Jewish creditors underscored the people's suffering:

> Now our flesh is the same as that of our kindred; our children are the same as their children; and yet we are forcing our sons and daughters to be slaves, and some of our daughters have been ravished; and we are powerless, and our fields and vineyards now belong to others. (5:5)

Nehemiah reproached the "nobles and officials" for taking their kinfolk as debt slaves and selling them to the nations (5:7–9). He exhorted them to stop this seizure of persons and lands and to restore them to their aggrieved kin along with the interest gained. This they evidently did (5:10–12). Nehemiah continued with his own defense as a responsible governor, in contrast to his predecessors. He maintained that he and his kin never ate the governor's bread/food allowance (לחם הפחה), whereas his predecessors "laid heavy burdens [הכבידו] on the people, and took food and wine from them, besides forty shekels of silver" (5:15). He then bragged about the 150 Jews, officials, and assorted others who feasted at his table (5:17).[41] The daily provision for these lavish banquets was one ox, six choice sheep, and fowl and wine in abundance. Yet, unlike the earlier governors, Nehemiah did not dip into his own governor's bread/food allowance (לחם הפחה) for his banquets, "because of the heavy burden of labor [כבדה העבדה] on the people" (5:18). The burden (כבד) that the former governors laid upon the people was the heavy extraction of their agricultural resources (5:15). The burden (כבד) upon the people here

---

[38] José Severino Croatto, "The Debt in Nehemiah's Social Reform: A Study of Nehemiah 5:1–19," in *Subversive Scriptures: Revolutionary Readings of the Christian Bible in Latin America*, ed. and trans. Leif E. Vaage (Valley Forge, PA: Trinity Press International, 1997), 39–59; Rainer Albertz, *From the Exile to the Maccabees*, vol. 2 of *A History of Israelite Religion in the Old Testament Period* (Louisville: Westminster John Knox, 1994), 493–97; Joseph Blenkinsopp, *Ezra-Nehemiah: A Commentary*, OTL (Philadelphia: Westminster, 1988), 253–60; Gottwald, "Expropriated and the Expropriators," 1–9.

[39] Bob Becking, "Drought, Hunger, and Redistribution: A Social Economic Reading of Nehemiah 5," in *The Historian and the Bible: Essays in Honour of Lester L. Grabbe*, ed. Philip R. Davies and Diana V. Edelman, LHBOTS 530 (New York: T&T Clark, 2010), 137–49.

[40] Peter Altmann, "Tithes for the Clergy and Taxes for the King: State and Temple Contributions in Nehemiah," *CBQ* 76 (2014): 215–29.

[41] This hospitality was designed to ease tensions among the elite and strengthen Nehemiah's leadership, according to Wright, "Commensal Politics in Ancient Western Asia: (Part II)," 351.

in 5:18 was one of labor (עבדה). This labor was not specified. It could have referred to the extraction of men to build the wall (5:16). It might have referred to the labor involved in the sowing, growing, and harvesting the crops (cf. 5:15). But it probably did *not* refer to the labor of those who prepared, cooked, and served the delicious and generous meals at these rich tables. It is to these invisible laborers that we now turn.

II. "King Solomon Conscripted Forced Labor out of All Israel" (1 Kings 5:13): Labor and Food Preparation for Whom?

Archaeological studies of ancient banquets reveal that a large and elaborate feast drew heavily on the provisions extracted from the people who effectively "funded" the occasion with their goods and labor.[42] Because securing labor was the major issue in the ancient Near East, this study will focus on the workforce responsible for banquet preparation. Except for the detail that the king will take Israel's "daughters" to toil as "flavorers,[43] cooks, and bakers" for the court (1 Sam 8:13), there is little information in the Hebrew Bible about those who labored in Israelite royal kitchens to prepare the feast. Used with caution, however, ancient Near Eastern sources can be helpful here. A banquet would have entailed a large professional staff of chefs, bakers, butchers, sommeliers, managers, and waiters, along with lower personnel who sliced, diced, skinned, filleted, and performed the myriad other tasks involved in food processing.[44] According to Bottero, the Neo-Assyrian staff in the "House of the Queen" included 300 various domestic servants, 220 cupbearers, 400 cooks, and 400 pastry chefs, among others.[45] The tables of the Israelite and Judean kings probably did not reach the level of haute cuisine as did their Egyptian and Mesopotamian counterparts.[46] They certainly, however, surpassed the nutritionally deficient diet of ordinary Israelites,[47] and their extravagance was definitely an object of prophetic critique (Amos 6:4–7; cf. 4:1; Isa 5:11–12, 22; 28:1, 7–8).

The "house of the father" was the symbolic basis of an embedded social order from the bottom upward, replicating the same structure at different levels.[48] It

---

[42] Pollock, "Towards an Archaeology of Commensal Spaces," 13.

[43] See n. 5 above.

[44] In fourteenth- to thirteenth-century documents from Nippur, 17 percent of the servant population who were listed with an occupation were identified as food preparers, which included millers, brewers, cooks, and butchers, 17.8 percent of whom were female. See Jonathan S. Tenney, *Life at the Bottom of Babylonian Society: Servile Labour at Nippur in the 14th and 13th Centuries BC*, CHANE 51 (Leiden: Brill, 2011), 99–100.

[45] Bottéro, *Oldest Cuisine in the World*, 81.

[46] Meyers, "Menu: Royal Repasts," 146–47.

[47] Meyers, *Rediscovering Eve*, 53–58.

[48] The biblical texts also refer to the "house of the mother," which seems to be the counterpart

legitimated royal rule by means of the very same patriarchal ideology that underpinned each ordinary household.[49] Feasting becomes a significant mechanism to conjoin nodal points of the patrimonial household (בית־אב), lineage, and larger political entities.[50] Indeed, 1 Kgs 4:6–7 recorded a bureaucrat named Ahishar who oversaw the running of Solomon's royal household (הבית), and twelve officials provided food for the king and his household (ביתו) one month in the year. When bodies were pulled off the village communes to work on the royal estates and prepare meals and feasts for the royal household, their needs for survival changed. Rather than rely on the traditional kinship-household for subsistence, one's survival was now contingent on his or her attachment to a particular estate, which *in name* did not differ from the kinship-household (בית).[51] One's affiliation with a royal estate, however, was qualitatively different from one's village commune, in that relations in the former were economically exploitative.

Along with Ahishar, who supervised Solomon's estate, an individual named Adoniram son of Abda was in charge of forced or corvée labor (מס, 1 Kgs 4:6). Corvée labor was needed for crucial times during the agricultural calendar (plowing, sowing, and harvesting) and for building projects. First Kings 5 recorded a levy of 30,000 men to collect timber in Lebanon for the temple (v. 13), 70,000 laborers and 80,000 stonecutters to quarry rock, and 3,300 hundred supervisors overall (vv. 15–16).[52]

In order to meet the subsistence needs of these corvée laborers, Michael Dietler and Ingrid Herbich argue that, because the forced labor was sponsored by

---

of the "house of the father." It apparently was a distinct kinship unit within the "house of the father" that had social and economic control over the marriage brokering of a daughter who would marry out. See Carol L. Meyers, "'To Her Mother's House': Considering a Counterpart to the Israelite *Bêt ʾāb*," in *The Bible and the Politics of Exegesis: Essays in Honor of Norman K. Gottwald on His Sixty-Fifth Birthday*, ed. David Jobling, Peggy L. Day, and Gerald T. Sheppard (Cleveland: Pilgrim, 1991), 39–51; Cynthia Ruth Chapman, "The Biblical 'House of the Mother' and the Brokering of Marriage: Economic Reciprocity among Natal Siblings," in *In the Wake of Tikva Frymer-Kensky*, ed. Steven Holloway, JoAnn Scurlock, and Richard Beal, Gorgias Précis Portfolios 4 (Piscataway, NJ: Gorgias, 2009), 143–69.

[49] J. David Schloen, "Economy and Society in Iron Age Israel and Judah: An Archaeological Perspective," in *The Wiley Blackwell Companion to Ancient Israel*, ed. Susan Niditch (Malden, MA: Wiley Blackwell, 2016), 433–53; Schloen, *The House of the Father as Fact and Symbol: Patrimonialism in Ugarit and the Ancient Near East*, Studies in the Archaeology and History of the Levant 2 (Winona Lake, IN: Eisenbrauns, 2001); Daniel M. Master, "State Formation Theory and the Kingdom of Ancient Israel," *JNES* 60 (2001): 117–31, here 130–31.

[50] Cf. the discussion of habitus and the dyadic nodes of the patrimonial household model in Fu and Altmann, "Feasting: Backgrounds," 18–21.

[51] See Susan Pollock, "Feasts, Funerals, and Fast Food in Early Mesopotamian States," in *The Archaeology and Politics of Food and Feasting in Early States and Empires*, ed. Tamara L. Bray (New York: Kluwer Academic, 2003), 17–38, here 28.

[52] Hermann Michael Niemann thinks that forced labor did exist in Solomon's time but that the actual numbers were beyond speculation ("The Socio-political Shadow Cast by the Biblical Solomon," in Handy, *Age of Solomon*, 252–99, here 280).

a royal state apparatus, the laborers were fed through "obligatory" work feasts in which people had to work because a ruler, religious leader, or public institution had the moral or ideological authority to require their presence as a form of labor tribute. They went on to say that, unless rulers provided a generous quantity of food and drink for their subjects' labor, they would face protests and resistance.[53] First Kings 5 did not specify how Solomon's labor force was fed.[54] In a parallel passage, however, 2 Chr 2:9–10, Solomon told Huram (Hiram in 1 Kings) that his workers would work with Huram's workers to cut timber for the temple and that he would provide twenty thousand cors of crushed wheat (חטים), twenty thousand cors of barley (שערים), twenty thousand baths of wine, and twenty thousand baths of oil for Huram's workers.[55] One presumes that Solomon's workers partook of this largess. Nevertheless, the burdens of his corvée demands eventually resulted in the breakdown of his kingdom and the stoning of Adoniram (1 Kgs 12:1–18), which suggest that inadequate attention to the workers' subsistence needs might have been a factor.

Labor extracted from the village communes was therefore responsible for providing and processing food for two population groups. The first were all the workers on the royal estate, including the food preparers themselves, who were given subsistence-level rations of milled barley.[56] Corvée workers and personnel who worked in other areas of the land were also in the tally. The second group, at significantly higher levels of expense and labor, was the royal court with its daily meals (1 Kgs 4:22–24) and its feasts for special occasions (1 Kgs 3:15, 8:65, 10:5). As mechanisms of hierarchical redistribution, feasts allowed the lower classes to partake in the conspicuous consumption extracted from them (see 2 Sam 6:18–19, 1 Kgs 3:15, 8:65–66, 1 Chr 29:21–22), but in a way that reinforced their dependence

---

[53] Michael Dietler and Ingrid Herbich, "Feasts and Labor Mobilization: Dissecting a Fundamental Economic Practice," in Dietler and Hayden, *Feasts*, 240–64, here 244.

[54] Pollock argues that the mass-produced pottery vessels in the Uruk period were used to distribute food rations (fast food) to dependent laborers ("Feasts, Funerals, and Fast Food," 29–32). Seymour Gitin argues that scoops found in large quantities in Israel during Iron II might have had a similar function in food distribution ("Scoops: Corpus, Function and Typology," in *Studies in the Archaeology and History of Ancient Israel in Honour of Moshe Dothan*, ed. Michael Heltzer, Arthur Segal, and Daniel Kaufman [Haifa: Haifa University Press, 1993], 99–126). I thank Jennie Ebeling for directing me to "Scoops."

[55] The quality of wine and oil, of course, was inferior to that reserved for elites. For a discussion of the cheap wine given to corvée workers, see Gershon Galil, "*YYN HLQ?*: The Oldest Hebrew Inscription from Jerusalem," *Strata: Bulletin of the Anglo Israel Archaeological Society* 31 (2013): 11–26; and on aged wine and fine oil sent to the court in Iron Age Samaria, see Roger S. Nam, "Power Relations in the Samaria Ostraca," *PEQ* 144 (2012): 155–63.

[56] Estate and corvée workers most likely received grain already ground by millers. Heimpel asks, "Would a 'slave or maid' take 'home' 30–60 liters of barley at the end of a month, mill it, and bake it?" Given their living conditions, it was more likely that the estate absorbed the cost of grinding and the recipient received "ready-made food as pay" (Heimpel, *Workers and Construction Work*, 90).

on the estate for subsistence and preserved the reputation of elites as those divinely blessed to be the dispensers of meat and other rare food items.[57] It is in this twofold context that we must situate the extraction of labor for royal feasts. This extraction of workers for food processing and preparation for both groups would have an adverse impact on the domestic subsistence needs of the village communes, since none of the labor for food was invested in the kinship households.

III. "Your Daughters as Flavorers and Cooks and Bakers" (1 Samuel 8:13): Women's Labor in Grain Processing and Bread Making

First Samuel 8:13 and Neh 5:1, 5 highlight the plight of women laborers. For the remainder of this article, we turn to the "daughters" taken as bakers.[58] Bread was a major component in the subsistence diet, accounting for 50 percent of a person's daily caloric intake.[59] Carol L. Meyers has consistently drawn attention to the labor-intensive, often tedious, process of bread making by Israelite women in the domestic household.[60] Reaped, threshed, and winnowed grain had to be soaked

---

[57] Justin Lev-Tov and Kevin McGeough, "Examing [sic] Feasting in Late Bronze Age Syro-Palestine through Ancient Texts and Bones," in *The Archaeology of Food and Identity*, ed. Katheryn C. Twiss, Occasional Paper 34 (Carbondale: Center for Archaeological Investigations, Southern Illinois University, 2007), 85–111, here 93–94, 100–102; Pollock, "Feasts, Funerals, and Fast Food," 33–34.

[58] If Samuel's assertion was historically accurate, women evidently were included as cooks in the royal kitchens of Israel. In Egypt and Mesopotamia, cooking for the elite was the preserve of men, who took women's recipes to the level of haute cuisine. The exception was Africa, where women cooked for the royal court but the menu was the same as for the ordinary citizen because royal women cooked as wives, not servants. See Goody, *Cooking, Cuisine and Class*, 101–2; Jean Bottéro, "The Cuisine of Ancient Mesopotamia," *BA* 48 (1985): 36–47, here 46.

[59] MacDonald, *What Did the Ancient Israelites Eat?*, 19.

[60] Carol L. Meyers, "From Field Crops to Food: Attributing Gender and Meaning to Bread Production in Iron Age Israel," in *The Archaeology of Difference: Gender, Ethnicity, Class and the "Other" in Antiquity; Studies in Honor of Eric M. Meyers*, ed. Douglas R. Edwards and C. Thomas McCollough, AASOR 60/61 (Boston: American Schools of Oriental Research, 2007), 67–84; Meyers, "Having Their Space and Eating There Too: Bread Production and Female Power in Ancient Israelite Households," *Nashim: A Journal of Jewish Women's Studies & Gender Issues* 5 (2002): 14–44, here 21–23; Meyers, *Rediscovering Eve*, 128–32; Meyers, "Material Remains and Social Relations: Women's Culture in Agrarian Households of the Iron Age," in *Symbiosis, Symbolism, and the Power of the Past: Canaan, Ancient Israel, and Their Neighbors from the Late Bronze Age through Roman Palaestina; Proceedings of the Centennial Symposium, W. F. Albright Institute of Archaeological Research and American Schools of Oriental Research, Jerusalem, May 29/31, 2000*, ed. William G. Dever and Seymour Gitin (Winona Lake, IN: Eisenbrauns, 2003), 425–44, here 430–32; Meyers, "Everyday Life: Women in the Period of the Hebrew Bible," in

or parched before it was milled into flour, made into dough, and leavened.⁶¹ Baking was the very last step in this lengthy bread-making process.⁶² Meyers estimates that it would have taken three hours daily to provide edible grain for six people.⁶³

The daily grinding of grain was the most demanding part of producing bread.⁶⁴ Appearing regularly in ancient Near Eastern texts were the large numbers of millers of grain working on the estates.⁶⁵ These grain grinders were usually female, and they were responsible for processing grain for the two populations just discussed⁶⁶—barley rations given out to estate and corvée laborers⁶⁷—as well as the high-grade flour for the tables and feasts for the royal court. These milled grains had their own positions in the social hierarchy, which factored into the workload of our millers. The hardier grain, barley (שערה), could be grown in less-favorable environs. Wheat (חטה), however, needed more rainfall and less-saline conditions than barley. Barley became the food for the poor, workers, and animals (1 Kgs 4:28), while the rich consumed the products of wheat.⁶⁸ Furthermore, the additional time and labor invested in the higher grades of wheat flour gave it greater standing on the culinary ladder. Solomon's court demanded thirty cors of choice flour (סלת) and sixty cors of regular flour (קמח; 1 Kgs 4:22 [MT 5:2]) daily. This choice flour was twice as great in cost and prestige as regular flour.⁶⁹

Women's Bible Commentary, ed. Carol A. Newsom and Sharon H. Ringe, expanded ed. (Louisville: Westminster John Knox, 1998), 251–59, here 254.

⁶¹ See the description of the process from grain to grindstone in Jean-Pierre Grégoire, "The Grain-Grinding-Households (E₂-Har.Har) of Southern Mesopotamia at the End of the 3rd Millennium before the Common Era: Major Units for the Transformation of Cereals," *Bulletin of the Anglo-Israel Archeological Society* 17 (1999): 7–38, here 20–24.

⁶² For an excellent documentary by Jennie Ebeling on traditional bread baking in northern Jordan, which can give one a glimpse of bread making in the ancient Near East, see https://www.academia.edu/14152018/Video_Traditional_Bread_Baking_in_Northern_Jordan_Part_I, and https://www.academia.edu/14151992/Video_Traditional_Bread_Baking_in_Northern_Jordan_Part_II_The_Oven.

⁶³ Meyers, "Having Their Space and Eating There Too," 21–22.

⁶⁴ For a discussion with images of the different ground-stone implements for food processing and how they were used, see Jennie R. Ebeling and Yorke M. Rowan, "The Archaeology of the Daily Grind: Ground Stone Tools and Food Production in the Southern Levant," *NEA* 67 (2004): 108–17.

⁶⁵ Grégoire, "Grain-Grinding-Households," 7–38.

⁶⁶ This is not even including the bread for the deity. For example, 486 liters of barley flour and 162 liters of spelt flour were needed for the 243 loaves for the god Anu (Bottéro, *Oldest Cuisine in the World*, 112).

⁶⁷ For a detailed discussion of the barley, bread, and beer rations given to workers at Garšana, see Heimpel, *Workers and Construction Work*, 90–122. For Babylonia in the first millennium, see Jursa, "Labor in Babylonia," 345–96.

⁶⁸ Philip J. King and Lawrence E. Stager, *Life in Biblical Israel*, LAI (Louisville: Westminster John Knox, 2001), 94–95; MacDonald, *What Did the Ancient Israelites Eat?*, 19–21.

⁶⁹ Cf. 2 Kgs 7:16, where "a measure of choice meal [סלת] was sold for a shekel" while "two measures of barley [שערים] for a shekel."

In bookkeeping texts from Ur III, the number of days that these millers worked and liters of grain that they processed were rigorously documented. The time tallies took into consideration the degrees of flour quality: the coarser meal involved less grinding time; the finer flour, much longer.[70] The grinding technique was also different for fine flour. Instead of pushing the handstone forward on the quern, our grinder must now move the handstone in a circular movement, repeating the grinding process fifteen to sixteen times to obtain a finer flour. While she could produce up to 9.5 liters of groats at the end of the day, she would be able to produce only 3.5 liters of fine flour.[71]

Furthermore, ancient Near Eastern texts note that, in addition to grinding grain, the female millers took part in agricultural activities performed by their male counterparts, such as harvesting, threshing, winnowing, maintaining irrigation installations, and excavation works. The expected labor performance for these millers was probably beyond the abilities of the normal worker, given their overall workload. There were no incentives to produce more, since their compensation was no more than the minimum amount of grain and clothing to keep them able to produce.[72] A grinder might have been one of the unlucky ones who were seized in the open streets if womanpower was needed for grain-grinding.[73] Finally, grinders were less likely to flee to escape their difficult situations than their male counterparts if they had children on the estate.[74]

Because these female grain grinders performed this backbreaking labor primarily for the needs of the estate instead of their own families, they most likely did not attain the social, personal, and sociopolitical power that Meyers argues for Israelite women in village households.[75] The labor conditions of the grinders were classic illustrations exemplifying Marx's alienation of the worker. The grinder was alienated from the means of production, since the grindingstones (mortars, querns), cooking vessels (griddles, trays, pots), and ovens (tabun and תנור) belonged to the estate.[76] She was alienated from bread, the product of her labor, in that she toiled not for herself or her family but for rations for other servile workers like herself and the conspicuous consumption of bread for the elite.[77] Bread became a

---

[70] Robert K. Englund, "Hard Work—Where Will It Get You? Labor Management in Ur III Mesopotamia," *JNES* 50 (1991): 255–80, here 270–73.

[71] Grégoire, "Grain-Grinding-Households," 18–19, 22, 25.

[72] Englund, "Hard Work—Where Will It Get You?," 255–80.

[73] Grégoire, "Grain-Grinding-Households," 16–17.

[74] Tenney, *Life at the Bottom of Babylonian Society*, 110–11.

[75] Meyers, "Having Their Space and Eating There Too," 30–33.

[76] This contrasts with the cooperative use of these materials for baking in Iron Age rural contexts; see Aubrey Baadsgaaard, "A Taste of Women's Sociality: Cooking as Cooperative Labor in Iron Age Syro-Palestine," in *The World of Women in the Ancient and Classical Near East*, ed. Beth Alpert Nakhai (Newcastle: Cambridge Scholars, 2008), 13–44.

[77] The haute cuisine of the Mesopotamian diet included three hundred kinds of bread with different combinations of ingredients; see Bottéro, "Cuisine of Ancient Mesopotamia," 38.

commodity for the estate, not the source of subsistence for her and her family. Finally, she was alienated from the activity of labor; her work was not chosen but coerced. It was not directly for herself or her family that she worked but for others who did not work and who had no kin-group relation to her but on whom she was dependent for survival.[78]

IV. Conclusion

This article focused on those who carried the economic burden for royal banquets in the Hebrew Bible—the invisible producers and preparers of feasts—rather than on their royal consumers. During the time of the monarchy, two economic structures—one allocative, the other extractive—conflicted with each other in their agenda regarding the agricultural production of food for feasts. The village communes practiced conservative risk-averse strategies of farming primarily for subsistence, keeping surpluses of crops and flocks to allocate to those in need during difficult periods. The nonproducers of the temple/palace extracted not only agricultural and animal surpluses but, more importantly, labor from the village communes. The elites needed cheap and unpaid labor not only to farm their own estates but also to work in their building and military projects. The diversion of human bodies away from subsistence farming placed a heavy burden on the villages, threatening the sustainability of the economic system on which the elites themselves relied.

When men and women were taken from the rural sectors to work on royal projects, the sources for their survival needs changed. Instead of relying on the traditional kinship household for their subsistence, the people now depended for their survival on their connection to a particular royal estate or endeavor. Food processors and preparers were therefore needed to provide food for two distinct social groups. The first were those who farmed the estates and those pressed into corvée labor camps, who primarily received subsistence-level rations of barley. These included the food processors and preparers themselves. The second group was the elites, who required rich daily provisions along with food for their lavish banquets.

First Samuel evidenced the extraction of female bakers in Samuel's warning against the monarchy in Israel. In this discussion, I highlighted the invisible arduous labor performed by female workers in the milling of different types of flour for the two social groups. The women's labor conditions epitomized the alienation not only of the female miller but also of all those individuals whose labor was extracted from the villages to contribute to the feasting of their "betters." These workers were

---

[78] See "Alienated Labor," in Karl Marx, *Writings of the Young Marx on Philosophy and Society*, ed. and trans. Loyd D. Easton and Kurt H. Guddat (Garden City, NY: Doubleday, 1967), 287–301.

alienated from the products of their labor, such as the food grown, harvested, baked, stewed, and cooked and the animals raised, culled, butchered, and boiled. They were alienated from the means of production, such as the land that produced the crops and flocks and the array of kitchen tools and implements needed to process and cook food. And they were especially alienated from the activity of their labor. Very little was invested in their own kinship-households; they worked for the benefit of a tiny oppressive minority. Although elites probably allowed estate and corvée laborers to eat some part of the richness of their feast, such as meat, the "beneficence" of the elites also cemented the class differentials between them and the laborers and reinforced the dependence of the latter on the former for their subsistence needs.

Yahwistic Appropriation of Achaemenid Ideology and the Function of Nehemiah 9 in Ezra-Nehemiah

DAVID JANZEN
david.janzen@durham.ac.uk
Durham University, Durham DH1 3RS, United Kingdom

The prayer of Neh 9:6–37, and particularly its final two verses, presents the imperial monarchy in a very negative light. This portrayal is far different from the depictions of the Achaemenids found everywhere else in Ezra-Nehemiah, where the Persian kings are great benefactors of the Judean assembly. The presence of this anti-imperial language points to the existence of a group that hoped that God would grant them independence from Persia. In Neh 8–13 as a whole, however, the inclusion of the prayer functions not to promote this view but to present it as terribly misguided. The prayer includes a description of the people that is drawn from Achaemenid ideology, a picture used by the Persian kings to contrast the beneficence bestowed on loyal subjects and the tortures inflicted on the disloyal. Nehemiah 8–13 demonstrates that independence from the Achaemenid king, the figure responsible for sending proper leadership to Judah in order to keep the people faithful to the law, would lead to divine destruction of the community. Here as elsewhere in Ezra-Nehemiah, God permits the continued existence of the assembly only because the figures sent by the king force the people to remain loyal to the law. The best possible life is one under Achaemenid rule, and life without it would be a disaster, which is precisely the claim of Achaemenid imperial ideology.

I. NEHEMIAH 9 AND EZRA-NEHEMIAH

One of the most puzzling aspects of the prayer of Neh 9:6–37 is its uncomfortable fit within Ezra-Nehemiah as a whole. Commentators often note that the negative portrayal of the imperial monarchy in the final section of the prayer, and especially its final two verses, contrasts markedly with the positive portrait of the Persian kings everywhere else in the book. This negative picture would seem to fit more easily in the context of early Persian-period works that include prophecies announcing a great divine overthrow of the existing imperial order, such as Hag 2:21–23 and Zech 2:1–4 [1:18–21], 10–17 [2:6–13]. We know, of course, that not everyone in the Persian-period assembly was content with the community's colonized status; certainly the early postexilic prophecies mentioned above attest to that fact. It is hardly outside the realm of possibility that anti-imperial sentiment lived on, even if there was almost no clear representation of this view in later extant Persian-period literature. The anti-imperial language of Neh 9 suggests that such sentiment was still present in the community when Ezra-Nehemiah was put together, at least a century after the time of Haggai and Zechariah. In the context of Ezra-Nehemiah as a whole, however, the prayer does not encourage this pro-independence attitude but rather presents it as terribly misguided. As we shall see, the final verses of the prayer use language Persian-period readers would recognize as reflecting Achaemenid imperial ideology. This language both points to Judah's status as a colonized people and contains an implicit warning of grievous punishment for those subjects of the empire who choose rebellion. Moreover, while the final verses of Neh 9 acknowledge the presence of proindependence sentiment within the community, chapters 8–13 as a whole demonstrate that freedom from Persian rule would result in the utter destruction of the community by divine order. In Ezra-Nehemiah's Yahwistic appropriation of Achaemenid ideology, the community will survive only under Persian rule; the prayer of Neh 9, even with its anti-imperial sentiment, functions as part of an argument in chapters 8–13 against precisely such an attitude. Although 9:36–37 may acknowledge the existence of such sentiment, chapters 8–13 argue that only Achaemenid leadership stands between the community and its destruction.

We begin by summarizing the tensions between Neh 9 and the rest of Ezra-Nehemiah in regard to their views of the Persians and the Persians' relationship to the Judean assembly. The first section of the prayer, verses 6–31, refers to God's interactions with the ancestors in the past, a negative portrayal of the earlier generations that consistently uses the third-person plural to refer to their sins and apostasies, to the gifts of law and land they received, and to their punishments at the hands of foreign peoples for their sins. Verses 32–37, the second section of the prayer, turns to the present situation with the word ועתה ("and now") and uses the first-person plural to refer to the sins of the current generation,[1] sins that have

---

[1] For further discussion of this point, see Waldemar Chrostowski, "An Examination of Conscience by God's People as Exemplified in Neh 9,6–37," *BZ* 34 (1990): 253–61, here 253–55; Samuel E. Balentine, *Prayer in the Hebrew Bible: The Drama of Divine–Human Dialogue*, OBT (Minneapolis: Fortress, 1993), 114; Rolf Rendtorff, "Nehemiah 9: An Important Theological Witness of Theological Reflection," in *Tehillah le-Moshe: Biblical and Judaic Studies in Honor of Moshe Greenberg*, ed. Mordechai Cogan, Barry L. Eichler, and Jeffrey H. Tigay (Winona Lake, IN: Eisenbrauns, 1997), 111–17, here 114; Tamara Cohn Eskenazi, "Nehemiah 9–10: Structure and Significance," in *Perspectives on Hebrew Scriptures I: Comprising the Contents of Journal of Hebrew Scriptures, Volumes 1–4*, ed. Ehud Ben Zvi, PHSC 1 (Piscataway, NJ: Gorgias, 2006), 365–78, here 371–72.

resulted, as verses 36–37 state, in the community's status as עֲבָדִים ("slaves") in the very land given to the ancestors, "and its great wealth belongs to kings whom you set over us because of our sins, and they rule over our bodies and our livestock as they wish, and we are in great distress." The final verses make perfect sense in the prayer as a whole, for verses 26–31 imitate the Deuteronomistic cycle of rebellion, saying that "many times" Israel's unfaithfulness in regard to the law was met with divine punishment manifested by foreign enemies.[2] Such punishments were always followed by divine rescue. In this context, verses 36–37 point out that sin has once again been followed by punishment, although the verses say nothing in any explicit way about a divine intervention to follow.

What makes the second section of the prayer, and especially its final two verses, seem so odd in the context of Ezra-Nehemiah is its portrayal of the foreign kings and their relationship to the current community. Verses 36–37 state that these kings rule over the land, its people, and their livestock and that the community serves them as "slaves." The kings are thus responsible, at least in part, for the "great distress" the assembly now experiences, and the prayer asks that God not look upon this "hardship" as "insignificant" (v. 32). In the context of Ezra-Nehemiah as a whole, these kings are, of course, the Achaemenids, but such a seemingly negative portrayal of them in Neh 9 contrasts markedly with their role as benefactors of the postexilic assembly everywhere else in the work.[3] In Ezra-Nehemiah's narrative, YHWH "roused" Cyrus, who claims that YHWH "has given to me all the kingdoms of the earth" and "charged me to build for him a house in Jerusalem" (Ezra 1:1–2). Cyrus asks Judeans in Babylonia to go and build the temple, gives them the temple vessels Nebuchadnezzar brought to Babylon (1:3, 7–11; 6:5), and has the crown pay for the construction (6:4). Darius enforces Cyrus's orders in regard to the temple and has the Persian government pay for the sacrifices there as well (6:6–12). Artaxerxes donates money and cultic vessels to the temple and continues Darius's policy of paying for the sacrifices in Jerusalem and even remits the tax the

---

[2] As H. G. M. Williamson points out, this cycle appears in its full form in Neh 9:26–27 and again in 9:28. Verses 29–31 begin a third turn of the cycle, but it is not completed. See Williamson, "The Torah and History in Presentations of Restoration in Ezra-Nehemiah," in *Reading the Law: Studies in Honour of Gordon J. Wenham*, ed. J. G. McConville and Karl Möller, LHBOTS 461 (London: T&T Clark, 2007), 156–70, here 168.

[3] Reference to this stark contrast is a point commonly made by commentators. See, e.g., Chrostowski, "Examination of Conscience," 261; Rodney Alan Werline, *Penitential Prayer in Second Temple Judaism: The Development of a Religious Institution*, EJL 13 (Atlanta: Scholars Press, 1998), 58; Michael W. Duggan, *The Covenant Renewal in Ezra-Nehemiah (Neh 7:72b–10:40): An Exegetical, Literary, and Theological Study*, SBLDS 164 (Atlanta: Society of Biblical Literature, 2001), 231–32; H. G. M. Williamson, "Structure and Historiography in Nehemiah 9," in *Studies in Persian Period History and Historiography*, FAT 38 (Tübingen: Mohr Siebeck, 2004), 282–93, here 289–90; Lena-Sofia Tiemeyer, "Abraham—A Judahite Prerogative," *ZAW* 120 (2008): 49–66, here 61; Klaas A. D. Smelik, "Nehemiah as a 'Court Jew,'" in *New Perspectives on Ezra-Nehemiah: History and Historiography, Text, Literature, and Interpretation*, ed. Isaac Kalimi (Winona Lake, IN: Eisenbrauns, 2012), 61–72, here 71–72.

temple personnel owe (7:15–24). He orders Ezra to teach "the laws of your God" throughout the satrapy of Across-the-River and is clear that he will enforce this law (7:25–26). Moreover, although the assembly's adversaries bribe officials to lie to Artaxerxes in order to have him prevent the building of Jerusalem's wall (4:1–23),[4] after Nehemiah's intervention he not only permits this construction but even provides wood for it (Neh 2:1–8). There is not the slightest hint in these or other passages in the work—Neh 9 excepted—that Persian rule is an evil from which Judeans should long to be free. Nehemiah 9:32–37 does not explicitly ask God for this freedom, although commentators widely conclude that these verses imply this kind of plea and so see here a radical break with the rest of the work, which is satisfied with the political status quo.[5]

As an instructive example of this conclusion that the negative presentation of foreign kings in Neh 9:32–37 does not appear neatly to suit Ezra-Nehemiah's otherwise very positive portrayal of the Persian monarchy, some point to the differences in this regard between the prayer of Neh 9 and that of Ezra in Ezra 9:6–15. Both are penitential prayers that rehearse the sins of the ancestors and claim that those sins were punished by foreign control of the land. The two prayers share many expressions;[6] Ezra 9:9 even refers to the current assembly as עבדים, just as Neh 9:36

---

[4] Specifically, Artaxerxes is told that Jerusalem was destroyed because it rebelled against previous imperial sovereigns (4:15) and that, if the walls are completed, the king can expect an end to the tax paid from the region (4:13). Neither of these things is true according to the narrative. Jerusalem was destroyed because its people angered their God (5:12), not because it revolted against its suzerains. And even when, as the city walls near completion, the people complain of the financial hardships caused by "the tax of the king" (Neh 5:4), Nehemiah claims that the difficulty lies with wealthy community members who loan money at interest (5:6–13), not with the royal tax, for which payment is not diminished.

[5] So, e.g., Joseph Blenkinsopp, *Ezra-Nehemiah: A Commentary*, OTL (London: SCM, 1989), 307–8; Mark A. Throntveit, *Ezra-Nehemiah*, IBC (Louisville: John Knox, 1992), 106; Balentine, *Prayer in the Hebrew Bible*, 115; Volker Pröbstl, *Nehemia 9, Psalm 106 und Psalm 136 und die Rezeption des Pentateuchs* (Göttingen: Cuvillier, 1997), 27–28; Werline, *Penitential Prayer*, 58–59; Mark J. Boda, *Praying the Tradition: The Origin and Use of Tradition in Nehemiah 9*, BZAW 277 (Berlin: de Gruyter, 1999), 190; Pablo R. Andiñach, "Nehemías 9,5b–37: Oración y denuncia de la opresión," in *Los caminos inexhauribles de la Palabra (Las relecturas creativas* en *la Biblia y de la Biblia)*, ed. Guillermo Hanson (Buenos Aires: Lumen, 2000), 241–53, here 252–53; Duggan, *Covenant Renewal*, 231–32; Richard J. Bautch, *Developments in Genre between Post-exilic Penitential Prayers and the Psalms of Communal Lament*, AcBib 7 (Atlanta: Society of Biblical Literature, 2003), 135; Williamson, "Structure and Historiography," 289–90.

[6] Michael Duggan, in fact, identifies thirty-two expressions that the two prayers share ("Ezra 9:6–15: A Penitential Prayer within Its Literary Setting," in *Seeking the Favor of God*, ed. Mark J. Boda, Daniel K. Falk, and Rodney A. Werline, 3 vols., EJL 21–23 [Atlanta: Society of Biblical Literature, 2006–2008], 1:165–80, here 175–77). He is not the only one to point to similarities between the two passages, however; see also, e.g., Charles C. Torrey, *Ezra Studies*, LBS (Chicago: University of Chicago Press, 1910; repr., New York: Ktav, 1970), 275–76; Harm van Grol, "'Indeed, Servants Are We': Ezra 9, Nehemiah 9 and 2 Chronicles 12 Compared," in *The Crisis of Israelite Religion: Transformation of Religious Tradition in Exilic and Post-exilic Times*, ed. Bob

does, but Ezra 9:9 says that God has "extended to us steadfast love before the kings of Persia, to give us life to raise up the house of our God and to build up its ruins." Slavery under the Persian kings appears to be a good thing here, a manifestation of God's mercy toward the people that has resulted in a rebuilt temple, and the point of this prayer is certainly not to ask for liberation from Persian rule. The danger the assembly faces, Ezra warns in Ezra 9:10–15, is that the community's failure to keep God's law in regard to intermarriage will end the current situation of divine mercy and Persian rule over the assembly as "slaves" and cause God to destroy them utterly, leaving them "without remnant or survivor." The prayer of Ezra 9 demonstrates that "the favour of the Persians is the form in which they [the assembly] experience the favour of their God."[7] It is no wonder that scholars who have concluded that Neh 9:32–37 includes an implicit plea for independence have also concluded that Neh 9 is quite different from Ezra 9 in the portrayal of imperial rule.[8]

Only Manfred Oeming argues at any length that Neh 9 is entirely compatible with the view of Persian rule found throughout the rest of Ezra-Nehemiah.[9] As part of his argument, Oeming touches on a matter that I will explore at greater length in the following section: the use of עבדים as a translation of the Old Persian *bandaka-*, a word the Achaemenids used to describe their subjects. My examination of this Old Persian term will show that Oeming is right to see the Hebrew word as reflecting *bandaka-* but that it is not so clear that we should understand עבדים in 9:36 as meaning "well-regarded allies of the Persian Empire," as Oeming believes.[10] He argues as well that the use of עבדים in 9:36 is meant to portray the current assembly positively in comparison to their ancestors, who, according to the previous verse, לא עבדוך, "did not serve you [God]." Assembly readers, he says, would conclude that they are עבדים in the sense that they are properly serving God, unlike their ancestors.[11] For Oeming, verses 32–37 portray the community as righteous servants of God whose status as "well-regarded allies of the Persian Empire" is their reward for their righteousness. This, however, is not a conclusion that really works

---

Becking and Marjo C. A. Korpel, OtSt 42 (Leiden: Brill, 1999), 209–27, here 209; Juha Pakkala, *Ezra the Scribe: The Development of Ezra 7–10 and Nehemia 8*, BZAW 347 (Berlin: de Gruyter, 2004), 183–84.

[7] D. J. A. Clines, *Ezra, Nehemiah, Esther: Based on the Revised Standard Version*, NCBC (Grand Rapids: Eerdmans, 1984), 125.

[8] So, e.g., Williamson, "Structure and Historiography," 282–83; Tiemeyer, "Abraham," 61; Gili Kugler, "Present Affliction Affects the Representation of the Past: An Alternative Dating of the Levitical Prayer of Nehemiah 9," *VT* 63 (2013): 605–26, here 616.

[9] Manfred Oeming, "'See, We Are Serving Today' (Nehemiah 9:36): Nehemiah 9 as a Theological Interpretation of the Persian Period," in *Judah and the Judeans in the Persian Period*, ed. Oded Lipschits and Manfred Oeming (Winona Lake, IN: Eisenbrauns, 2006), 571–88.

[10] Ibid., 579. For an analysis of the word that supports Oeming's conclusion, see Christine Mitchell, "Achaemenid Persian Concepts Pertaining to Covenant and Haggai, Zechariah, and Malachi," in *Covenant in the Persian Period: From Genesis to Chronicles*, ed. Richard J. Bautch and Gary N. Knoppers (Winona Lake, IN: Eisenbrauns, 2015), 291–306.

[11] Oeming, "'See, We Are Serving,'" 579–80.

in the context of the prayer's final verses. The prayer does not say that the community is in great distress because they are "about to" abandon Torah, which is how Oeming puts it;[12] verse 37 refers to "our sins" that have resulted in the great distress. The prayer does not imply that the assembly is now rightly serving God; it says they are already sinning. According to the prayer, the community's status as עבדים is the result of their sin, not a reward for their righteousness. Just as the ancestors "did not serve you," the current community is not rightly serving God either, which is why they confess their sin.[13] Further, it is because of their sin that they are now עבדים to the Persians.

Given the prayer's insistence in its final verse that the land's yield now goes to foreign kings "because of our sin," Oeming's reading of the end of Neh 9 as reflecting positively upon the Achaemenids, the community, and their relationship, does not really seem to fit. As the immediate agents of the community's "great distress," the Persians are not cast in a positive light in the prayer, even if the assembly's sin is ultimately responsible for the distress they suffer. The negative portrayal of imperial rule that virtually all other scholars see in 9:32–37 would seem to reflect the view of proindependence members of the assembly or, at the very least, members unhappy with Persian rule. This would include especially those who still held to the earlier messages of Haggai and Zechariah of a coming divine geopolitical action, a view politically out of step with the rest of Ezra-Nehemiah. Oeming is correct, though, that the prayer reflects Achaemenid imperial ideology, and it is to that issue we now turn. The prayer's use of imperial language will likely tell us something important as to how the empire is being portrayed.

II. The Slave in Achaemenid Imperial Ideology

Our knowledge of Achaemenid imperial ideology comes primarily from stelae carved in Iran, but we know that the Achaemenids' view of the legitimacy of their kingship and their relationship to the colonized was broadcast widely throughout their empire.[14] Inscriptions of Darius have also been found in Suez (DZa; DZb; DZc), and the statue of Darius in the Egyptian style discovered in Susa and inscribed in Egyptian, Elamite, Akkadian, and Old Persian (DSab) was carved in Egypt and likely stood originally in the temple of Atum in Heliopolis,[15] and Herodotus describes Darius as erecting inscriptions on his campaign to Greece (4.87–88, 91). Darius writes in the Bisitun inscription of his interest in widely broadcasting the

---

[12] Ibid., 582.

[13] For more discussion of this point, see Williamson, "Structure and Historiography," 290.

[14] For texts and translations of the Old Persian inscriptions, see Roland G. Kent, *Old Persian: Grammar, Texts, Lexicon*, 2nd ed., AOS 32 (New Haven: American Oriental Society, 1953).

[15] For this as the scholarly consensus as to the statue's original location, see Shahrokh Razmjou, "Assessing the Damage: Notes on the Life and Demise of the Statue of Darius from Susa," *ArsOr* 32 (2002): 81–104, here 86–87.

inscription's message, for he says there that he had it translated and distributed throughout the empire on clay and parchment (DB 4.88–92), a claim borne out in the discovery of an Aramaic copy in Elephantine (*TAD* C2.1)[16] and fragmentary Akkadian copies in Babylon.[17] Indeed, the text Darius had carved at Bisitun is so high that it cannot be read from the mountain's base, and the only way to make the specifics of its message known was to have the text circulate in readable form; it is thus quite possible that the text existed first on clay and parchment, circulating throughout the empire, and only later as an inscription carved into the stone at Bisitun.[18] Moreover, since the Aramaic copy of Bisitun also includes some lines from Darius's burial inscription,[19] the Bisitun inscription was clearly not the only official Achaemenid writing that circulated throughout the empire.[20] Before the Achaemenids, multilingual royal inscriptions were rare in the Near East, but the Persian kings made them the norm, apparently so that their ideology could be more widely understood.[21] Darius claimed at various points that writing is an important way to convey the truth that the king wants to communicate (DB 4.41–43, 45–50, 54–59; DNb 50–57), and so we should not be surprised that an Aramaic copy of Bisitun was circulating a century after the inscription was first carved. The kings obviously wanted the colonized to be aware of the reasons why the Achaemenids should rule them, and they made these reasons widely available. As a result, we find Greek writers who were clearly aware of claims made on these inscriptions; Herodotus, for example, knew of at least parts of the narrative from Bisitun,[22] telling us that its basic story was well known a century after Darius's time. Numerous classical authors, to take one more example, seem to be well informed of the

---

[16] Bezalel Porten and Ada Yardeni, *Textbook of Aramaic Documents from Ancient Egypt*, 4 vols. (Jerusalem: Hebrew University Press, 1986–1993), 3:60–71.

[17] For the Babylonian text, see Elizabeth N. von Voightlander, *The Bisitun Inscription of Darius the Great: Babylonian Version*, Corpus Inscriptionum Iranicarum 1.2.1 (London: Lund Humphries, 1978).

[18] For a discussion of the placement of the text at Bisitun, see Donald C. Polaski, "What Mean These Stones? Inscriptions, Textuality, and Power in Persia and Yehud," in *Approaching Yehud: New Approaches to the Study of the Persian Period*, ed. Jon L. Berquist, SemeiaSt 50 (Atlanta: Society of Biblical Literature, 2007), 37–48, here 37–40. For the claim that the Bisitun inscription first existed in documents that circulated throughout the empire, see Josef Wiesehöfer, *Ancient Persia from 550 BC to 650 AD*, trans. Azizeh Azodi (London: I. B. Tauris, 2001), 18–19.

[19] *TAD* C2.1.66–70 parallels DNb 50–60.

[20] See Jonas C. Greenfield and Bezalel Porten, *The Bisitun Inscription of Darius the Great: Aramaic Version*, Corpus Inscriptionum Iranicarum 1.5.1 (London: Lund Humphries, 1982), 3–4; and Amélie Kuhrt, "Achaemenid Images of Royalty and Empire," in *Concepts of Kingship in Antiquity: Proceedings of the European Science Foundation Exploratory Workshop Held in Padova, November 28th–December 1st, 2007*, ed. Giovanni B. Lanfranchi and Robert Rollings, HANE/M 11 (Padua: SARGON, 2010), 87–105, here 98–99.

[21] Hannes D. Galter, "Cuneiform Bilingual Royal Inscriptions," *IOS* 15 (1995): 25–50, here 41.

[22] See Maria Brosius, "Greek Sources on Achaemenid Iran," in *The Oxford Handbook of Ancient Iran*, ed. D. T. Potts (Oxford: Oxford University Press, 2013), 658–68, here 662.

physical and moral virtues with which Darius and Xerxes claim to be endowed, the qualities that make them good rulers.[23]

There were other media besides inscriptions through which the Persian kings broadcast their justifications for ruling and their virtues as rulers, such as coins, bullae, and palace reliefs,[24] and we have no reason to believe that the Judean elite who could read Ezra-Nehemiah would not have been aware of this ideology since it was widespread. There was a Persian palace at Ramat Raḥel, close to Jerusalem, that would have contained officials and iconography, and leaders of the assembly and province like Ezra and Nehemiah came to Judah from the center of the empire.[25] It is reasonable to assume that assembly readers of the work would have been aware, for example, of the strict hierarchy in Achaemenid ideology that separated the Great King from all his subjects. As Oeming notes, Darius uses the Old Persian word *bandaka-* to refer to his generals,[26] a word Oeming understands to be "a title of honor for vassals."[27] Clearly, Darius does use it to refer to high-ranking individuals, but the term applies to any and all of the Achaemenids' subjects,[28] as is the case when Darius uses it in the plural to refer to all of the peoples whom he rules (DB 1.19). Oeming is correct when he writes that עבדים in Neh 9:36 is an attempt to reflect the Old Persian word, since the Akkadian version of Bisitun consistently

---

[23] Compare DNb 5–49 and XPl 5–50 with Herodotus 1.36; Xenophon, *Cyr.* 1.2.6–8; *Anab.* 1.9.2–19; Strabo 15.3.8. See also Bruce Lincoln, "On Persian Pedagogy and Greek Machismo," in *"Happiness for Mankind": Achaemenian Religion and the Imperial Project*, Acta Iranica 53 (Leuven: Peeters, 2012), 335–54, here 335–45.

[24] There is a large amount of material that discusses the ways in which Persian imperial ideology was communicated through these different media. Helpful studies include Margaret Cool Root, *The King and Kingship in Achaemenid Art: Essays on the Creation of an Iconography of Empire*, Acta Iranica 19 (Leiden: Brill, 1979); Peter Vargyas, "Darius I and the Daric Reconsidered," *IrAnt* 35 (2000): 33–46; Mark B. Garrison and Margaret Cool Root, *Seals on the Persepolis Fortification Tablets*, OIP 117 (Chicago: Oriental Institute, University of Chicago, 2001); Cindy L. Nimchuk, "The 'Archers' of Darius: Coinage or Tokens of Royal Esteem?," *ArsOr* 32 (2002): 55–79; Mark B. Garrison, "Royal Achaemenid Iconography," in Potts, *Oxford Handbook of Ancient Iran*, 566–95.

[25] On the palace, see Oded Lipschits, "Shedding New Light on the Dark Years of the 'Exilic Period': New Studies, Further Elucidation, and Some Questions Regarding the Archaeology of Judah as an 'Empty Land,'" in *Interpreting Exile: Displacement and Deportation in Biblical and Modern Contexts*, ed. Brad E. Kelle, Frank Ritchel Ames, and Jacob L. Wright, AIL 10 (Atlanta: Society of Biblical Literature, 2011), 57–90, here 57–61; Oded Lipschits et al., "Palace and Village, Paradise and Oblivion: Unraveling the Riddles of Ramat Rahel," *NEA* 74 (2011): 2–49, here 31–37; O. Lipschits, Y. Gadot, and D. Langgut, "The Riddle of Ramat Raḥel: The Archaeology of a Royal Persian Period Edifice," *Transeu* 41 (2012): 57–79.

[26] In the Achaemenid inscriptions, the word appears only in the Bisitun inscription. See DB 1.19; 2.20, 30, 49–50, 82; 3.13, 31, 56, 85; 5.8.

[27] Oeming, "'See, We Are Serving,'" 579.

[28] See Christopher Tuplin, "All the King's Men," in *The World of Achaemenid Persia: History, Art and Society in Iran and the Ancient Near East*, ed. John Curtis and St John Simpson (London: I. B. Tauris, 2010), 51–61, here 54–55.

uses *qallu* ("slave") in its translation of the word (lines 44, 48, 53, 62, 73, 79, 86), and the Aramaic version uses ʿ*ylm* ("servant," *TAD* C2.1.19). Thus, the term is not really one that indicates any kind of honor so much as it is a basic way to refer to all subjects of the Great King. They are all *bandakā*, as DB 1.19 tells readers, even the satraps at the very highest rung (but one) of the political ladder, as DB 3.56, which uses the term in reference to a satrap, demonstrates. The word itself is related to the Old Persian verb *band-* ("to bind"); it derives from the Indo-European **bhendh-* and so is cognate with words like Avestan *banda-* ("bond, fetter"), Greek πεῖσμα ("rope, cable"), and Latin *defendo* ("to free from entanglement"), not to mention English *bond*.[29] Everyone within the empire, then, is "bound" to the Achaemenids;[30] and, given that *bandaka-* was translated in official documents by words that referred to servitude, it is not surprising that the Greeks concluded that the Great King considered all of his subjects, even the high-ranking ones, to be δοῦλοι ("slaves") bound in subjection to the royal will.[31]

Persian imperial ideology, however, works to validate the Achaemenids' rule; and, even if the Great King's subjects are "slaves," this is still greatly to their advantage. Imperial power is good power and far better than an absence of empire, according to the inscriptions. For example, as Darius explains on his burial inscription, the world was "in turmoil [*yaudantim*]" before Ahura Mazda made him king (DNa 31–32), but, by Ahura Mazda's will, he acted to restore order (33–38). In an inscription from Susa, he writes again that "the lands were in turmoil [*ayaudan*], one fought another" (DSe 32–34), but, by Ahura Mazda's will, Darius put an end to this violence (34–41). Achaemenid inscriptions frequently open by referring to Ahura Mazda as creator of the world and its *šiyāti-*,[32] a word that derives from the Indo-European root **kweyĕ-*, which has the general sense of "to rest comfortably" and is cognate not only with words like Latin *quies* and English *quiet* but with

---

[29] For Indo-European **bhendh-*, see Julius Pokorny, *Indogermanisches etymologisches Wörterbuch*, 2 vols. (Bern: Francke, 1959–1969), 1:127.

[30] The *-ka-* suffix of the word indicates that it is an adjective with substantive meaning; see Kent, *Old Persian*, 51. Given its relationship to the verb "to bind," *bandaka-* reflects the "boundness" of all of the Achaemenids' subjects.

[31] See the discussion in Anna Missiou, "Δοῦλος τοῦ βασιλέως: The Politics of Translation," *ClQ* 43 (1993): 377–91. Missiou argues that *bandaka-* was not meant in a pejorative sense but was understood as such by the Greeks.

[32] This line became the standard opening to many Achaemenid inscriptions: "A great god is Ahura Mazda, who created this earth, who created that sky, who created humanity, who created *šiyātim* for humanity, who made Darius king, one king of many, one lord of many." It appears in DNa 1–8; DPg 1–5; DSe 1–7; DSf 1–8; DSab 1–8; DZc 1–4; DE 1–11; XPa 1–6; XPb 1–11; XPc 1–5; XPd 1–8; XPf 1–8; XPh 1–6; A¹Pa 1–8; A³Pa 1–8. Xerxes, Artaxerxes I, and Artaxerxes III alter the wording only in order to replace Darius's name with their own. For the last inscription and its attribution to Artaxerxes III, see Rüdiger Schmitt, *The Old Persian Inscriptions of Naqsh-i Rustam and Persepolis*, Corpus Inscriptionum Iranicarum 1.1.2 (London: School of Oriental and African Studies, 2000), 119.

Avestan *šaiti-š* ("joy") and *šyāta-* ("pleased").[33] By banishing turmoil and violence from the world, the Achaemenids restore the *šiyāti-* that Ahura Mazda intended humanity to enjoy at creation.[34] The king brings not just quiet and an absence of the warfare that had earlier plagued the peoples; he brings joy and pleasure and general well-being. The colonized, therefore, are fortunate to live under his rule. While his subjects are to bring him *bāji-* ("tribute"), a word that includes the sense of something owed to the king,[35] Persian iconography always portrays the colonized support of the Achaemenids as done with dignity and little exertion.[36] Those who are bound to (or below) him are much better off than they would be otherwise, a view that Ezra-Nehemiah's portrayal of the beneficent Persian kings endorses.

Since *bandaka-* can be applied to all of the Great King's subjects, it is not precisely a term of honor, although one certainly understands it as referring to a close relationship between king and subject, who might be said to be bound together.[37] Oeming is correct to conclude that the term was used only in reference to loyal vassals,[38] since Darius uses it in no other context. Achaemenid imperial ideology almost never overtly refers to the fate of disloyal subjects, and the Bisitun inscription, a narrative of Darius's defeat of various rebellions, is the obvious example that proves this rule. Here, Darius uses the word *basta*, a participial form of the verb *band-*, in order to explain what he did to those who rebelled against his power. His enemies are *basta* ("bound") so that he can kill them (DB 1.82–83; 5.25–27), impale them (3.88–92), or publicly display them as tortured and mutilated before he puts them to death (2.73–76, 86–91). It is this contrast between being bound in servitude to the Achaemenids or bound in preparation for death—or worse—that we see in Ezra's prayer, when he claims that the community's very state of slavery—the people's status as *bandakā*, in other words—is the manifestation of God's "steadfast love before the kings of Persia." According to the prayer, the community's current failure to act rightly would end in destruction "without remnant or survivor." It is God rather than the Achaemenids who ultimately controls the people's fate, but this kind of Yahwism is really just an appropriation of Achaemenid ideology: life under

---

[33] For Indo-European **kweyĕ-*, see Pokorny, *Indogermanisches etymologisches Wörterbuch*, 1:638; Thomas V. Gamkrelidze and Vjačeslav V. Ivanov, *Indo-European and the Indo-Europeans: A Reconstruction and Historical Analysis of a Proto-language and a Proto-culture*, trans. Johanna Nichols, 2 vols., Trends in Linguistics: Studies and Monographs 80 (Berlin: de Gruyter, 1995), 1:205.

[34] See Bruce Lincoln, "À la recherche du paradis perdu," in *"Happiness for Mankind,"* 3–19.

[35] See Heleen Sancisi-Weerdenburg, "Bāji," in *Studies in Persian History: Essays in Memory of David M. Lewis*, ed. Maria Brosius and Amélie Kuhrt, AchH 11 (Leiden: Nederlands Instituut voor het Nabije Oosten, 1998), 23–34.

[36] For studies of this aspect of Achaemenid iconography, see Root, *King and Kingship*, 131–61.

[37] So, e.g., Pierre Briant, *From Cyrus to Alexander: A History of the Persian Empire*, trans. Peter T. Daniels (Winona Lake, IN: Eisenbrauns, 2002), 65; and Wiesehöfer, *Ancient Persia*, 31.

[38] Oeming, "'See, We Are Serving,'" 579.

Persian rule is the best possible life available, and the alternative is destruction. Certainly even the nonelite among the colonized peoples of the Achaemenids would have been well aware that being slaves of the Great King was not the worst fate that could befall them. When Darius writes that he kept leaders of rebellions "bound" at the entrance of his palace after cutting off noses and ears and putting out eyes (DB 2.73–75, 88–90), part of the point of this is so that "all the people" could witness the fate of the rebels (2.75–76, 90). While Bisitun is the only Achaemenid inscription to refer to such torture,[39] it was hardly necessary for the Great Kings to use their inscriptions to advertise the dire consequences of failing to be loyally bound to the king. Xenophon writes that it was common in the Persian Empire to see convicted criminals without feet, hands, or eyes (*Anab.* 1.9.13); the consequences were written on the bodies of disloyal subjects. When Darius claims that he punishes those who cause injury (DB 4.66–67; DNb 17–21) and that the colonized peoples are afraid of him (DPe 9) and of his law (DSe 37–39), we have no particular reason to believe he is lying. If the classical sources are any indication, the kinds of tortures to which the Achaemenids subjected the disloyal were gruesome and well known.[40]

As Oeming has pointed out, then, it is true that referring to the Judean assembly as "slaves" does not in and of itself reflect negatively on the Persians nor necessarily contradict Ezra-Nehemiah's positive portrayal of the relationship between the assembly and the empire, even though, in the context of 9:32–37, one could read עבדים in this contradictory manner. Insofar as the word reflects the Old Persian *bandaka-*, it may not be a term of honor, but it is a concept at home both in Achaemenid royal ideology and in Ezra-Nehemiah's understanding of the nature of the relationship between the assembly and the Great King. They are his subjects, as is everyone else in the empire; Persian rule has brought well-being (*šiyāti-*) to Judah; and the assembly's fate could clearly be worse, as Ezra says in his prayer. But the word עבדים does not appear by itself in 9:32–37, and the prayer's conclusion also refers to the "hardship" and "great distress" for which the foreign kings who rule the assembly are at least partly responsible. If *bandaka-* can be understood as referring to a king and subject bound together in harmony, it can also be understood as referring to a subject bound in servitude to the king, as the use of words like the Akkadian *qallu* and Aramaic ʿ*ylm* in official translations of the Bisitun

---

[39] On the general Achaemenid disinclination to refer to violence in their iconography, especially in comparison with their Neo-Assyrian predecessors, see Margaret Cool Root, "Imperial Ideology in Achaemenid Persian Art: Transforming the Mesopotamian Legacy," *BCSMS* 35 (2000): 19–27. As Bruce Lincoln points out, there are fifty-three known Achaemenid inscriptions that postdate Bisitun, and not one of them refers to any specific armed struggle; see his *Religion, Empire, and Torture: The Case of Achaemenian Persia with a Postscript on Abu Ghraib* (Chicago: University of Chicago Press, 2007), 12.

[40] See, e.g., Herodotus 3.119, 130; 5.25; Diodorus 17.30.4; Plutarch, *Art.* 14.5; 16.2–4; Strabo 15.3.17; and see also Bruce Lincoln, "Happiness, Law, and Fear," in *"Happiness for Mankind,"* 406–24, here 420–22.

inscription clearly show. Insofar as עבדים in Neh 9:36–37 appears to reflect *bandaka-*, it reflects the latter understanding of the word, as the broader context of 9:32–37 demonstrates.

The question is why Ezra-Nehemiah includes 9:32–37 and its negative sense of *bandaka-*, since this is hardly the picture of imperial rule in the rest of the book. As we shall see in the next section, these verses seem to reflect an anti-Persian sentiment, the same attitude toward Persia that we find in Haggai and First Zechariah. This view coexisted in the Judean assembly with the pro-Achaemenid stance displayed in a passage like Ezra 9, where עבדים manifests the more positive interpretation of *bandaka-*. In the context of the concluding section of Ezra-Nehemiah, chapter 9 depicts Judah faced with the choice of being "bound" in subjection to the Achaemenids or "bound" in preparation for torture and death at God's hand. In this appropriation of Achaemenid ideology into Yahwism, Neh 8–13 works to convince readers that the Persians are indeed responsible for the people's well-being and that the disappearance of Achaemenid rule would lead to God's destruction of the people. Ezra-Nehemiah's conclusion presents one side of a debate in the Persian-period assembly, and if it is the side that dominates everywhere else in the book, it at least acknowledges in Neh 9 the existence of a different view in regard to the colonized status of Judah. But, in the end, Neh 8–13, like Ezra 9, is a Yahwistic appropriation of Achaemenid imperial ideology, which asserts that the best possible life is one under Persian rule and that the alternative is one of complete disaster.

III. The Slaves' Failure in Nehemiah 8–13

Scholarly consensus sees Neh 9:32–37 as containing an implicit request for divine liberation from Persia. After the prayer surveys God's gifts to the people's ancestors from the time of Abraham to the period of wilderness wanderings (9:7–15), it moves on to refer to the ancestors' rebellion in the wilderness (9:16–17), an ethical failure met with divine mercy and the gift of the land (9:17–25). But in 9:26–31 a Deuteronomistic cycle of rebellion is now met not with mercy but with punishment of foreign oppression. According to 9:28, this cycle happens "many times," but divine mercy consistently follows and the people are saved. In 9:29–31, this consistent failure in the face of repeated prophetic warnings over "many years" caused God to give the ancestors into "the hand of the peoples of the lands." Divine mercy now functions only to ensure that the people are not completely destroyed. Verses 29–31 may appear to be the beginning of another cycle of rebellion, one that is not yet complete. Verses 32–37 refer to the sins of the current community (vv. 33–34, 37) but ask God not to treat their situation lightly. Readers of the prayer, both ancient and modern, might therefore conclude that God's grace and mercy, mentioned frequently earlier in the prayer (vv. 17, 19, 27, 28, 31), would follow in response to the community's admission of sin and their "great distress" under foreign rule. A righteous God (vv. 8, 33) who keeps covenant (vv. 8, 32) would take the control of the land away from the foreign kings and return it to the people once they demonstrated their righteousness, something they swear to do in the following chapter.[41]

It is possible that 9:6–37 was developed for use in a covenant renewal ceremony,[42] and in this original context the understanding might have been that renewed attention to covenant, law, and commandments would lead God to respond to an implicit plea for independence. The context of Neh 10 might suggest such an implicit plea in an original context of a covenant renewal ceremony. The verse that immediately follows the prayer, 10:1 [9:38], refers to an אמנה ("agreement") by the community. Led by Nehemiah and the heads of the priests, Levites, and people (10:2–28 [1–27]), the rest of the people and the temple personnel join this agreement (10:29–30 [28–29]), and its details are spelled out in the rest of the chapter: they will keep the law, commandments, judgments, and statutes (10:30 [29]); specifically, they will not marry outside of the community (10:31 [30]) or engage in commerce with "the peoples of the land" on the Sabbath (10:32 [31]);

---

[41] For arguments like this, see, e.g., Frederick C. Holmgren, "Faithful Abraham and the ᵃmānâ Covenant: Nehemiah 9,6–10,1," ZAW 104 (1992): 249–54; Throntveit, Ezra-Nehemiah, 106; Pröbstl, Nehemia 9, 27–28; Werline, Penitential Prayer, 58–59; Eskenazi, "Nehemiah 9–10," 377; Williamson, "Torah and History," 168–69; Katherine E. Southwood, "'But Now ... Do Not Let All This Hardship Seem Insignificant before You': Ethnic History and Nehemiah 9," SEÅ 79 (2014): 1–23, here 20–21.

[42] So, e.g., Ulrich Kellermann, Nehemia: Quellen, Überlieferung und Geschichte, BZAW 102 (Berlin: Töpelmann, 1967), 90–92; H. G. M. Williamson, Ezra, Nehemiah, WBC 16 (Waco, TX: Word, 1985), 275–76; Boda, Praying the Tradition, 32–34. The date of the prayer is widely discussed. Some see it as preexilic (e.g., A. C. Welch, "The Source of Nehemiah ix," ZAW 47 [1929]: 130–37; Martin Rehm, "Nehemias 9," BZ 1 [1957]: 59–69; Kugler, "Present Affliction"), but it is mainly dated to the Persian period or the exile (e.g., Chrostowski, "Examination of Conscience," 258; Gary A. Rendsburg, "The Northern Origin of Nehemiah 9," Bib 72 [1991]: 348–66, here 364–66; Hans-Peter Mathys, Dichter und Beter: Theologen aus spätalttestamentlicher Zeit, OBO 132 [Fribourg: Universitätsverlag; Göttingen: Vandenhoeck & Ruprecht, 1994], 19; Pröbstl, Nehemia 9, 103–4; Boda, Praying the Tradition, 189–95; Tiemeyer, "Abraham," 62–63; Richard J. Bautch, "An Appraisal of Abraham's Role in Postexilic Covenants," CBQ 71 [2009]: 42–63, here 53 n. 44; Mark Leuchter, "Inter-Levitical Polemics in the Late 6th Century BCE: The Evidence from Nehemiah 9," Bib 95 [2014]: 269–79, here 272). There are some who argue for at least the possibility of a post-Persian-period date; see Antonius H. J. Gunneweg, Nehemia, KAT 19.2 (Gütersloh: Gütersloher Verlagshaus, 1987), 129; Blenkinsopp, Ezra-Nehemiah, 302–3; Andiñach, "Nehemías 9:5b–37," 253; Jacques Vermeylen, "The Gracious God, Sinners and Forgiveness: How Nehemiah 9 Interprets the History of Israel," in History and Identity: How Israel's Later Authors Viewed Its Earlier History, ed. Núria Calduch-Benages and Jan Liesen, DCL.Y 2006 (Berlin: de Gruyter, 2006), 77–114, here 105–11. One often encounters in arguments for a Hellenistic dating the presupposition that the entire Judean elite saw the Persians as benevolent rulers and that it is out of the question that a negative portrayal of them could come from the Persian period. Although it is true that Ezra-Nehemiah portrays the Persians positively, we need not assume that everyone in the assembly viewed the Achaemenids this way. There is nothing in the prayer that demands an original date of composition later than the Persian period.

and they will fully fund the temple cult and financially support the priests and Levites (10:33–40 [32–39]).

If the context of 9:6–37 is expanded to include chapter 10, these two chapters might signal that a faithful community that sedulously follows the law will win from God the reward of independence from Persia. Adding chapter 8 to the context (or really 7:73b–9:5, the section that provides the opening context for the prayer) neither supports nor undermines this conclusion. When Ezra and the Levites teach the people the law, the people respond by weeping (8:1–9). While the narrative does not explicitly explain this response, 9:1–2 says they fasted, wore sackcloth, put dust on their heads, and confessed their sins and those of their ancestors. Their grief suggests that they realize that they and their ancestors have sinned, precisely the claim of 9:6–37. Readers of Ezra-Nehemiah, who have already encountered Ezra's prayer in Ezra 9:6–15, might conclude that further violations of the commandments will result in complete destruction, the same lesson that Ezra communicated in his prayer. As readers reach Neh 9 and 10, they might also conclude that a community that confesses its sin and works faithfully to keep the law might win political independence as a divine gift.

Nehemiah 10, however, is not the conclusion of the work—chapter 13 is. Following the lists and the story in Neh 11–12 of the dedication of the wall, Nehemiah returns to Judah after meeting Artaxerxes in Babylon to find that the community has violated all of the specific aspects of the agreement it vowed to keep in chapter 10. The people have not provided financial support for the temple personnel, and the Levites and musicians have had to go to their fields to support themselves, with the result that the temple cult has been abandoned (13:10–11). Further, foreigners are trading in Jerusalem on the Sabbath (13:15–16), and Judeans—even a son of the high priest—have been intermarrying with foreigners (13:23, 28). These chapters present the picture of a community that has been exposed to the law in chapter 8, has been reminded of the awful consequences of violating that law in chapter 9, has sworn to uphold it in chapter 10, and has returned immediately to its sinful ways. In the Deuteronomistic cycle of rebellion in the prayer of chapter 9, verses 26–28 say that "many times" divine mercy saved the ancestors from deserved punishment at the hands of foreigners, and in verses 29–31 divine mercy functioned not to restore the people's earlier independence but to avoid a complete annihilation of them. Although one could interpret verses 32–37 as placing the community at the nadir of a cycle that began in verse 29, a cycle that will continue to divine deliverance from foreign rule, the text does not actually say that this will happen. There is no explicit expectation that God's mercy will now operate as it did many times before; by 9:29–31 God's mercy is limited merely to maintaining the existence of the community, precisely Ezra's message in the prayer of Ezra 9, where divine mercy is extended only to ensuring the survival of the community as "slaves" to the Achaemenids. The very fact that Ezra-Nehemiah includes Neh 9, which can be read as an implicit plea for independence, suggests there were some in the Judean assembly who hoped God would effect precisely such a political change if the community faithfully followed the law. Yet the prayer is followed by the assembly's agreement to keep the law and then their failure to observe each specific part of that agreement. Their failure sends a message that the community's merited punishment of servitude to the Persians cannot be changed; the people are portrayed as utterly unable to keep from sinning, just as their ancestors were. It is no wonder that the people of Neh 8 are grieved when they hear the law, for, as the prayer suggests, they deserve a fate no better than that of their ancestors. They are potentially faced with a God who is now less inclined to show mercy than in the time of their ancestors. If they are "bound" as "slaves" now, perhaps God will arrange events so that they will be "bound" for torture and death soon.

Nehemiah 8–13 portrays a community congenitally unable to keep God's law, and in Neh 13, just as in Ezra 9, the community's native leadership is as guilty as the rest of the people. When Ezra is told of the intermarriages, which he sees as an existential threat to the community, he is informed that "the hand of the leaders and the officials [השרים והסגנים]⁴³ was first in this rebellion" (Ezra 9:2). While Nehemiah is in Babylon, the high priest has permitted one of his sons to marry a foreigner (Neh 13:28), and the חרים ("nobles")⁴⁴ of the people have permitted trading with foreigners in Jerusalem on the Sabbath (13:17). As a result of the failure of the assembly's native leadership, it is up to leaders sent by the Achaemenids to impose order and rein in the community's self-destructive impulses. Just as Ezra

---

⁴³ H. G. M. Williamson points out that שרים is used as a synonym for the "elders" and "heads," the leadership of the postexilic community ("The Family in Persian Period Judah: Some Textual Reflections," in *Symbiosis, Symbolism, and the Power of the Past: Canaan, Ancient Israel and Their Neighbors from the Late Bronze Age through Roman Palaestina*, ed. William G. Dever and Seymour Gitin [Winona Lake, IN: Eisenbrauns, 2003], 469–85, here 475). The term סגן is a loanword from Akkadian *šaknu*, a word that could be used for someone who oversaw professional groups dependent on the state or even someone serving as governor; see Israel Eph'al, "Changes in Palestine during the Persian Period in Light of Epigraphic Sources," *IEJ* 48 (1998): 106–19, here 117; M. A. Dandamaev, "Neo-Babylonian and Achaemenid State Administration in Mesopotamia," in Lipschits and Oeming, *Judah and the Judeans in the Persian Period*, 373–98, here 375–76. The Nehemiah Memoir uses the word to refer to leaders within the assembly itself; in addressing them in Neh 5, Nehemiah refers to the Judeans as their "kin" (5:1, 7, 8). They appear in the same context as the community's חרים ("nobles"; see below) in 2:16; 4:8, 13 [14, 19]; 5:7; 7:5. The סגנים were recognized as Persian officials in some fashion, perhaps because they held leadership positions in the assembly.

⁴⁴ The Judean community at Elephantine writes that they had sent a letter addressed to the high priest in Judah and to *ḥry yhwdy*ᵓ to ask for support in rebuilding their temple (*TAD* A4.7.19), which suggests that they identified this group as the leadership within the Judean assembly, along with the priests. The Nehemiah Memoir also uses the term חרים to refer to the leadership within the community. The חרים appear together with the priests and/or other officials as an important group within the people as a whole in Neh 2:16; 4:8, 13 [14, 19]; 5:7; 7:5. In 6:17, as in 13:17, Nehemiah depicts the חרים as leaders among the people and figures who appear to wield local power in the province; in 5:7 Nehemiah portrays them as wealthy figures, for he blames them for taking interest from the Judeans—whom he describes as their "kin" (5:1, 7, 8)—and driving them into poverty.

leads the fight to impose the law in Ezra 9–10, Nehemiah brings the Levites back to the temple and remonstrates with the community's leadership until tithes are again brought to support the cultic personnel (13:11–14), has the gates of Jerusalem guarded on the Sabbath so foreign merchants are unable to bring in their products (13:17–22), and has the people swear not to continue to marry foreigners (13:25–27). In the last two cases, he warns the people that their ancestors acted in the same ways (13:18, 26), making the point, as 9:32–37 does, that the current community is no different from their ancestors in their continual predilection to sin. "Did not your ancestors act this way," Nehemiah asks the community after they have profaned the Sabbath, "and did not our God bring upon us and upon this city all this evil?" (13:18). The community is sinful; the assembly leadership from Judah itself is sinful; and, were it not for the leadership the Achaemenids send from the center of the empire, God would already have destroyed the assembly "without remnant or survivor." The final picture of the assembly left by Ezra-Nehemiah is one of a community that is unable to gain political independence through adherence to the law; the assembly is confronted by a choice between continuing to be bound in slavery to Persia or being bound for torture and utter annihilation. YHWH, not the king of Persia, is the ultimate actor here, and adherence to God's law and not the king's command is what defines Judah's loyalty. Achaemenid ideology has clearly been appropriated into this version of Yahwism.

In Ezra-Nehemiah, then, the very existence of the assembly depends on the leaders supplied by the Achaemenids. It is Ezra, sent under written orders from Artaxerxes (Ezra 7:11), who brings the law that he enforces in Ezra 9–10 and so steers the community away from destruction "without remnant or survivor." And it is Nehemiah, also under written command from Artaxerxes (Neh 2:7–9), who gains royal support to build the wall and who enforces the law in Neh 13. It appears to be a key tenet of Ezra-Nehemiah that the immigrant community in Judah cannot survive without the leadership the Persian kings send to them from the diaspora;[45] they need Ezra and Nehemiah to lead them in proper observance of the law so they

---

[45] As is often noted, Ezra-Nehemiah portrays the Judeans as dependent on the diaspora for their leadership and texts; see, e.g., Peter R. Bedford, "Diaspora: Homeland Relations in Ezra-Nehemiah," *VT* 52 (2002): 147–65; Sara Japhet, "'History' and 'Literature' in the Persian Period: The Restoration of the Temple," in *From the Rivers of Babylon to the Highlands of Judah: Collected Studies on the Restoration Period* (Winona Lake, IN: Eisenbrauns, 2006), 152–68, here 166–67; John Kessler, "The Diaspora in Zechariah 1–8 and Ezra-Nehemiah: The Role of History, Social Location, and Tradition in the Formulation of Identity," in *Community Identity in Judean Historiography: Biblical and Comparative Perspectives*, ed. Gary N. Knoppers and Kenneth A. Ristau (Winona Lake, IN: Eisenbrauns, 2009), 119–45, here 128–34; Gary N. Knoppers, "Exile, Return and Diaspora: Expatriates and Repatriates in Late Biblical Literature," in *Texts, Contexts and Readings in Postexilic Literature: Explorations into Historiography and Identity Negotiation in Hebrew Bible and Related Texts*, ed. Louis Jonker, FAT 2/53 (Tübingen: Mohr Siebeck, 2011), 29–61, here 47–49; Dalit Rom-Shiloni, *Exclusive Inclusivity: Identity Conflicts between the Exiles and the People Who Remained (6th–5th Centuries BCE)*, LHBOTS 543 (New York: Bloomsbury T&T Clark, 2013), 83–92.

can avoid complete destruction at the hands of the Persians as further divine punishment. Left to their own devices and to the leadership from the province itself, the community cannot survive. They are fortunate that they are slaves to the Persians, who send them leaders. Nehemiah even claims that he was משקה ("cupbearer") to Artaxerxes (Neh 1:11), a position at court held only by Persian nobility,[46] which suggests that he was not merely an emissary of the crown but one with the closest of ties to the Great King. The prayer of Neh 9, and Neh 9–10 as a whole, may well reflect part of a debate in the Persian-period assembly concerning the possibility of a divine overthrow of Achaemenid power. Ezra-Nehemiah as a whole, however, rejects the argument that a Torah-abiding community will win its political freedom with God's help, portraying instead an assembly that will not keep the law unless it is forced to do so by leaders sent from the Persians. By including the anti-Achaemenid sentiment of 9:32–37 and juxtaposing it with the community's agreement to keep the law, the narrative seems to adopt the premise of anti-Achaemenid thinking: a righteous assembly can win divinely provided freedom from Persia. Nehemiah 13 depicts the community violating each aspect of the law they vowed to keep in Neh 10 and portrays Nehemiah, the Achaemenid governor, as the one who enforces the law. In Nehemiah 8–13, therefore, as in Ezra 7–10, it is the people themselves who are the problem and the Persian administration and its representative who are the solution. Nehemiah 9:6–37 portrays a God who becomes less and less merciful, and being "bound" in servitude to the Achaemenids is what keeps the assembly from destruction. The prayer demonstrates that God is willing to "bind" them for punishment and death. Nehemiah 8–13 as a whole, like the rest of Ezra-Nehemiah, appropriates Achaemenid ideology for its version of Yahwism. Whatever šiyāti- ("well-being") the assembly enjoys is due to the fact that the representative sent by the Achaemenids forces them to be faithful to God's laws so that YHWH does not utterly destroy them.

As Neh 8–13 presents the issue, the last thing the assembly needs is independence. It needs the Achaemenids to keep sending leaders from the center of the empire, since the native leadership is as sinful as the rest of the people. If the prayer refers to "great distress" in the fact that foreign kings rule the people and take of the produce of the land, the context of Neh 8–13 suggests no real alternative. Nehemiah's warning in 13:18 concerning destruction as punishment for failure to

---

[46] For example, Darius himself was the quiver bearer to Cyrus (Aelian, *Var. hist.* 12.43), while Herodotus 3.34.1 refers to a Persian aristocrat as the king's οἰνοχόος ("cupbearer"), exactly the position Nehemiah says that he holds (LXX^A uses the word οἰνοχόος to translate משקה in Neh 1:11), and, Herodotus says, "this is no small honor." DNc and DNd refer to Persians as spear bearers and clothes bearers to the king; see Schmitt, *Old Persian Inscriptions*, 45–46, for short discussions of the inscriptions. Herodotus 7.40.4 refers to a Persian as the king's chariot driver, and there are other such examples of Persian nobility serving in such capacities to the king. As mundane as such positions sound, they were filled only by the upper ranks of Persians. Nehemiah 1:11, as part of the Nehemiah Memoir, is generally assigned to Nehemiah himself, and Nehemiah was likely exaggerating his importance at court.

keep even one aspect of the law is precisely the same warning Ezra gives in Ezra 9:6–15. According to Neh 8–13, the community can be "bound" in colonized servitude and live or be "bound" in preparation for torture and death. The inclusion of language such as "great distress" hardly fits the beneficent picture of Persian rule elsewhere in Ezra-Nehemiah. These elements likely reflect anti-Achaemenid sentiment within the assembly and perhaps even the existence of a proindependence party, ideological descendants of the anti-imperial view of Haggai and Zechariah. In the end, however, imperial rule is conducted "by kings whom you [God] have set over us because of our sins" (Neh 9:37). Sin appears to be an activity in which the community excels unless controlled by a stern hand sent from the Persian king. Nehemiah 8–13 portrays the anti-imperial sentiment as deeply misguided, since the people cannot survive without the leadership the Achaemenids send to them. For Ezra-Nehemiah, this is as much a part of Persian beneficence as the imperial contributions to the construction of the temple and its cultic maintenance.

Since the redactor included in 9:36–37 the reference to the foreign kings' control of the land and its produce, readers who reach the end of the work and are persuaded by its pro-Achaemenid viewpoint will conclude that this control is the price the community pays for their sin. For Ezra-Nehemiah as a whole, even this conforms to the presentation in Achaemenid ideology of the ease with which the colonized support the king. By the time readers of the work reach Neh 9, they have encountered the narrative of chapter 5, where the people complain about "the king's tax," but that story frames the issue as an intracommunal problem. As 5:1 introduces the problem, the "great outcry of the people and their wives" here is directed not against the king but against "their kin, the Judeans." The problem in this chapter lies not with the king's tax per se but with the wealthy leadership of the assembly who have been lending money at interest to their kin and impoverishing them (5:1, 6–12). The *bāji-* ("tribute") owed to the Achaemenids is something the community can pay, according to this narrative, and they encounter hardship only when "the nobles" (החרים) and "the officials" (הסגנים) take economic advantage of them through their practice of lending at interest. Then Nehemiah, the Achaemenids' representative, has to step in and solve the problem by having the native leadership end this practice and restore the land, produce, and money of the poor that they had taken (5:10–13). As far as Ezra-Nehemiah is concerned, if there is "great distress" linked to financial obligations to Persia, it is really the native leadership, not the Great King, who has caused the problem. It is the Great King who, through his governor, resolves the problem. The prayer of Neh 9 allows at least a trace of an anti-Achaemenid argument to enter Ezra-Nehemiah, one voiced by some within the assembly who continued to promote a belief in a great divine geopolitical action of the sort articulated by Haggai and Zechariah at the beginning of the Persian period. In the end, however, readers encounter a narrative that uses Yahwistic language to articulate the Achaemenids' own claims in regard to the virtues of Persian rule and the disaster of its alternative.

Job 2 and 42:7–10 as Narrative Bridge and Theological Pivot

PAUL K.-K. CHO
pcho@wesleyseminary.edu
Wesley Theological Seminary, Washington, DC 20016

This article reexamines the literary relationship between the prose frame (Job 1–2, 42:7–17) and the poetic core (3:1–42:6) of the book of Job. Building on previous work that identifies Job 1, 42:11–17 as an older and independent composition, I argue that the author of the poetic core composed Job 2, 42:7–10 as a narrative bridge and a theological pivot from the prose frame to the poetic core. Job 2, 42:7–10 narratively connects the prose frame to the poetic dialogue, principally through the introduction of Job's friends, and broaches pivotal theological themes to prepare for the contentious dialogue to come.

The sharp transitions between the prose frame (Job 1–2, 42:7–17) and the poetic core (3:1–42:6) of the book of Job continue to be an interpretive crux. On the one hand, the numerous and real tensions between the prose frame and the poetic core—for example, the contrastive personalities of Job and God,[1] the apparent differences in genre and language,[2] and the diametrically opposed nature of the theological questions that animate the two sections[3]—appear to be evidence of different authorship.[4] On the other, the narrative connections between the two sections—for example, the friends who come to comfort Job in the prose prologue (2:11–13) engage in conversation with him in the poetic core (3:1–31:40) and are, in the prose epilogue, judged for their folly and for not having spoken what is right

---

[1] See, e.g., H. L. Ginsberg, "Job the Patient and Job the Impatient," *Conservative Judaism* 21 (1966–1967): 12–28.

[2] N. H. Tur-Sinai, *The Book of Job: A New Commentary*, rev. ed. (Jerusalem: Kiryath Sepher, 1967), xxx–xl.

[3] Susannah Ticciati, *Job and the Disruption of Identity: Reading beyond Barth* (London: T&T Clark, 2005), 2.

[4] For a list of contrastive characteristics of the prose frame and the poetic core, see Yair Hoffman, "The Relationship between the Prologue and the Speech-Cycles in Job: A Reconsideration," *VT* 31 (1981): 160–70.

about God (42:7–8)—suggest compositional unity.⁵ In short, the prose and the poetry appear to stand apart and opposed; yet, as C. L. Seow recently put it, "neither the prose tale nor the poetic middle can stand alone."⁶

Over the centuries since Richard Simon in 1678 first opined that the prose prologue is a late addition to the poetry on account of their "diverse styles," critical scholars have proposed and defended a variety of compositional histories in efforts to explain how the two contrastive, yet strangely coherent, compositions came to be juxtaposed.⁷ The typical historical-critical strategy has been to dissect the book along its seams and to attribute the disjointedness to the history of composition: the prose frame and the poetic dialogue were originally independent compositions and were stitched together by a later redactor;⁸ the prose was written expressly as a frame for the poetry;⁹ or the Joban poet used the prose folktale as the starting point of his own poetic work.¹⁰ These historical-critical proposals, however, have not been without their critics, and some have argued that the prose and poetry were written by the same author.¹¹ In short, there is a split within the interpretive tradition concerning the relationship between the prose and the poetic sections of Job.¹²

---

⁵ Ibid.; Bruce Zuckerman, *Job the Silent: A Study in Historical Counterpoint* (Oxford: Oxford University Press, 1991), 25–33; Carol A. Newsom, *The Book of Job: A Contest of Moral Imaginations* (New York: Oxford University Press, 2003), 32–71.

⁶ C. L. Seow, *Job 1–21: Interpretation and Commentary*, Illuminations (Grand Rapids: Eerdmans, 2013), 29.

⁷ Richard Simon, *A Critical Study of the Old Testament*, trans. variously attributed to Henry Dickinson and Richard Hampden (London: Walter Davis, 1682), bk. 1, ch. 4, 34.

⁸ Bernhard Duhm, *Das Buch Hiob*, KHC 16 (Freiburg: Mohr Siebeck, 1897), viii, 1–11.

⁹ Samuel Rolles Driver and George Buchanan Gray, *A Critical and Exegetical Commentary on the Book of Job, together with a New Translation*, 2 vols., ICC (New York: Scribner, 1921), 1:xxxv; Tur-Sinai, *Book of Job*, xxxviii; Raik Heckl, *Hiob—Vom Gottesfürchtigen zum Repräsentanten Israels: Studien zur Buchwerdung des Hiobbuches und zu seinen Quellen*, FAT 70 (Tübingen: Mohr Siebeck, 2010).

¹⁰ Marvin H. Pope, *Job: Introduction, Translation, and Notes*, AB 15 (Garden City, NY: Doubleday, 1965), xxii; Georg Fohrer, *Das Buch Hiob*, KAT 16 (Gütersloh: Gütersloher Verlagshaus, 1963), 29–33.

¹¹ Matitiahu Tsevat opines that the author of the poetic core either adapted an older prose story or himself wrote the prose frame ("The Meaning of the Book of Job," *HUCA* 37 [1966]: 73–106, here 73); Édouard Dhorme argues that a single author composed the book of Job in stages, with the exception of the Elihu speeches (*A Commentary on the Book of Job*, trans. Harold Knight [London: Nelson, 1967], lxi–cxi); H. H. Rowley essentially agrees with Dhorme (*Job*, NCB [London: Nelson, 1970], 8–18); Norman C. Habel argues for the unity of the entire book at the level of narrative and thematic development (*The Book of Job: A Commentary*, OTL [London: SCM, 1985], 25–35, 49–57); Seow admits of the possibility of a complex compositional history but, in reviewing the scholarship, favors arguments for the unity of the book (*Job 1–21*, 26–39). For a review of scholarly opinions, see Newsom, *Book of Job*, 3–11.

¹² Michael Cheney also takes note of this exact bifurcation in the interpretive tradition (*Dust, Wind and Agony: Character, Speech and Genre in Job*, ConBOT 36 [Stockholm: Almqvist & Wiksell, 1994], 3–4).

Despite these disagreements, however, the vast majority of scholars agree on one crucial point: the generic divide between the prose frame and the poetic core constitutes the major challenge to the unity of the book, whether one understands it as indicative of multiple authorship or as the result of stylistic variation on the part of a single author.

In a previous article, I challenged the validity precisely of this point of agreement, which has led to the conflation of the problem of compositional history and the issue of genre.[13] I argued that the principal redactional seam in the book of Job lies not between the prose and the poetic sections along generic lines but rather between chapters 1 and 2 and between verses 10 and 11 in chapter 42, that is, between the outer prose frame (Job 1, 42:11–17) and the inner prose frame (Job 2, 42:7–10). I argued for the structural and, to a limited extent, theological integrity of the outer prose frame—what we might call, in its original form, the "Joban tale"—and, correspondingly, began to defend the affinity between chapters 2 and 3 on theological grounds. In this article, I turn my attention directly to the inner prose frame in order to argue that, if the interpretive tradition of the relationship between the prose frame and the poetic core is split, it is because the inner prose frame is Janus-faced. I will argue that the Joban poet expressly composed the inner frame as a narrative bridge between the Joban tale and his own poetic dialogue and as a theological pivot away from the pietism of the former toward the anthropocentric agon of the latter.

I. The Narrative and Theological Disjunction between the Joban Tale and the Poetic Core

I have argued elsewhere that the Joban tale (Job 1, 42:11–17) is an older and independent literary unity not authored by the Joban poet.[14] If we consider the disjunctive relationship between the Joban tale and the poetic core (Job 3:1–42:6) only—not taking into consideration the inner prose frame (Job 2, 42:7–10), which we will place under scrutiny below—we can begin better to understand the bridging and pivotal function that the inner frame plays in the book of Job.

In the Joban tale, Job is a hyperbolically pious and blessed man who endures the calamitous loss of all his property and all his children—as the readers are informed in the heavenly scene of Job 1:6–12—at the divinely sanctioned hand of the satan (1:12) and yet does not curse God. Far from it, he blesses God:

---

[13] Paul K.-K. Cho, "The Integrity of Job 1 and 42:11–17," *CBQ* 76 (2014): 230–51. See also Albrecht Alt, "Zur Vorgeschichte des Buches Hiob," *ZAW* 55 (1937): 265–68; Fohrer, *Das Buch Hiob*, 29–33; and Ulrich Berges, "Der Ijobrahmen (Ijob 1,1–2,10; 42,7–17): Theologische Versuche angesichts unschuldingen Leidens," *BZ* 39 (1995): 225–45.

[14] Cho, "Integrity of Job."

> Naked I came out from my mother's womb,
> And naked I will return there.
> YHWH gave, and YHWH took;
> YHWH's name be blessed. (Job 1:21)[15]

After Job's piety is proven true (1:22), Job's brothers and sisters come to eat bread with him, to comfort him, and to give him money and gold (42:11). Indeed, God richly blesses Job with double the property and double the number of children (42:12–15)—readers are left to suppose—as recompense for the loss Job has had to suffer to demonstrate that God's faith in him was not without reason.[16] The tale teaches a relatively simple, if difficult, lesson on the importance of piety toward God.[17] It is also a coherent and self-contained narrative unit, a beautiful example of ring composition.[18]

The literary and theological world of the poetic core stands in stark contrast to that of the Joban tale. In terms of narrative and dramatic setting, the two sections share the characters of Job and God, but they are augmented by three new characters (Eliphaz, Bildad, and Zophar) in the poetic core. The two sections also share the fact of Job's suffering, but the frenetic activity of the tale—the destruction of Job's property and the death of his sons, which we must presume includes his ten children, are recounted in six speedy verses (1:14–19)—is replaced by impassioned and intricate dialogue. Narrative gives way to speech.[19] Without the benefit of the inner prose frame, the narrative and dramatic connection between the Joban tale and the poetic core is far from obvious. Where did Eliphaz, Bildad, and Zophar come from? Who are they? Is the verbose and impatient Job of the core the same pithy and pious Job of the tale?

In addition to the literary gap, there is a theological and hermeneutical gap between the Joban tale and the poetic core. David J. A. Clines throws the theological divide into sharp relief.[20] He argues that there is an incompatibility between the philosophy, or theology, of the prose frame and that of the poetic body. (The observations Clines and other scholars below make concerning the prose frame as a whole apply more aptly to the Joban tale.) The prose frame, Clines argues, espouses a doctrine of moral retribution in which "one is rewarded or punished in strict conformity with the moral quality of one's deeds." He correctly characterizes the

---

[15] Unless otherwise noted, English translations of the Hebrew are my own.

[16] Dhorme argues that שבענה in Job 42:13 should be translated as a dual form of seven, so as "fourteen" (*Commentary on the Book of Job*, 651–52).

[17] See Michael V. Fox, "Job the Pious," *ZAW* 117 (2005): 351–66.

[18] See Cho, "Integrity of Job."

[19] The Joban tale contains dialogue and speech (1:7–12, 14–19, 21); and the poetic core, narrative (3:1, 32:1–5, 38:1, etc.). The difference between the two sections is a matter of degree.

[20] David J. A. Clines, "Deconstructing the Book of Job," in *The Bible as Rhetoric: Studies in Biblical Persuasion and Credibility*, ed. Martin Warner, Warwick Studies in Philosophy and Literature (London: Routledge, 1990), 65–80; quotations in this paragraph are from 66 and 69.

divine decision to subject the exceptionally righteous Job to exceptional suffering—which seems to contradict the doctrine of retribution—as a narrative and not a philosophical feature. It is a complication in the plot that drives the story forward, something "we should expect of any narrative," something that should not be abstracted into a philosophical position. In fact, the narrative complication makes it possible to reaffirm the doctrine of retribution more strongly at the end, for Job again receives blessings commensurate with his piety. "There is no deconstruction going on" in the prose frame, Clines concludes. Rather, on the whole, the frame affirms the doctrine of retribution: Job begins in a state of blessedness because he is pious (1:1-3) and ends up in a state of double blessedness because he demonstrates extraordinary piety in not cursing God despite the unwarranted suffering (42:12-17).

Clines argues that the poetic core, in contrast, proves "over and over again that the doctrine of retribution is wrong."[21] The dramatic failure of Job's friends to defend the doctrine and Job's stirring opposition to it, presenting himself as one who is righteous yet suffers as the primary argument against the doctrine, directly undermine the philosophy of the prose frame. There exists a contradiction, philosophically speaking, between the prose frame and the poetic dialogue such that, when read together, they deconstruct each other. The book of Job "undermines the philosophy it asserts," and the deconstructive fault line lies between the prose frame and the poetic core.[22]

The theological contradiction between the Joban tale and the poetic core is not a feature only of a self-consciously deconstructionist reading such as Clines's. For example, the diverging reading strategies of two recent works that attempt to provide a coherent interpretation of the theological message of the entire book of Job by Carol A. Newsom and by Michael V. Fox bring to light the hermeneutical divide between the Joban tale and the poetic core. Fox and Newsom, in choosing to privilege the hermeneutics of either the prose or the poetry, respectively, produce divergent readings of the theology of Job, which, together, unwittingly confirm Clines's deconstructive observation.

Carol A. Newsom, in her highly insightful work *The Book of Job: A Contest of Moral Imaginations*, analyzes the book of Job as a polyphonic text in which different genres represent different "modes of perception that conceptualize aspects of reality in distinctive ways."[23] She argues that we should read the various genres found in the book, such as the didactic tale of the prose frame and the wisdom dialogue of the poetic body, as engaged in a dialogue in which "a plurality of unmerged voices" come together to present each its own distinctive perception of

---

[21] Ibid., 69.
[22] Ibid., 65, citing Jonathan Culler, *On Deconstruction: Theory and Criticism after Structuralism* (London: Routledge & Kegan Paul, 1983), 66.
[23] Newsom, *Book of Job*, 12.

reality and to challenge those of others.²⁴ The book, therefore, offers a dialogic truth in which no perspective is "subordinated to a single controlling perspective that represents the author's own voice" and in which each perspective enjoys equal footing with all others.²⁵ To offer an imperfect analogy, Newsom sees the individual perspectives, embodied in genres and articulated by different characters, as the cells of a beehive that together constitute the one superstructure.

Yet, even in a beehive, there is the queen's super cell. For Newsom, among the several generic boundaries that riddle Job, the most important one divides the didactic prose frame from the poetic wisdom dialogue. According to Newsom, the prose frame is "intensely monologic" and has a simple and predetermined truth.²⁶ It describes "a world where everything is certain, clear, a unity of coherent meaning."²⁷ In contrast, the worldview of the wisdom dialogue of the poetic body is already "dialogic," featuring a plurality of distinct and competing voices (those of Job and Job's friends). Newsom suggests that we can see in wisdom dialogues "something akin to what [Mikhail] Bakhtin meant by genuine dialogue and the dialogic sense of truth."²⁸ No surprise, then, that it is the wisdom dialogue, with its dialogic sense of truth, that provides the hermeneutical key to the entire book for Newsom. Newsom reads the book itself as a wisdom dialogue—one that takes place among different genres—and treats the monologic worldview of the prose frame, ironically, as a contributing participant in the presentation of an overall dialogic truth of the book. The various voices of the book of Job, God's voice along with those of the human characters, engage in an ongoing dialogue about "the moral nature of reality" in which each voice contributes a valuable and unique perspective and where no one voice dominates.²⁹ It is a utopian vision of nonjudgmental inclusivity and interminable debate.

Michael V. Fox, in contrast to Newsom, finds the hermeneutical key to the book of Job in the prose frame and, by privileging the theocentric perspective of the prose frame over the anthropocentric perspectives found in the rest of the book, aims to bring the contest of moral imaginations that Newsom elegantly brought to light to a close. More specifically, Fox directly engages Newsom's claim that "the author [of Job] gives up the type of control exercised in monologic works and attempts to create several consciousnesses that will be truly independent of the author's and interact with genuine freedom"³⁰ and argues that "the author [of Job] does maintain control" and, in the prose frame, presents a theocentric and monologic perspective meant to control how readers interpret all other (human)

---

²⁴ Ibid., 86.
²⁵ Ibid., 260.
²⁶ Ibid., 24.
²⁷ Ibid., 54.
²⁸ Ibid., 85.
²⁹ Ibid., 17. See the review by Jon D. Levenson, *JR* 84 (2004): 271–72.
³⁰ Newsom, *Book of Job*, 23; cited in Fox, "Job the Pious," 358.

perspectives of the book.³¹ Fox explains that the narrator, in chapters 1 and 2, tells the reader more than he tells Job, namely, that God makes Job suffer not because of any moral deficiency but precisely because of his moral quality. In other words, the reader is made to see the Joban drama from God's perspective as disclosed in the frame narrative and to know that Job's suffering-without-reason is a divinely sanctioned opportunity, a great privilege in disguise, for Job to honor God and foil the satan by demonstrating piety-without-reason, something God values highly. In his own words, Fox states that "the narrative frame of Job is meant to be read with full seriousness and is determinative for the meaning of the book."³² It, "like a picture frame ... defines the setting that controls the way we view the picture," that is, the poetic core.³³ Fox, in contrast to Newsom, subordinates all other perspectives of the book of Job under the theocentric perspective of the prose frame. If the book of Job is a contest of moral imaginations, as Newsom characterizes it, for Fox, the God of the prose frame wins.

In summary, the interpretations of Clines, Newsom, and Fox demonstrate the theological and hermeneutical divide between the prose frame and the poetic body that coincides with and so reinforces the literary gap. The divergent philosophies, hermeneutics, and points of view of the two sections suggest split authorship with conflicting goals—though that they are coordinated opposites, taking opposite sides on the same issue, suggests some dependence. It would appear that Clines's deconstructive reading and the contrastive hermeneutics of Newsom and Fox, as outlined above, leave little room for doubt that there exists a considerable gap between the Joban tale and the poetic core of the book of Job.

II. Comparative Examples

Examples of poetry set within a narrative framework that parallel the structure of the book of Job exist both in the Hebrew Bible and in comparative ancient Near Eastern literatures. These comparative examples, however, are substantially different from Job and do not help to explain the idiosyncratic difficulties of the biblical book.

Claus Westermann, fully acknowledging that the narrative frame of Job "does not agree in places with the events which the poet depicts" in the poetic core, nevertheless finds the phenomenon unremarkable.³⁴ He notes that this type of

---

³¹ Fox, "Job the Pious," 358.

³² Michael V. Fox, "Reading the Tale of Job," in *A Critical Engagement: Essays on the Hebrew Bible in Honour of J. Cheryl Exum*, ed. David J. A. Clines and Ellen van Wolde, HBM 38 (Sheffield: Sheffield Phoenix, 2011), 145–62, here 145.

³³ Ibid., 159.

³⁴ Claus Westermann, *The Structure of the Book of Job: A Form-Critical Analysis*, trans. Charles A. Muenchow (Philadelphia: Fortress, 1981), 7.

disjuncture between poem and narrative setting "frequently shows up" in the Hebrew Bible.[35] Among several examples, he highlights the Song of Hannah (1 Sam 2) and notes that the narrative context, a barren woman giving birth to a child, ill fits the content of the song, a psalm of descriptive praise whose only clear narrative connection to Hannah's situation is the half verse "The barren woman bears seven, / but the one with many children languishes" (1 Sam 2:5b).[36] The structure of the book of Job and the mismatch between the prose frame and the inserted poetry is far from unique in the Hebrew Bible and, so Westermann contends, does not deserve to be the object of scholarly obsession.

Seow, looking to extrabiblical literatures, mentions several ancient Near Eastern parallels in which a poetic core is set within a narrative frame.[37] Most interesting is the Egyptian Tale of the Eloquent Peasant, a text that dates back at least to the nineteenth century BCE.[38] The narrative prologue recounts a simple tale of the injustice an innocent peasant suffers at the hand of an evil landowner, and the core is a series of nine versified speeches by the peasant that eloquently address the issue of justice before judicial authorities. The peasant is richly rewarded for his suffering and, it appears, for his eloquence in the prose epilogue. Seow concludes, "The point here is not the possible *influence* of one text upon another but *analogy*: there are other texts from elsewhere in the ancient Near East that manifest such prose framing of poetry as we find in Job."[39]

These comparative examples from the Hebrew Bible and ancient Near Eastern literature suggest that the structure of the book of Job in itself does not make the incongruence between the prose frame and the poetic core a point of particular interest. Nor does it speak necessarily against the compositional integrity of the book. Westermann's analogies, however, have not convinced many interpreters to regard the incongruence simply as a sign of "authenticity," because the Joban incongruence points not to compositions with "different origins" that were redacted together but rather to a literary history in which one composition was likely written as a direct response to the other.[40] Both the prose and the poetry wrestle with the same situation (Job's unjust suffering) and the questions it raises but respond to them in contrasting ways. The incongruence is not random but coordinated, not

---

[35] Westermann mentions "the song of praise which a king sings at the high point of his reign (2 Sam. 22 = Ps. 18), the lament of an ill king (Isa. 38), the lament of a childless woman (1 Sam. 2), the song of the prophet Jonah, and the songs of the community in Chronicles, which are constructed out of psalms" (ibid.).

[36] Ibid.

[37] Seow mentions: Eloquent Peasant, Admonition of Ipuwer, Prophecies of Neferti, and Instructions of Ankhsheshonq among Egyptian wisdom texts and Proverbs of Aḥiqar among Aramaic texts (*Job 1–21*, 27–28).

[38] See Miriam Lichtheim, *Ancient Egyptian Literature: A Book of Readings*, 3 vols. (Berkeley: University of California Press, 1971–1980), 1:169–83.

[39] Seow, *Job 1–21*, 28.

[40] Westermann, *Structure of the Book of Job*, 7.

the result of a chance pairing but the effect of calculated intent. Furthermore, the ancient Near Eastern parallels Seow mentions exhibit a basic continuity between the frame narrative and the poetic core, unlike the book of Job. "There is no deconstruction going on" in those texts as there is in Job.

In sum, neither the structure of the book of Job nor its mix of genres necessarily calls for special attention. Yet the idiosyncratic matrix of the structure of the book, its mix of genres, and the presence of coordinated theological oppositions justifies the scholarly attention that the issue of the compositional history of Job has elicited and received. How did the Joban tale and the poetic core come together —and in such a way as to convince one group of scholars that they belong together organically and compositionally and another group the very opposite?

III. Job 2 and 42:7-10 as Narrative Bridge and Theological Pivot

The solution to the enigma of the bifurcation in the interpretive tradition concerning the relationship between the prose frame and the poetic core lies in the inner prose frame (Job 2, 42:7–10). The ways in which the inner prose frame functions as a narrative connection between the Joban tale and the poetic core are simple but also demonstrate what Clines aptly called "false naivety."[41] The inner prologue, for example, almost artlessly brings the world of the Joban tale to a close and sets the scene narratively for the poetic dialogue. At the same time, each narrative connection also functions as a theological hinge and introduces new concepts, themes, characters, and questions that, when fully developed, challenge the theology of the Joban tale and anticipate the probing theological discussion to come. The inner frame is not only a straightforward narrative bridge but also a sophisticated theological pivot away from the concerns of the Joban tale to the world of the dialogue. It is a work of poetic and theological genius and is marked by both a simplicity of style and penetrating insight.

The inner prose frame comprises four distinct scenes: scene A (2:1–7a) recounts a second heavenly dialogue between YHWH and the satan concerning Job; scene B (2:7b–10) recounts the earthly consequences of the heavenly dialogue, that is, of Job's suffering and his dialogue with his wife; scene C (2:11–13) recounts the arrival of Job's three friends and their silent response to Job's pitiable state; and scene D (42:7–10) stages the exit of the three friends.

The first three scenes make up the inner prologue. Scene A, which is a virtual repetition of the first heavenly dialogue recounted in chapter 1, firmly anchors the narrative in the world of the Joban tale. Scene C complements scene A and anchors the narrative in the world of the poetic dialogue. It introduces Job's three friends,

---

[41] David J. A. Clines, "False Naivety in the Prologue of Job," *HAR* 9 (1985): 127–36.

Eliphaz, Bildad, and Zophar, who will engage in dialogue with Job in the poetic core. Scene B binds the two opposing ends of the inner prologue (chapter 2). It mimics the earlier scene of earthly consequences (Job 1:14–22) but also introduces themes and motifs that anticipate the dialogue to come, with Job's wife serving as a kind of keystone to the bridge that connects heaven and earth, narrative and dialogue, piety and defiance. Scene D is the inner epilogue.

Scene A (Job 2:1–7a)

Scene A anchors chapter 2, the narrative bridge between the outer prologue and the poetic core, firmly in the world of the Joban tale. It does this by the virtual repetition of the first scene of heavenly dialogue (1:6–12). When chapter 2 opens, "One day, the divine beings came to present themselves before YHWH," the reader is thrust back into a familiar scene, the heavenly scene at the center of the Joban tale (1:6–12). The return to heaven gives rise to the readerly expectation that the debate that began there may finally come to an end. Indeed, God's acknowledgment that Job "still persists in his purity" though God destroyed him "for no reason [חנם]" (2:3)—which effectively invalidates the satan's charge against Job's integrity: "Does Job fear God for no reason [חנם]?" (1:9)—seems to signal such an end. The story continues, however, because the Joban poet employs the trope of repetition for two opposing reasons, first, to link chapter 2 to the world of the Joban tale and, second and crucially, to extend and augment the narrative. Instead of coming to an end, the debate between God and the satan continues because the return to heaven is also a return to the pattern of heavenly debate and earthly consequences. Thus, in repetition of the prior heavenly scene, the satan counters God's (re)presentation of Job the (still) pious with yet another trial:

> Skin after skin. All that a man has, he will give for his life [נפש]. But indeed stretch out your hand and strike his bone and his flesh [עצם ובשר], and he will surely curse you to your face! (2:4b–5)

God does not challenge the satan's proposal but hands Job into his hands for a new round of trials—again, in repetition of the first heavenly scene. At the same time that the repeated heavenly scene anchors chapter 2 in the narrative world of the Joban tale, it opens up the story to augmentation, which comes in the form of scene B.[42]

Scene A is not only a part of the narrative bridge but also a theological turning point away from chapter 1 to the poetic core, introducing two key themes in service of the latter purpose. First is the thematic word חנם, "for no reason." Scholars have noted that the thematic word occurs twice in the prose prologue (1:9, 2:3) and twice in the poetic dialogue (9:17, 22:6) and have identified it as a link between the prose

---

[42] For further discussion, see Cho, "Integrity of Job," 241–47.

and the poetry.⁴³ Against the compositional history proposed in the present article, one might argue that the thematic word connects the outer prose frame, the inner prose frame, and the poetic core. Upon closer examination, however, the important thematic word is better understood as a connection that, *in nuce*, encapsulates the hinge function of chapter 2.

The satan first uses the word חנם to challenge the integrity of Job's piety:

> Is it for no reason [חנם] that Job fears God? Have you not put a fence around him, around his house, and around all that he has on every side? You have blessed the work of his hands, and his livestock have burst forth in the land. (1:9b–10)

The satan posits God's blessings as the reason that Job acts piously and asks whether blessings, which were intended as the effect of piety, have instead become the cause. Furthermore, it is important to note that the satan's accusation that Job's piety may not be unmotivated is precisely the reason that God hands over all that Job has into the satan's hands (1:12). Fox, in his incisive reading of the prose frame, emphasizes this very point: "God will not, perhaps *can* not … allow the integrity of human righteousness to be impugned and permanently left in question."⁴⁴ God allows Job to suffer the loss of all his possessions in order that or, better, in the hope that the integrity of Job's piety will prove pure and true against the satan's claim to the contrary.

The thematic word חנם appears again in Job 2:3, where it is used in a way that is contrary to its use in 1:9 and reflects a human perspective and not the perspective of heaven.⁴⁵ In the opening statement in chapter 2, God makes a surprising admission that he "destroyed [Job] for no reason [חנם]" (2:3). To gloss over this statement as a mere thematic connection to chapter 1 is to miss its subtle and important function within the book. First, God's admission in 2:3 that he destroyed Job for no reason directly contradicts what the reader has learned in chapter 1, which is that God has a reason for destroying Job. Second, God's statement in 2:3 reflects a human perspective concerning Job's suffering—though not that of the reader. For Job and his wife, the catastrophes appear to have been "for no reason." As Job will articulate fully in the poetic core, he cannot begin to fathom why he was made to suffer. From his perspective, he was destroyed "for no reason," and it is because he wants to know the reason for his suffering that he seeks audience with God. In this way, the seemingly simple use of the thematic word חנם in chapter 2 reveals itself as distinct and distant from its use in chapter 1 and as anticipating the anthropocentric question about God's justice that will occupy the poetic core.

---

⁴³ Seow, *Job 1–21*, 28.
⁴⁴ Fox, "Job the Pious," 358–59.
⁴⁵ For a contrary interpretation of חנם in 1:9 and 2:3, see Tod Linafelt and Andrew R. Davis, "Translating חנם in Job 1:9 and 2:3: On the Relationship between Job's Piety and His Interiority," *VT* 63 (2013): 627–39.

The next use of חנם, in 9:17, mirrors exactly its use in 2:3 over against its use in 1:9. In a speech in which Job first begins to entertain the possibility of a legal confrontation with God (ch. 9),[46] Job declares,

> For he bruises me with tempest
> and multiplies my wound for no reason [חנם]. (9:17)

The "tempest" may refer to the "great wind" (1:19) that caused the death of Job's children and demonstrates that the Joban poet was aware of the Joban tale.[47] Important for our argument is the observation that Job characterizes God as causing him tremendous pain "for no reason [חנם]." This is the exact way חנם is used in chapter 2 but not in chapter 1. It is used in 9:17 to ascribe to God the sole responsibility for Job's suffering (cf. 2:10a) and to deny knowledge of any reason, whether one thinks it is legitimate or not, that God might have caused Job pain.[48] In chapter 9, Job accuses God of exactly what God confesses in chapter 2 in contradistinction to chapter 1.

In sum, the thematic word חנם, far from forming a connection between the prose frame and the poetic core concisely illustrates the perspectival and theological affinity between the inner prologue and the poetic core over against the perspective and theology of the outer prologue. The outer prologue privileges the divine perspective as the hermeneutical lens through which to interpret the Joban drama and asks, "Are human beings capable of pure piety? Can humanity be pious for no reason?" The inner prologue and the poetic core give voice to human perspectives and ask, "Is God just? Why does God allow humanity to suffer for no reason?"

The satan's response to God's opening statement further anticipates the narrative extension and the poetic dialogue. The satan ignores God's apparent claim to victory and proposes a new test (2:4b–5). In so doing, the satan identifies Job's "bone and flesh" (עצם ובשר) as the object of torment and anticipates the narrative in scene B. The satan also introduces a distinction between one's נפש and one's עצם ובשר and, in this way, signals the rising importance of human interiority.[49]

---

[46] On the legal metaphor in Job, see Habel, *Book of Job*, esp. 54–57.

[47] Other narrative connections between the prose frame and the poetic core (i.e., the depiction of Job as blameless [תם; 1:1, 8; 2:3; 4:6; 8:20; 9:20, 21, 22; 22:3]; allusions to the death of Job's children [1:18–19; 8:4]; etc.) do not necessarily point to common authorship (*pace* Seow, *Job 1–21*, 28–29) but may indicate that the Joban poet builds on the Joban tale.

[48] The word חנם appears once more, in Eliphaz's final speech, in which he accuses Job of injustices: "For you exact a pledge from your brother for no reason [חנם] / and strip the clothing of the naked" (22:6). Eliphaz depicts Job as being as cruel as Job accuses God of being.

[49] David A. Lambert criticizes the tendency in modern interpretations of Job to privilege the human interiority ("The Book of Job in Ritual Perspective," *JBL* 134 [2015]: 557–75, here 572–75). As I argue below (see also "Job and Human Interiority: Perspectives, Repetitions, and Speech [Job 1–2]," paper presented at the Annual Meeting of the Society of Biblical Literature, San Francisco, CA, 2011) and as others (Linafelt and Davis, "Translating חנם") have noted, the

The literal sense of the phrase "bone and flesh" (עצם ובשר) is clear; its referent, however, is ambiguous. On the one hand, the phrase refers to Job's physical body. This becomes apparent when the satan exits heaven and in scene B "inflicts Job with terrible sores from the soles of his feet to the crown of his head" (2:7). On the other hand, a person's physical body is not called her "bone and flesh" (עצם ובשר) anywhere in the Hebrew Bible. Rather, the phrase always refers to one's kin.[50] Thus, it has sometimes been noted that the satan sardonically refers to Job's children, whom he has already struck dead, or possibly to his siblings.[51] The more likely referent, however, is Job's wife.[52] Recall that Adam refers to the woman, just after her creation (Gen 2:22) and before the etiological notice about marriage (2:24), as "bone of my bones and flesh of my flesh" (2:23).[53] Thus, the idiom עצם ובשר may anticipate the appearance of Job's wife in the next scene and recognize that she too has been struck by the satan. It is a subtle indication that the satan will afflict both Job's body and his wife—attack Job both physically and socially—as a means of testing the extent of his piety.[54] More than the physical torment, however, it is the affliction of Job's wife that functions as the narrative and theological keystone of Job 2, the bridge between the Joban tale and the poetic core.

Also important in the satan's second challenge is the distinction he makes between נפש and עצם ובשר. What the satan means by נפש is not obvious. But it is clear, if we take the link between the inner prologue and the poetic core seriously, that the usual and colorless translation of נפש as "life" (NRSV, JPS, NIV) is inadequate.[55] Clines argues that נפש refers to a person's "simple existence" in Job 2:4 in contrast to עצם ובשר, which refer to "the bodily structure of the human individual" or "the physical, external being of a person."[56] I would argue for a more substantive understanding of נפש, something like the feeling and thinking faculty of a human being.[57] The Joban poet uses the term נפש twenty-four times to refer to a variety of

---

internal thoughts and motivations that animate human action—as opposed to outward ritual actions and words—are the very things that interest God and the satan.

[50] Werner Reiser, "Die Verwandtschaftsformel in Gen 2,23," *TZ* 16 (1960): 1–4; Walter Brueggemann, "Of the Same Flesh and Bone (GN 2,23a)," *CBQ* 32 (1970): 532–42.

[51] Seow, *Job 1–21*, 293; Clines, *Job 1–20*, 46.

[52] David Shepherd, "'Strike His Bone and His Flesh': Reading Job from the Beginning," *JSOT* 33 (2008): 81–97.

[53] The Genesis usage is likely an adaptation of the shorter idiom. So Reiser, "Die Verwandtschaftsformel," 3.

[54] That the Joban poet reuses traditions from Genesis in Job 3:3–13 (see Michael Fishbane, "Jeremiah IV 23–26 and Job III 3–13: A Recovered Use of the Creation Pattern," *VT* 21 [1971]: 151–67) and possibly in Job 31:33, 38–40 (see Habel, *Book of Job*, 438, 439–40) makes it more likely that he does so also in Job 2.

[55] Clines, *Job 1–20*, 45.

[56] Ibid.

[57] See Hans Walter Wolff, *Anthropology of the Old Testament*, trans. Margaret Kohl (Philadelphia: Fortress, 1974), 17–18. Jon D. Levenson likewise identifies נפש as something more than

concepts.⁵⁸ In its first use in the poetic core (3:20), נפש does not refer to a person's "simple existence": "Why does he give light to the troubled / and life [חיים] to the bitter of נפש" (3:20; see also 7:11, 10:1, 21:25, 27:2). The poet, here as elsewhere, differentiates נפש from "life" (חיים; see 10:1, 12:10).⁵⁹ The poet uses נפש also to refer to that part of the human anatomy that is capable of experiencing bitterness (see 7:11, 10:1, 21:25, 27:2) and, therefore, capable of responding to that experience, presumably by either cursing or blessing God. In this light, the reason that God safeguards Job's נפש is not in order to keep Job alive—the satan also does not desire Job's death, which would annul the very possibility of the contest—but in order to safeguard the integrity of Job's feeling and thinking faculty. God is making certain that the satan does not rig the result of the contest by manipulating Job's נפש one way or the other. The question at the heart of the debate between God and the satan is this: Will Job's נפש, made bitter by the experience of physical and social torment (עצם ובשר), choose to bless (ברך) God to his face? The response comes in scene B.

Scene B (2:7b–10)

At the end of scene A, the satan takes leave of God (2:7a) and immediately finds himself on earth, where he strikes Job with a physical ailment (שחין, a skin disease of unspecified nature) from the sole of his feet to the crown of his head.⁶⁰ (The repeated references to Job's skin disease in the poetic core [7:5, 30:30] are yet another attestation to the continuity of the inner prologue with the poetic core.)⁶¹ Job, sitting on an ash heap, "takes a potsherd with which to scrape himself" (2:8) in ritual mourning.⁶² Yet the sores are not the end of Job's torment, nor is his silent ritual action his final response. Job's wife, struck by the satan, says to Job, "Still you

---

simply life; it refers to "one's vitality, vigor, energy, selfhood, inner forcefulness, and the like" (*The Love of God: Divine Gift, Human Gratitude, and Mutual Faithfulness in Judaism* [Princeton: Princeton University Press, 2015], 70).

⁵⁸ Job 3:20; 6:7, 11; 7:11, 15; 9:21; 10:1; 11:20; 12:10; 13:14; 14:22; 16:4; 18:4; 19:2; 21:25; 23:13; 24:12; 27:2, 8; 30:16, 26; 31:30, 39; 41:13.

⁵⁹ Note, however, that in Job 9:21, חיים stands in parallel to נפש.

⁶⁰ On שחין, see Clines, *Job 1–20*, 48. "Sores" (שחין), in Levitical law, were understood to appear on the "skin" (עור) or the "body" (בשר) (Lev 13:18, 20). "Terrible sores [שחין רע]" are, in Deuteronomy, punishment for covenantal unfaithfulness (28:27, 35). If Job 2 is to be understood as raising the stakes of the debate about the purity of Job's righteousness, "the terrible sores" (שחין רע) can hardly fit the bill. The phrase "terrible sores" appears one other time in the Hebrew Bible in reference to the sores with which God inflicted the Egyptians—the sixth plague (Deut 28:35; cf. Exod 9:8–11). Deuteronomy uses the same verb (נכה) and the phrase (מכף רגלו ועד קדקדו) as Job 2:7, thus thickening the intertextuality between Job and Deuteronomy. If we take seriously the exodus background, Job's sores, however terrible, cannot be greater than the loss of his children, which one may compare to the tenth plague. Rather, the increasing of the stakes likely has something to do with Job's wife and Job's נפש, as we will see below.

⁶¹ Clines, *Job 1–20*, 49.

⁶² See Lambert, "Ritual Perspective," 559–60.

persist in your purity. Curse God and die!" (2:9), to which Job gives a rather flat response: "You speak as any foolish woman [הנבלות] would speak. Shall we receive the good from God, and not receive the bad?" (2:10a). Then the narrator provides an evaluative summation: "In all this Job did not sin with his lips" (2:10b). Each of these elements fulfills prior narrative expectations: the satan strikes Job's "bone and flesh," that is, his body and possibly his wife, as indicated in scene A; and Job responds to his torment with ritual acts of mourning and with pious words, concerning which the narrator provides a summary judgment, in expected repetition of chapter 1. But more than forming a narrative bridge, these elements also turn away theologically from the Joban tale and anticipate the probing, tortured dialogue to follow.

The central figure in this regard is Job's wife, and the central event is the dialogue she initiates with Job. It has often been noted that the advice Job's wife gives to the suffering Job echoes the satan's words (cf. 1:11; 2:5, 9). This observation has led to a diabolical characterization of Job's wife, perhaps most famously by Augustine, who called her *adjutrix diaboli*. Yet Job's wife echoes God's words more closely than the satan's. Compare 2:3bα and 2:9aβ:

2:3bα (the LORD speaking to the satan):
He still persists in his integrity (NRSV)　　　　　　　עדנו מחזיק בתמתו

2:3aβ (Job's wife speaking to Job):
Do you still persist in your integrity? (NRSV)　　　　עדך מחזיק בתמתך

In short, the words of Job's wife echo both the satan and God and, in this way, replicate the heavenly dialogue on earth. In terms of narrative technique, it is an efficient means of changing the scene and perspective of the drama: the satan and God find their counterpart and are, in a sense, replaced by Job's wife. No longer will the debate concerning human piety and suffering happen in heaven among divine beings from a divine perspective but on earth among human interlocutors from a human perspective. Job's verbal engagement with his wife further concretizes the change in scene from heaven to earth and anticipates the dominant literary form of dialogue that characterizes the poetic core.[63] In the space of a few verses, the Joban poet briskly moves from heaven to earth and from prose narrative to poetic dialogue. Job's wife represents the central point of transition from the Joban tale to the poetic core. She is the fulcrum on which the book turns.

Job's wife also introduces a theology of defiance that challenges the piety of the Joban tale and anticipates the theological agon of the poetic core. She demonstrates that for a human being to ask the same question that God and the satan ask of Job is to ask, in effect, a very different question.

---

[63] Fohrer, who reads the dialogue between Job's wife and her husband as poetry, also notes that these verses introduce poetry into the prose frame just as there is prose in the poetic core (*Das Buch Hiob*, 35).

That new question, articulated with words stolen from heaven and turned back against it, represents the central theological axis in the book of Job. It might be said that Job's wife sets the theological agenda for the rest of the book and lays bare the impossible choice that stands before Job—and his readers. She speaks six words and three statements: (1) "Still you persist in your integrity" (עדך מחזיק בתמתך); (2) "curse God" (ברך אלהים); and (3) "and die" (ומת). The first statement, understood either as a straightforward statement or a rhetorical question, describes Job's current state of piety. The next two statements are imperatives and ambiguously connect the act of cursing or blessing (ברך)⁶⁴ God and dying. The principal ambiguity turns on what Tod Linafelt has called the "undecidability of ברך." Scholars generally agree that ברך is used in Job 1–2 both literally to mean "to bless" (1:10, 23; 42:12) and euphemistically to mean "to curse" (1:5, 11; 2:5, 9) as a means of avoiding directly cursing God.⁶⁵ Some, however, have questioned whether we can know what ברך means with certainty:⁶⁶ Does Job's wife advise Job antiphrastically to curse God or literally to bless God? The uncertain function of the connecting *vav*, whether it is a coordinating *vav* or a subordinating *vav*, further magnifies the undecidability of ברך.⁶⁷ Does Job's wife think that Job will die inevitably whether he curses or blesses God, or is she advocating that Job take the initiative to die? Two major interpretations are the following:

1. You still persist in your purity. Good. Bless God, though you should die.
2. Do you still persist in your purity? Just curse God and die!⁶⁸

The choice set that Job's wife lays before Job will animate the poetic dialogue but is alien to the Joban tale, in which the principal reference point is God. Even Job's relationship to his children, servants, and property is secondary to his primary relationship to God; and his relationship to himself hardly concerns the tale. In response to the tragedies that befall his household in chapter 1, Job engages in ritual acts of mourning: "Job stood up, tore his robe, and shaved his head" (1:20a), but then he immediately (re)establishes a pious relationship with God: "then he fell to the ground and worshiped" (1:20b). The relevant choice set in the Joban tale is whether Job will bless God or curse God in response to the calamities. The question of Job's relationship to himself, whether he will choose to live or die, does not materialize. Yet Job's relationship to himself is precisely the question Job's wife forces upon him. Will Job passively receive whatever God metes out, whether woe

---

⁶⁴ Tod Linafelt, "The Undecidability of ברך in the Prologue to Job and Beyond," *BibInt* 4 (1996): 154–72.

⁶⁵ See 1 Kgs 21:10, 13; and Ps 10:3. Cf. Exod 22:27, Lev 24:11–16, Isa 8:21.

⁶⁶ Edwin M. Good, *In Turns of Tempest: A Reading of Job, with a Translation* (Stanford, CA: Stanford University Press, 1990), 196; Linafelt, "Undecideability of ברך."

⁶⁷ Paul Joüon, S.J., *Grammaire de l'Hébreu biblique*, 2nd ed. (Rome: Institut biblique pontifical, 1947) §116c; see also *IBHS* 32.2.2.

⁶⁸ Linafelt sees a similar choice set ("Undecideability of ברך," 167).

or weal, or will Job rise to make a claim for himself before God and before other human beings?

We should therefore understand the words of Job's wife as introducing a dramatically new choice set from that found in the Joban tale, a choice set that turns on Job's relationship to God and, critically, to himself. The first choice is for Job to affirm God as one deserving unquestioning piety ("Bless God") and to accept death as inevitable ("though you should die"). This choice, which Job's friends will vigorously advocate, is to embrace the traditional conception of God and to abandon the possibility that any person might have a claim against God. The second choice is for Job to abandon a God who would permit a righteous person to suffer ("Curse God") and to embrace, in a final, desperate act, the human right to self-determination and to end his suffering and die ("and die!"). Job's response to his wife indicates that he understands her to advocate the latter option, to abandon God and to embrace the suffering person. Though Job's full response falls beyond the scope of this article, Job himself, throughout the poetic core, will struggle mightily to hold on both to himself as a righteous person (27:5–6, 31:5–6) and to the possibility of a God who remains worthy of human piety.[69] Job chooses to will to be himself (a suffering righteous person) before God (whose existence or worth Job refuses easily to dismiss).[70] To summarize, Job's wife, with six short impactful words, transforms the tenor of the theological landscape from one of admirable piety to one in which a variety of human responses, including defiance, are possible.[71]

After Job's flat response to his wife's probing statements in which he names God as the source of both the good and the bad and neither blesses nor curses God, the narrator manages a summary statement that raises more questions rather than provides a satisfying conclusion: "In all this Job did not sin with his lips" (2:10b). In qualifying Job's response in reference to his lips, that is, his speech, the Joban poet may be understood to suggest that, just as Job's skin disease, which according to Deuteronomy (28:35) is a visible sign of covenantal unfaithfulness, belies Job's

---

[69] I understand Job's desire for a legal confrontation with God as not only an occasion for Job to discover that he is righteous and why God made him suffer (these issues, in terms of the entire book, have already been disclosed in the prose frame) but also an opportunity for God to justify himself. Indeed, God's speech is the dramatic apex of the poetic core: What will God say for himself?

[70] Borrowing language from Søren Kierkegaard, *The Sickness unto Death: A Christian Psychological Exposition for Upbuilding and Awakening*, ed. and trans. Howard V. Hong and Edna H. Hong, Kierkegaard's Writings 19 (Princeton: Princeton University Press, 1980). I thank R. Kendall Soulen for referring me to this book and for our conversations about Joban questions.

[71] Patricia Kirkpatrick likewise notes, "Then suddenly, out of the blue she utters a fateful phrase which will determine the outcome of the book," and characterizes Job's wife as an instigator "of important shifts of theological perspective … the catalyst … to her husband's salvation" ("Curse God and Die—Job's Wife and the Struggle for Job's Transformation," in *Evil and Death: Conceptions of the Human in Biblical, Early Jewish, and Greco-Roman and Egyptian Literature*, ed. Beate Ego and Ulrike Mittmann, DCLS 18 [Berlin: de Gruyter, 2015], 43–55, here 46).

inner righteousness, so too his speech ill represents his internal thoughts. The narrator's statement suggests that more than rote piety, perhaps even its opposite, willful sin, may lurk behind Job's words.

The narrator's ambivalence toward Job's speech reflects the larger biblical attitude toward words. The Hebrew Bible recognizes that speech not only can exteriorize internal thoughts (Prov 16:23, 24:2) but can also state other than what the heart truly thinks (Isa 29:13, Prov 26:23).[72] Human speech can both reveal and conceal, obfuscate and clarify, the human interiority. Linafelt and Davis, after pointing out that Job does not reveal what he really thinks in 2:10a, optimistically write that the purpose of Job's trials is "to force him to say what he really thinks, to make manifest his inner life via speech."[73] Linafelt and Davis's statement and the biblical ambivalence toward speech, taken together, underline the importance of the dialogues to come, in which one hopes Job will reveal his inner life, his נפש. They also dampen expectation that we can ever fully know Job's interiority, his נפש, for there is no guarantee that his many words can reveal what a few words have concealed. This is the doubt that the friends' unwillingness to believe what Job verbalizes thematizes throughout the poetic dialogue.

In sum, there is a mysterious opaqueness to the human heart that even God cannot penetrate; it must wait on human words to break open. But human words are double—capable of revealing and concealing. Thus, the human heart remains gloriously free and frustratingly hidden in the book of Job. The book acknowledges that it is easier to judge a person by the condition of her skin (e.g., Job's skin disease)—as Job's friends do—rather than carefully weigh her words. The book also acknowledges that outer appearances can mislead and lead to sinfulness. Do not the friends misinterpret Job's grotesque skin disease as a sign of his inner sinfulness? Does not God rebuke them for so doing (42:7–9)? In the book of Job, the human נפש, as opposed to her עצם ובשר, is presented as the seat of a person's true worth and being and, at the same time, as hidden, mysterious, free—not open to divine manipulation or access.

Scene C (Job 2:11–13)

As Georg Fohrer recognized, the Joban poet modeled scene C after the scene in the Joban tale in which Job's siblings and acquaintances visit him (42:11).[74] In the overall design of the Joban drama, however, the three friends play almost the opposite role of the original visitors. First, whereas the visitation of Job's siblings and acquaintances brings the tale to a close, the introduction of the three friends anticipates the extended dialogue to come and functions as the narrative transition

---

[72] See Walter Vogels, "Job's Empty Pious Slogans," in *The Book of Job*, ed. W. A. M. Beuken, BETL 114 (Leuven: Leuven University Press, 1994), 369–76.

[73] Linafelt and Davis, "Translating חנם," 623.

[74] Fohrer, *Das Buch Hiob*, 32.

from the outer prologue to the poetic core. Even their silent ritual companionship of seven days and nights—almost as if they are mourning Job's death[75]—is an anticipatory foil to the imminent explosion of words. Second, whereas the original visitors comfort and restore Job to health and wealth, the friends are agents of Job's social torment. They assume and then accuse Job of heinous sins, of which, they say, his sufferings are indisputable evidence. Indeed, the friends, with Job's wife, represent the ethical and social face of the Joban drama, and the Joban poet uses them as means of exploring a wide range of human responses to the following questions: How do you console, counsel, and correct a suffering person?[76] How do you relate to God in light of suffering, whether deserved or innocent? Can a person be righteous before God? Is God innocent before human suffering? These are the vital questions that animate the inspired poetic core.

Scene D (Job 42:7–10)

The inner epilogue, which comes after the tortured dialogue between Job and his would-be comforters and Job's confrontation with the majesty of God, consists of a single scene (scene D). It completes the narrative arc that began in scene C and stages the friends' exit as the scene transitions abruptly and somewhat awkwardly back to the world of the Joban tale. The Joban poet, nevertheless, manages to provide a theological and ethical conclusion to the inner frame and the poetic dialogues.

Theologically, God says that Job's friends committed folly (נבלה) in contrast to Job, who spoke "what is right" (נכונה, 42:7, 8). This statement is a concluding judgment not only on the poetic dialogue—which it obviously is in unsurprising ways—but also on Job's wife. Recall that Job characterized her words as the speech of fools (נבלות, 2:10a). God suggestively reverses Job's earlier judgment by calling the words of Job's friends, who spoke almost the very opposite of what Job's wife said, folly and Job's words, which embody the audacity of Job's wife, right. Job's wife, in retrospect, was no fool but intimated "what is right."

Ethically, God commands the friends to reconcile with Job, whose prayer is to accompany their burnt offerings to seal their forgiveness. Job's honor, called into extreme question by the friends' silent assumptions and then explicitly attacked in the dialogues, is not only restored but elevated above that of his friends. God makes Job priest and prophet who intercedes for them. After the theological and ethical conclusion, the friends exit the scene, and the scene returns to the world of the Joban tale.

The final verse of the inner epilogue deserves comment for its awkward effectiveness.

---

[75] Clines, *Job 1–20*, 64.
[76] For a sympathetic reading of Job's friends, see Newsom, *Book of Job*, 90–129.

> And YHWH restored Job's fortunes when he prayed for his friends; and YHWH gave double of all that Job had. (42:10)

The verse bids goodbye to Job's friends and the poetic dialogue of which they were a part. It prematurely and proleptically announces the restoration of Job's fortunes, even before Job's siblings and acquaintances arrive on the scene. It effectively links the poetic core and the framing tale but without the artfulness characteristic of the Joban poet. It is perhaps his least accomplished composition. It announces, deus ex machina, we are back again.

IV. The Significance of the Literary History and Shape of the Book of Job

The literary history of the book of Job proposed above explains the presence of continuity and discontinuity between the prose frame and the poetic core. The Joban poet, by means of the inner prose frame, skillfully expands the narrative world of the Joban tale and inserts the poetic dialogue in the created space. The resulting shape is a series of dialogues—among human interlocutors (chs. 3–27) and between God and human beings (29:1–31:40, 38:1–42:10)[77]—framed by prose narrative at the beginning and the end. Because the poet uses the dialogues critically to examine the Joban situation and, with daring and imagination, to explore perspectives seemingly at odds with the innocent pietism of the tale, the resulting shape is also of a pen of bulls—questioning and speculative discourse about God and creation that push hard and threaten to breach the narrative fence. Thus, the literary shape gives rise to questions of significance: Why does the Joban poet preserve the Joban tale not only as the narrative and dramatic starting point but also as the narrative and theological conclusion of his work? Why does the poet embark from the pietistic shores of the tale for the turbulent and tortured sea of traumatized discourse, only to return, awkwardly, abruptly, to the Joban tale? Why does he not write away the ending of the Joban tale, erase it from the Joban tradition?

These important questions cannot be answered fully here. The answer, which can only be intimated, is not, I suggest, in order to incorporate the viewpoint of the Joban tale as one among the multiple voices of the poetic core, for the poet has enclosed the core with the tale as a prominent hermeneutical framework. Nor is the answer to give poetic expression to human voices of deep anguish, fear, and confusion in the dialogues only to suppress them under the theocentric perspective

---

[77] The literary history of the poetic core is complex and deserves more attention than can be given here. I suspect, with many critical scholars, that chapters 28 and 32–37 are later additions to the Joban poet's original composition, which too may have undergone disruption, particularly in chapters 22–27.

of the framework, for the poet has invested the human words with much genuine pathos and beauty. I would venture that the Joban poet tried, with his composite work, to affirm the piety of the Joban tale and, at the same time, to make room for the defiant questions and the daring moral imaginations that he saw on the lips of his contemporaries and that he himself entertained in his heart. He tried to be a poet of the love of God and the love of neighbor, both to exhort his doubting neighbors to love God in suffering and also to console them without hypocrisy, that God embraces the anguished sufferer with love. He tried, with bold liberality and compassionate traditionalism, to uphold the two pillars of biblical faith: "Love YHWH your God with all your heart and with all your soul and with all your might" (Deut 6:5) and "Love your neighbor as yourself" (Lev 19:18; cf. Matt 22:37–40; b. Šabb. 31a). The literary history and shape of the book of Job simultaneously commend the Job who demonstrates pure piety and embrace the Job who raises his voice before God in faithful defiance.

THE CULMINATING WORK OF A LEADING ARCHAEOLOGIST OF THE BIBLICAL WORLD

BEYOND THE TEXTS

An Archaeological Portrait of Ancient Israel and Judah
William G. Dever

William G. Dever offers a welcome perspective on ancient Israel and Judah that prioritizes the archaeological remains to render history as it was—not as the biblical writers argue it should have been. Drawing from the most recent archaeological data as interpreted from a nontheological point of view and supplementing that data with biblical material only when it converges with the archaeological record, Dever analyzes all the evidence at hand to provide a new history of ancient Israel and Judah that is accessible to all interested readers.

FROM SBL PRESS

More than 80 maps and illustrations
Hardcover ISBN 978-0-88414-218-8
E-book ISBN 978-0-88414-217-1
Hardcover or E-book $49.95

Order online at
https://tinyurl.com/SBLPressDeverBeyond

Phone: 877-725-3334 (toll-free) or 802-864-6185
Fax: 802-864-7626

SBL PRESS

הבל as "Worthless" in Qoheleth: A Critique of Michael V. Fox's "Absurd" Thesis

MARK SNEED
mark.sneed@lcu.edu
Lubbock Christian University, Lubbock, TX 79407

This essay critiques the thesis that Michael V. Fox first published in 1986 and has since supplemented that the word הבל in Ecclesiastes (38x) should always be translated as "absurd." Fox's argument has convinced many other Qoheleth experts to adopt this translation. In this essay, I will demonstrate that Fox's argument is untenable for the following reasons: it constitutes a new usage for הבל not found in the rest of the Hebrew Bible and, thus, is lexically and semantically fallacious; it is anachronistic both for Qoheleth and for the ancient Near East; it downplays the carpe-diem ethic and, thus, Qoheleth's primarily ethical intent. Following the critique and relying on Klaus Seybold, I propose that a word in the sphere of values such as "worthless" is a better translation of הבל for the majority of usages in Qoheleth.

The meaning of הבל has been a source of contention among Qoheleth experts for many years. One reason is that Qoheleth uses the term in a way that other biblical writers do not. Usually הבל as a descriptor is used for things like the fleeting nature of human existence (e.g., "Abel" in Gen 4, Ps 78:33), the uselessness of idols (e.g., Jer 8:19), or the futility of human effort (e.g., Job 9:29). But Qoheleth describes "everything" "under the sun" as הבל and uniquely applies the term to events and situations (e.g., 6:1–2), not just to activities and things. This situation is further complicated because he often indicates the referent of הבל with an ambiguous "this" (זה; e.g., 2:26). Moreover, the meaning and function of this term constitute in large measure the overall message of the book.[1] The term, which occurs thirty-eight

---

I would like to thank my colleagues Jesse Long Jr. and Michael Martin for helpful suggestions in revising the manuscript.

[1] C. L. Seow, "Beyond Mortal Grasp: The Usage of *Hebel* in Ecclesiastes," *ABR* 48 (2000): 1–16, here 1–2.

times in the book, serves as a catchword for Qoheleth's dominant theme.² It is part of the inclusion that envelops the book as a whole: הבל הבלים הכל הבל ("vanity of vanities, everything is vanity"; 1:2, 12:8). In order to understand both the term and the book, therefore, a hermeneutical move back and forth from the term to the book as a whole is necessary, a circularity that cannot be avoided.

The most influential article on the meaning of the term was by Michael V. Fox in 1986. Relying on Albert Camus, Fox argued that the term הבל should be translated uniformly throughout the biblical book as "absurd."³ The influence of Fox's article is evidenced by the many commentators who have adopted this translation and by the many reactions to it.⁴ No one who attempts to analyze the meaning of הבל in Qoheleth and, therefore, to discern the message of the book as a whole can afford to ignore Fox's thesis. Fox defines "absurdity" in the following Camusian way:

> The essence of the absurd is a disparity between two terms that are supposed to be joined by a link of harmony or causality but are, in fact, disjunct. The absurd is an affront to reason, in the broad sense of the human faculty that looks for order in the world about us. The quality of absurdity does not inhere in a being, act, or event in and of itself ... but rather in the tension between a certain reality and a framework of expectations.⁵

Though Fox does not believe Qoheleth's usage of the notion of the absurd is identical to Camus's in every respect, he argues that the similarities run deeper than the dissimilarities. According to Fox, the Camusian nuances that fit Qoheleth's mentality include "alienation, frustration, resentment, a stale taste of repeated and meaningless events, even resentment at the 'gods.'"⁶

> *Hebel* for Qohelet, like "absurd" for Camus ... is oppressive, even tragic. The divorce between act and result is the reality upon which human reason founders; it robs human actions of significance and undermines morality. For Qohelet *hebel* is an injustice, nearly synonymous with *rāʿâ*, "inequity, injustice." In 6:1–2,

---

²See Aarre Lauha, *Kohelet*, BKAT 19 (Neukirchen-Vluyn: Neukirchener Verlag, 1978), 18.

³Michael V. Fox, "The Meaning of *Hebel* for Qohelet," *JBL* 105 (1986): 409–27, https://doi.org/10.2307/3260510.

⁴For a recent negative response, see Scott C. Jones, "The Values and Limits of Qohelet's Sub-celestial Economy," *VT* 64 (2014): 21–33, here 26; for a positive reaction, see Antoon Schoors, *Ecclesiastes*, HCOT (Leuven: Peeters, 2013), 40–47. Those who accept the translation "absurd," though not necessarily in the Camusian sense, include Sibley Towner, "The Book of Ecclesiastes," *NIB* 5:265–360, here 279–80, 282–84; William H. U. Anderson, "The Semantic Implications of הבל and רעות רוח in the Hebrew Bible and for Qohelet," *JNSL* 25 (1999): 59–73, here 70–71; James L. Crenshaw, *Ecclesiastes: A Commentary*, OTL (Philadelphia: Westminster, 1987), 57; Benjamin Lyle Berger, "Qohelet and the Exigencies of the Absurd," *BibInt* 9 (2001): 141–79, here 145 n. 5.

⁵Fox, "Meaning of *Hebel*," 409.

⁶Ibid., n. 3.

for example, Qohelet first refers to a situation as a *rāʿâ*, then calls it *hebel* and *ḥŏlî rāʿ*, an "evil sickness." Similarly, in 9:1–3, a single situation (all people receiving the same fate) is called both *hebel* (9:1-2 …) and a *rāʿ* (9:3); see also 2:21 and 4:8.[7]

Fox argues that all the other senses of הבל in the Hebrew Bible do not fit for Qoheleth: "ephemeral" (e.g., Prov 21:6, Job 7:16), "inefficacy" (e.g., Isa 30:7, Job 9:29), and "deceit" or "lie" (Zech 10:2, Ps 62:10, etc.).[8] He also points out that idols are often characterized with the term because of their inefficacy and deceitfulness (e.g., Jer 16:19, 2 Kgs 17:15) and observes, "But Qoheleth's usage cannot be simply and directly derived from the lexical meanings it has elsewhere."[9]

Fox cites Qoh 8:14 to illustrate the notion of the absurd:

> There is a *hebel* that occurs on the earth: namely, that there are righteous people who receive what the deeds of the wicked deserve and there are wicked people who receive what the deeds of the righteous deserve. I say that this too is a *hebel*.[10]

Fox then argues against all other translations that have been suggested for the word הבל elsewhere in the Hebrew Bible and also in Qoheleth.[11] He points out that there is no antecedent for "this" except the whole situation.[12]

> To call this situation "vaporous" gives no information about it: none of the qualities usually associated with vapors seem to apply. It is not "transitory" or "fleeting"—if it were, that would be all to the good. Nor is it a "Nichtiges," a zero, an absence; it is quite substantive, very much a reality. Nor is it "vain" in the sense of futile; it is true that the deeds of the righteous may prove futile, but the passage also describes what happens to the wicked, and that fate cannot be said to show the futility of *their* actions. Nor does "incomprehensible" adequately denote the quality that troubles Qohelet in observing this situation. Although the injustice described in 8:11–14 is indeed incomprehensible, it is not the mysteriousness of the situation that pains Qohelet, but its inequity.[13]

In the rest of the article, Fox attempts to show how "absurd" best fits Qoheleth's usage of הבל in the biblical author's assessment of human behavior (toil and its fruits, pleasure, wisdom, words), living creatures and their times, and divine behavior (divine justice and "everything" of "everything is vanity").

In conclusion, Fox presents some propositions that necessarily follow if הבל is understood as denoting the absurd. First, the carpe-diem ethic is not really the dominant message of the book: "Qohelet's evaluation of human effort as absurd is

---

[7] Ibid., 410.
[8] Ibid., 412.
[9] Ibid.
[10] Ibid. (Fox's translation).
[11] Ibid., 412–13.
[12] Ibid., 412.
[13] Ibid., 412–13.

thus not (contrary to a common understanding of the purpose of the book) meant as advice to take it easy, to enjoy life's gifts as they come. Taking it easy is not really something one can choose."[14] The latter supposition Fox deduces from 2:26, 3:13, and 6:2, where God determines who can enjoy life's goods and who cannot.[15] Second, Fox offers his précis of the purpose of the biblical book:

> Qohelet speaks of futile activities not to warn against those activities so much as to muster the fact of that futility as evidence for his contention that life is absurd. The book of Qohelet, taken as a whole, is not primarily lamenting the brevity of life or exposing the vanity of worldly wealth and pleasures. Qohelet is not at root saying that everything is insubstantial, or transitory, or nothingness, or trivial. He does indeed observe these qualities in many beings and actions, but he mentions them mainly to reinforce and exemplify his main complaint—the irrationality of life as a whole, which is to say, of divine behavior.[16]

Then Fox argues that Qoheleth's הבל-judgments assume that the system should be rational and that Qoheleth "believes in the rule of divine justice."[17] But since this justice is not evident, the world appears absurd and perverse. Finally, Fox emphasizes that the phrase "'Everything is absurd' itself implies a complaint against God."[18]

In subsequent publications, Fox has supported his thesis but also revised it in two ways.[19] First, he affirms that Qoheleth is not simply deconstructing life's values ("to tear down") but is also reconstructing them ("to build up"). This move represents backtracking from his earlier argument that the biblical book is primarily descriptive and not prescriptive. Second, Fox adds examples of other ancient Near Eastern works that he believes also reflect the notion of the absurd: the Egyptian Dispute between a Man and His Ba, the Harper Song, the Babylonian Theodicy, the Emar text Ballad of the Heroes, and the Dialogue of Pessimism.[20] In addition, he considers the following three Egyptian works as expressing absurdities: Prophecies of Neferti, Instruction of Khakheperre-Sonb, and Admonitions of Ipuwer.[21] These are singled out because they represent rhetorical uses of the theme of absurdity.

---

[14] Ibid., 426.

[15] On the compatibility of divine determinism and human freedom with Qoheleth, see Mark Sneed, review of *Determinism in the Book of Ecclesiastes*, by Dominic Rudman, RBL 2002, https://www.bookreviews.org/pdf/1662_2745.pdf.

[16] Ibid.

[17] Ibid.

[18] Ibid., 427.

[19] For his additional support of the thesis, see *Qohelet and His Contradictions*, JSOTSup 71 (Sheffield: Almond, 1989); for his revisions, see *A Time to Tear Down and a Time to Build Up: A Rereading of Ecclesiastes* (Grand Rapids: Eerdmans, 1999), 138–44.

[20] Fox, *Time to Tear Down*, 11–14.

[21] Ibid., 32–33.

These parallels represent Fox's attempt to counter the claim that the notion of the absurd he sees in Qoheleth is anachronistic.

I. Critique of Fox's Thesis

Anachronism

The three Egyptian works that Fox cites as expressing the notion of the absurd (Nerferti, Khakheperre-Sonb, and Ipuwer) may, he admits, be *ex eventu* "prophecies." They seemingly bemoan the reign of a former king but actually place the contemporary ruler in a positive light by comparison.[22] In other words, these works function rhetorically to legitimate the reign of a particular king by contrasting a seemingly chaotic reign with a peaceful one. Yet Fox insists that they still express the notion of the absurd. Here is an example from Ipuwer as quoted by Fox:[23]

> Lo, citizens are put to the grindstones,
> Wearers of fine linen are beaten with [sticks].
> Those who never saw daylight go out unhindered.
> Those who were on their husband's beds,
> "Let them lie on boards," [one repeats]. (*AEL* 1:153)

Yet, rather than convey the absurd, these verses display what scholars refer to as the topsy-turvy motif.[24] Most Egyptologists, however, view Ipuwer and similar works composed after the First Intermediate period not as actual descriptions of earlier periods but as gross exaggeration for effect.[25] In fact, the First Intermediate was not actually chaotic but rather an era of decentralization during which there were regional rulers instead of a single, centralized power. One could describe it more as a democratic period, during which persons of formerly lower status experienced more freedom and self-determination.[26] Miriam Lichtheim points out that the Egyptian scribes who penned these anarchic portrayals were disturbed by this period because it appeared to challenge orthodox views of divine retribution.[27]

---

[22] Ibid.

[23] Ibid., 33.

[24] See S. Luria, "Die Ersten werden die Letzen sein (Zur 'sozialen Revolution' in Altertum)," *Klio* NS 4 (1929): 1–27; for a sophisticated discussion of the topsy-turvy motif in Proverbs, see Raymond C. Van Leeuwen, "Proverbs 30:21–23 and the Biblical World Upside Down," *JBL* 105 (1986): 1–27, https://doi.org/10.2307/3261208.

[25] Cf. Barry J. Kemp, "Old Kingdom, Middle Kingdom and Second Intermediate Period c. 2686–1552 BC," in *Ancient Egypt: A Social History*, by B. G. Trigger et al. (Cambridge: Cambridge University Press, 1983), 71–182, here 75–76, 115–16; William W. Hallo and William Kelly Simpson, *The Ancient Near East: A History* (New York: Harcourt Brace Jovanovich, 1971), 237.

[26] See Miriam Lichtheim, *AEL* 1:83.

[27] Ibid., 1:9.

Once this "upside-down" topos was created, it was used repeatedly, mainly for rhetorical purposes, not for solving or treating the problem of a lack of divine retribution. Egyptologists, however, do not view this motif as expressing the absurd.

Fox describes the Egyptian Dispute between a Man and His Ba as an example of the absurd, as "nihilistic toward this world."[28] The Ba (a spiritual entity analogous to the soul) tries to prevent the man from committing suicide because the man wanted to leave this oppressive world and enjoy the afterlife. The Ba reminds him that no one really knows what happens after death. The Ba suggests that it is best to enjoy life in the meantime (carpe-diem ethic). The man refuses, but the Ba, who had threatened to leave him, agrees to remain to prevent his suicide. This work reflects skepticism about the afterlife and the possible remedy of suicide but not the notion of the absurd.

Fox also enlists one of the Harper Songs as an example of the notion of the absurd. These songs, written in tombs, usually praise the afterlife and depict a harper playing as if accompanying the song. The song to King Intef, however, expresses skepticism about the afterlife and the efficacy of the mortuary cult:

> (Yet) those who build tombs,
> their places are gone,
> what has become of them?
> I have heard the words of Imhotep and Hardedef,
> whose sayings are recited whole.
> What of their places?
> their walls have crumbled,
> their places are gone,
> as though they had never been!
> . . . .
> Follow your heart as long as you live!
> Put myrrh on your head,
> dress in fine linen,
> anoint yourself with oils fit for a god.
> . . . .
> Make holiday,
> do not weary of it!
> Lo, none is allowed to take his goods with him,
> lo, none who departs comes back again![29]

The wording of the carpe-diem ethic is strikingly similar to Qoh 9:7–10, the most fully developed of Qoheleth's carpe-diem passages. (One could also compare this to the Siduri's [the barfly] advice to Gilgamesh, when he is about to make his quest for immortality.[30]) The harper questions the efficacy of famous sages building tombs and paying for mortuary service. He counsels enjoying the present rather

---

[28] Fox, *Time to Tear Down*, 12.
[29] *AEL* 1:196–97
[30] *ANET*, 90.

than counting on the afterlife. Again, it is hard to discern the sentiment of the absurd here—only skepticism.

In *A Time to Tear Down*, Fox also refers to several Mesopotamian texts that he believes connote the sense of the absurd. He includes the Babylonian Theodicy, which describes a dialogue between a sufferer and a friend.[31] The orthodox friend tries to convince the sufferer that if he practiced proper ritual, all would be well. The sufferer complains that he is not being listened to (cf. Job 6:14–30). Finally, the friend ends the dialogue when he admits that the gods made humans prone to error. The sufferer then prays that the god punishing him stop his attack. I do not find here any sense of the absurd, at least as represented by Camus. This work is often compared to the book of Job, but Job does not evidence the notion of the absurd.

Among these works, Fox argues that the closest parallel to Qoheleth's "absurdism" is the Babylonian Dialogue of Pessimism, in which a master and slave debate various proposed activities that reflect customary Babylonian values, for example, making an offering to a god, starting a family, and so on.[32] The slave sycophantically defends each proposal offered by his master, even though with each proposal its exact opposite is simultaneously proffered. The dialogue ends on a negative note when the master asks the servant, "What, then, is good?" To which the slave responds:

"To have my neck and your neck broken
And to be thrown into the river is good.
'Who is so tall as to ascend to the heavens?
Who is so broad as to encompass the underworld?'"
"No, slave, I will kill you and send you first."
"And my master would certainly not outlive me by even three days!"[33]

Fox describes this work as nihilistic in that it presents each activity and its opposite as both valid, thus, essentially nullifying both of them.

The interpretation of this passage is hotly disputed; some view it as satire and humor, others as a serious contemplation of suicide.[34] Though this piece is certainly melancholic, to suggest that it connotes the absurd is going too far. It represents the typical combination of skepticism (about societal values and discerning the will of the gods) and pessimism. This combination is also present in Qoheleth. The presence of this kind of dark and "unorthodox" material among the works in the school archives of the Mesopotamia and Syria, as well as in Egypt, demonstrates that scribes took great delight in such emotive and dark forms of literature.[35] Their

---

[31] Fox, *Time to Tear Down*, 13.
[32] Ibid., 13–14.
[33] W. G. Lambert, *BWL*, 149.
[34] See ibid., 139–41.
[35] For a comprehensive discussion of ancient Near Eastern scribes, their literature, and their social location, see Mark Sneed, *The Social World of the Sages: An Introduction to the Israelite and Jewish Wisdom Literature* (Minneapolis: Fortress, 2015), 1–215.

interest in such forms may reflect scribes' complex social location as retainers situated between the truly powerful/wealthy and the poor, who sometimes resented the former. Their interest also reflects their nature as saucy intellectuals who often enjoyed exploring subjects that were taboo. It may have also served to help them mature culturally, enabling them to function more successfully in their later scribal roles. Fox's attempt to categorize these works as expressing the notion of the absurd fails to take account of these nuances and the functional role of skepticism/pessimism in the training of scribes.

Karel van der Toorn has argued persuasively that ancient Near Eastern dialogues such as the Babylonian Theodicy, the Dispute between a Man and His Ba, and the Dialogue of Pessimism do not appear seriously to challenge the notion of divine retribution or justice. Rather, they serve to relativize this teaching and to emphasize the limitations of human cognition: one cannot comprehend the ways of the gods.[36] For van der Toorn, what is important is not the solution the dialogue might provide but the debate or discussion itself. The dialogue serves to create room for flexibility in the ideological system as a whole, which is beneficial in itself.

Another text that Fox cites as an example of the notion of the absurd is a Syrian text from Emar and, in a variant form, from Ugarit, which apparently is the Ballad of the Heroes, a text also found among Babylonian writings.[37] It reflects on the finality of death, looking back to the great heroes of the past, as does the Harper's Song. In it, the poet begins by listing the great heroes (Gilgamesh) and kings of the past, some of whom lived for thousands of years. Then the poet asks:

> Where are they—the great kings [Ugaritic Version 1] // Where are the great kings from past days up to now [Emar Version]?
> They are not (anymore) engendered, are not born.
> Life without light—how can it be better than death?
> Young man let me teach you truly about (the nature of) your god.
> Chase away grief *from* depression; have nothing to do with silence.
> In exchange for a single day of happiness let pass a time of silence of tens of thousands of days. [Ug. and Emar combined].[38]

Note the connection of brooding over the finality of death and the carpe-diem ethic. Yoram Cohen, an expert on Western Periphery literature of the Late Bronze Age, interprets the poem as teaching that even the great heroes of the past eventually died.[39] These heroes were chosen because they represented two related

---

[36] Karel van der Toorn, "The Ancient Near Eastern Literary Dialogue as a Vehicle of Critical Reflection," in *Dispute Poems and Dialogues in the Ancient and Mediaeval Near East: Forms and Types of Literary Debates in Semitic and Related Literatures*, ed. G. J. Reinink and H. L. J. Vanstiphout, OLA 42 (Leuven: Peeters, 1991), 59–75.

[37] Fox, *Rereading of Ecclesiastes*, 13.

[38] Yoram Cohen, *Wisdom from the Late Bronze Age*, WAW 29 (Atlanta: Society of Biblical Literature, 2013), 141.

[39] Ibid., 143.

issues: wisdom and mortality—and wisdom has its limits.⁴⁰ Cohen views the poem as expressing not the absurdity of life but rather its futility and consequently the necessity of adopting a carpe-diem perspective while life is available.⁴¹ Thus, the Ballad of the Heroes does not express the absurdity of life but rather instructs on the limits of wisdom and the illusion of immortality; humanity must resign itself to its status as mortal.

Similarly, the Sumerologist Bendt Alster categorizes the poem as a scribal "student song" that involves nostalgic humor.⁴² Looking back on the longevity of ancient rulers, the poem offers the following message: "Have you ever heard this before: things aren't what they used to be and they never were, so now, hurry up: find a way to rejoice before it's too late."⁴³ Alster points out that this and other Syro-Mesopotamian wisdom texts not only were used for scribal training but also "served to promulgate new and deeper insight into the conditions of human life."⁴⁴ Nowhere does Alster describe the poem as promulgating the absurdity of human existence.

Alster also presents a related work (which Fox does not mention) in his section on the theme of vanity in Sumerian literature, whose title he translates as "Nothing Is of Value." This work, like the preceding, connects the theme of vanity with a carpe-diem ethic. Here is one version of it:

> Nothing is of value, but life itself should be sweet-tasting.
> Whenever a man does not own some piece of property, that man owns some property.
> . . . .
> (Even) the tallest one cannot reach to the sky;
> (Even) the broadest one cannot go down to the Netherworld.
> (Even) the strongest one cannot [stretch himself] on Earth.
> The good life, let it be defiled in joy!
> Let the "race" be spent in joy!
> A man's good house is the house in which he has to live!⁴⁵

The reference near the beginning to the piece of property appears to be saying that poverty is in fact a type of riches.⁴⁶ The reference to the inability of humans to reach heaven or the underworld is similar to Job 11:8, Deut 30:12–13, and the slave's remark in the Dialogue of Pessimism. The reference in the last line to the "good house" may refer to being content with the home one already has.⁴⁷ Again, the point

---

⁴⁰ Ibid.
⁴¹ Ibid., 144.
⁴² Bendt Alster, *Wisdom of Ancient Sumer* (Bethesda, MD: CDL, 2005), 288–97.
⁴³ Ibid., 294–95.
⁴⁴ Ibid., 288.
⁴⁵ Ibid., 270–71.
⁴⁶ Ibid., 271.
⁴⁷ Ibid.

is obvious that this "pessimistic" poem is meant to express skepticism about the values that most Sumerians would have held and points to the limitations of human existence and the need to enjoy the present while it lasts. One version of the poem mentions the inevitability of death,[48] and some versions question the usefulness of ritual activities.[49]

These works demonstrate that the carpe-diem ethic in the ancient Near East is bound to the fact that human beings are not gods and must resign themselves to their divinely ordained fate of death. The best advice is to enjoy oneself before the inevitable comes. These texts often express skepticism about traditional values. This is not, however, the notion of the absurd but a coming to grips with the harsh reality of death and the attempt to make the most of life. The reality is that the modern notion of the absurd, as best expressed by Camus, is possible only in the disenchantment of the world brought on by the Renaissance and the Industrial Revolution. Only with the dissolution of the premodern religious and ethical moorings does humanity become exposed to the truly absurd character of the world.

These ancient Near Eastern works fail to demonstrate a clear notion of the absurd, and neither does Qoheleth, at least in terms of modern existentialism and especially Camus. Robert Gordis, years before Fox, demonstrated that, while there is an affinity between Camus and Qoheleth, Qoheleth never goes as far as Camus in proclaiming the world to be absurd.[50] Qoheleth may not fully discern the meaning of life and may view the world as largely irrational, but this does not equate with seeing the world as meaningless or absurd. Martin Shuster has shown that Qoheleth is no proto-existentialist.[51] Similarly, historian Matthew Schwartz has also contrasted Camus and Qoheleth and, while certainly finding an affinity between them, sees striking differences. Whereas in Camus's *Myth of Sisyphus* the tragic hero must accept the world as absurd, "Koheleth's world is neither meaningless nor absurd, and man may work, learn and be happy."[52] Although Qoheleth may find God oppressive, to a degree, that does not mean that life has no meaning for him. Karl Haden suggests:

> For Qoheleth, meaning may be elusive and cause the feeling of *hebel*, but nevertheless, meaning exists because God exists.... There is a higher level of meaning,

---

[48] Ibid., 273.

[49] Ibid., 276.

[50] Robert Gordis, *Koheleth, the Man and His World: A Study of Ecclesiastes*, 3rd augmented ed. (New York: Schocken, 1968), 112–21; cf. Tilmann Zimmer, *Zwischen Tod und Lebensglück: Eine Untersuchung zur Anthropologie Kohelets*, BZAW 286 (Berlin: de Gruyter, 1999), 27 n. 26, 32 n. 61.

[51] Martin Shuster, "Being as Breath, Vapor as Joy: Using Martin Heidegger to Re-read the Book of Ecclesiastes," *JSOT* 33 (2008): 219–44, here 219, 232; cf. Kenneth W. James, "Ecclesiastes: Precursor of Existentialists," *TBT* 22 (1984): 85–90.

[52] Matthew J. Schwartz, "Koheleth and Camus: Two Views of Achievement," *Judaism* 35 (1986): 29–34, here 30–31.

that is, there is a level of meaning known only to God. When God serves as the reference point—or hub of existence for the individual—one finds equanimity in the belief that although he does not have the answers, God does.[53]

That Qoheleth believed in an absolute being,[54] even if he was frustrated by aspects of that being's behavior, means that Qoheleth could never be an absurdist, and this is what fundamentally separates him from Camus. Modern existential philosophy is not the best background for interpreting Qoheleth's message.

II. Lexical-Semantic Fallacies

Perhaps the strongest argument against Fox's thesis is that it is faulty on lexical-semantic grounds. Fox is essentially arguing for a meaning for the word הבל that is not found elsewhere in the Hebrew Bible. While this in itself does not exclude the possibility of a unique meaning in Qoheleth, the burden of proof falls on Fox to demonstrate this. But Fox only asserts that "Qoheleth's usage cannot be simply and directly derived from the lexical meanings it has elsewhere."[55] Stuart Weeks's critique is telling and significant:

> It faces the substantial objection, however, that *hebel* does not have this meaning elsewhere, and it is difficult to see either how "breath" could have come to mean "absurd," or how the original readers were supposed to deduce this meaning. To put it another way, if *hebel* were a completely unknown word, then Fox would have supplied an excellent understanding from its use in the context of Ecclesiastes, but it is not, and his definition jars with the meanings and connotations established from numerous other contexts.[56]

In other words, while what Fox says about determining a word's sense directly from the other meanings is true in itself, the opposite does not hold true: that a word's meaning can be determined by its context alone! The word must have some connection in meaning with its other usages outside the book. Fox has failed to show how "absurd" can be connected at all with either the concrete meaning of "vapor" or "wind" or with the word's metaphorical senses, such as "transient," "futile," "vain," or "insubstantial." Instead, Fox simply describes what he perceives Qoheleth to be doing with the situations he describes as הבל. This is not sound from a lexical-semantic perspective.

---

[53] N. Karl Haden, "Qoheleth and the Problem of Alienation," *CScR* 17 (1987): 52–66, here 66 n. 59.

[54] Thanks goes to Thomas Bolin of St. Norbert College for this wording here (private communication).

[55] Fox, "Meaning of *Hebel*," 412.

[56] Stuart Weeks, *An Introduction to the Study of Wisdom Literature*, T&T Clark Approaches to Biblical Studies (London: T&T Clark, 2010), 81.

What is interesting is that Fox violates his own tenet when he tries to infer that the connection between הבל and what he calls a "nearly synonymous" term, *evil* (as in 6:1–2) (רעה and רע), should determine its meaning.[57] First of all, רעה is not a true synonym of הבל; it is rather a contiguous term. The two terms together complement each other. The terms "evil" or "evil sickness," when used in conjunction with הבל, characterize the injustice of the situation. Fox is correct that Qoheleth expresses frustration with the situations described as הבל because of their injustice, but that in itself does not dictate that הבל means "absurd." Again, Qoheleth sees the world as irrational and unjust, but that in itself would not justify translating הבל as "absurd."

More closely synonymous with הבל is the phrase that Qoheleth often pairs with it: "and a chasing after the wind" or "a pursuit of wind" (ורעות רוח, 1:14; 2:11, 17, 26; 4:4; 6:9; cf. 4:6). This phrase by itself clearly denotes the sense of futility, which is one of the meanings of הבל in the Hebrew Bible. Strangely, Fox tries to argue that this phrase too means the absurd, translating it idiosyncratically as "senseless," rather than letting this phrase shed light on the particular nuance of הבל.[58] It demonstrates that Fox has started with a preconception and then tried to fit the evidence to it.

Another problem is the fallacious character of Fox's argument that all the other possible senses for הבל will not work. Fox argues that one cannot use "futility" for the situation of 8:14 because the efforts of the wicked are not futile in that they are rewarded.[59] There are two things wrong here. First, Fox is equivocating in that he moves from the situation as a whole to part of the situation: what happens to the wicked. Second, if we use Fox's reasoning and if we focus on the wicked alone, one could also argue that the situation is not properly absurd because the wicked expect their actions to result in beneficial outcomes; otherwise they would not choose to be wicked. It depends, therefore, on one's perspective whether a situation is either absurd or futile, worthless, or delusory. It is unlikely that Qoheleth's implied audience would be tempted to become wicked. Rather, he is demonstrating to them that piety does not always pan out: "Don't put all your eggs in the one basket of piety." Any wicked person reading this text would simply disagree with it. Thus, "futile," "worthless," and "delusory" are just as suitable for describing this situation as "absurd" would be. To the righteous, 8:14 is a "futile" or "worthless" or "delusive" situation. It does not work to their benefit as righteous people.

A final lexical-semantic difficulty with Fox's proposal is that he has taken a word that operates within the realm of axiology and transposed it to that of epistemology, an inappropriate move. In other words, הבל is not meant to answer the question of what or how we can know or not know but rather the question of what is of value or not. Jaco Gericke points out that the abundance of the use of the word

---

[57] Fox, "Meaning of *Hebel*," 410.
[58] Fox, *Time to Tear Down*, 175.
[59] Fox, "Meaning of *Hebel*," 412–13.

טוב ("good"; 51x) and its opposite רעה ("bad"; 30x) in a book of 222 verses is an indication that Qoheleth is primarily interested in axiology and not epistemology.[60] Similarly, Norbert Lohfink has argued that, although Qoheleth is skeptical of human epistemological capacity, he never uses הבל to express this.[61] Lohfink concludes, "When Qohelet speaks of הבל, then he speaks of actions, things, situations, results. He speaks of the objective world, not of the subject and his epistemological possibilities."[62]

Fox's "absurd" thesis is, thus, suspect for the following reasons: it constitutes a new usage for הבל not found in the rest of the Hebrew Bible and is, thus, lexically semantically fallacious; it is anachronistic both for Qoheleth and for the ancient Near East; it downplays the carpe-diem ethic and, thus, Qoheleth's primarily ethical intent (though Fox attempts to balance this out in his later work).

III. הבל AS "WORTHLESS" IN QOHELETH

What Is Worthless?

In my opinion, the best lexical-semantic analysis of הבל in Qoheleth is still that of Klaus Seybold. He finds that the term has the sense of null, worthless, vain, and futile.[63] None of these translation possibilities is unique to him.[64] What is

---

[60] Jaco W. Gericke, "Axiological Assumptions in Qohelet: A Historical-Philosophical Clarification," *VeEc* 33 (2012): 1–6, here 1, http://dx.doi.org/10.4102/ve.v33i1.515.

[61] Norbert Lohfink, "Ist Kohelets הבל-Aussage erkenntnistheoretisch gemeint?," in *Qohelet in the Context of Wisdom*, ed. Anton Schoors, BETL 136 (Leuven: Leuven University Press, 1998), 41–59.

[62] Ibid, 59 (my translation).

[63] Klaus Seybold, "הֶבֶל *hebhel*," *TDOT* 3:318–20, here 319.

[64] A variety of translations have been proffered by various scholars: "incomprehensible," "beyond mortal grasp," "senseless," "arbitrary," or "unpredictable" (Seow, "Beyond Mortal Grasp," 1–16; Seow, *Ecclesiastes: A New Translation with Introduction and Commentary*, AB 18C [New York: Doubleday, 1997], 102); "senseless" (Martin A. Shields, *The End of Wisdom: A Reappraisal of the Historical and Canonical Function of Ecclesiastes* [Winona Lake, IN: Eisenbrauns, 2006], 121); "enigmatic/mysterious" (Graham Ogden, *Qoheleth*, Readings [Sheffield: JSOT Press, 1987], 22; Ogden, "'Vanity' It Certainly Is Not," *BT* 38 [1987]: 301–7; Craig G. Bartholomew, *Ecclesiastes*, BCOTWP [Grand Rapids: Baker Academic, 2009], 104); "empty," "nothing," "useless," "senseless," and "bad" (Rainer Albertz, "הֶבֶל *hebel* breath," *TLOT* 1:352); "incongruence" or "ironic" (Edwin M. Good, *Irony in the Old Testament* [Philadelphia: Westminster, 1965], 182; Timothy Polk, "The Wisdom of Irony: A Study of *Hebel* and Its Relation to Joy and the Fear of God in Ecclesiastes," *SBTh* 6 [1976]: 3–17, here 7–9); "inconstant" (R. Christopher Heard, "The Dao of Qoheleth: An Intertextual Reading of the *Daode Jing* and the Book of Ecclesiastes," *Jian Dao* 5 [1996]: 65–93, here 89); "contingency" (Shuster, "Being as Breath," 229; John E. McKenna, "The Concept of Hebel in the Book of Ecclesiastes," *SJT* 45 [1992]: 19–28, here 28); "transient," "insubstantial," and "foul" (Douglas B. Miller, *Symbol and Rhetoric in Ecclesiastes: The Place of Hebel in Qohelet's Work*, AcBib 2 [Atlanta: Society of Biblical Literature, 2002], 61; cf. Miller, "Qohelet's Symbolic Use of הבל,"

unique is his contextualization of Qoheleth's use of the term. He notes the importance of the following words and phrases: רעות רוח or רעיון רוח, "chasing after the wind" or "feeding on the wind" (1:14, 17), which point to its meaning as "vanity."[65] He also points out that יתרון ("profit, advantage, gain"), which is used in antithesis to הבל, is significant for understanding it. It means "'that which counts or matters,' 'that which results or issues from all our work.' It forces upon *hebhel* the special sense of 'that which does not count or matter,' 'null,' 'vain,' 'that which yields no results.'"[66]

Further, the parallel words צל ("shadow," 6:12) and רוח ("wind," 5:15), as well as חלי ("affliction," 6:2) and רעה ("evil," 5:12) further clarify the meaning of הבל. Antithetical terms include חלק ("portion/lot," 2:10), טוב ("good," 2:3), and יתר ("profit, advantage," 6:11). Seybold concludes:

> The dominant use of *hebhel* in a nominal statement shows that for Qoheleth too the word serves the purpose of evaluation, or, more accurately, devaluation, with a critico-polemic intention. The total equalization of all earthly, human activity in 1:14 runs contrary to a sapiential value system; such a radical disqualification is directed against the norm of *yithron* thinking which underlies this system.[67]

Qoheleth's polemic against traditional wisdom has been widely recognized. Seybold's connection of this polemic with הבל is a significant contribution.

Specific items that are devalued include striving after wisdom (1:17, 2:15), laughter and pleasure (2:2), the life work of the wise (2:19, 21, 23, 26), energy expended by the skillful (4:4), wealth (4:8, 5:9), the career of the wise (4:16), zeal (6:9), the wise (7:7), decisions of the mighty (8:10), and confidence in the law of

---

JBL 117 [1998]: 437–54, https://doi.org/10.2307/3266441); "Abel-ness" (Russell L. Meek, "The Meaning of הבל in Qohelet: An Intertextual Suggestion," in *The Words of the Wise Are Like Goads: Engaging Qohelet in the 21st Century*, ed. Mark J. Boda, Tremper Longman III, and Cristian G. Rata [Winona Lake, IN: Eisenbrauns, 2013], 241–56); "Nichtigkeit" (Lauha, *Kohelet*, 19); "nothing" (John Jarick, "The Hebrew Book of Changes: Reflections on *Hakkōl Hebel* and *Lakkōl Zᵉmān* in Ecclesiastes," *JSOT* 90 [2000]: 79–99, here 79–83); "shit" (Frank Crüsemann, "The Unchangeable World: The 'Crisis' of Wisdom' in Koheleth," in *God of the Lowly: Socio-historical Interpretations of the Bible*, ed. Willy Schottroff and Wolfgang Stegemann, trans. Matthew J. O'Connell [Maryknoll, NY: Orbis, 1984], 57–77, here 57); "temporary" (Daniel C. Fredericks, *Coping with Transience: Ecclesiastes on the Brevity of Life*, BibSem 18 [Sheffield: JSOT Press, 1993]); "illusory or deceptive" (Weeks, *Study of Wisdom Literature*, 81); *déception* or the notion of disappointing or dissatisfying (Étienne Glasser, *Le procès du bonheur par Qohelet*, LD 61 [Paris: Cerf, 1970], 20; cf. François Rousseau ["Structure de Qohélet I 4–11 et plan du livre," *VT* 31 (1981): 200–217, here 208], who adopts Glasser's delineation.

[65] Seybold, *TDOT* 3:319; this is similar to the proverb about sowing the wind and reaping the whirlwind, which indicates the results of wickedness (Hos 8:7; cf. Job 4:8, Ps 126:5–6, Prov 11:29, 22:8).

[66] Ibid., citing Kurt Galling, "Der Prediger," in *Die Fünf Megilloth*, ed. Ernst Würthwein, Kurt Galling, and Otto Plöger, 2nd ed., HAT 1/18 (Tübingen: Mohr Siebeck, 1969), 73–125, here 79; cf. "Nichtigkeit" (Lauha, *Kohelet*, 18).

[67] Seybold, *TDOT* 3:319.

just retribution (8:14). All of these, Seybold notes, are particular ways and goals of life that wisdom holds in high esteem. "Thus, הבל serves as 'destructive judgment,'[68] a devaluation of the system of norms established by traditional wisdom, a polemic against its sensible value regulations, a defamation of the wisdom ideal of life. It proves to be an effective catchword in that it extends those values into the grotesque."[69] Finally, Seybold resists any translations such as "incomprehensible" or "unintelligible," which are based on the cult mysteries.[70]

Three aspects of Seybold's analysis of Qoheleth's use of הבל bear repeating. First, הבל is a judgmental term, used to evaluate various human aspirations. Second, it is a polemical term aimed specifically at critiquing traditional wisdom. Third, it never means "incomprehensible" or "unintelligible," the domain of cognition or rationality.

In contrast to Seybold, what Fox has essentially attempted is a redirection of the aim of Qoheleth's polemical use of הבל from traditional wisdom toward God! Qoheleth's concern, however, is not primarily about God but about human aspirations and labor, especially wisdom. This correlates with Stephan de Jong's thesis that Qoheleth's main message is *human limitation*.[71] All of Qoheleth's argumentation and advice are geared toward advancing that message. His concern is primarily anthropology, not theology.[72] A theology of Qoheleth can be derived only artificially through his inferences and indirect statements. Thus, Qoheleth is not using הבל to proclaim God's world absurd but rather as his favorite tool to punch holes in the suppositions of traditional wisdom. As an axiological concept for Qoheleth הבל expresses the worthlessness of many of traditional wisdom's tenets and reveals them to be shams.

What Is Worthwhile?

Qoheleth's assessment of the goals of traditional wisdom as "futile" or "worthless" points to what he finds "worthwhile," or what I would call his alternative ethical system. The carpe-diem ethic is not some minor theme in Qoheleth but, in addition to God-fearing (3:14, 5:6, 7:18, 8:12–13), is the main ethical counsel of the book, occurring seven times—the Hebrew magical number (2:24; 3:12–13, 22; 5:18–20; 8:15; 9:7–10; 11:7–10). While pleasure has its liabilities (it does not

---

[68] Ibid., 320, citing R. Albertz, *THAT* 1:467–69, s.v. הבל.

[69] Seybold, *TDOT* 3:320. Though הבל does have a negative connotation, translating it as "bad" (Albertz, *TLOT* 1:352) or "foul" (Miller, *Symbol and Rhetoric*, 95–97) is not justified; see D. M. Clemens, review of *Symbol and Rhetoric in Ecclesiastes: The Place of Hebel in Qohelet's Work*, by Douglas B. Miller, *JNES* 66 (2007): 216–21, here 220.

[70] Seybold, *TDOT* 3:318.

[71] Stephan de Jong, "God in the Book of Qohelet: A Reappraisal of Qohelet's Place in Old Testament Theology," *VT* 47 (1997): 154–67, here 166; cf. de Jong, "A Book on Labour: The Structuring Principles and the Main Theme of the Book of Qohelet," *JSOT* 54 (1992): 107–16.

[72] See de Jong, "God in the Book," 161–64.

accomplish anything [2:2] and it does not endure⁷³), Qoheleth advises a eudaemonistic ethic that preaches finding happiness in the simple and limited pleasures of life, pleasures that do not endure for long but are the best that one can hope for, pleasures that come from one's regular toil.⁷⁴ R. N. Whybray's famous characterization of Qoheleth as a "Preacher of Joy" is too optimistic, but one could legitimately speak of Qoheleth as a "Preacher of Limited Joy"!⁷⁵ This ethic is his primary advice that he hopes his readers will adopt, if God enables them. Life "under the sun" as הבל is then the foundation for this ethic. In a world where traditional wisdom offers little help, it makes sense to live for the moment and seize the day. For the majority of usages, הבל as "worthlessness/worthless" fits Qoheleth's larger strategy of lowering the expectations of his readers so that they can better adapt to the difficult circumstances in which they find themselves during the Ptolemaic period (the consensus for the book's date).⁷⁶ This coheres with ancient Near Eastern literature that combines pessimism/skepticism about traditional beliefs with the carpe-diem ethic. These ancient Near Eastern works, then, are primarily about ethics, not about making observations about the irrationality of the world.

IV. Conclusion

Fox's attempt to provide a more modern and relevant translation of the majority of occurrences of הבל in Qoheleth by translating them as "absurd" misses the mark in a number of respects. First, it is anachronistic. None of the ancient Near Eastern examples he enlists as parallels to the supposed absurdism in Qoheleth is convincing. Second, from a lexical-semantic perspective, Fox's argument is faulty for not relying on the broader semantic range of the use of הבל in the Hebrew Bible, which never carries the sense of "absurd." Third, Fox's proposal illegitimately downplays the carpe-diem ethic in the book; he therefore misses the role that הבל plays in foregrounding this ethic. Fourth, Fox's proposal mistakenly places the term הבל within the domain of rationality, cognition, or epistemology instead of in its rightful place within the sphere of axiology or values. A better translation would be "worthlessness" or "worthless" and other related terms ("futility," "vanity," and "null") that function polemically in critiquing traditional wisdom and ultimately point to an alternative ethic and the ultimate message of the book: seize the day!

---

[73] Glasser, *Le procès du bonheur*, 52.

[74] See ibid., 52–53; and Marie Maussion, "Qohélet VI 1–2: 'Dieu ne permet pas …,'" *VT* 55 (2005): 501–10.

[75] R. N. Whybray, "Qoheleth, Preacher of Joy," *JSOT* 23 (1982): 87–98.

[76] See Mark Sneed, *The Politics of Pessimism in Ecclesiastes: A Social-Science Perspective*, AIL 12 (Atlanta: Society of Biblical Literature, 2012), 30 n. 68, 125–54, 177–253.

JBL 136, no. 4 (2017): 895–904
doi: http://dx.doi.org/10.15699/jbl.1364.2017.198627

Naqia and Nineveh in Nahum: Ambiguity and the Prostitute Queen

GREGORY D. COOK
greg@bookofjonah.net
Huntington, West Virginia

Throughout the book of Nahum, the prophet taunts an unnamed female adversary. Clues in the text identify this woman as personified Nineveh, but ambiguity allows for multiple interpretations. In this article, I propose that the description of the woman in Nah 3:4 matches Queen Naqia. Biblical scholarship has not yet considered this link, probably because of her age when Nahum wrote. Nahum 3:4, however, mirrors a biblical depiction of Jezebel. When the verse is reconsidered in light of Jezebel, Naqia becomes a strong candidate for Nahum's female enemy.

Despite the relentlessness with which Nahum prophesies the demise of a female adversary, biblical scholars have not paid much attention to "the feminine element in Nahum" until recently.[1] The first "feminist discussion focused on Nahum" did not appear in scholarly literature until twenty-five years ago.[2] Although others have since addressed this theme,[3] much remains to be done. In this article,

I would like to thank the anonymous reviewers, as well as the *JBL* editors, for their work and the helpful feedback they provided.

[1] Laurel Lanner, *"Who Will Lament Her?" The Feminine and Fantastic in the Book of Nahum*, LHBOTS 434 (New York: T&T Clark, 2006), 1.

[2] Julia M. O'Brien, *Nahum*, 2nd ed., Readings (London: Sheffield Academic, 2009), 81. The article O'Brien so labels is Judith E. Sanderson, "Nahum," in *The Women's Bible Commentary*, ed. Carol A. Newsom and Sharon H. Ringe (Louisville: Westminster John Knox, 1992), 217–21.

[3] Lanner's monograph and O'Brien's commentary both offer feminist readings of Nahum. References to Nahum increasingly appear in Old Testament feminist scholarship: see, e.g., F. Rachel Magdalene, "Ancient Near Eastern Treaty-Curses and the Ultimate Texts of Terror: A Study of the Language of Divine Sexual Abuse in the Prophetic Corpus," in *A Feminist Companion to the Latter Prophets*, ed. Athalya Brenner, FCB 8 (Sheffield: Sheffield Academic, 1995), 326–52, here 333; Elke Seifert, *Tochter und Vater im Alten Testament: Eine ideologiekritische Untersuchung zur Verfügungsgewalt von Vätern über ihre Töchter*, NThDH 9 (Neukirchen-Vluyn: Neukirchener Verlag, 1997), 308; Cynthia R. Chapman, *The Gendered Language of Warfare in the Israelite-Assyrian Encounter*, HSM 62 (Winona Lake, IN: Eisenbrauns, 2004), 108.

895

I will explore one question that has not yet entered into the discussion—the likelihood that Nahum patterned his description of the Assyrian prostitute (3:4) after Queen Naqia.

Naqia was the "wife of Sennacherib, king of the world, king of Assyria, daughter-in-law of Sargon (II), king of the world, king of Assyria, mother of Esarhaddon, king of the world (and) king of Assyria."[4] She supervised the transfer of power to Assurbanipal, her grandson, after Esarhaddon died. She stands apart in an empire that rarely mentioned its queens, and ample archaeological information attests to Naqia's importance. For example, in Assyrian artworks, "there are depictions of only two of the Assyrian royal consorts: Naqia/Zakutu and Libbali-šarrat. The scarcity of the appearance of royal women in Neo-Assyrian art stands in sharp contrast to the numerous, elaborate and detailed portrayals of almost all the Assyrian male rulers, and in itself is a significant fact."[5] Records demonstrate that she had "exceptional abilities. That these abilities were recognized throughout the Assyrian empire can also be verified."[6] It is hypothesized here that the Assyrian yoke was heavy enough in Nahum's day—and Naqia's influence so well known—that at least some of Nahum's original audience would have recognized Naqia's likeness in the prophet's words.[7]

I. Nahum's Ambiguous Female

Nahum's judgment against an unnamed female foe pours forth throughout the vision. Nahum almost always refers to her by pronouns. The first instance

---

[4] See Erle Leichty, *The Royal Inscriptions of Esarhaddon, King of Assyria (680–669 BC)*, RINAP 4 (Winona Lake, IN: Eisenbrauns, 2011), 179. The possibility that Naqia is the mysterious female enemy adds a double meaning to the charge "From you [fem. sg.] has one gone forth [יצא] devising evil against YHWH" (Nah 1:11). The verb יצא would then acquire the connation of Naqia giving birth to Esarhaddon. Assurbanipal likewise, but not as literally, "went forth" from Naqia. The verb is used with a similar connotation in Gen 17:6: "And I will make you extremely fruitful, and I will make nations from you, and kings will come out [יצאו] from you." Other examples include Gen 10:14 and 1 Chr 1:12. Unless otherwise noted, all translations are mine.

[5] Tally Ornan, "The Queen in Public: Royal Women in Neo-Assyrian Art," in *Sex and Gender in the Ancient Near East: Proceedings of the 47th Recontre Assyriologique Internationale, Helsinki, July 2–6, 2001*, ed. Simo Parpola and Robert M. Whiting, 2 vols. (Helsinki: Neo-Assyrian Text Corpus Project, 2002), 2:463–64.

[6] Sherry Lou Macgregor, "Women in the Neo-Assyrian World: Visual and Textual Evidence from Palace and Temple" (PhD diss., University of California, Berkeley, 2003), 167.

[7] Scholars generally agree that Nahum knew Assyrian ideology. See Klaas Spronk, *Nahum*, HCOT (Kampen: Kok Pharos, 1997), 6; Adam S. van der Woude, *Jona, Nahum*, POuT (Nijerk: Callenbach, 1978), 71–72. Peter Machinist argues convincingly that Isaiah's audience would have been familiar with Assyrian propaganda ("Assyria and Its Image in the First Isaiah," *JAOS* 103 [1983]: 719–37).

comes in 1:8, where the prophet foretold, "And with an overwhelming flood, he [YHWH] will make a complete end of her place [מקומה]."⁸ Many commentators find this reference to "her" so confusing that they ignore it.⁹ This anonymity continues throughout the book, however, occurring in 1:11; 2:2 [Eng. 2:1], 8 [7], 14 [13]; 3:5, 6, 7, 8, 11, 12, 13, 14, 15, 16, and 18.¹⁰ In each of these verses, the prophecy addresses a single feminine adversary as "you."

A few clues to this woman's identity do present themselves. First, Nah 1:1 proclaims the book an "oracle against Nineveh." Since the OT frequently speaks of cities as women, personified Nineveh becomes a likely candidate. Second, Nah 2:9 [2:8] directly links the city of Nineveh to the second-person feminine pronoun: ונינוה כברכת־מים מימי היא ("And Nineveh was as a pool of water. She is of old"). Third, Nah 3:4 identifies this woman as a witch and a prostitute. Fourth, Nah 3:7 links the city of Nineveh to a singular feminine pronoun. Fifth, Nahum personifies Thebes as a woman (3:8–10) when comparing it to Nahum's feminine adversary.

Because Nah 1:1, 2:9, and 3:7–10 point to Nineveh as YHWH's female adversary, most scholars take that position. Some scholars, however, believe that the

---

⁸ It is possible that this verse uses wordplay on an Assyrian city to further implicate Naqia. The Hebrew word כלה occurs in Nah 1:8, 9, where it means "complete end." It may contain a double meaning, though, as a homonym for the Assyrian city Calah (modern Nimrud). Naqia participated in cultic ceremonies in the three major cities of Assyria: Assur, Calah, and Nineveh (Sarah Melville, *The Role of Naqia/Zakutu in Sargonid Politics*, SAA 9 [Helsinki: Neo-Assyrian Text Corpus Project, 1999], 13). A homonym for the city Assur also appears in Nahum. The Hebrew word for "Assyria" (אשור, 3:18) is the same as the name of the city of Assur. Therefore, the names of the three most important cities in Assyria may appear in the book of Nahum, though this has not yet been mentioned in scholarly literature. Interestingly, the homonym for an Assyrian city mentioned in Gen 10:11, Rehoboth-Ir, also appears in Nah 2:4 [Eng. 2:5]. There the word ברחבות means "in the city squares." Rehoboth-Ir remains unknown, however. The correspondence between Nahum and the four names in Gen 10:11—אשור, נינוה, רחבת, and כלח—in the book of Nahum has likewise gone without comment, and whether these find their way into Nahum by coincidence or intention remains to be explored.

⁹ This word is one of many places in Nahum where the difficulty of the text has resulted in numerous proposed emendations. As in this case, variants often go back to early versions, including the LXX. See Duane L. Christensen, *Nahum: A New Translation with Introduction and Commentary*, AYB 24F (New Haven: Yale University Press, 2009), 198–200. I take the position that the variants in 1:8 arose in order to make sense of "her place" as the pronoun lacks an antecedent and seems out of context. It is argued here that Nahum intended "her," and the many other pronouns that lack an antecedent, to remain ambiguous.

¹⁰ Adele Reinhartz points out that "the details of and gaps within the text, such as role designations and the absence of the name, are meaningful" (*Why Ask My Name? Anonymity and Identity in Biblical Narrative* [New York: Oxford University Press, 1998], 14). Reinhartz clarified that biblical texts use anonymity in a variety of ways. Lanner elucidates how the concept of anonymity functions in Nahum: "I support [Alfred] Haldar's suggestion that the anonymity of the enemy allows the political enemy to be equated with the cultic one. This very anonymity also allows multiple events to be read. Like [Carl] Keller, I consider the vagueness of much of the text as indicating a supernatural event" (Lanner, *"Who Will Lament?,"* 26).

mysterious references allude to Ishtar, the patron goddess of Nineveh. The most thorough exposition of this view comes in Laurel Lanner's monograph, which endeavors "to show that it is possible that a feminine deity is present in the text of Nahum."[11] Lanner claims that the "obvious choice would be the goddess of the Assyrians and their capital Nineveh, Ishtar."[12] Other scholars who argue for Ishtar imagery in Nahum include Judith Sanderson, Aron Pinker, J. H. Eaton, and John D. W. Watts.[13] Notably, Julia O'Brien disagrees: "Although Sanderson ... identifies 'she' as Ishtar, the city goddess of Nineveh, a more logical identification is Nineveh itself, addressed with a feminine pronoun in 2.2 and soon to be named explicitly as Nineveh in 2.9."[14]

Biblical scholars have not yet examined a third possibility—that Nahum based this female adversary on the life of an Assyrian queen. Even Lanner concludes, "The identification of this 'female adversary' is difficult. There is no known historical human figure who would seem a likely candidate. No Assyrian or Israelite woman would appear to have been a particular threat in the mid-seventh century."[15] I do not dispute that Nahum intended judgment against the city of Nineveh and Ishtar. Instead, I suggest that the prophet intended multiple interpretations—a reasonable hypothesis since such ambiguity is one mark of Hebrew poetry.[16] According to the standard text on literary ambiguity, "'Ambiguity' itself can mean an indecision as to what you mean, an intention to mean several things, a probability that one or other or both of two things has been meant, and the fact that a statement has several meanings."[17] Such multivalent meaning could certainly exist in a "perfect poem,"

---

[11] Lanner, *"Who Will Lament?,"* 2. Lanner explores the relationship between Ishtar and Nahum in many places, but especially in 37–43.

[12] Ibid., 87.

[13] Sanderson, "Nahum," 218; Aron Pinker, "Descent of the Goddess Ishtar to the Netherworld and Nahum II 8," *VT* 55 (2005): 89–100, here 95–100; John D. W. Watts, *The Books of Joel, Obadiah, Jonah, Nahum, Habakkuk, and Zephaniah*, CBC (Cambridge: Cambridge University Press, 1975), 105; J. H. Eaton, *Obadiah, Nahum, Habakkuk and Zephaniah: Introduction and Commentary*, TBC (London: SCM, 1961), 67–68).

[14] O'Brien, *Nahum*, 53.

[15] Lanner, *"Who Will Lament?,"* 86–87.

[16] S. E. Gillingham, *The Poems and Psalms of the Hebrew Bible*, OBS (Oxford: Oxford University Press, 1994), 21–23.

[17] William Empson, *Seven Types of Ambiguity* (London: Chatto & Windus, 1930; repr., New York: New Directions, 1966), 11. This book changed the way literary critics viewed ambiguity. Before Empson, critics tended to interpret ambiguity as a defect, but Empson demonstrated that it often marked literary skill. Although Empson wrote about ambiguity in English literature, his book notes the pervasiveness of ambiguity in Hebrew poetry and the effect Hebrew had on the development of ambiguity in English poetry: "The study of Hebrew, by the way, and the existence of English Bibles with alternatives in the margin, may have had influence on the capacity of English for ambiguity; Donne, Herbert, Jonson, and Crashaw, for instance, were Hebrew scholars, and the flowering of poetry at the end of the sixteenth century corresponded with the first thorough permeation of the English language by the translated texts" (193–94). The profusion of

as Robert Lowth termed Nahum; a poet capable of writing such a poem had the ability to craft words in this manner.[18] While Queen Naqia would not have been the primary target of Nahum's prophecy, the original audience might have recognized her likeness.

II. Naqia and Jezebel

The description in Nah 3:4 portrays Nineveh's queen as a type of Jezebel.[19] Readers imagining a youthful, gorgeous seductress will not find Naqia a compelling candidate. By changing this perception, however, and recognizing a link with Jezebel, Naqia becomes a remarkable match.

The primary basis for suggesting this connection comes from an intertextual link between Nah 3:4 and 2 Kgs 9:22. In 2 Kgs 9:22, Jehu retorted to Joram, מה השלום עד־זנוני איזבל אמך וכשפיה הרבים ("What peace as long as the fornications of your mother Jezebel and her great sorceries abound?"). Similar vocabulary appears in Nah 3:4: מרב זנוני זונה טובת חן בעלת כשפים המכרת גוים בזנוניה ומשפחות בכשפיה ("Because of the abundant fornications of the prostitute, gracefully alluring, mistress of sorceries. She sells nations by her fornications and clans by her sorceries"). The conspicuous occurrence of זנונים, כשף, and רב in both passages has been noticed before, but with little comment. Both O'Brien and Sanderson briefly mention it: "Just as Jehu expressed his contempt by accusing her of promiscuity and sorceries (2 Kings 9:22), so Nahum applied the same two words to Nineveh";[20] "As in 2 Kgs 9.22 and Isa. 57.3, the charge of zônâ is paired with witchcraft."[21] These similarities suggest that Nahum may have shaped his female enemy in the image of Jezebel.

Linking Nahum's foe with Jezebel simplifies the identification of a historical queen. The careers of Naqia and Jezebel correspond in four ways. First, Jezebel and Naqia stand out as women who exercised power in male-dominated monarchies.[22]

---

ambiguous pronouns—masculine and feminine—in Nahum is cited by some as evidence of redaction; see, e.g., Heinz-Josef Fabry, *Nahum*, HThKAT (Freiburg im Breisgau: Herder, 2006), 32. I contend the opposite. Following Empson, I believe that ambiguity is a complex literary device indicative of a brilliant mind.

[18] Robert Lowth, *Lectures on the Sacred Poetry of the Hebrews*, trans. G. Gregory (Boston: Crocker & Brewer, 1829), 180. Commentators, regardless of whether they love or loathe Nahum, acknowledge the poetic talent of the author.

[19] It is widely recognized that, besides being a historical person, Jezebel became a literary type for biblical authors. For instance, Jezebel is the first biblical character to receive a section in Athalya Brenner-Idan, *The Israelite Woman: Social Role and Literary Type in Biblical Narrative*, 2nd ed. (London: Bloomsbury T&T Clark, 2015), 21–28.

[20] Sanderson, "Nahum," 219.

[21] O'Brien, *Nahum*, 62.

[22] According to Brenner-Idan, "Unlike any other king's wife or mother in the Hebrew bible,

Assyrian kings styled themselves as the "perfect man, virile warrior."[23] They emphasized masculine characteristics to demonstrate their right to rule.[24] Despite this, Naqia wielded significant authority in the empire. The "one surviving letter attesting to the correspondence between the king [Esarhaddon] and his mother" shows unusual respect.[25] Another letter shows that Naqia held military authority, as the writer asked her directly for reinforcements.[26] In addition, "high officials from the whole country" sent her deferential letters that credit her "with powers usually reserved for the king."[27] Naqia built a palace for Esarhaddon, which "was unprecedented. With this single act, the message of Naqia's status and authority was unambiguously presented to the public."[28] She had an "extraordinary" role in Assyrian cultic rituals.[29] Statues "of her were displayed in different cities, either in temples or in the public areas of towns."[30] These statues required a "staggering" amount of gold.[31] Not only did Naqia achieve a high position, but the empire celebrated and publicized her power.

Second, Jezebel and Naqia both ruled as queen mothers. The Assyrian records describe Naqia's influence during the reign of her son, Esarhaddon.[32] This culminates in Naqia's administering the loyalty oath at Assurbanipal's coronation; the oath implies that she has authority equal to Assurbanipal's: "All known Assyrian loyalty oaths were imposed by the kings for themselves or for the son chosen to be the crown prince—except for this one. It should be stressed that, for Naqia to have the prestige, the influence and the power to institute such an oath, and then presumably to enforce it, made her a unique and exceptional queen."[33] The oath uses

---

Jezebel was a real queen, assistant and partner in government to her husband Ahab (and, as contended above, regent after his and his sons' death)" (*Israelite Woman*, 21).

[23] A. Kirk Grayson and Jamie Novotny, *The Royal Inscriptions of Sennacherib, King of Assyria (704–681 BC)*, RINAP 3.1 (Winona Lake, IN: Eisenbrauns, 2012), 32.

[24] Chapman, *Gendered Language*, 1.

[25] Saana Svärd, "Power and Women in Assyrian Palaces" (PhD diss., University of Helsinki, 2012), 110–11.

[26] Frances Reynolds, ed., *The Babylonian Correspondence of Esarhaddon: And Letters of Assurbanipal and Sin-Šarru-Iškan from Northern and Central Babylonia*, SAA 18 (Helsinki: Helsinki University Press, 2003), 85.

[27] Svärd, "Power and Women," 110.

[28] Melville, *Role of Naqia*, 38. Melville's work, the only book devoted to Naqia, dwarfs previous scholarly treatments of this figure. Numerous scholars who mention Naqia cite Melville's work as their source. Macgregor and Svärd have added to Melville's work, but both rely heavily on Melville. These three have combined to give a much better portrait of Naqia than was previously available.

[29] Ibid, 42.

[30] Macgregor, "Women in the Neo-Assyrian World," 202.

[31] Svärd, "Power and Women," 108.

[32] Melville, *Role of Naqia*, 74–75.

[33] Macgregor, "Women in the Neo-Assyrian World," 171.

Naqia's other name, Zakutu, which is a translation of Naqia.³⁴ It begins with the words, "The treaty of Zakutu, the queen of Senna[cherib, ki]ng of Assyria, mother of Esarhaddon, king of Assyria."³⁵ Naqia made this treaty "with the whole nation concerning her favourite grandson [Assurba]nipal."³⁶ It concludes with the order to crush any rebellion: "seize and [kill] them and bring them to Zakutu [his mother and to Assurbani]pal, [king of Assyria, your lord]."³⁷ This remarkable document anticipates that Naqia will continue to rule into the reign of Assurbanipal.

The third link between Jezebel and Naqia requires speculation. On the basis of her West Semitic name, it is possible that Naqia came from outside Assyria. Sarah Melville finds this inconclusive: "Naqia's name alone cannot tell us where she came from, nor does it indicate that she was born outside Assyria proper."³⁸ Yet, if Naqia was not native to Assyria, she joins Jezebel as a woman who rose to the heights of power in a foreign nation.

The most important resemblance comes from Jezebel's and Naqia's involvement in what Nah 3:4 calls "sorceries." Assyrian texts demonstrate that Naqia had great interest, belief, and participation in Assyrian cultic rituals. These records reveal "oracles and prophecies addressed to Naqiʾa (*SAA 9* 1.8, *SAA 9* 5, *SAA 9* 2.1 and a reference to one in *SAA 10* 109)," which "are a unique phenomenon" regarding Assyrian women.³⁹ When Naqia became seriously ill, only one physician was assigned to attend her, while three exorcists labored to release her from the effects of witchcraft.⁴⁰ This indicates that Naqia truly believed in the power of magic.

Similar activities, when performed by Jezebel, were considered witchcraft and harlotry by the Hebrew prophets. Mordecai Cogan and Hayim Tadmor make this point: "Harlotry is the standard biblical metaphor for abandoning YHWH to take up the ways of foreign gods (e.g. Exod 34:16; Lev 17:7; Deut 31:16; Judg 2:7). With reference to Jezebel, 'harlotry' expresses the contempt in which Israel held pagan practice, seen as suffused with improper sex and magic (cf. Lev 18)."⁴¹ T. R. Hobbs gives a similar interpretation of Jezebel while explicitly linking her to Nah 3:4: "there is nothing in the preceding chapters that the queen was anything but a loyal wife to her husband. This being the case, there is here the continuation of the tradition of apostasy as adultery which is found in Judg 2:17; 8:33, and which is traced

---

³⁴ Melville, *Role of Naqia*, 16.

³⁵ Simo Parpola and Kazuko Watanabe, eds., *Neo-Assyrian Treaties and Loyalty Oaths*, SAA 2 (Helsinki: Helsinki University Press, 1988), 62 (brackets in original).

³⁶ Ibid. (brackets in original).

³⁷ Ibid. (brackets in original).

³⁸ Melville, *Role of Naqia*, 13.

³⁹ Svärd, "Power and Women," 108. Svärd cites Simo Parpola, ed., *Assyrian Prophecies*, SAA 9 (Helsinki: Helsinki University Press, 1997).

⁴⁰ Melville, *Role of Naqia*, 84.

⁴¹ Mordecai Cogan and Hayim Tadmor, *II Kings: A New Translation with Introduction and Commentary*, AB 11 (New York: Doubleday, 1988), 110.

through the later prophets (Jer 2:1–13; Nah 3:4; Hosea)."⁴² If Naqia had exercised control in Assyria and Nahum had considered her cultic activities to be part of that control, it is reasonable to conclude that the prophet utilized her image in constructing Nah 3:4.

III. Historical Context

The primary barrier to considering Naqia as the subject of Nahum's prophecy comes from her age. She does not seem to qualify as a beautiful and seductive woman at the time of Nahum. Simo Parpola dates Esarhaddon's birth to "713 at the latest."⁴³ Naqia would therefore have been no younger than sixty-five at the time of the sack of Thebes—mentioned in Nah 3:8–10—in 663 BC. Unless one accepts an early date for Nahum's prophecy, she likely would have been too old to still wield power—and most likely dead.⁴⁴ The perspective of Naqia as a type of Jezebel, however, reorients the interpretation of Nah 3:4. While טובת חן suggests powerful physical beauty, it does not demand it. The NRSV translation as "gracefully alluring," for instance, could describe a woman of Naqia's talents. As Klaas Spronk observes, "power is attractive."⁴⁵ The language in 3:4 proves flexible enough to describe a queen—such as Jezebel or Naqia—endowed with charm, power, and acumen.

Naqia had an unlikely rise to power. When she entered Sennacherib's harem, she did not do so as Sennacherib's primary queen. Unexpectedly, her son Esarhaddon became crown prince despite illness and having at least four eligible older brothers. It is likely that this decision led to Sennacherib's murder.⁴⁶

After Sennacherib's death, Esarhaddon overcame his brothers and their armies with unexpected ease. He managed to keep control of Assyria, and the empire

---

⁴² T. R. Hobbs, *2 Kings*, WBC 13 (Waco, TX: Word, 1985), 116–17.

⁴³ Simo Parpola, *Letters from Assyrian Scholars to the Kings Esarhaddon and Assurbanipal*, 2 vols. (Kevelaer: Butzon & Bercker; Neukirchen-Vluyn: Neukirchener Verlag, 1983; repr., Winona Lake, IN: Eisenbrauns, 2007), 231 n. 390.

⁴⁴ Nahum provides a limited range for its chronological setting. "Hardly anybody doubts that the book of Nahum or part of it has to be dated somewhere between 663 (the fall of Thebes) and 612 BCE (the fall of Nineveh)" (Spronk, *Nahum*, 12). The question of when the book reached its final form is another matter. Theories range from shortly after Thebes fell to the Maccabean period. For a recent summary of proposed dates, see Christensen, *Nahum*, 52–58. I advocate a date of 639 BCE based on the theory that שלמים in Nah 1:12 alludes to Assurbanipal's destruction of Elam in 639 and the peace that came over the ancient Near East from 639 to 627. Even if one accepts this relatively early date, however, Naqia would have been at least eighty-nine years old.

⁴⁵ Spronk, *Nahum*, 122.

⁴⁶ See Simo Parpola, "The Murderer of Sennacherib," in *Death in Mesopotamia: Papers Read at the XXVIe Rencontre Assyriologique International*, ed. Bendt Alster, Mesopotamia 8 (Copenhagen: Akademisk, 1980), 171–82.

prospered despite his "chronic" illness.⁴⁷ People in the ancient Near East would probably have credited Esarhaddon's successes to Naqia's magical abilities. This would explain the deference accorded Naqia in Assyria—a nation fixated on military power. The adoration and reverence paid to Ishtar in Assyrian writings suggest that the empire would have respected and submitted to a queen who could give them victory.⁴⁸

Melville, Sherry Lou Macgregor, and Saana Svärd rightly argue that earlier scholars who credited Esarhaddon's triumph to Naqia's machinations did so without evidence.⁴⁹ No Assyrian text links Sennacherib's decision regarding Esarhaddon to Naqia, and no text links Esarhaddon's success against his brothers to Naqia. But by comparing Nahum's mistress of sorceries with Assyrian textual evidence, I hypothesize that Nahum concluded that Naqia's machinations and magic drove Assyrian policy. According to Nah 3:4, the macabre scenes in 3:1–3 occurred "because of the abundant fornications of the prostitute." If this hypothesis is correct, Nahum claimed that the atrocities of the late Neo-Assyrian Empire stemmed from Naqia's religious perversions.

While it cannot be shown that Naqia influenced Sennacherib or Esarhaddon, Assyrian texts reveal that Naqia made use of divination regarding Esarhaddon's succession.

> For Naqia, Esarhaddon's appointment [as crown prince] must have seemed ideal: the future was assured for her and her son. When, in the subsequent months, the situation began to change and opposition to the nomination started to gain momentum, naturally she would have striven to counteract the negative reports about Esarhaddon that were reaching the king. That she was not entirely successful in doing so may indicate that she did not have as much influence on Sennacherib as has previously been assumed. On the other hand, in spite of growing pressure, Sennacherib did not change the succession, and this may be a point in favor of Naqia's influence. Naqia, evidently stymied in her efforts to restore Esarhaddon to Sennacherib's good graces, resorted to extispicy, astrology and oracles for favorable signs.⁵⁰

What Melville considers a last resort Nahum likely would have considered a powerful—and evil—tool. Many of Nahum's contemporaries, both inside and outside

---

⁴⁷ Parpola, *Letters from Assyrian Scholars*, 231; for details about Esarhaddon's illness, see 230–38.

⁴⁸ Sennacherib and Esarhaddon pay homage to Ishtar for the power she granted them (Grayson and Novotny, *Royal Inscriptions of Sennacherib*, 238–39; Leichty, *Royal Inscriptions of Esarhaddon*, 11–26). Artistic representations of Ishtar's warlike nature are discussed in Marie-Thérèse Barrelet, "Les déesses armées et ailées," *Syria* 32 (1955): 222–60; and Wolfgang Fauth, "Ištar als Löwengöttin und die löwenköpfige Lamaštu," *WO* 12 (1981): 21–36.

⁴⁹ Macgregor quotes nine such scholars in *Beyond Hearth and Home: Women in the Public Sphere in Neo-Assyrian Society*, SAAS 21 (Winona Lake, IN: Eisenbrauns, 2012), 96–97.

⁵⁰ Melville, *Role of Naqia*, 27.

Assyria, would have credited these events to Naqia's use of magic. The knowledge that Naqia used divination for Esarhaddon's sake, the linguistic link between Nah 3:4 and 2 Kgs 9:22, and the analogous lives of Naqia and Jezebel combine to make Naqia a likely candidate for Nahum's "mistress of sorceries."

IV. Conclusion

Much of Nahum's prophecy concerns YHWH's judgment against an unnamed female adversary. I have argued the prophet intended the ambiguity in these references; they pertain to the city of Nineveh, to the goddess Ishtar, and also to Queen Naqia. The linguistic analogy between Nah 3:4 and 2 Kgs 9:22 suggests that Nahum portrays the Assyrian queen as a type of Jezebel. Naqia and Jezebel had parallel careers as powerful queen mothers in patriarchal societies. Both gained a reputation for magical power. If Nah 3:4 is read from such a perspective, Naqia fits the description precisely. It is certainly possible that Nahum's original audience—many of whom had lived during the height of Naqia's power—would have recognized the resemblance. Therefore, without being able to prove intention, the hypothesis that Naqia's life influenced Nahum's description of the Assyrian prostitute queen deserves consideration.

A Newly Reconstructed Calendrical Scroll from Qumran in Cryptic Script

ESHBAL RATZON
eshbal@gmail.com
University of Haifa, Haifa 3498838, Israel

JONATHAN BEN-DOV
jonbendov@gmail.com
University of Haifa, Haifa 3498838, Israel

In this article we offer a reconstruction and edition of one of the last unpublished Dead Sea Scrolls. It is an extremely fragmentary calendrical scroll written in the Cryptic A code. While images of 4Q324d were included in the DJD series, no formal edition of it exists. The suggested jigsaw-puzzlelike reconstruction integrates forty-two extremely small fragments into a stretch of five consecutive columns of what we consider to be one continuous scroll (*pace* earlier preliminary editions). In terms of its content, the calendar contained in this scroll resembles the one found at the top of 4Q394 3–7 (a copy of 4QMMT) and in 4Q394 1–2. An intriguing interlinear gloss in both shape and content offers a ruling on the Festival of Wood Offering that follows the halakic rulings of the Temple Scroll.

A distinctive corpus of scrolls written in cryptic script stands out among the scrolls found in Qumran.[1] While the final publication of all Qumran scrolls is often celebrated, several scrolls in cryptic script are the only scrolls left that have not been

This study was written with the support of the Israel Science Foundation, grant number 1330/14. We would like to express our gratitude to Asaf Gayer, who has been deeply involved in the material reconstruction of this scroll and offered invaluable help. Composite images in this article are based on the PAM images, supplied to us courtesy of the Leon Levy Dead Sea Scrolls Digital Library, Israel Antiquities Authority. In addition, we gained much benefit from the new multispectral images supplied to us by the same library (photographer: Shai Halevy).

[1] For a description of this corpus, see Stephen J. Pfann, "The Character of the Early Essene Movement in the Light of the Manuscripts Written in Esoteric Scripts from Qumran" (PhD diss., The Hebrew University, Jerusalem, 2001); Pfann, "Writings in Esoteric Script from Qumran," in *The Dead Sea Scrolls Fifty Years after Their Discovery: Proceedings of the Jerusalem Congress, July 20–25, 1997*, ed. Lawrence H. Schiffman, Emanuel Tov, and James C. VanderKam (Jerusalem: Israel Exploration Society, 2000), 177–90.

furnished with a full scientific edition. In effect, they are the last unpublished Dead Sea Scrolls. We are privileged to have completed an edition of one of these last scrolls and present it here. We assign the scroll presented here the number 4Q324d.[2]

The reconstruction suggested here for one of these extremely fragmentary scrolls presented outstanding difficulties and required extraordinary efforts, much like assembling a jigsaw puzzle with individual pieces measuring 1.5 cm × 1.5 cm on average. Important preliminary work on this scroll was carried out by József T. Milik and Stephen J. Pfann, to whom we are greatly indebted. The final result, as presented here, is a calendar text covering a 364-day year, with pronounced concluding formulas at the conclusion of each of the seasons. A calendar list of the same kind was famously preserved at the top of 4Q394 3–7, a copy of the important halakic scroll Miqṣat Ma'aśe haTorah. There only its last line can be read, but more information can be gleaned from the better-preserved scroll 4Q394 1–2.[3] Notwithstanding the partial information of the above scrolls, we are now able to trace the structure of the whole year according to that—or a very similar—order.

A complete publication of this modest-looking scroll is significant for Qumran studies, even for the entire field of biblical studies, in several respects. It alerts scholars to the opportunities that are still present in the Dead Sea Scrolls corpus if older editions are reexamined with the proper attention and with new technologies available today.[4] The scribal practice of this little scroll adds particularly telling

---

[2] The number 324d was used by Pfann for only a small part of the sixty or so fragments discussed here, as he divided them into six different copies 4Q324d–i. Since we now see all fragments as constituting a single copy, we name it 4Q324d, the first available siglum in the sequence. Although we are alert to the confusion that choosing this siglum may cause, we prefer to use it in order to preserve the direct flow of 4Q324 numbers, rather than invent a whole new siglum. Since no publication was written about this scroll beyond the mere editions, the risk of confusion seems limited.

[3] See the initial publication of 4Q394 1–2 and 3–7 in Elisha Qimron and John Strugnell, *Qumran Cave 4.V: Miqṣat Ma'aśe ha-Torah*, DJD X (Oxford: Clarendon, 1994), 6–9, 44–45. While DJD X assigns frags. 1–2 and 3–7 to one and the same manuscript, Strugnell (ibid., 203) doubted this association, and VanderKam concluded against it; see James C. VanderKam, "The Calendar, 4Q327 and 4Q394," in *Legal Texts and Legal Issues: Proceedings of the Second Meeting of the International Organization for Qumran Studies, Cambridge, 1995*, ed. Moshe Bernstein, Florentino García Martínez, and John Kampen, STDJ 23 (Leiden: Brill, 1997), 179–94. In his title, VanderKam called frags. 1–2 by the old designation "4Q327." His arguments were accepted by Shemaryahu Talmon; see S. Talmon, J. Ben-Dov, and U. Glessmer, *Qumran Cave 4.XVI: Calendrical Texts*, DJD XXI (Oxford: Clarendon, 2001), 158. Elisha Qimron leaves the question open in his new edition: *The Dead Sea Scrolls: The Hebrew Writings* [in Hebrew] (Jerusalem: Yad Ben-Zvi, 2013), 2:204. For the relation between MMT and the calendar of 4Q394, see Hanne von Weissenberg, *4QMMT: Reevaluating the Text, the Function, and the Meaning of the Epilogue*, STDJ 82 (Leiden: Brill, 2009), 33–38.

[4] See, e.g., Jonathan Ben-Dov, Daniel Stökl Ben Ezra, and Asaf Gayer, "Reconstruction of a Single Copy of the Qumran Cave 4 Cryptic-Script Serekh haEdah," *RevQ* 29 (2017): 21–77;

examples to the record of scribal practices assembled by Emanuel Tov.[5] In addition, our reconstruction adds several significant details about the 364-day calendar, specifically about the nature of the Feast of Wood Offering and about the *təqûpôt*, that is, the days standing at the turn of the seasons. Finally, the reconstruction of 4Q324d as a single scroll rather than as a collection of six separate scrolls, as suggested in earlier research, is significant for assessing the nature and scope of encryption in sectarian circles. The religious phenomenon of secrecy and encryption in the ancient Near East, Judaism, Christianity, and other late-antique religions, keeps attracting scholarly attention and will benefit from the finds of the present project.[6] These three aspects are discussed below, followed by a detailed edition of 4Q324d. The extent of material work performed here requires an extensive technical apparatus, without which the more general results cannot stand.

I. The 364-Day Calendar Tradition

The calendar constituted a central part of the sectarian identity. Members of the Yaḥad adhered to a year of 364 days, which was different from the luni-solar year of the Jerusalem temple and the Hasmonean state.[7] The sectarian calendrical tradition is well represented in a variety of documents from Qumran and outside it.[8] It is a highly schematic year with ideal relations between its numerical

---

Chanan Ariel, Alexei Yuditsky, and Elisha Qimron, "The *Pesher on the Periods* A–B (4Q180–4Q181): Editing, Language, and Interpretation" [in Hebrew], *Meghillot* 11–12 (2015): 3–39.

[5] Emanuel Tov, *Scribal Practices and Approaches Reflected in the Texts Found in the Judean Desert*, STDJ 54 (Leiden: Brill, 2004).

[6] See, e.g., Alan Lenzi, *Secrecy and the Gods: Secret Knowledge in Ancient Mesopotamia and Biblical Israel*, SAAS 19 (Helsinki: Neo-Assyrian Text Corpus Project, 2008); Adela Yarbro Collins, "Messianic Secret and the Gospel of Mark: Secrecy in Jewish Apocalypticism, the Hellenistic Mystery Religions, and Magic," in *Rending the Veil: Concealment and Secrecy in the History of Religions*, ed. Elliot R. Wolfson (New York: Seven Bridges, 1999), 11–30.

[7] For the role of the calendar in sectarian polemics, see the ever-relevant Shemaryahu Talmon, "Yom Hakippurim in the Habakkuk Scroll," *Bib* 32 (1951): 549–63. Although much of the criticism leveled against Talmon by Sacha Stern ("Qumran Calendars and Sectarianism," in *The Oxford Handbook of the Dead Sea Scrolls*, ed. Timothy H. Lim and John J. Collins [Oxford: Oxford University Press, 2010], 232–53) is valid, the core sectarian value of the calendar cannot be denied.

[8] Uwe Glessmer, "Calendars in the Qumran Scrolls," in *The Dead Sea Scrolls after Fifty Years: A Comprehensive Assessment*, ed. Peter W. Flint and James C. VanderKam, 2 vols. (Leiden: Brill, 1999), 2:213–78; James C. VanderKam, *Calendars in the Dead Sea Scrolls: Measuring Time*, Literature of the Dead Sea Scrolls (London: Routledge, 1998); Jonathan Ben-Dov, "The 364-Day Year in the Dead Sea Scrolls and Jewish Pseudepigrapha," in *Calendars and Years II: Astronomy and Time in the Ancient and Medieval World*, ed. John M. Steele (Oxford: Oxbow, 2011), 69–105. The Qumran calendrical texts 4Q319–324c and 4Q325–330 were published by Talmon, Ben-Dov, and Glessmer in DJD XXI.

constituents. The number of 364 days is neatly divided by seven, a typological number with significant religious connotation. Each 364-day year contains exactly fifty-two weeks, a fact that allows anchoring the festivals to fixed weekdays, thus avoiding their coincidence with the Sabbath. In addition, the number 364 divides neatly by four as well, yielding a good symmetry of the four seasons, each season containing exactly 91 days. Finally, the synchronization of the 364-day year with a schematic lunar calendar of alternating twenty-nine- and thirty-day months is easily achieved, using an intercalation of one thirty-day month every three years (a triennial cycle of three years of 364 days = three lunar years of 354 days + an intercalary month of thirty days).

A distinct part of the 364-day calendar tradition appears in a collection of calendar texts from Qumran that present the characteristics mentioned above in the form of detailed rosters in addition to the following: the triennial cycle involving lunar months; a six-year cycle that incorporates the times of service of priestly families (*mišmārôt*) in the temple; and a detailed record of lunar phases along the six-year cycle. Each type of calendrical scroll represents only some of these traits, and thus a variety of calendrical "genre" is created.[9] The scroll 4Q324d represents the Sabbaths and festivals as well as a simple record of the names of priestly courses but does not go into the details of either the *mishmarot* service or of the lunar phenomena. It is unique in phrasing a distinct type of formula indicating the dates of transition between the seasons.[10]

The vocabulary and style of the calendrical texts are typically very limited and monotonous, a fact that eases the task of reconstructing fragmentary scrolls. We benefited greatly from this characteristic when assembling the jigsaw puzzle of 4Q324d.

The account of annual festivals recorded in 4Q324d generally agrees with the record of festivals in other scrolls. An exception pertains to the Festival of Wood Offering, as explained below. In this case, a long marginal note specifies some details about the performance of this particular feast, in accordance with the halakah of the Temple Scroll and in contrast to other practices reflected in Second Temple literature.[11] The inclusion of this note seems to indicate an awareness of halakic disagreements and the need of additional clarification.

---

[9] For a classification of types of calendar texts, see DJD XXI:7–14.

[10] For these transition days, see Jonathan Ben-Dov, *Head of All Years: Astronomy and Calendars at Qumran in Their Ancient Near Eastern Context*, STDJ 78 (Leiden: Brill, 2008), 31–52.

[11] For this festival, see mainly Cana Werman, "The Wood-Offering: The Convoluted Evolution of a Halakhah in Qumran and Rabbinic Law," in *New Perspectives on Old Texts: Proceedings of the Tenth International Symposium of the Orion Center for the Study of the Dead Sea Scrolls and Associated Literature, 9–11 January, 2005*, ed. Esther G. Chazon, Betsy Halpern-Amaru in collaboration with Ruth A. Clements, STDJ 88 (Leiden: Brill, 2010), 151–81.

II. The Cryptic Script and Esotericism

While more than one code was employed in the Dead Sea Scrolls, the main one in use was dubbed Cryptic A by its decipherer, J. T. Milik.[12] The general aim of encryption in Qumran is not entirely clear, as we hope to discuss elsewhere. Most of the encrypted texts are attested elsewhere in a completely unesoteric edition, such as the Rule of the Congregation from Cave 1 and the present calendrical scroll 4Q324d, which resembles other calendrical scrolls written in the square Jewish script. Those that are not encountered elsewhere—insofar as we can read them in their current condition—do not betray any sign of exceptional secrets or hidden wisdom. Such is the case, for example, with 4Q249 Midrash Moshe or even 4Q317 Phases of the Moon. It generally seems that encryption was a means of conveying prestige to the initiated but not a means of 100-percent security or preventing comprehension by other community members.[13]

Cryptic A is a simple replacement code, with each letter represented by a designated sign. Some of these signs correspond to paleo-Hebrew or Greek letters, while others seem arbitrary. These signs played a part in the sectarian scribal practice, as some of them appear as scribal marks in various scrolls.[14] As it seems now, about eight scrolls were written in the Cryptic A script; some of these texts are known from other Dead Sea Scrolls, while others are uniquely attested. The inventory includes Midrash Moshe (4Q249); the Rule of the Congregation (4Q249a); a yet-unknown composition written on papyrus 4Q250; Words of the Maskil to the Sons of Dawn (4Q298); Phases of the Moon (4Q317); the calendrical scroll 4Q324d; and several other smaller fragments.[15] Of these, the first three are written on

---

[12] J. T. Milik, "*Milkî-ṣedeq* et *Milkî-rešaᶜ* dans les anciens écrits juifs et chrétiens," *JJS* 23 (1972): 94–144; Milik, *The Books of Enoch: Aramaic Fragments of Qumran Cave 4* (Oxford: Clarendon, 1976), 68–69; Émile Puech, "L'alphabet cryptique A en 4QSᵉ (4Q259)," *RevQ* 18 (1998): 425–35. For the story of the decipherment, see Frank Moore Cross, *The Ancient Library of Qumran*, 3rd ed., BibSem 30 (Sheffield: Sheffield Academic, 1995), 45. See also the publications by Pfann mentioned in n. 1 above. The Cryptic B script is represented in the fragments 4Q362, 4Q363, and 4Q363b, while Cryptic C is represented in 4Q363a.

[13] This general feature of encryption resembles the find in other ancient cultures. See Jacco Dieleman, *Priests, Tongues, and Rites: The London-Leiden Magical Manuscripts and Translation in Egyptian Ritual (100–300 CE)*, RGRW 153 (Leiden: Brill, 2005); Kathryn Stevens, "Secrets in the Library: Protected Knowledge and Professional Identity in Late Babylonian Uruk," *Iraq* 75 (2013): 211–53; Mladen Popović, "Physiognomic Knowledge in Qumran and Babylonia: Form, Interdisciplinarity, and Secrecy," *DSD* 13 (2006): 150–76.

[14] See Tov, *Scribal Practices*, 203–6.

[15] These last pieces are 11Q23 CryptA Unidentified Text, and 4Q313 MMT (the latter document was divided into three different scrolls in Stephen J. Pfann, *Qumran Cave 4.XXVI: Cryptic Texts and Miscellanea, Part 1*, DJD XXXVI [Oxford: Clarendon, 2000], 697–701). The identification of MMT remains dubious. The hundreds of tiny fragments contained under the

papyrus, while the rest are on skin. In contrast to the earlier discussions by Pfann, we are inclined to see each of these works as represented by one copy only, a position that will be defended in detail below for 4Q324d.

Since 4Q298 is explicitly connected with the figure of the Maskil by means of its title (written in square letters), other cryptic scrolls used by the Maskil may indicate the fields of interest of that functionary. Maintaining times and seasons seems to have taken pride of place among these interests, as corroborated also by the Hymn of the Maskil in 1QS X–XI.[16] Another significant find is that the Cryptic A script find amounts to no more than eight to ten scrolls, which places the entire phenomenon of encryption relatively in the margins of the sectarian discourse on mystery and secrecy.[17] The fine-grained material work on 4Q324d and other scrolls can lead the way to a better assessment of secrecy and esotericism in the Yaḥad.

III. 4Q324d

Against this background, we now turn to an edition of 4Q324d, which, as indicated above, remains as one of the few Dead Sea Scrolls of which there has not yet been a detailed edition.

Milik did not publish 4Q324d even preliminarily, but his opinion may be recalled from the way he placed the fragments on the historical PAM plates.[18] 4Q324d contains nearly sixty poorly preserved fragments. None of these fragments contains more than four lines of script, and no line contains more than three broken words. The general content of the scroll was revealed by means of the vocabulary legible on some of the fragments. The recurring word *Sabbath* alongside numbers and date formulas, together with several names of priestly families, reveals that 4Q324d comprises a calendar and a *mishmarot* list. In 1992, as Milik released all scrolls remaining in his responsibility, the cryptic scrolls were assigned to Pfann.

---

umbrella name 4Q249 (DJD XXXVI:547–677) may represent more than the two scrolls mentioned here. Their meager content, however, renders any further judgment difficult.

[16] See Carol A. Newsom, *The Self as Symbolic Space: Constructing Identity and Community at Qumran*, STDJ 52 (Leiden: Brill, 2004), 178–86.

[17] Cf. Samuel I. Thomas, *The "Mysteries" of Qumran: Mystery, Secrecy, and Esotericism in the Dead Sea Scrolls*, EJL 25 (Atlanta: Society of Biblical Literature, 2009).

[18] Only a few fragments with cryptic script are found on the early images PAM 40.985, 40.979 (taken in 1954). Milik left notes with numbers ranging from 1 to 4 next to some of the fragments on PAM 41.692 (taken in 1955). Most fragments are represented on PAM 42.429, 42.430 (taken in 1957), and PAM 43.333, 43.340 (taken in 1960). Apart from his work on the cryptic fragments, Milik prepared reconstructions of the calendrical scrolls, which he classified into groups and subgroups (thus, e.g., 4Q327, which he called "Mishmarot E^b"). We do not have any transcription by Milik of the present cryptic scroll, however.

Pfann wrote an insightful dissertation on this corpus and documented his significant discoveries in various volumes of the DJD series.[19] His work on 4Q324d remained incomplete, however. Images of the fragments with new joins appeared in DJD XXVIII, presenting Pfann's new division of the fragments into six different scrolls, which he designated 4Q324d–i.[20] An edition of these fragments was published by Martin Abegg, retaining the DJD division of copies.[21] Until today this is the only available edition of 4Q324d.

We accept Pfann's joins and follow his path in adding many more similar joins. Since approximately two-thirds of the fragments can now be reconstructed to a single, physically joined and textually coherent copy, there is no reason to assume that 4Q324d comprised more than one scroll.[22] As is often the case, most of the preserved fragments are concentrated around a certain area of the scroll, in this case around the bottom parts of five consecutive columns. The present framework does not allow for publishing a full edition of the scroll, which we hope to achieve elsewhere. Here we present only an overall material reconstruction of the scroll and the readings resulting from it, as support for our view that 4Q324d comprises a single scroll. No detailed notes on readings will be presented, but pertinent comments are unavoidable.

According to the classification principles offered by Talmon in DJD XXI, this

---

[19] Pfann, "Character of the Early Essene Movement"; Pfann, "Cryptic Texts," in Pfann, DJD XXXVI:515–701. Pfann's preliminary transcription was presented to the late Shemaryahu Talmon as he was working on DJD XXI. One line of this reconstruction was accordingly quoted in DJD XXI:5, "courtesy of S. J. Pfann."

[20] Stephen J. Pfann, "Cryptic A Calendrical Documents," in D. Gropp, *Wadi Daliyeh II: The Samaria Papyri from Wadi Daliyeh* and *Qumran Cave 4.XXVIII: Miscellanea, Part 2*, DJD XXVIII (Oxford: Clarendon, 2000), pls. LII–LXII.

[21] Martin G. Abegg, "4Q324i (4QcryptA Mishmarot J)," "4Q324f (4QcryptA Liturgical Calendar^c?)," "4Q324g (4QcryptA Cal. Doc. F?)," "4Q324h (4QcryptA Cal. Doc. G?)," "4Q324d (4QCryptA Liturgical Calendar^a)," "4Q324e (4QcryptA Liturgical Calendar^b)," in *The Dead Sea Scrolls Reader*, ed. Donald W. Parry and Emanuel Tov, 6 vols. (Leiden: Brill, 2004), 4:14–15, 52–56 ("Calendrical and Sapiential Texts"). The same edition is reproduced in the electronic databases Accordance and DSS Electronic Library.

[22] Pfann seems to have supported his division of the fragments by a newly introduced method of discerning the direction of hair follicles, although he never applied this method specifically to 4Q324d (see Pfann, DJD XXXVI:517–23; Pfann, in T. Elgvin et al., in consultation with J. A. Fitzmyer, *Qumran Cave 4.XV: Sapiential Texts, Part 1*, DJD XX [Oxford: Clarendon, 1997], 2–4; and Pfann, "Character of the Early Essene Movement," 94–95). See also Emanuel Tov, "The Sciences and the Reconstruction of the Ancient Scrolls: Possibilities and Impossibilities," in *The Dead Sea Scrolls in Context: Integrating the Dead Sea Scrolls in the Study of Ancient Texts, Languages, and Cultures*, ed. Armin Lange, Emanuel Tov, and Matthias Weigold, 2 vols., VTSup 140 (Leiden: Brill, 2011), 1:3–25, here 17–18. This evidence, however, is not sufficient grounds for dividing the tiny fragments of 4Q324d into separate scrolls. As clarified to us by Ira Rabin (November 2015), this method is difficult to apply to such small fragments.

reconstructed scroll should be classified as "Calendrical Document/Mishmarot C" since it contains lists of two kinds: a table of festivals and Sabbaths as well as a *mishmarot* list (see in detail below).

For the sake of the present discussion it was essential to assign a new number to each fragment of 4Q324d, with each of these numbers corresponding to a DJD fragment number. We allocated the numbers according to the placement of the fragments in our suggested reconstruction. The following table facilitates the conversion between the various methods of naming the fragments. The two rightmost columns refer the reader to all known images of each fragment.

Although we joined many fragments into a continuous scroll, the table below assigns a number for each separate piece of leather, called here a "fragment." This methodological decision required us to disband some of Pfann's earlier joins, which had been assigned one number in DJD although they contain several pieces of leather.

New Numbering	DJD XXI	Plate	PAM
1	4Q324h 12	Plate 240, frag. 14	42.428, 43.333
2	4Q324d 4	Plate 241, frag. 5	41.692, 42.429, 43.340
3	4Q324d 12	Plate 241, frag. 14	41.692, 42.429, 43.340
4	4Q324d 11	Plate 241, frag. 6	41.692, 42.430, 43.340
5	4Q324d 5	Plate 241, frag. 31	42.430, 43.340
6	4Q324d 3 i	Plate 241, frag. 25	41.692, 42.429, 43.340
7	4Q324d 6	Plate 241, frag. 21	40.979, 41.692, 42.429, 43.340
8	4Q324d 3 ii	Plate 241, frag. 31	41.372, 42.430, 43.340
9	4Q324d 3 ii	Plate 240, frag. 9	41.867, 42.430, 43.333
10	4Q324d 2	Plate 240, frag. 1	42.430, 43.333
11	4Q324d 2	Plate 240, frag. 16	43.333
12	4Q324d 7	Plate 241, frag. 9	40.985, 41.692, 42.429, 43.340
13	4Q324d 3 ii	Plate 241, frag. 23	41.692, 42.429, 43.340
14	4Q324d 3 ii	Plate 241, frag. 24	41.692, 42.429, 43.340
15	4Q324d 2	Plate 241, frag. 38	42.426, 43.340
16	4Q324d 2	Plate 240, frag. 4+18	42.430, 43.333
17	4Q324d 7	Plate 240, frag. 8	41.867, 42.430, 43.340
18	4Q324f 1	Plate 240, frag. 12	42.430, 43.333
19	4Q324e 6	Plate 240, frag. 15	42.428, 43.333
20	4Q324f 2	Plate 240, frag. 13	41.643, 42.430, 43.333

21	4Q324e 1	Plate 241, frag. 26	40.985, 41.692, 42.429, 43.340
22	4Q324d 7	Plate 241, frag. 9	40.985, 41.692, 42.429, 43.340
23	4Q324d 8	Plate 241, frag. 12	41.692, 42.429, 43.340
24	4Q324e 9	Plate 241, frag. 19	41.692, 42.429, 43.340
25	4Q324e 4	Plate 241, frag. 11	41.692, 42.429, 43.340
26	4Q324e 4	Plate 240, frag. 2	41.867, 42.430, 43.333
27	4Q324d 9	Plate 241, frag. 15	41.692, 42.429, 43.340
28	4Q324d 9	Plate 241, frag. 32	42.430, 43.340
29	4Q324d 10	Plate 309, frag. 8	41.867, 42.430, 43.333
30	4Q324e 12	Plate 241, frag. 33	41.692, 42.429, 43.340
31	4Q324h 3	Plate 241, frag. 18	41.692, 42.429, 43.340
32	4Q324h 8	Plate 241, frag. 37	41.867, 42.430, 43.340
33	4Q324e 5	Plate 240, frag. 5	41.461, 42.430, 43.333
34	4Q324e 8	Plate 241, frag. 10	41.692, 42.429, 43.340
35	4Q324e 3	Plate 241, frag. 16	41.692, 42.429, 43.340
36	4Q324i 1 c	Plate 241, frag. 3	41.692, 42.429, 43.340
37	4Q324i 1 a	Plate 241, frag. 1	41.692, 42.429, 43.340
38	4Q324i 1 a	Plate 241, frag. 2	41.692, 42.429, 43.340
39	Not found in the DJD edition	Not on the IAA website	41.867
40	4Q324i 1 b	Plate 241, frag. 17	41.692, 43.340
41	4Q324h 9	Plate 241, frag. 36	41.457, 42.429, 43.340
42	4Q324d 1	Plate 241, frag. 39	42.430, 43.340
43	4Q324e 13	Plate 240, frag. 3	41.660, 42.430, 43.333
44	Not found in the DJD edition	Plate 240, frag. 6	42.429, 43.333
45	4Q324f 4	Plate 240, frag. 7	43.333
46	4Q324f 3	Plate 240, frag. 10	41.867, 42.430, 43.333
47	4Q324h 10	Plate 240, frag. 11	43.333
48	Not found in the DJD edition	Plate 240, frag. 17	Cannot be found in the PAM photos
49	4Q324i 2	Plate 241, frag. 4	41.692, 42.429, 43.340

50	4Q324e 2	Plate 241, frag. 7	41.692, 42.429, 43.340
51	4Q324h 1	Plate 241, frag. 8	41.692, 42.429, 43.340
52	4Q324h 2	Plate 241, frag. 13	41.692, 42.429, 43.340
53	4Q324h 4	Plate 241, frag. 20	42.429, 43.340
54	4Q324e 7	Plate 241, frag. 22	42.430, 43.340
55	4Q324g 2	Plate 241, frag. 27	40.985, 43.340
56	4Q324g 1	Plate 241, frag. 28	40.985, 42.429, 43.340
57	4Q324g 6	Plate 241, frag. 29	40.985, 43.340
58	4Q324h 5	Plate 241, frag. 30	43.340
59	4Q324e 10	Plate 241, frag. 34	40.985, 42.429, 43.340
60	4Q324e 11	Plate 241, frag. 35	40.985, 41.692, 42.429, 43.333
61	4Q324h 7	Plate 241, frag. 40	42.426, 43.340
62	4Q324h 11	Plate 241, frag. 41	42.430, 43.340

Material Description, Paleography, and Measurements

The fragments vary in size from 3.9 cm × 2.8 cm for the largest fragment to many small fragments not larger than 1.5 cm × 1.5 cm. The color of all fragments is dark brown but not black, so that all fragments can be read in the original without recourse to the infrared images. Fragments 21, 30, 59, and 60 are slightly lighter. Four fragments (numbers 18, 19, 20, 24) accumulated a whitish granular residue.[23]

When one compares 4Q324d with the two other cryptic scrolls written on leather—4Q298 and 4Q317—it emerges that 4Q324d is more similar to 4Q317 than to 4Q298. The latter scroll manifests better preparation work of the leather and a more formal hand, as well as dry rulings limiting the columns and lines, while no such rulings are preserved on 4Q324d and 4Q317. Since the dimensions of 4Q324d are considerably smaller than both 4Q317 and 4Q298, it seems to have been a more provisory copy, in keeping with the material characteristics of many other calendar scrolls from Cave 4.

The present framework does not suffice for presenting a full analysis of the cryptic paleography. Such an analysis will be offered by Daniel Stökl Ben Ezra in a separate publication. While Pfann has developed a classification of the cryptic hands and used it to date the various scrolls, we doubt whether such a scant corpus is sufficient for establishing this typology.[24] Since the cryptic corpus is by definition

---

[23] What seems like a white substance on frags. 44 (which is absent from the images published in DJD XXVIII) and 53 is in fact remnants of the rice paper used during the reconstruction.

[24] Pfann, "Character of the Early Essene Movement," 179–203; Pfann, "The Ancient 'Library' or 'Libraries' of Qumran: The Specter of Cave 1Q," in *The Dead Sea Scrolls at Qumran and the*

less stable than the persistent tradition of the Jewish script, the establishment of a rigid typology seems less secure. Generally speaking, the scroll 4Q298 Words of Maskil to All the Sons of Dawn is written in the most formal book hand of Cryptic A, while the two other leather scrolls 4Q324d and 4Q317 use a less-ordered hand. Letters in 4Q324d are sometimes irregularly executed: for example, the head of the *bet* can often be round and open but sometimes also sharp and closed; the right downstroke of *tav* can be either horizontal or tilted inward. Special attention should be given to the curly left leg of *vav*, in contrast to the vertical orientation of this leg in other cryptic hands. Largely, the hand of 4Q324d is close to that of 4Q317 and the papyri. Compared to the latter, 4Q324d is unique in its *alef*, which stands vertically rather than spreading horizontally; in its *samek*, which contains only the upper right strokes of the composite letter of 4Q317 and the papyri; and in its *tav*, whose right stroke is much longer and more open than the spiked *tav* of 4Q317 and the papyri.

It is mainly the bottom part of this scroll that has survived, preserving two to five lines from the bottom of each column and a bottom margin of 1.2 cm on average. Three fragments are preserved at the top of column IV, showing a top margin of 0.8 cm, but it seems that the original margin was larger than this figure.

Letters are normally 4 mm high (disregarding the shorter letters *yod* and *ayin*). The height of lines is not uniform, approximately 7.5 mm on average, measured from the top of one line to the top of the next. According to the reconstruction below, each column contained ten lines. Thus, the approximate height of a column is 10 lines + 2 margins of 1.5 cm each = 10.5 cm in height.

The width of a column can be reconstructed in the places where the entire width has been preserved on the joined fragments. We estimate that the width of column II is 12.2 cm (containing 31 letter spaces); column III is 12.2 cm (31 letter spaces); column IV is 13.3 cm (33 letter spaces); column V is 10.8 cm (25 letter spaces); and column VI is 10.7 cm (20 letter spaces). The space between columns measures 0.9 cm between columns II and III; 1.7 cm between columns III and IV; and 1.4 cm between columns IV and V. If, as we posit below, the scroll consisted of at least seven columns, the overall length of these columns would have been approximately 90 cm.

An interlinear addition appears in column III between lines 9 and 10. In addition, an especially long marginal gloss appears to the left of column III. The scribe started a gloss in the margin between columns III and IV, writing it downward as is often the case in the Dead Sea Scrolls; after writing all the way down the margin, the scribe rotated the scroll and continued writing the gloss on the bottom margin,

---

Concept of a Library, ed. Sidnie White Crawford and Cecilia Wassen, STDJ 116 (Leiden: Brill, 2016), 168–213, here 205–7. The analysis by Pfann (DJD XXXVI:525–32) relates primarily to the cursive script on the papyri and is thus less relevant for 4Q324d. For a critique of Pfann's system of dating, see Jonathan Ben-Dov and Daniel Stökl Ben Ezra, "4Q249 Midrash Moshe: A New Reading and Its Implications," *DSD* 21 (2014): 131–49; Puech, "L'alphabet cryptique A."

with the letters appearing upside down from the point of view of the observer. This peculiar setting supplied us with an invaluable tool for reconstructing the jigsaw puzzle. Pfann had noticed it but did not trace the 90-degree turn. He thus suggested that the inverted line "may serve to convey some hidden meaning in an esoteric text."[25] In contrast, we think that this line was written upside down not as a means of encryption but simply because the scribe ran out of space between the columns and had to continue his note at the bottom of the column.[26]

4Q324d Column II

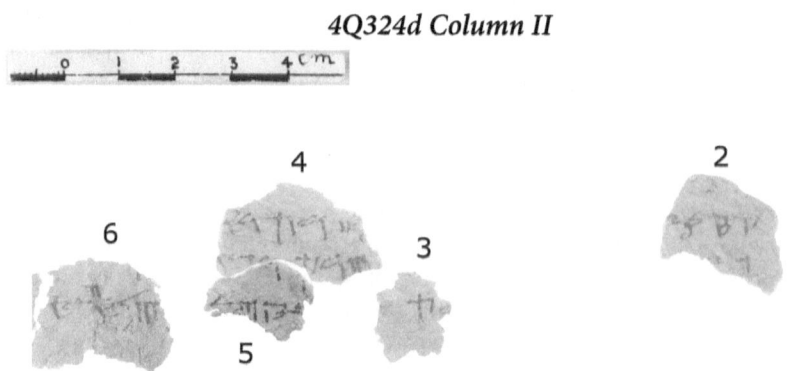

FIGURE 1. Reconstruction of Column II (frags. 2–6). PAM 41.692, 42.430

7   י̇ו̇ם] השלישי נואספ vacat הרביעי יום הרביעי[
8   תקופ̇]ה בארבעה ב[ו̇ שבת בא̇]חד עשר בו[
9   שב̇ת̇] בשמונה עשר ב[ו̇ שבת בעש̇]רים[
10 וחמשה בו ש[ב̇ת י̇]ום [ח̇מישי̇] ב[ו̇ שלושׁים

7. [(Week)d]ay[three is additional. vacat (The beginning of the) fourth (month) is on (week)day four.]
8. Tequf[ah. On the fourth in] it – Sabbath. On the e[leventh in it –]
9. Sabbath.[On the eighteenth in] it – Sabbath. On the twe[nty-]
10. [fifth in it – Sab]bath. (Week)d[ay] five[– in] it (falls) the thirtieth (day of the month).

---

[25] Pfann, "Character of the Early Essene Movement," 126.

[26] A similar scribal practice is found in 4QJer[a] III (Jer 7:30–8:3), where a scribe added three lines between lines 5 and 7, continued them vertically alongside the text (four lines), and moved on below the column in upside-down writing (one line). See Emanuel Tov, "4QJer[a]," in E. Ulrich et al., *Qumran Cave 4.X: The Prophets*, DJD XV (Oxford: Clarendon, 1997), 155–56; Tov, *Scribal Practices*, 223–27. Unlike in 4Q324d, the addition in 4QJer[a] seems to be a correction due to the erroneous omission of the first scribe.

The first reconstructed column does not preserve a text from the beginning of the year but rather from the fourth month onward (see below). We calculate that an additional previous column was required to accommodate the beginning of the year; hence we designate the first preserved column as column II. A reconstruction of the hypothetical column I is suggested below.

Joins and Layout

In contrast to columns III–VI, most fragments in column II are not physically joined. Regardless of whether the scroll was rolled from the beginning or from the end, it seems that the middle part is best preserved while the beginning and end are less so. Thus, the reconstruction of column II, although appearing here first in chronological order, is the least convincing one. The details of this column depend on the more-established guidelines of the subsequent columns. Since the text of 4Q324d is highly formulaic and repetitive, most reconstructions are hard to contest.

The anchor for the reconstruction is frag. 6, which physically touches the remains of a left margin and of the subsequent column III. Fragments 4–5 must be joined due to the agreement in physical contours and to the continuation of subject matter. The letters *tav* and *bet* in line 9 spread across the two fragments and buttress the join.[27] The composite frags. 4–5 does not touch frag. 6, and thus its placement depends on our reconstruction of the formula for describing the end of the month (see in detail below). At the top of frag. 4, the blank space without lettering is somewhat larger than the normal space between lines. We are reluctant to see this space as the remains of a top margin, not only because the scroll preserves almost exclusively bottom parts of columns but also because the space is only slightly larger than the normal space between lines. We explain this space as a short *vacat* inserted in line 7, before the beginning of the fourth month.

Fragment 3 contains the bottom margin, remains of two letters in line 10, and faint remains of another letter to the left of the same line and on the line above. We place it here according to content.

Fragment 2 preserves three lines from the righthand side of a column. It does not physically join frags. 3–6, and its placement here is based on considerations of content presented below. Altogether, column II comprises ten lines, as do all other reconstructed columns in 4Q324d.

Comments

The lines reconstructed here recount the very end of the third month as well as the entire fourth month of the year. Fragment 2 preserves the significant term

---

[27] We thus disagree with the present placement of the fragments on IAA plate 241, where frag. 5 (our new numbering) is joined with our frag. 8. Curiously, this join is not represented in the plates of DJD XXVIII. Close examination of the joins reveals, however, that frag. 4 offers a far better match than frag. 8.

tequfah, indicating that it refers to the beginning of a season (months 1, 4, 7, or 10). Two of the four annual days of *tequfah* are already incorporated in the reconstruction below: the *tequfah* of the seventh month in III, 10 and that of the tenth month in IV, 9. The only possible dates are thus the beginnings of the first and fourth months. Since another annotation precedes the *tequfah* in line 1, the fragment cannot be related to the first day of the year. Hence, it must be the *tequfah* of the fourth month, located in II, 7–9. 4Q324d employs an exceptionally long and somewhat unusual formula for indicating the end of each season, placing greater emphasis on the days of the week than do other cognate calendrical texts. For the reconstruction of the *tequfah* formula, see the excursus below. For the awkward reconstructed spelling נואספ in line 7, see the note on IV, 9 below.

The column preserves all Sabbaths of month 4 as expected. At the end of the month, however, the occurrence of the word חמישי is surprising,[28] and so is the proximity of that word to שלושים at the end of the line on frag. 5. This must in some way relate to the end of the month, but we are dealing here with the end of the fourth month, not the fifth. The mention of the ordinal number חמישי ("fifth") must thus be a reference to the fifth day of the week. In the fixed 364-day year, the fifth day of the week appears at the end of months 1, 4, 7, and 10, of which the end of month 4 is encountered here.

4Q324d Column III

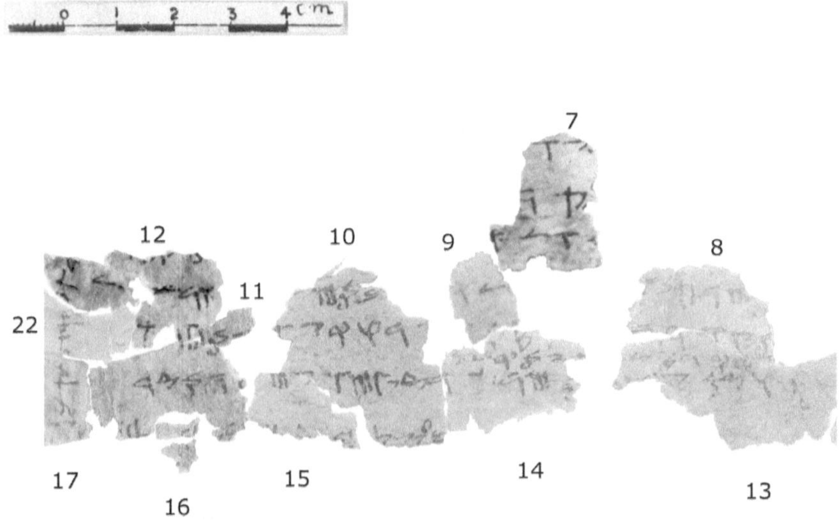

Figure 2. Reconstruction of Column III (frags. 7–17, 22). PAM 40.979, 40.985, 41.372, 41.692, 41.867, 42.426, 42.430, 43.333

---

[28] The letter *yod* at the end of the word is clearer on PAM 42.430, verifying that the word is not the cardinal number חמישה but rather the ordinal.

[השש]י אחר השבת בש[בעה] בו שבת]   5
[בארבעה עשר בו שב]ת ב[עשרים ואחד בו שבת]   6
[אחר השבת מוע]ד היצ[הר בעשרים ושׁ]מֹוֹנָה   7
ב[וֹ] שבת הׁ[יום השנ]י בֹ[ו שׁ]לוֹשׁיֹ[ם הׁ]שׁביֹ[ע]י   8
י[וֹם הרֹבֹ]יעי [תֹקוֹפֹה בארעה בוֹ שבת   9
ב[עשר בו יוֹ]ם הׁ[כפורים]   9a
בֹאחד עשֹ[ר ב]וֹ שבת בחמשה עשר בו חג   10

5. [The (beginning of the) sixth (month) is after the Sabbath. On the se]venth [in it – Sabbath.]
6. [On the fourteenth in it – Sabba]th. On [the twenty-first in it – Sabbath.]
7. [After the Sabbath (is) the Festiva]l of Oi[l. On the twenty-e]igh[th]
8. [in] it – Sabbath. [(Week)day tw]o – in [it (falls) the th]irt[ieth (day of the month). The] (beginning of the) sev[en]th (month)
9. [(is on) (week)d]ay fou[r]. *Tequfah*. On the fourth in it (= the seventh month) – Sabbath.
9a. [On the] tenth in it – the Da[y of At]onement
10. On the eleven[th in] it – Sabbath. On the fifteenth in it – the Feast of

The foundation for the reconstruction of column III was laid by Pfann, who joined frags. 10, 11, 15, and 16 into a cluster, apparently based on the gloss written upside down at their bottom margin. Pfann also assembled a second cluster, containing frags. 6, 8, 9, 13, and 14. This second cluster preserves the remains of columns II–III with the margin separating them. A third cluster comprises frags. 12, 17, and 22 and shows the vertical part of the gloss. We now suggest combining these three clusters together. Fragments 17 + 12 physically join the left side of frag. 16. The righthand side of frag. 10, in turn, joins perfectly with frag. 14; note the completion of words and even letters across the join.

Joins and Layout

Abegg read Pfann's first cluster (i.e., frags. 10, 11, 15, 16) as follows and interpreted it to refer to the third month of the year.

בשׁ[לוֹשׁיֹ]ם בו שבת   1
[○ בארעהׁ [29] עשר [בֹו שבֹ]ת   2
[בחמשה עשר בו חג   3
השבועים   [○○○○]]וֹ[ ]○○○[ ]○○[ ]שׁ[4

According to the new join suggested here, however, there is not enough space for the word עשר in the lacuna in line 2, since the word בו immediately follows בא(ר)עה.[30] The date of the Sabbath in line 2 should thus be the fourth day of the

---

[29] Note the scribal mistake in this word by the omission of *bet*.
[30] The exact layout of this join is further verified by the subsequent line 3, which is based on the continuous text and the physical contact of the two pieces.

month, rather than the fourteenth. Since in the 364-day year the dates are anchored to specific days of the week, this Sabbath cannot occur in the third month, as previously assumed, but rather in month 1, 4, 7, or 10. The next line lists a feast on the fifteenth of the same month and thus narrows our options to either month 1 or month 7 (with either the Feast of Unleavened Bread or the Feast of Tabernacles, respectively). This column ends with the word חג, with the identity of that feast left to the next column. The line quoted as line 4 is in fact the upside-down part of the marginal gloss. While Abegg thought that this was the last line of the column, which continues line 3, we now know that this is not the case and that this line constitutes the end of the gloss. The reading "Feast of Weeks" thus cannot be accepted. We perceive the continuation of line 3 as referring to the Feast of Tabernacles חג הסוכות, with the letters סו[preserved on frag. 18 at the righthand top of the next column.

Abegg read the second cluster (frags. 6, 8, 9, 13, 14) as follows:

		Column ii		Column i	
1	] ○○				
2	ב[ו שבת ה̇] [○יו ב̇]				
3	י[ום הרב]יעי [ת̇קופ̇]ה		] ○	1
4a	[עשר בו יו]ם ה[כ̇פורים]				
4	באחד עש̇ר] ב]ו שבת ב[חמשה עשר בו		שלוש̇ים]○	2

We place this cluster to the right of the previous one, preceding it in the scroll. It preserves the beginnings of lines of frag. 8, describing the festivals of the seventh month, as well as the tip of the preceding column. The join is confirmed by the *bet* of ב̇]חמשה, which continues over from frag. 14 to frag. 10. So does the upside-down *mem* on the marginal note, which can be detected on the new IAA images of frag. 14 and should be joined to the partial *mem* on frag. 10. Faint traces of the righthand end of the marginal note can possibly be traced also on frag. 13, which further substantiates the join. To this cluster we add frag. 7, which touches frag. 9 and completes the expected text perfectly.

Fragments 12, 17, and 22 contain two columns as well as a marginal note, which is the key for the placement of this cluster. At the end of the vertical gloss on frag. 17, the new IAA images show how the writing direction switches 90 degrees to the left and continues in an upside-down manner with regard to the main written column. Fragment 12 may accordingly be joined with fragments 11 and 16.

Comments

These lines describe the end of month 6 and the beginning of month 7, together with an expanded *tequfah* formula. Such an expanded formula is the norm in 4Q324d, as will be shown below. In this particular case, however, it is abbreviated. The text then continues to describe the initial days of month 7, albeit with substantial omissions, some of which were subsequently corrected. The scribe had omitted the Day of Atonement, which was later added between the lines (9a). The omitted Festival of Wood Offering was completed in a long marginal gloss, for which see below. Omitted also is the holiday of the first day of the seventh month (called יום הזכרון in 4Q320 III, 6; 4Q321 V, 2; etc.), which is represented here only as the day of *tequfah* and as heading the month, not as a holiday. In addition, the thirty-first day of the sixth month is omitted. These omissions were not corrected. Finally, the omitted letter *bet* in the word באר(ב)עה, and the letter *he* in the word בעשר(ה) constitute minor copying mistakes. While the multiple omissions admittedly raise doubt about the reconstruction of the column, two factors make it compelling: the completion of two broken letters across frags. 14 and 10 and the fact that the omission (and subsequent completion) of the Day of Atonement is not a matter of reconstruction but rather is attested quite clearly on frags. 13–14.

The Marginal Gloss

Column III ends with the words בחמשה עשר בו חג, "on the fifteenth in it (the seventh month) – the feast of." We expect that the next column will begin with the word הסוכות (Tabernacles). Luckily enough, frag. 18 with the remains of the top right margin of an unknown column preserved the letters סו[.[31] The text thus runs directly from column III to column IV. Fragments 19 and 20, which, like frag. 18 accumulated white residue and preserve a part of the top margin, are placed at the top of column IV and make good sense as the continuation of the text.

Similar to the interlinear mention of the Day of Atonement in line 9a, the gloss completes information that had been left out of the main calendar by mistake—the Festival of Wood Offering. As mentioned above, Pfann and Abegg did not connect the vertical, intercolumnar gloss between columns III and IV to the upside-down note on the bottom margin. Both of them read the bottom note as a record of the Feast of Weeks.[32] They differ regarding the intercolumnal note. Abegg's reading חש[בנות הימים, "[cal]culations of days," is difficult for several reasons. Abegg assumes a deficient spelling of the word חשבנות without *vav* following the *bet*. The absence of the *vav* is very clear in frag. 12. The spelling חשבן is very frequent in Aramaic, in which the *bet* is pronounced with the long vowel *ā* (*ḥušbān*). 4Q324d is a Hebrew

---

[31] This feast is always called חג הסוכות with the definite article *he* (e.g., 4Q320 4 III, 9; V, 7; VI, 2). Its designation here חג סוכות is admittedly awkward but hard to deny. The letters סו are not part of the calendrical vocabulary in any other way. Close examination of the new multispectral images of frag. 18 at the top of the column reveals the faint remains of *shin*, written perpendicularly to the main text. This trace is best seen on plate 240 frag. 12, IAA image number B-360071. It may indicate another, albeit shorter, marginal gloss.

[32] Pfann's reading of the gloss in the bottom margin was בחמשה עשר בו חג השב[וע]ים] והב[כ<ו>ר<י]>ם ביום א[חד (see n. 19 above). Abegg did not read a substantial statement here.

scroll, however, and the spelling חשבונות should be expected (cf. 1Q27 1 II, 2). In addition, the second letter of the second word cannot be a *yod*. The right curve of an *ayin* is clearly seen on frag. 22. Finally, a comparison with *mem* at the end of the word makes it highly unlikely that the middle letter is *mem*.

Pfann's suggestion that the vertical gloss recounts the Wood Offering solves all of the above reservations.[33] In this case the vertical note should read קר[בנות העצים. The gloss begins exactly next to III, 7, where, according to our reconstruction, the Wood Offering is mentioned. Admittedly the shape of the *ṣade* is somewhat unusual (compared with the same letter in III, 6 on frag. 7), but a similar *ṣade* is found in the cryptic document 4Q298 (1 I, 9 and 3, 2). This fact supports the possibility that the gloss was written by a second hand.

Since the upside-down gloss in the bottom margin continues the vertical gloss, we expect it to take up the theme of the Wood Offering rather than the Festival of Weeks. The preservation of the bottom gloss is extremely bad; therefore, we offer the following reading cautiously:

ששׁת̇] י̇[מ̇י̇מ̇] [שׁנ̇]י̇[מ̇ ביומ]

The composite gloss thus yields a curious statement on the Festival of Wood Offering:

קר[בנות העצימ ששׁת̇] י̇[מ̇י̇מ̇] [שׁנ̇]י̇[מ̇ ביומ]

The Off]erings of Wood [pl.] (last) six [d]ays, t[w]o in (each) day [

This note is quite interesting for halakic reasons, as it clearly echoes the sectarian view of the Festival of Wood Offering and disagrees with the rabbinic opinion.[34] 11QT[a] XI, 12 mentions ובששת ימי̇ קרבן העצים, based on a certain reconstruction since it is the feast immediately following the Feast of Oil (cf. 4Q394 1–2 col. V and DJD XXI:165). In these six days, the twelve tribes of Israel offer trees, two on each day, as mentioned in 11QT[a] XXIII–XXIV. A similar account is preserved in the rewritten Pentateuch scroll 4Q365 frag. 23, which is often considered the source of the Temple Scroll.[35] In contrast, m. Taʿan. 4:5 assigns the wood offerings to nine days spread throughout the year (cf. Josephus, *J.W.* 2.17.6 §§429–430). The author of the gloss in 4Q324d thus found it appropriate to complement the mention of the Wood Offering in III, 7 with a gloss expanding the conduct of that festival.

---

[33] Pfann, "Ancient 'Library' or 'Libraries,'" 192.

[34] For a detailed discussion of this festival, see Werman, "Wood-Offering."

[35] Molly M. Zahn, "4QReworked Pentateuch C and the Literary Sources of the Temple Scroll: A New (Old) Proposal," *DSD* 19 (2012): 133–58.

4Q324d Column IV

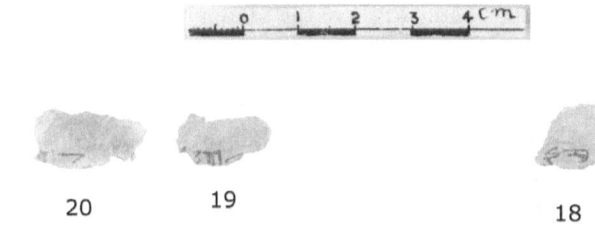

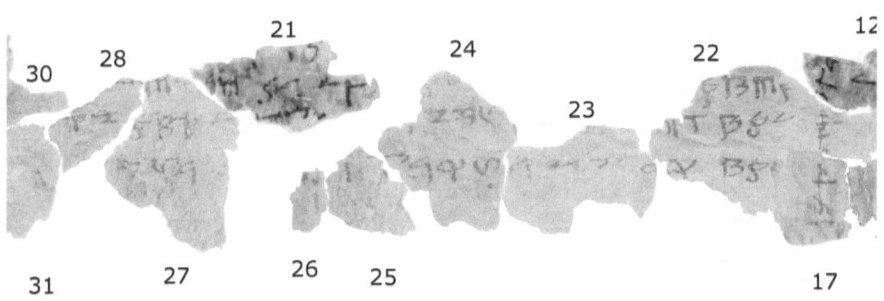

FIGURE 3. Reconstruction of Column IV (frags. 21–28). PAM 40.985, 41.692, 41.867, 42.430.

1   סו[כות יום רביעי [בּ]שמ[ונה [עש]ר בו שבת]

7   [בו שבת בעשרים ואח[ד בּ]וֹ] שבת בעשרים]
8   ושמו[נה בו שבת [יו]ם ש[ני בו שלושי]ם]
9   יום השׁ[לי]שׁ[י נו[אסף בּ]אחד [בּעשרי תקופה
10 יום רביעי בארבעהׁ בוֹ שׁ[ב]תֹ באחדׁ

1. Tab[ernacles on (week)day four]. On the ei[ghte]ent[h in it – Sabbath.]
....
7. [in it – Sabbath. On the twenty-firs]t in it – [Sabbath. On the twenty-]
8. eigh[th in it – Sabbath]. (Week)da[y t]wo – in it (falls the) thirti[eth (day of the month)]
9. (Week)day th[ree is additio]nal. On [the first day of] the tenth (month) – Tequfah
10. (on) (week)day four. On the fourth in it (= the tenth month) – S[ab]bath. On the eleve[

Joins and Layout

Fragments 19 and 20 share the same physical characteristics as frag. 18: all three fragments preserve the remains of a top margin and show white residue on the leather.[36] They should thus all be taken as one sequence.

The first words of the bottom lines of column IV are preserved on fragment 22, where days of the week are listed in lines 9–10. Since after the Feast of Tabernacles there are no more holidays in the seventh month, these two weekdays must belong to the formula which concludes the *tequfah*, as attested earlier in column III and as partly reconstructed in 4Q394 1–2 II, 3–14 and 4Q394 3–7 I, 1–3.[37] These lines thus correspond to the end of the ninth month and the beginning of the tenth.

We join frags. 22 and 23 based on the continuity of the lines. These two fragments were associated by Milik already on PAM 41.692. The composite piece reveals that line 9 mentions the third day of the week (השלישי), while line 10 mentions the fourth day (רביעי).[38] The fourth day of the week is the beginning of month 10, and the next Sabbath of this month thus falls on the fourth day of the month. This contiguity confirms the join of frag. 24, which mentions the fourth day of a certain month in the line right above a bottom margin. In addition, its contours perfectly fit those of frag. 23. The join of frags. 24 and 23 requires a refinement of the readings suggested by Abegg.[39] We reconstruct in the penultimate line: וֹאסף נ[לי]שׁ[י יום הש, "The third da[y (of the week) is additio]nal." Despite the unique spelling of נואסף, this exact term describes the epagomenal thirty-first day at the end of the season in the cognate calendar scroll 4Q394 3–7 I, 2. A Sabbath on the fourth day of the following month, reported in the bottom line 10, lends yet more credibility to the join of frags. 22–23–24 and to the suggested reconstruction.

Considerations of content allow the placement of frags. 21, 25–28 at the ends of the lines begun in frags. 22–24, together forming column IV. Fragments 25 and 26 contain a bottom margin and adjoin each other perfectly according to the

---

[36] The similarity of these three fragments was acknowledged by Milik, who placed them side by side on PAM 43.333. Pfann, however, considered frag. 19 part of a third scroll (4Q324e 6). We reinstate Milik's insight and consider these three fragments part of 4Q324d.

[37] See DJD XXI:164.

[38] Note that the serial number of the day can be preceded by the definite article but also stand without it, seemingly with no regularity. Cf. similarly the awkward formulation חג סוכות (IV, 10–V, 1) without the definite article.

[39] Abegg reads frag. 24 as follows:

1]יוֹם
2 חג [הֹאסף ○]
3 ב[ארבע]ה

This reconstruction is difficult for several reasons. First, there is no important date on the 4th, 14th, or 24th of the month in which the Feast of Tabernacle (= אסיף, "ingathering," Exod 34:22) occurs. Second, the biblical term חג האסיף is never used in the Dead Sea Scrolls. Third, that feast appears already in frag. 18, where it is named חג (ה)סוכות as expected. Last, the traces of the first letter in line 2 protrude below the line and can thus only be *dalet* or *vav*.

breakage of lines; they thus form a natural sequel to the previous cluster. Despite the fact that frag. 21 does not touch any of the other fragments, it shares with frag. 27 both the letter *lamed* of the word שלושים on line 8 and the word העשרי on line 9. Note that the word עשרים in line 7 exceeds the end of the column and reaches column V. The remains of its *mem* are visible on frag. 30. Although Pfann assigned some of these fragments to separate scrolls, we consider it improbable to see such a perfect match of text and contour across so many fragments and thus consider them as stemming from one scroll.

4Q324d Column V

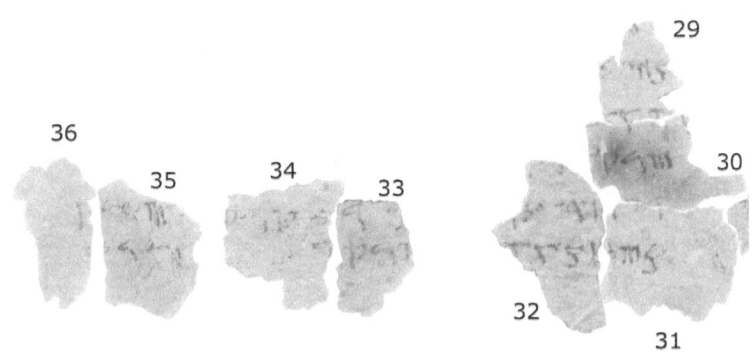

FIGURE 4. Reconstruction of Column V (frags. 29–36). PAM 41.461, 41.692, 41.867.

5 [בעשרימ] שבת בששה עשר בו שבת בעשרימ[ב]וֹ[
6 ושל[ושה בו שבת בשלושימ בו שבת]
7 שׁנימֹ[עשר החודש אחר השבת בשבעה בו]
8 שבת בֹּאַ[רבעה עשר בו שבת]
9 בֹּעַשׂרימֹ[ואח]דֹ בו שבתֹ [ב]עַשׂרימֹ
10 ושמֹונהֹ[בו] vacat ב [שֹבת ש]נֹי בוֹ

5. [in] it[– Sabbath. On the sixteenth in it – Sabbath. On the twenty-]
6. thi[rd in it – Sabbath. On the thirtieth in it – Sabbath.]
7. (The beginning of the) twelf[th month is after the Sabbath. On the seventh in it –]
8. Sabbath. On the fo[urteenth in it – Sabbath.]
9. On the twenty-[firs]t in it – Sabbath. [On the] twenty-
10. eighth [in it –] Sabbath. On *vacat* [(weekday)tw]o – in it (falls)

Joins and Layout

After composing the bottom strip of columns II–IV, we are left with only nine fragments attesting to a bottom margin and not containing names of *mishmarot*.[40] We were able to arrange six of them in column V, despite Pfann's earlier assigning of them to various separate scrolls. Fragments 30 and 31 contain the right margin and can be joined to frag. 28, standing at the left end of column IV. In addition, the last letter of line 7 in column IV is visible on frag. 30. Fragment 32 was joined already by Pfann in the plates of DJD XXVIII to frag. 31. The four other fragments are joined here based on their content. In addition, the contours of frag. 30 touch frags. 31 and 32, and it shares two letters with frag. 31. Fragment 29 also touches frag. 30 and shares the *shin* and the *nun* with it.

Comment

These lines cover half of month 11 and the entire month 12. If our reconstruction is correct, another line describing the thirty-first day of month 12, the very last day of the year, would have been written at the beginning of the next column (VI). It would not have employed more than the first line, and hence one may expect that another list or composition was copied in the rest of that column.

4Q324d Columns VI–VII

Joins and Layout

In addition to the fragments discussed thus far, seven fragments in Cryptic A script of a similar hand were preserved. Six of the fragments are physically joined here, preserving a bottom margin, while the seventh preserves a top margin. These fragments record names of priestly families (*mishmarot*) and are thus different from the content of columns I–V. Since the *mishmarot* list is rather short, it is the perfect candidate to fit into the next column (VI) of the scroll. The single fragment preserving a top margin would have belonged in yet another column VII. Although no physical join can be proven for the placement of frags. 37–41 in column VI, their overall material pattern resembles that of the previous columns.

An additional consideration supports the placement of the list in column VI. Most calendrical documents from Cave 4 constitute anthologies of various calendar lists. Some of these lists contain *mishmarot* in various constellations and some do not. Thus, lists of *mishmarot* follow the calendar in 4Q319.[41] In addition, a list of the twenty-four *mishmarot* without any calendrical notation next to them appears preceding the calendar in 4Q329 and in the reconstructed "master list" that probably underlay that scroll.[42]

---

[40] For those fragments containing names of *mishmarot*, see below.
[41] The miscellaneous calendrical lists are collected in 4Q319 7 II and on frags. 9–73 (DJD XXI:221–44).
[42] See DJD XXI:145.

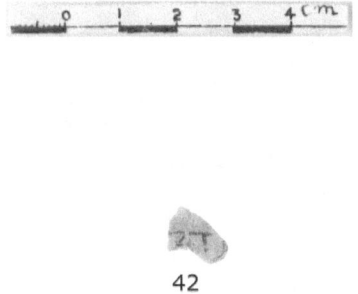

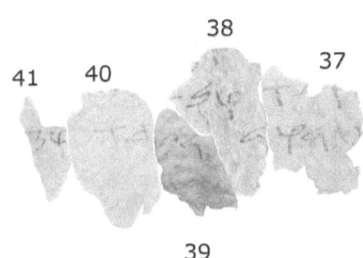

FIGURE 5. Reconstruction of Column VI (frags. 37–41). PAM 41.457, 41.692, 41.867, 43.340

6 [גמול דליה מעזיה]
7 [יהויריב ידעיה חרים שערים]
8 [מלכיה מימן] הקֹ[וץ אביה]
9 [ישוע שכ]נֹיה אלישׁיֹבֹ[יקים]
10 [חופה י]שׁובאב בלגה אמֹ[ר

6. [Gamul Delaiah Maʿoziah]
7. [Yoiarib Yedaʿiah Ḥarim Seʿorim]
8. [Malkiah Miyyamin] Haqq[oṣ Abiah]
9. [Yešuʿa Šek]aniah Eliašib[Yaqim]
10. [Ḥuppah Ye]šubab Bilgah ʾImme[r

Milik had seemingly believed that the *mishmarot* fragments belong to a different scroll than the calendar, hence there are no images of these fragments on PAM 42.429 and 42.430 (taken in 1957). He later changed his mind, as the *mishmarot* fragments are placed next to the calendar on PAM 43.340 (taken in 1960). Pfann regards frags. 37, 38, and 40 as part of 4Q324i; frag. 41 as 4Q324h 9; and frag. 42 as 4Q324d 1. Fragment 39 is not included in Pfann's edition.

The reconstructed sequence of fragments is based on the match of contours as well as on letters split between the pieces. Fragments 37 and 38 were squeezed together in PAM 41.692, 42.429; thus the right side of frag. 37 rose above the left side of frag. 38. Though they seem to have been torn when separated, it is still possible to join them quite neatly. Fragment 39 exists only on PAM 41.692 and can no longer be traced in the IAA collection. It contains the first two letters of the name בלגה and joins well with frag. 38. The rest of the name בלגה is found on frag. 40. Fragment 41 contains the first two letters of אִמ[ר, which is the next priestly family in order, and joins frag. 40.

Column VI commenced with one or more lines recording the end of the calendar year, as the previous column V ends at day 28 of month 12. One would expect that the formula ending the year is at least as long as the earlier *tequfah* formulas in 4Q324d or that of 4Q394 3–7 I, 1–3. Be that as it may, the *mishmarot* list would have begun at line 6 (assuming ten lines in column VI), leaving a place in the first five lines for the concluding formula of the year.

Column VI ends with the mishmar name אמר. The additional five *mishmarot* names expected at the end of the list would have been contained in the subsequent column VII. Remains of the names [חזי]ר̇ and הפ[צץ are preserved on frag. 42, just below the top margin. The fact that column VII contains only one line of *mishmarot* names implies that at least one more list or composition was copied on this scroll.[43] Unfortunately, nothing was preserved from this list or composition.

Comments

The priestly name ישבאב (1 Chr 24:13) is variously spelled ישיבאב (4Q319 VII, 6) and appears here as [י]שׁוּבאב (frag. 37; legible only on the older images). Since *yod* and *vav* are graphically similar only in the square script, the variation might indicate that the scroll, or at least the list of the *mishmarot*, was copied from an earlier list written in the square script.

Fragments 1, 43–62

Fragments 1 and 43–62 are either too small to be identified and are placed too far away from the rest of the joined fragments or their placement in the scroll is equivocal. They are thus not discussed here but will be presented in the full edition of 4Q324d.

---

[43] It is also possible that the *mishmarot* list preceded the calendar, but the option chosen here fits better with the material reconstruction.

IV. Excursus: The *Tequfah* Formula and the Description of the Ends of Months

The *tequfah* formula describes the point of transition between seasons: the end of the third month of every season, followed by the beginning of the next season.[44] In the unique structure of the 364-day year, regular months contain thirty days while the third (i.e., the last) month of each season contains thirty-one days. The *tequfah* formula appears in fragmentary form in the scrolls 4Q394 1–2, 4Q394 3–7, and 6Q17, where special effort is invested in naming the weekdays at the transition of the seasons. These occurrences, however, are highly fragmentary, so that our knowledge of the indication of the *tequfah* can be enriched from 4Q324d, where this formula is exceptionally pronounced. Since the latter scroll is also far from complete, problems arise when one attempts to reconstruct the *tequfah* formula.

One may expect to find full *tequfah* formulas three times in 4Q324d: in the third–fourth months (col. II), in the sixth–seven months (col. III), and in the ninth–tenth months (col. IV). Partial formulas are also expected to appear at the beginning of the first month and the end of the twelfth month. In the suggested reconstruction of 4Q324d, we have remains of all formulas but one, the opening line of the year. Their exact content is not entirely consistent, however.

The best-preserved formula is found in column IV, describing the transition between months 9 and 10. That formula begins with the thirtieth day of month 9, which falls on the second day of the week (Monday). This day is described as follows (IV, 8):

[יו]ם ש[ני בו שלושי]ם

The seco[nd da]y (of the week) – in it (is day) thirt[y (of month X)

Although the syntax of this phrase is awkward, it gains support from a parallel in the small calendrical fragment 6Q17, which reads:[45]

[שני בו 30

M. Baillet reconstructed here: ה[חדש ה]שני בו 30, "the second month – in it (are) 30 (days)," assuming that the preserved words count the number of days in the second month.[46] What we know today, however, about the recording of weekdays in 4Q324d suggests that 6Q17 rather records the second weekday on the thirtieth day of an unknown month. A reference to the second day of the week, on the thirtieth day of the third month, is found also in the *tequfah* formula of 4Q394 1–2 II,

---

[44] For the significance of the seasons in the 364-day year, see Ben-Dov, *Head of All Years*, 31–52.

[45] Maurice Baillet, in *Les 'petites grottes' de Qumran*, 2 vols., DJD III (Oxford: Clarendon, 1962), 1:132–33.

[46] Talmon followed this reconstruction in DJD XXI:7.

5–7. That unit also mentions the previous day, the twenty-ninth, named after its weekday designation אחר השבת, "the day after the Sabbath." The above sources demonstrate how important it was for the authors of this type of calendar to specifically mention and number the weekdays at the transition of the seasons.

Going back now to 4Q324d IV, 9, the next day in the formula is the third day of the week (Tuesday) = the thirty-first of the month. This day is designated here by the adjective נואסף, "an additional/epagomenal day," indicating the simple fact that a thirty-first day is a special addition, enacted only at the end of the season. A parallel to this expression is fragmentarily attested at the end of the year in 4Q394 3–7, 1–2: יֹום [וארבעה ושלש]ים סאת שלוש השנה ושלמה וסֹף[נו, "additio]nal and the year is complete three hundred and six[ty-four] days."[47]

Subsequently in 4Q324d IV, 9, the first day of month 10 is mentioned by its weekday רביעי (the fourth day, i.e., Wednesday) and is named תקופה.

The *tequfah* formula at the transition from month 6 to 7 is also preserved in 4Q324d column III. That text suffered substantial omissions, however, neglecting to mention holidays and elements of the *tequfah* formula and attesting to several spelling mistakes. Thus, in this occurrence of the *tequfah* formula, the second day of the week (= the thirtieth of month 6) was specified, but the following day, the third weekday (= the thirty-first), was omitted. Word order is also different: while on column IV the order is: month name – *tequfah* – weekday (fourth), the order in column III is: month name – weekday (fourth) – *tequfah*. It is difficult to determine whether this difference is a simple mistake like other omissions in column III or whether it indicates flexibility—or maybe indeterminacy—of the formula.

The preservation of column II, at the end of the first season, is even worse than the columns discussed so far in the excursus. Here, only the word תקופה remains from the entire *tequfah* formula (II, 8).

Finally, at the end of month 12 the evidence is spread across the (extant) end of column V and the (not extant) beginning of column VI. For this month only a reference to the second day of the week, even without its date, has survived. The word יום ("day") itself is missing in that line, and a *vacat* appears instead.

We turn now to the special way in which the endings of months are enumerated in 4Q324d. This matter bears on the *tequfah* formula but does not entirely overlap it since not all months stand at the end of seasons. Of the three months in each season, the *tequfah* formula demanded a reference to the weekday of the thirtieth and thirty-first days of the third month of every season. In addition, the weekday of the thirtieth day of the second month of every season was also mentioned, by force of its being a Sabbath day. It seems likely, therefore, that the author of 4Q324d sought to make the records of the thirtieth day of every month more systematic, unlike the author of 4Q394, and thus recorded even the ending of the first

[47] DJD X:8.

month in each season. An example of that practice is partly preserved at the end of month 4 (4Q324d II, 10; frags. 3–6): יום ה[חמשי] ב[ו שלושי]ם.

To conclude, it turns out that the author of 4Q324d was exceptionally keen on recording weekdays in his calendrical notations, keener than the authors of comparable calendrical texts.[48]

V. Textual Reconstruction of 4Q324d
(See fig. 6, p. 932.)

Column I

1 [   ]
2 [   ]
3 [הראשונ י]וֹמ[הרביעי תקופה בארבעה]
4 [בו שבת בא]חֹד עשר בו שבת בארבעה
5 [עשר בו הפסח יום שלישי בחמישה עשר]
6 [בו חג המצות יום רביעי בשמונה עשר]
7 [בו שבת בעשרים וחמישה בו שבת הנפ]
8 [העומר בעשרים וששה בו אחר השבת יומ]
9 [החמשי בו שלושים השני יום הששי בשנימ]
10 [בו שבת בתשעה בו שבת בששה עשר בו]

3. [(The beginning of the) first (month) on (week)d]ay[four. *Tequfah*. On the fourth]
4. [in it – Sabbath.] On the e[leventh in it – Sabbath. On the four-]
5. [teenth in it – the Passah, (week)day three. On the fifteenth]
6. [in it – the Feast of Mazzot, (week)day four. On the eighteenth]
7. [in it – Sabbath. On the twenty-fifth in it – Sabbath. The Waving]
8. [of the Sheaf is on the twenty-sixth in it, after the Sabbath. (Week)day]
9. [Five – in it (falls) the thirtieth (day of the month). (The beginning of the) second (month) is on (week)day six. On the second]
10. [in it – Sabbath. On the ninth in it – Sabbath. On the sixteenth in it –]

---

[48] For the insertion of weekdays in dating formulas, see Ben-Dov, *Head of All Years*, 62–67.

FIGURE 6. 4Q324d Columns II–VI

Column II

1. [שבת בעשרים ושלושה בו שבת בשלושימ]
2. [בו שבת השלישי אחר השבת בשבעה]
3. [בו שבת בארבעה עשר בו שבת בחמשה]
4. [עשר בו אחר השבת חג השבועימ]
5. [בעשרימ ואחד בו שבת בעשרימ]
6. [ושמונה בו שבת יום שני בו שלושים]
7. י[ומ] השלישי נואספ vacat הרביעי יומ הרביעי
8. תקופ[ה בארבעה ב]וֹ שבת בא[חד עשר בו]
9. שבֹתֹ[בשמונה עש]רֹ[ב]וֹ שבֹת בֹּעשֹ[רימ]
10. [וחמשה בו ש]בֹת יֹ[ום]חֹמישי[ב]וֹ שלושׁים

bottom margin

1. [Sabbath. On the twenty-third in it – Sabbath. On the thirtieth]
2. [in it – Sabbath. (The beginning of the) third (month) is after the Sabbath. On the seventh]
3. [in it – Sabbath. On the fourteenth in it – Sabbath. On the fif-]
4. [teenth in it, after the Sabbath, the Feast of Weeks.]
5. [On the twenty-first in it – Sabbath. On the twenty-]
6. [eighth in it – Sabbath. (Week)day two – in it (falls) the thirtieth (day of the month).]
7. [(Week)d]ay [three is additional. vacat (The beginning of the) fourth (month) is on (week)day four.]
8. Tequf[ah. On the fourth in] it – Sabbath. On the e[leventh in it –]
9. Sabbath. [On the eighteenth in] it – Sabbath. On the twe[nty-]
10. [fifth in it – Sab]bath. (Week)d[ay] five – [in] it (falls) the thirtieth (day of the month).

Column III

1. [החמישי יומ הששי בשנימ בו שבת]
2. [בשלושה בו מועד התירוש אחר השבת]
3. [בתשעה בו שבת בששה עשר בו שבת בעשרימ]
4. [ושלושה בו שבת בשלושימ בו שבת]
5. [הששי אחר השבת בש]בֹּעה[בו שבת]
6. [בארבעה עשר בו שב]ת ב[עשרימ ואחד בו שבת]
7. [אחר השבת מוע]דֹ היצ[הר בעשרימ]וֹ[ש]מֹוֹנֹ[ה]
8. ב[וֹ] שבת הֹ[יומ השנ]יֹ ב[ו ש]לֹושיֹ[מ ה]שֹביֹ[ע]יֹ
9. יֹ[ומ הרֹבֹ[יעי]תֹקוֹפֹה בארעהֹ בו שבֹת
9a. ב[עשר בו יו]ֹמ ה[]כֹפורימֹ
10. באחד עשֹ[ר ב]וֹ שבת בחמשה עשרֹ בו חג

bottom margin

שֹשֹתֹ[ ] יֹ[מֹיֹמֹ] [שֹנֹ]יֹ[מ ביומ]

1. [The (beginning of the) fifth (month) is on (week)day six. On the second (day) in it – Sabbath.]
2. [On the third in it – The Feast of Wine, after the Sabbath.
3. [On the ninth in it – Sabbath. On the sixteenth in it – Sabbath. On the twenty-]
4. [third in it – Sabbath. On the thirtieth in it – Sabbath.]
5. [The (beginning of the) sixth (month) is after the Sabbath. On the se]venth [in it – Sabbath.]
6. [On the fourteenth in it – Sabba]th. On [the twenty-first in it – Sabbath.]
7. [After the Sabbath (is) the Festiva]l of Oi[l. On the twenty-e]igh[th]
8. [in] it – Sabbath. [(Week)day tw]o – in [it (falls) the th]irti[eth (day of the month). The] (beginning of the) sev[en]th (month)
9. [(is on) (week)d]ay fou[r]. *Tequfah*. On the fourth in it (= the seventh month) – Sabbath.
9a. [On the] tenth in it – the Da[y of At]onement
10. On the eleven[th in] it – Sabbath. On the fifteenth in it – the Feast of

Marginal gloss:
The Off]erings of Wood [pl.] (last) six [d]ays, t[w]o in (each) day

Column IV

top margin

1 סו[כות יום רביעי [בּשמ]ונה [עשרׄ בּ]ו שבת]
2 [בעשרים וחמשה בו שבת יום חמשי בו שלושימ]
3 [השמיני יום הששי בשנימ בו שבת בתשעה]
4 [בו שבת בששה עשר בו שבת בעשרימ]
5 [ושלושה בו שבת בשלושימ בו שבת התשיעי]
6 [אחר השבת בשבעה בו שבת בארבעה עשר]
7 [בו שבת בעשרימ ואח[דׄ בֹּ]וׄ] שבת בעשרי[מׄ
8 ושמו[נה בו שבת [יֹו]מׄ ש[נׄ]י בו שלושי[מׄ]
9 יום הש[לׄ]לי[/שׄ]י נו[אסף בֹּ]אחד [בֹּעשׂרׂי תקופה
10 יום רׄביעי בארבעהׄ בֹּוׄ שׄ[ב]תׄ באחדׄ

bottom margin

1. Tab[ernacles on (week)day four]. On the ei[ghte]ent[h] in it – Sabbath.]
2. [On the twenty-fifth in it – Sabbath. (Week)day five – in it (falls) the thirtieth (day of the month).]
3. [The (beginning of the) eighth (month) is on (week)day six. On the second in it – Sabbath. On the ninth]
4. [in it – Sabbath. On the sixteenth in it – Sabbath. On the twenty-]
5. [third in it – Sabbath. On the thirtieth in it – Sabbath. (The beginning of the) ninth (month)]
6. [is after the Sabbath. On the seventh in it – Sabbath. On the fourteenth]
7. [in it – Sabbath. On the twenty-firs]t in it – [Sabbath. On the twent]y-

8. eigh[th in it – Sabbath.]. (Week)da[y t]wo – in it (falls) the thirti[eth (day of the month)]
9. (Week)day th[ree is additio]nal. On [the first (day) of]the tenth (month)- *Tequfah*
10. (on) (week)day four. On the fourth in it – S[ab]bath. On the eleve-

Column V

1 [עשר בו שבת בשמונה עשר בו]
2 [שבת בעשרים וחמישה בו שבת יומ]
3 [החמשי בו שלושימ עשתי עשר החודש]
4 [יומ הששי בשנימ בו שבת בתשעה]
5 [ב]וֹ[ ] שבת בששה עשר בו שבת בעשרימ[]
6 ושל[ושה בו שבת בשלושימ בו שבת]
7 שנימׄ[עשר החודש אחר השבת בשבעה בו]
8 שבת בֹאׄ[רבעה עשר בו שבת]
9 בֹעׄשרימׄ[ואח]דׄ בו שבתׄ [ב]עׄשרימׄ
10 ושמׄונהׄ[בו [שׁבת ב *vacat* [ש]נׄי בוֹ

bottom margin

1. [-nth in it – Sabbath. On the eighteenth in it –]
2. [Sabbath. On the twenty-fifth in it – Sabbath. (Week)day]
3. [five – in it (falls) the thirtieth (day of the month). (The beginning of the) eleventh (month)]
4. [is on (week)day six. On the second in it – Sabbath. On the ninth]
5. [in] it[– Sabbath. On the sixteenth in it – Sabbath. On the twenty-]
6. thi[rd in it – Sabbath. On the thirtieth in it – Sabbath.]
7. (The beginning of) twelf[th month is after the Sabbath. On the seventh in it –]
8. Sabbath. On the fo[urteenth in it – Sabbath.]
9. On the twenty-[firs]t in it – Sabbath. [On the] twenty-
10. eighth [in it –] Sabbath. On *vacat* [(weekday) tw]o – in it (falls)

Column VI

1 [שלושימ יומ השלישי נואספ]
2 [ ]
3 [ ]
4 [ ]
5 [ ]
6 [גמול דליה מעזיה]
7 [יהויריב ידעיה חרימ שערימ]
8 [מלכיה מימנ]הקׄ[וצ אביה]
9 [ישוע ש]בׄנׄיה אלישׁיׄבׄ[יקימ]
10 [חופה י]שׁובאב בלגה אמׄ[ר

bottom margin

1. [the thirtieth day (of the month). (Week)day three is additional]
6. [Gamul Delaiah Maʿoziah]
7. [Yoiarib Yedaʿiah Ḥarim Seʿorim]
8. [Malkiah Miyyamin] Haqq[oṣ Abiah]
9. [Yešuʿa Šek]aniah Eliašib[Yaqim]
10. [Ḥuppah Ye]šubab Bilgah ʾImme[r

Column VII

top margin

1 [ ]חזי[ ]ֹר הפ[צץ פתחיה יחזקאל יכינ]

1. [Ḥezi]r Happ[iṣṣeṣ Petaḥia Yeḥezqel Yakin]

VI. Conclusion

Meticulous work led us to a material reconstruction of a well-preserved sequence of text from the calendrical scroll 4Q324d. Only the main lines of our work are presented here, as we intend to present the full edition elsewhere. We hope to have proven that what had been formerly conceived as the remains of six different scrolls can now stand as one scroll only. Other cryptic scrolls from Cave 4 should be treated similarly.[49] The limited circulation of the cryptic script in the Yaḥad is useful for the study of secrecy and esotericism in that community. It is also valuable for enriching our knowledge about other cases of cryptology in writings from antiquity, a well-known and intriguing aspect of ongoing research.

The calendrical document 4Q324d resembles the one contained at the beginning of the scroll 4Q394 3–7 (4QMMTª). 4Q324d differs from 4Q394 in the way it assigns special attention to weekdays included in the *tequfah* formula. In addition, a unique intercolumnar gloss surprisingly aligns this text with the halakah of the Temple Scroll. This scroll thus adds a small albeit unique detail to the study of the sectarian calendar.

We feel privileged to have achieved the publication of one of the last unpublished Dead Sea Scrolls. It is our contention that further study of the scrolls, whether published or unpublished, with renewed attention and newly available techniques, will be able to produce more new and exciting information for students of Second Temple Judaism.

---

[49] For a similar claim with regard to the Cryptic A copies of Serekh haEdah from Cave 4 see Asaf Gayer, Daniel Stökl Ben Ezra, and Jonathan Ben-Dov, "A New Join of Two Fragments of Serekh haEdah from Cave 4 and Its Implications," *DSD* 23 (2016): 139–54.

Jesus's Question to Pilate in Mark 15:2

JONATHAN SCHWIEBERT
schwiebertj@lr.edu
Lenoir-Rhyne University, Hickory, NC 28601

A narrative-critical reading of Jesus's ambiguous reply to Pilate in Mark 15:2 is significantly enhanced if that reply is interpreted as a question. Although this interpretation has occasionally been suggested, a full case for its value has so far not been advanced, despite the linguistic, grammatical, and narrative plausibility of the interpretation. This article makes that case, with special attention to the relationship of this question to the characterization of Jesus in Mark.

Jesus's enigmatic reply to Pilate's question of Jesus's status as king of the Jews in Mark 15:2 (σὺ λέγεις, "you say") comes at a crucial moment in the narrative and has dire ramifications for Jesus's fate in that narrative. Nevertheless, narrative critics have tended to overlook Jesus's reply in their otherwise insightful readings. While other critical approaches may have recourse to Mark's broader theological or ideological imagination, narrative criticism must explore the narrative implications of Jesus's reply, especially as it emerges from and impacts the character Jesus. But precisely at this point, narrative critics have had little to say. For instance, Jack Dean Kingsbury, contending that Jesus is being proclaimed "king" in Mark, interprets σὺ λέγεις as a tacit affirmation on the narrator's part, albeit a "circumlocutory" one.[1] Kingsbury thus ascribes Jesus's evasiveness to the *narrator*'s perception that this title, on Pilate's lips, amounts to a charge of insurrection—a misleading perception the narrator wishes to correct. Yet why the *character* Jesus would affirm this charge, however tacitly, is left unexplained—a puzzling omission, given the stakes for Jesus in the narrative. In Mary Ann Tolbert's reading, Jesus's reply (which she translates: "You say so") is, so to speak, the beginning of the silence that falls once Jesus has made his confession before the high priest (14:62) and "has nothing more to admit to the present tenants of the vineyard."[2] Thus, his reply serves no

I would like to thank Eric Thurman and Scott Elliott for constructive feedback and encouragement on earlier drafts of this paper and Adele Reinhartz and an anonymous reviewer for helpful suggestions that improved this final draft.

[1] Jack Dean Kingsbury, *The Christology of Mark's Gospel* (Philadelphia: Fortress, 1983), 125–28, 151–52, 163–64, 171.

[2] Mary Ann Tolbert, *Sowing the Gospel: Mark's World in Literary-Historical Perspective*

meaningful narrative purpose in Tolbert's reading, least of all for the character Jesus. Edwin Broadhead admits as much: "the brief exchange between Pilate and Jesus offers little substance"; Jesus merely "blunts the attempt to label him a king."[3] Richard A. Horsley, who sees in Pilate's question an element of the climax of Mark's plot, says of Jesus's reply merely that he "never admits" to the title of "king."[4] Elizabeth Struthers Malbon, finally, emphasizing once more the misleading nature of Pilate's question ("Are you the king of the Jews?"), labels Jesus's reply "begrudging."[5] But what induces Jesus to offer this "begrudging" reply she does not say. Her reading would be unchanged had Jesus offered no reply at all.

Narrative critics appear unable to make sense of Jesus's words to Pilate. In their readings, he may as well have remained silent. Nevertheless, the awkward fact remains that Jesus does offer a brief, ambiguous reply, almost his last words in the narrative. That ambiguity is quickly perceived. Reading Jesus's reply as a qualified or tacit admission ("Yes, you could say that") proves problematic or even counterproductive for the plot, not to mention the character Jesus. As Morna D. Hooker has pointed out, any sort of affirmation here, no matter how "circumlocutory" or "begrudging," makes Pilate's subsequent reluctance to execute Jesus extremely awkward.[6] Meanwhile, these words are at least as suggestive of a mild *refusal* as they

---

(Minneapolis: Fortress, 1989), 278. Of the trial before Pilate, she writes, "Jesus need not defend himself against the charge of insurrection" (228). So why does he answer Pilate at all, and what does his answer actually mean?

[3] Edwin Broadhead, *Prophet, Son, Messiah: Narrative Form and Function in Mark 14–16*, JSNTSup 97 (Sheffield: JSOT Press, 1994), 167, 188. Broadhead seems to attribute Jesus's reply wholly to the demands of a parallel structure with the Sanhedrin trial. Thus, Jesus's words in 15:2 are structurally necessary but carry little narrative force (162–67).

[4] Horsley's interpretation of Jesus's reply in 15:2 can be found embedded in his interpretation of Jesus's reply to the high priest; his interest in this verse lies exclusively with Pilate's question rather than Jesus's reply (*Hearing the Whole Story: The Politics of Plot in Mark's Gospel* [Louisville: Westminster John Knox, 2001], esp. 99, 252).

[5] This one word is, indeed, virtually all she says about it. See Elizabeth Struthers Malbon, *Mark's Jesus: Characterization as Narrative Christology* (Waco, TX: Baylor University Press, 2009), 118, 172. See also David Rhoads, Joanna Dewey, and Donald Michie, *Mark as Story: An Introduction to the Narrative of a Gospel*, 2nd ed. (Minneapolis: Fortress, 1999), 86–87 and 111: "He gives truthful evidence for his death sentence to the Judean authorities, and he does not compromise that faithful witness before Pilate." Authors do not say, however, how Jesus's enigmatic response (perhaps a refusal) does not "compromise that faithful witness." Again, in his thirty-page narrative reading of Mark, Robert C. Tannehill gives hardly a glance at the trial before Pilate (79) and says nothing of Jesus's reply ("The Gospel of Mark as Narrative Christology," *Semeia* 16 [1979]: 57–95). Finally, Paul Danove makes nothing of Jesus's exchange with Pilate in his lengthy and detailed study, *The Rhetoric of Characterization of God, Jesus, and Jesus' Disciples in the Gospel of Mark*, JSNTSup 290 (London: T&T Clark, 2005).

[6] Morna D. Hooker, *The Gospel according to Saint Mark*, BNTC (Peabody, MA: Hendrickson, 1991), 367–68; cf. Joel Marcus, *Mark 8–16: A New Translation with Introduction and Commentary*, AYB 27A (New Haven: Yale University Press, 2009), 1033–35. Note that Jesus gives the same reply

are an affirmation: "No, those are your words, not mine."⁷ But why, in that case, would Jesus not simply deny it outright ("No"; or "I am not")? A third option is simple ambiguity ("You say so"), but this interpretation likewise offers no compelling reason for Jesus to break his silence. Such an answer is no answer—and yet it carries significant risks. To what end? Taking Jesus's reply as ambiguously yes, ambiguously no, or simply ambiguously noncommittal leaves the narrative critic unable to explain the utterance within the fabric of a richly woven narrative.

A neglected alternative to all these interpretations would, however, allow Jesus's reply to Pilate to bear significantly more narrative weight, while also better fitting the portrait of Jesus that emerges in Mark, especially in the last chapters. That alternative is to repunctuate Jesus's reply. Jesus is not asserting anything; he is asking Pilate a question.

This alternative has obvious parallels with Pilate's question in the same verse:

σὺ εἶ ὁ βασιλεὺς τῶν Ἰουδαίων
Are you the king of the Jews?

σὺ λέγεις
Do you say so?

Neglecting this syntactical parallel, critics have tended to treat σὺ λέγεις on analogy with the σὺ εἶπας of Matt 26:64, the Matthean Jesus's reply to Caiaphas, which appears to redact Mark 14:62 (ἐγώ εἰμι) and which can hardly be read as a question.⁸ What held for Matt 26:64 has been taken to apply to Mark 15:2.⁹ But this approach has obvious flaws, especially if we accept Markan priority.¹⁰ Regardless of how Matt

---

in Luke, where the charge is explicitly that he makes himself a "king." Pilate, on hearing Jesus's words (σὺ λέγεις), finds him innocent of that charge, which is unthinkable if this is a tacit admission (Luke 23:2–4).

⁷ This is well noted by Bas M. F. van Iersel, *Mark: A Reader-Response Commentary*, trans. W. H. Bisscheroux, JSNTSup 164 (Sheffield: Sheffield Academic, 1998), 459.

⁸ Again, though, Westcott-Hort offers that as a possibility (see J. Henry Thayer, "Σὺ εἶπας, Σὺ λέγεις, in the Answers of Jesus," *JBL* 13 [1894]: 40–49, here 45, https://doi.org/10.2307/3268914).

⁹ An oft-cited article by David R. Catchpole sets the standard here: "The Answer of Jesus to Caiaphas (Matt. XXVI. 64)," *NTS* 17 (1971): 213–26; see, e.g., R. T. France, *The Gospel of Mark: A Commentary on the Greek Text*, NIGTC (Grand Rapids: Eerdmans, 2002), 628. The strategy both predates and postdates Catchpole; see, e.g., S. J. Andrews, "Matt. xxvi. 64," *JBL* 7 (1887): 90–93, https://doi.org/10.2307/3268782; and Raymond E. Brown, *The Death of the Messiah: From Gethsemane to the Grave; A Commentary on the Passion Narratives in the Four Gospels*, 2 vols., ABRL (New York: Doubleday, 1994), 1:489–93, 733.

¹⁰ Markan priority remains a contested issue; see, e.g., Alan Garrow, "Streeter's 'Other' Synoptic Solution: The Matthew Conflator Hypothesis," *NTS* 62 (2016): 207–26; Thomas Brodie, *Proto-Luke: The Oldest Gospel Account* (Limerick: Dominican Biblical Institute, 2006); and William R. Farmer, *The Gospel of Jesus: The Pastoral Relevance of the Synoptic Problem* (Louisville: Westminster John Knox, 1994). Even if Mark is the later text, however, my larger argument holds (see below).

26:64 may have interpreted Mark 14:62 and what that may imply for his interpretation of Mark 15:2, such a reading is not determinative for his redaction of the earlier text. Matthew may well have taken an ambiguous utterance, meant as a question, and "misread" it as a statement. Moreover, it is far from clear that Matthew and Luke did interpret Mark 15:2 as a statement. Jesus's reply to Pilate in both Matthew (27:11) and Luke (23:3) follows Mark 15:2 so closely that, if Mark 15:2 can be read as a question, the Matthean and Lukan replies can also be read this way.[11] Meanwhile, Luke's version of Jesus's reply to Caiaphas (here the Sanhedrin) in Luke 22:70, a pluralized form of σὺ λέγεις (ὑμεῖς λέγετε), can itself be read as a question.[12]

Matthew 26:64, therefore, ought to be bracketed as a foundation for reading Mark 15:2. When this is done, the syntactical parallel nearest to hand (i.e., in 15:2) suggests that Jesus's utterance is, like Pilate's, a question. Further, the formula Mark uses to introduce Jesus's reply is precisely what one would expect if the reply is meant to be taken as a question. That formula reads ὁ δὲ ἀποκριθεὶς αὐτῷ λέγει. Earlier in the narrative, Mark twice used exactly this formula (mutatis mutandis) to introduce what were clearly questions: ὁ δὲ ἀποκριθεὶς αὐτοῖς λέγει (9:19); ὁ δὲ ἀποκριθεὶς εἶπεν αὐτοῖς (10:3). Four additional instances from the prior narrative, again introducing what are clearly questions, are substantially identical to Mark 15:2: καὶ ἀποκριθεὶς αὐτοῖς λέγει (3:33); καὶ ἀποκριθεὶς αὐτῷ ὁ Ἰησοῦς εἶπεν (10:51); καὶ ἀποκριθεὶς ὁ Ἰησοῦς ἔλεγεν διδάσκων ἐν τῷ ἱερῷ (12:35); καὶ ἀποκριθεὶς ὁ Ἰησοῦς εἶπεν αὐτοῖς (14:48). In chapter 15 itself, some nine sentences after 15:2, Pilate's first question to the crowd is introduced with a remarkably similar formula: ὁ δὲ Πιλᾶτος ἀπεκρίθη αὐτοῖς λέγων (15:9). Still more similar is the introduction to Pilate's second question to the crowd a bit later: ὁ δὲ Πιλᾶτος πάλιν ἀποκριθεὶς ἔλεγεν αὐτοῖς (15:12). These eight instances, then, point to a characteristic Markan formula used to introduce a *question* that functions as a *response*.[13] This is precisely the formula used in 15:2.[14] Thus, a reader (and auditor) of Mark's text is well prepared to recognize Jesus's reply to Pilate as a question.

---

[11] Indeed, bizarrely, NA[27] offers a question mark as alternate punctuation in the apparatus for both Matt 27:11 and Luke 23:3, but not Mark 15:2.

[12] Like Matt 26:64, Luke 22:67–68 redacts Jesus's bare confession in Mark 14:62 to make it more evasive. When pressed, Jesus responds ὑμεῖς λέγετε, which may well be a question. One could argue that Luke's reading of Mark 15:2 (as a question) has influenced his interpretation of Jesus's reply to the Sanhedrin (turning it into a question), which reverses the standard exegetical argument. For Luke 22:70 as a question see, e.g., the textual apparatus in NA[27] loc cit.

[13] Two additional instances of the formula, in 10:25 and 11:22, could well be introducing questions. Five times the formula introduces what is clearly a statement, rather than a question: 6:37; 8:29; 9:5, 19; 11:14. Thus, at least half (and possibly well over half) of the speech elements introduced by this formula in Mark are questions.

[14] Apart from this particular formula, Mark characteristically introduces questions with λέγω, including in 12:15, 16, discussed below. See 1:24, 27; 2:8, 16, 18, 19, 24, 25; 3:4; 4:13, 21, 30, 38, 40, 41; 5:7, 30, 39; 6:2, 24, 38; 7:18; 8:12, 17, 21; 10:18, 26, 35, 36; 11:3, 5, 17, 28, 31; 13:2; 14:12, 14, 19, 37, [61], 63; 15:14; 16:3. This is clearly Mark's stylistic preference. Once, he employs simply

Raymond Brown's brief dismissal of this interpretive possibility relies on a slender stylistic argument. Responding to a virtually unknown note by Thomas Nicklin in 1939, which argued that Pilate's (sneering) question was met by a question, Brown counters that such a reading is "closer to John's development of basic tradition," while "Mark's account is singularly free of such psychological tone."[15] Brown's assertion is rather problematic: Mark's psychological tone is, to a great extent, in the eye of the beholder.[16] Meanwhile, John's interpretation of "basic tradition" stands no further from being definitive on this matter than Matthew's—also no closer.

A more profitable way to evaluate Nicklin's suggestion is by weighing it against Mark's own narrative portrayal of Jesus, especially in this portion of his gospel.[17] Would the Markan Jesus have answered such an important question with a counterquestion? Contextual evidence suggests that he would. Consider these instances:[18]

1. Jesus refuses to answer the chief priests', scribes', and elders' question about the source of his authority (11:27–33). An answer to their question would likely have furnished them with grounds for arresting and executing him. Instead, he responds with a counterquestion.

2. Jesus fails to answer, at least unambiguously, the question of whether to pay taxes to Caesar (12:13–17). A simple yes or no would have been damaging and even dangerous, alienating him from the populace (his primary source of protection at this moment in Mark [11:32, 12:12]) or making him appear

ἀποκρίνομαι (καὶ ἀπεκρίθησαν αὐτῷ οἱ μαθηταὶ αὐτοῦ, 8:4); ἐρωτάω and ἐπερωτάω are much less frequent.

[15] Brown, *Death of the Messiah*, 1:733. Nicklin's suggestion, given the ambiguity of Mark 15:2, was as follows: "If understood as 'Is it you who say this?' Jn 18^{34} is a fuller record which explains it.... Pilate's question is better understood as a slighting sneer" ("Thou Sayest," *ExpTim* 51 [1939–1940]: 155). Sherman E. Johnson responds, even more weakly, that a question in verse 2 would "conflict with Pilate's question" in verse 4; he admits (as seems more likely) that Pilate's question in verse 4 may only concern the fresh accusations in verse 3 (*A Commentary on the Gospel according to Mark*, HNTC [New York: Harper, 1961], 249).

[16] Among countless narrative-critical studies that demonstrate Mark's psychological complexity, Frank Kermode, *The Genesis of Secrecy: On the Interpretation of Narrative*, Charles Eliot Norton Lectures 1977–1978 (Cambridge: Harvard University Press, 1979), is one of the richest. Joel Marcus's commentary, largely redaction-critical in slant, also finds a great deal of psychological subtlety in this gospel (*Mark 8–16*).

[17] Henceforth I follow Malbon's usage: "By 'the Markan Jesus' I refer to the character who speaks and acts in the Gospel of Mark" as opposed to the more complex and layered "Mark's Jesus" produced by the interweaving of various narrative strands (*Mark's Jesus*, 231). In this study I limit my focus to "the Markan Jesus," even where I simply call him "Jesus."

[18] Compare item 3 on this list and the following paragraph to the insightful remarks of William Sanger Campbell, "Engagement, Disengagement and Obstruction: Jesus' Defense Strategies in Mark's Trial and Execution Scenes (14.53–64; 15.1–39)," *JSNT* 26 (2004): 283–300, esp. 284–91.

to instigate a rebellion, like Jesus's older contemporary and fellow Galilean, Judas. Instead, Jesus responds by posing a question.[19]

3. Jesus refuses to respond to a series of false witnesses introduced at his trial (14:55–61). The obvious danger is that, in defending himself, he would have only provided material that, in hostile hands, could be used against him. The wisdom of his tactic of silence is patent: the false witnesses contradict one another.

Taken together, these three confrontations exhibit a consistent strategy on the part of the Markan Jesus. While he has not treated influential or powerful opponents cautiously elsewhere in Mark's narrative (see, e.g., 3:1–6, 20–30; 7:1–13; 8:11–13; 11:5–19; 12:18–27, 35–40), in these three instances he responds in such a way as to elude traps set for him. Consistent with this strategy on almost any reading of 15:2, the answer σὺ λέγεις is ambiguous. At the very least, it avoids giving Pilate's question the definitive yes that would certainly seal Jesus's death sentence.[20] Further, these four episodes are linked thematically: the source of Jesus's authority, his position toward Caesar's authority, his (alleged) vow to destroy the temple, and his (alleged) claim to be "king of the Jews" are all politically inflammatory, explicitly designed to entrap Jesus in legally binding terms. To each he responds with a question, silence, or ambiguity. Characteristically, such responses shift the grounds of the confrontation, allowing Jesus to escape his enemies' designs without sacrificing his integrity or making claims not in keeping with his own aims.[21]

---

[19] For Judas, see Josephus, *Ant.* 18.1.1 §§4–6; Acts 5:36–37. Regardless of whether Mark (and hence the Markan Jesus) knew of Judas, he surely would know that teaching people not to pay taxes to Rome was political suicide. Indeed, the episode depends on the point. On the threat inherent in this question and the ambiguity of Jesus's reply, see Richard A. Horsley, *Jesus and the Spiral of Violence: Popular Jewish Resistance in Roman Palestine* (Minneapolis: Fortress, 1993), 306–17.

[20] The ambiguity of Jesus's reply emerges clearly enough from the scholarly discussion, even if not all scholars acknowledge that ambiguity. See esp. Thayer, "Σὺ εἶπας," 40–49; Catchpole, "Answer of Jesus," 218; Brown, *Death of the Messiah*, 1:489–93, 720, 733; Hooker, *Gospel according to St. Mark*, 367–68; Adela Yarbro Collins, *Mark: A Commentary*, Hermeneia (Minneapolis: Fortress, 2007), 713; Marcus, *Mark 8–16*, 1033–34.

[21] Many examples occur elsewhere in Mark of Jesus responding to questions with counterquestions. Specific examples, usually in a threatening context, occur in Mark 2:7–8 (scribes), 2:18–19 (Pharisees?), 2:24–25 (Pharisees), 6:37–38//8:4–5 (disciples), 7:17–19 (disciples), 8:11–12 (Pharisees), 9:11–13 (disciples), 10:2–3 (Pharisees), 10:17–18 (rich young man), 10:35–36 (James and John), 12:18–27 (Sadducees), 12:35 (an "answer" to his enemies' silence), 14:4–6 (some disciples). Most but not all of these questions are followed by an assertion of some kind. Some are clearly meant to teach, others to evade.

Jerome H. Neyrey contends that the *public* questions on such a list inherently challenge honor claims; the counterquestion, like the initiating question, is also aggressive in that context ("Questions, Chreiai, and Honor Challenges: The Interface of Rhetoric and Culture in Mark's Gospel," *CBQ* 60 [1998]: 657–81). Neyrey's contention would require us to interpret Jesus's

In 11:27, the challenge, coming from powerful elites and on the temple grounds, is raw and unvarnished: "On what authority are you doing these things?" Jesus's reply, a question, adroitly shifts the grounds of the confrontation: "Was the baptism of John from heaven?" (11:30). With the crowd's support (11:32), Jesus can safely deploy such a tactic, and so he slips out of the trap (11:33). In 12:14–15, by contrast, the challenge is more wily ("that they might catch him with a word," v. 13): "Is it lawful to pay the poll tax to Caesar or not?" Jesus's reply is accordingly more involved. He first responds with a question, the point of which is clearly to elude his interlocutors: he asks them to identify the image and name on the coin. Then comes the punch line, which shifts the grounds of this challenge even more effectively than did his question in 11:30. Here, in effect, the resolution of the question ("Should we pay taxes or not?") is thrown back on the audience, who must decide for themselves what belongs to Caesar and what belongs to God.

Jesus's reply to Pilate in 15:2, read as a question, fits perfectly within this pattern. The question "Do you say [that I am the king of the Jews]?" throws the decision back on Pilate, who might have wished for an unambiguous yes or no to quickly resolve the matter.[22]

There is, however, an exception to this pattern that I have so far intentionally avoided. In both interrogations, the one before "the high priest, and all the chief priests, the elders, and the scribes" (14:53) and the other before Pilate, Jesus will opt mostly for silence (14:61, 15:4–5)—but in both trials he speaks once. His answer to the high priest in 14:62 appears to depart from the pattern I have argued for here. It is this answer, moreover, that seals Jesus's fate in that first interrogation. Jesus gives here the only direct reply in the entire gospel to a question regarding his status or mission.

The question itself (14:61) deserves attention:

σὺ εἶ ὁ χριστὸς ὁ υἱὸς τοῦ εὐλογητοῦ
Are you the Messiah, the Son of the Blessed One? (NRSV)

This question is structurally parallel to Pilate's. Unlike Pilate's question, however, it asks Jesus his identity in language that the narrative has previously applied to Jesus. Jesus is never called "king of the Jews" prior to Pilate's question in chapter 15, but he has certainly been called God's son—twice by God (1:11, 9:7) and once by Jesus himself (12:6).[23] Intriguingly, a textual variant, albeit with slight support (Γ Φ ℵ), puts the high priest's question even more in line with the narrative's favored

---

counterquestion as a challenge to Pilate's concept of "kingship" or (more aggressively) Pilate's authority to pronounce judgment in Jesus's case.

[22] Alternatively, Pilate is asking a rhetorical question, which expects no answer and is (in that case) mockery. I return to this point briefly in my conclusion. See van Iersel, *Mark*, 459; Joel Marcus, "Crucifixion as Parodic Exaltation," *JBL* 125 (2006): 73–87, here 87, https://doi.org/10.2307/27638347.

[23] See Kingsbury, *Christology of Mark's Gospel*, 116–18. Malbon emphasizes that this is a

terminology: σὺ εἶ ὁ υἱὸς τοῦ εὐλογητοῦ (14:61); cf. σὺ εἶ ὁ υἱός μου (1:11). A reader or auditor of this gospel could well believe the Markan Jesus is ready to confess to being God's son, especially when asked directly. Jesus has already admitted as much in the parable of the tenants (12:1–12). Moreover, he does not let the confession sit without comment (14:62).[24]

From a narrative perspective, then, it appears that the Markan Jesus is confessing the truth openly even at the cost of his life, in direct contrast to Peter, whose denial brackets Jesus's confession (14:66–72). As James R. Edwards puts it, "The juxtaposition of bold confession and cowardly denial forces upon the reader the terrible gap between Jesus and Peter."[25] But this confession does not contradict Jesus's careful refusal elsewhere to answer in any straightforward way various challenges and false representations of himself, since it responds truthfully (within the narrative world) to a direct and accurate question regarding his identity.[26] In other words, Jesus's confession in 14:62 does not contradict his unwillingness to risk his life in answering *one-sided* questions or challenges that put his identity and mission on the wrong footing.[27] Such is Pilate's question in 15:2, with its misleading language of kingship (cf. the *titulus* "King of the Jews"; 15:26).[28] The exception in 14:62,

---

parable (*Mark's Jesus*, 175); nonetheless, Jesus does here adopt the term for himself (even if coyly) that God twice used earlier, showing that Jesus embraces this word from God as a true one.

[24] This pattern of confession-plus-elaboration connects to the Markan Jesus's pervasive (and much-studied) efforts to manage public interpretation of his identity.

[25] See James R. Edwards, "Markan Sandwiches: The Significance of Interpolations in Markan Narratives," *NovT* 31 (1989): 193–216, here 212. Jesus's faithfulness is thus highlighted.

[26] Cf. Tannehill, "Narrative Christology," 61–62, 74–75, 86–88; Kingsbury, *Christology of Mark's Gospel*, 118–20. By invoking the "narrative world," I refer to the "truth" about Jesus as constructed by the narrative itself. On this concept ("story world"), see David Rhoads, "Narrative Criticism and the Gospel of Mark," *JAAR* 50 (1982): 411–34, here 413–15.

[27] Different is Norman Perrin, "The Christology of Mark: A Study in Methodology," *JR* 51 (1971): 173–87, followed in this instance by Malbon, *Mark's Jesus*, esp. 169–71 and 209–10. Perrin contends that Jesus (i.e., Mark) embraces "Son of God" only to correct it with "Son of Man," while Malbon sees the "son of humanity" addendum as part of Jesus's strategy to deflect honor, which is more in character than the confession "I am." The difficulty she evinces in explaining Jesus's confession ("I am") suggests that her otherwise helpful distinction between the "Markan Jesus" and "Mark's Jesus" is strained on this point. Perhaps the author of Mark is guilty of a (mistaken) collapse of perspectives. But, given that Jesus elsewhere adopts the term for himself (albeit in parable), I think it more likely that the Markan Jesus is courageously speaking the truth in the face of suffering, thus exhibiting faithfulness to what God has twice said of him. On this question, see too Kingsbury, *Christology of Mark's Gospel*, 121–24.

[28] See the discussion and literature in Malbon, *Mark's Jesus*, 118–21; and Edwin Broadhead, *Naming Jesus: Titular Christology in the Gospel of Mark*, JSNTSup 175 (Sheffield: Sheffield Academic, 1999), 77–80. I find Malbon's and Broadhead's arguments persuasive here, but even for scholars who argue that Jesus really is being proclaimed "king" in Mark, the language of kingship is misleading, or flatly ironic, in Pilate's mouth (see, e.g., Tannehill, "Narrative Christology," 79–80 ["irony"]; Kingsbury, *Christology of Mark's Gospel*, 125–28; Marcus, "Crucifixion as Parodic Exaltation," 73–74, 86–87).

therefore, falls into place. Jesus's pattern of response to his interlocutors is broken only carefully, within strictly defined limits. Pilate's question in 15:2 does not fall within those limits.

Finally, a narrative-critical reading of Mark will find in 15:2, read as a question, a meaningful parallel to Jesus's important questions in 8:27 and 8:29:

τίνα με λέγουσιν οἱ ἄνθρωποι εἶναι
Who do people say that I am? (NRSV)

ὑμεῖς δὲ τίνα με λέγετε εἶναι
But who do you say that I am? (NRSV)

These two questions anticipate the two halves of Jesus's exchange with Pilate. In 15:12, as Pilate (echoing the Jewish authorities) volunteers the title "king of the Jews," the disciples (echoing the people) volunteer John the Baptist, Elijah, and one of the prophets (8:28). Neither Jesus's enemies nor his sympathizers (οἱ ἄνθρωποι) offer an adequate answer, and so Jesus probes his interlocutors further: "What do *you* say?" Both words in the question of 15:2 are present in the earlier question in 8:29, and in the same order: ὑμεῖς ... λέγετε becomes σὺ λέγεις. Each question comes near the end of its half of the narrative, 8:29 almost in the center of the gospel and 15:2 almost at its end. While Jesus initiates the first interrogation, his enemies initiate the second. While Jesus's audience in the first is his set of closest followers on their way from Herod Antipas's territory, his audience in the second is his most dangerous enemy, Rome's appointed ruler; and the exchange takes place at the heart of Jesus's enemies' power. Finally, while Jesus's first question elicits Peter's remarkable confession, his second goes unanswered.[29] In such comparisons and contrasts lies meaningful grist for a narrative-critical reading of Jesus's question to Pilate in Mark 15:2.

The difficulties that narrative critics encounter when σὺ λέγεις is read as a statement disappear when this reply is read as a question. With this question, Jesus does not utter insubstantial, unintelligible, "circumlocutory," or "begrudging" words. He instead evades the charge of insurrection and effectively distances himself from the title "king of the Jews." And he does so while shifting the grounds of the encounter, placing the decision regarding his identity and aims back on Pilate— just as he had shifted the decision about "what belongs to God" back on his opponents earlier in the narrative.[30] Pilate's subsequent inability to decide whether he really does "say" that Jesus is a king (15:3–15) further demonstrates the value of

---

[29] I leave aside here any effort to negotiate particular readings of each of these elements in the literature. The importance of 8:27–33 for narrative readings of Mark has been profound.

[30] Marcus similarly reads Jesus's reply (which he takes as a statement) as "cheekily shift[ing] the responsibility for a positive evaluation of Jesus' kingship onto Pilate himself" (*Mark 8–16*, 1034); cf. Hooker, *Gospel according to Saint Mark*, 368. Jesus's reply as a question more effectively accomplishes this shift without some of the risks attendant on a statement, risks that Marcus also rightly highlights.

this interpretation. Further, the question to Pilate evokes for the reader the similar, narratively significant question to the disciples earlier in the story. Thus, taking Jesus's reply to Pilate as a question allows these two words to take their rightful place as a meaningful utterance, in character, within the narrative.

In addition to removing narrative-critical difficulties, reading Jesus's reply to Pilate in 15:2 as a question opens new possibilities for interpretation and exploration. One such opportunity concerns the tone in which Jesus's question might have been asked. If, as some scholars contend, Pilate poses his question in mockery ("So *you're* the king of the Jews?"), then Jesus's reply might answer in kind: "Do I look like a king to *you*?"[31] Humor is, arguably, stock-in-trade for the Markan Jesus (2:21–22, 4:21, 7:18–19, 10:25, 14:48).[32] Alternatively, if Pilate's question is more sincere, then Jesus's reply begins to approximate developments in the Johannine tradition, where Jesus seems to hold out hope that Pilate, confronted with the truth, may yet embrace it (John 18:33–38).[33] Both possibilities in turn yield additional interpretive questions.

Meanwhile, Jesus's perceived tone is bound up with theological readings of his fate in Mark. For instance, popular interpretations of Jesus's death often emphasize his willingness to die, which for some readers approaches an almost suicidal eagerness to provoke his own execution.[34] Such a reading of Jesus's fate, tied up with particular theologies of atonement, loses considerable force if Jesus is still seeking to evade a death sentence in Mark 15:2. Instead of submitting to the inevitable, much less forcing Pilate's hand, Jesus puts the question to Pilate whether he, Pilate, really regards Jesus as a threat. If not, will Pilate summon the courage to act justly? In that interpretation, Jesus's stance offers a model for how his betrayed followers might speak with courage to powerful governors and kings, who will similarly misunderstand them (see 13:9–13). This reading can create space for new assessments of Mark's theology.

A third important opportunity is opened for further exploration of Mark's stance toward imperial authority. If Jesus poses a question in 15:2, the reader is left in doubt whether Jesus is any sort of "king," especially if one hears here an echo of Jesus's question to the disciples in 8:29. Maybe the cross should be seen as the epitaph rather than a monument to kingship. When readers imagine the *titulus* ("The King of the Jews") above that instrument of death and recall that Jesus questioned that title, they might draw radical conclusions regarding all claims to royal power.

---

[31] See van Iersel, *Mark*, 459; Marcus, "Crucifixion as Parodic Exaltation," 87; Marcus, *Mark 8–16*, 1033.

[32] See too Kelly R. Iverson, "Incongruity, Humor, and Mark: Performance and the Use of Laughter in the Second Gospel (Mark 8.14–21)," *NTS* 59 (2013): 2–19.

[33] See Brown, *Death of the Messiah*, 1:733, 749–53.

[34] On this point, see Campbell, "Engagement, Disengagement," 283. For an example, see Alan Carr, "Why Did He Go to Calvary?" in *The Sermon Notebook*, http://www.sermonnotebook.org/new testament/1Pet 1_18-20.htm.

These and other enticing avenues of interpretation are opened when we take seriously the possibility that Jesus, so far from offering an answer to Pilate, questions the ground upon which his interlocutor stands.

In sum, given (a) the structural parallels between Jesus's words in 15:2 and Pilate's, as well as the high priest's questions; (b) the formula used to introduce Jesus's words in 15:2; and, most of all (c) the consistency of the Markan Jesus's strategy of responding to challenges in this portion of the gospel, Jesus's reply to Pilate in Mark 15:2 can most plausibly be read as a question rather than a statement. The narrative evinces a consistent strategy for Jesus's interactions with those in power within the narrative world, and reading 15:2 as a question fits this strategy quite well. The contrast between 14:62 and 15:2, which poses a challenge to any interpretation of 15:2, can be explained in such a way that the Markan Jesus's strategy is *upheld* rather than contravened. Reading Jesus's reply as a question allows the important encounter with Pilate to hold its weight in a narrative reading of the Markan Jesus and the plot that leads to his death. This reading, in turn, opens new avenues of interpretation in the larger narrative of Mark's Gospel.

RECENT TITLES FROM **EERDMANS**

JESUS AND THE EYEWITNESSES
The Gospels as Eyewitness Testimony
SECOND EDITION
RICHARD BAUCKHAM

"A fresh and vivid approach to dozens, perhaps hundreds, of well-known problems and passages."
— N. T. WRIGHT

ISBN 9780802874313 • 704 PAGES • HARDCOVER • $50.00

INTERPRETING THE GOSPEL AND LETTERS OF JOHN
An Introduction
SHERRI BROWN and FRANCIS J. MOLONEY, SDB

"Embraces Israel's story, Rome's world, and the church's beginnings as a framework for a careful reading of the biblical texts."
— WILLIAM LOADER

ISBN 9780802873385 • 371 PAGES • PAPERBACK • $36.00

IN THE FULLNESS OF TIME
Essays on Christology, Creation, and Eschatology in Honor of Richard Bauckham
Edited by DANIEL M. GURTNER, GRANT MACASKILL, and JONATHAN T. PENNINGTON

"A fitting tribute to a great Christian scholar." — *Church Times*

ISBN 9780802873378 • 286 PAGES • HARDCOVER • $60.00

JESUS IN JOHN'S GOSPEL
Structure and Issues in Johannine Christology
WILLIAM LOADER
Foreword by Harold W. Attridge

"An engaging guide to new insights into the New Testament's most profound reflections on the incarnation, death, and exaltation of Jesus. This is a masterpiece!"
— R. ALAN CULPEPPER

ISBN 9780802875112 • 542 PAGES • PAPERBACK • $45.00

7021-C

eerdmans.com

At your bookstore,
or call 800.253.7521
www.eerdmans.com

Slow Sailing in Acts: Suspense in the Final Sea Journey (Acts 27:1–28:15)

TROY M. TROFTGRUBEN
ttroftgruben@wartburgseminary.edu
Wartburg Theological Seminary, Dubuque, IA 52003

In the narrative of Acts, the sea journey of 27:1–28:15 has long been a puzzle. While it resembles other sea-journey stories from antiquity, its relevance to the narrative is far from clear. Though most interpreters emphasize particular symbolic meanings discernible in the story, these emphases sidestep the most distinctive features of the passage: its length, vivid detail, and location near the end of the narrative. I seek to correct this oversight by drawing attention not simply to what the story says but also to what it does to the reader. Located where it is, the Final Sea Journey builds anticipation concerning Paul's fate, raises doubts about whether he will arrive and testify in Rome, slows the pace of the story dramatically, and suspends questions about the story's outcome in ways that provoke tension and expectation. In these ways, the "slow sailing" of Acts 27:1–28:15 gives an experiential dimension to the final two chapters, provokes the reader to engaged reflection, depicts openness and uncertainty as prime places for witness, and draws attention to the journey itself as sacred space for divine activity.

"This suspense is terrible. I hope it will last."[1]

In the narrative of Acts, the Final Sea Journey (27:1–28:15) has long been a puzzle.[2] Certainly the story is engaging, rivaling some of the most exciting sea journeys of ancient novels. Yet the passage takes up fifty-nine verses—about 6 percent of the entire book—to relate a story whose direct relevance to the larger narrative is hardly clear. The fact that Paul arrives in Rome is undoubtedly important, but does that justify a travel narrative more than four times longer than any other in Acts? Luke Timothy Johnson expresses the question pondered by many a reader:

---

[1] Gwendolen, in Oscar Wilde, *The Importance of Being Earnest: A Trivial Comedy for Serious People* (London: Leonard, Smithers, 1899), 146.

[2] For brevity's sake, throughout this article I refer to Acts 27:1–28:15 as "the Final Sea Journey."

"Why does [Luke] spend so much time and care on what was after all only a voyage?"[3]

Many scholars have proposed solutions to this puzzle. Advocates of the narrative's historicity propose that the Final Sea Journey is so long and detailed because it reflects actual events, recorded as the personal memoirs of the author. The "personal memoirs" interpretation has a long line of prominent supporters, from Irenaeus to Henry J. Cadbury and to this day.[4] This theory, however, often presumes that the Sea Journey's first-person references ("we") imply a firsthand witness as author. Scholars in recent decades have challenged this assumption based on the functions of such references in Acts and in ancient literature, showing at the very least that such accounts may reflect diverse motives.[5] In short, it is far from clear that the Final Sea Journey comprises the author's personal memoirs.

A second proposal for the distinctive length of the Sea Journey is expressed by Martin Dibelius: "Luke"[6] incorporated a preexisting story of voyage and shipwreck, into which he inserted his story of Paul.[7] Though interesting, this theory

---

[3] Luke Timothy Johnson, *The Acts of the Apostles*, SP 5 (Collegeville, MN: Liturgical Press, 1992), 450.

[4] Irenaeus, *Haer.* 3.14.1; Henry J. Cadbury, "We and I Passages in Luke-Acts," *NTS* 3 (1956): 128–32. J. B. Lightfoot is another who would almost certainly have been a supporter (see *The Acts of the Apostles: A Newly Discovered Commentary*, ed. Ben Witherington III and Todd D. Still, Lightfoot Legacy 1 [Downers Grove, IL: IVP Academic, 2014], 61–66). Other supporters are Martin Hengel, *Acts and the History of Earliest Christianity*, trans. John Bowden (Philadelphia: Fortress, 1979), 66–67; Colin J. Hemer, "First Person Narrative in Acts 27–28," *TynBul* 36 (1985): 79–109; Joseph A. Fitzmyer, *Luke the Theologian: Aspects of His Teaching* (New York: Paulist, 1989), 16–22; Jürgen Wehnert, *Die Wir-Passagen der Apostelgeschichte: Ein lukanisches Stilmittel aus jüdischer Tradition*, GTA 40 (Göttingen: Vandenhoeck & Ruprecht, 1989). See also Ernst Haenchen, "Acta 27," in *Zeit und Geschichte: Dankesgabe an Rudolf Bultmann zum 80. Geburtstag*, ed. Erich Dinkler (Tübingen: Mohr Siebeck, 1964), 235–54; Brian Rapske, "Acts, Travel and Shipwreck," in *The Book of Acts in Its Graeco-Roman Setting*, ed. David W. J. Gill and Conrad Gempf, BAFCS 2 (Grand Rapids: Eerdmans, 1994), 1–47; J. M. Gilchrist, "The Historicity of Paul's Shipwreck," *JSNT* 61 (1996): 29–61, https://doi.org/10.1177/0142064x9601806102; Jacob Jervell, *Die Apostelgeschichte*, KEK 3 (Göttingen: Vandenhoeck & Ruprecht, 1998), 612–14; Darrell L. Bock, *Acts*, BECNT (Grand Rapids: Baker Academic, 2007), 727–28.

[5] Vernon K. Robbins, "The We-Passages in Acts and Ancient Sea Voyages," *BR* 20 (1975): 5–18; Susan Marie Praeder, "The Problem of First Person Narration in Acts," *NovT* 29 (1987): 193–218, https://doi.org/10.1163/156853687x00083; Dennis R. MacDonald, "The Shipwrecks of Odysseus and Paul," *NTS* 45 (1999): 88–107, esp. 89; Samuel Byrskog, "History or Story in Acts—A Middle Way? The 'We' Passages, Historical Intertexture, and Oral History," in *Contextualizing Acts: Lukan Narrative and Greco-Roman Discourse*, ed. Todd C. Penner and Caroline Vander Stichele, SymS 20 (Atlanta: Society of Biblical Literature, 2003), 257–83; William Sanger Campbell, *The We Passages in the Acts of the Apostles: The Narrator as Narrative Character*, SBLStBL 14 (Atlanta: Society of Biblical Literature, 2007). See also A. J. M. Wedderburn, "The 'We'-Passages in Acts: On the Horns of a Dilemma," *ZNW* 93 (2002): 78–98.

[6] I use "Luke" in this article simply as a shorthand reference to the author of Luke and Acts.

[7] Martin Dibelius, *Studies in the Acts of the Apostles*, ed. Heinrich Greeven, trans. Mary Ling

implies that Luke was incapable of using sources in ways that are nuanced and subtle; there is very little in Acts to support this idea. If source-critical studies of Acts in the early twentieth century showed anything, it was a remarkable lack of agreement on where—if anywhere—there is evidence of the narrative as a patchwork of traditions.[8] In other words, incorporation of a preexisting narrative in the Sea Journey cannot be clearly demonstrated. More recently, scholars have nuanced this proposal further: Luke's Sea Journey reflects not *incorporation* but *imitation* of a preexisting journey story. Dennis MacDonald, for instance, suggests that the Final Sea Journey imitates scenes from Homer's *Odyssey*.[9] Indeed, classic and conventional shipwreck stories from ancient literature may well have influenced Acts 27:1–28:15, since perilous sea journeys were common in literary tradition. But evidence for such direct influence is not overwhelming—at least not enough to justify the passage's distinctiveness within the larger narrative of Acts. Most important of all, the proposals noted above sidestep questions of exegetical meaning: they explain and justify Acts 27:1–28:15 more than interpret its function and significance.

Richard Pervo has judiciously observed that discerning the meaning of the Final Sea Journey is inextricably bound to three factors: its length, its position in the narrative, and the symbolisms associated with sea voyage in ancient literature.[10]

(New York: Scribner's Sons, 1956), 204–6. Dibelius simply developed older suggestions, e.g., of Julius Wellhausen (*Kritische Analyse der Apostelgeschichte*, Abhandlungen der Königlichen Gesellschaft der Wissenschaften zu Göttingen: Philologish-historische Klasse 15.2 [Berlin: Weidmann, 1914], 2) and Paul Wendland (*Die urchristlichen Literaturformen*, 2nd ed., HNT 1.3 [Tübingen: Mohr, 1912], 324 and n. 4). Similar arguments, with various nuances, are issued by Ernst Haenchen (*The Acts of the Apostles: A Commentary*, trans. Bernard Noble et al. [Philadelphia: Westminster, 1971], 709), Hans Conzelmann (*Acts of the Apostles: A Commentary on the Acts of the Apostles*, trans. James Limburg, A. Thomas Kraabel, and Donald H. Juel, Hermeneia [Philadelphia: Fortress, 1987], 221), J. Roloff (*Die Apostelgeschichte*, NTD 5 [Göttingen; Vandenhoeck & Ruprecht, 1981], 358–60), Alfons Weiser (*Die Apostelgeschichte*, 2 vols., ÖTBK 5 [Gütersloh: Gütersloher Verlagshaus, 1981, 1985], 2:390–91, 659–60), and Gerhard Schneider (*Die Apostelgeschichte*, 2 vols., HThKNT 5 [Freiburg im Breisgau: Herder, 1980–1982], 2:387).

[8] F. J. Foakes-Jackson and Henry J. Cadbury summarize: "The truth seems to be that although there is a *prima facie* probability for the use of written sources in Acts…, the writer wrote too well to allow us to distinguish with certainty either the boundaries of his sources or the extent of his own editorial work" ("The Internal Evidence of Acts," in *The Acts of the Apostles*, part 1 of *The Beginnings of Christianity*, ed. F. J. Foakes-Jackson and Kirsopp Lake, 5 vols. [London: Macmillan, 1920–1933], 2:133).

[9] Dennis R. MacDonald, "Shipwrecks of Odysseus." Many interpreters—not just MacDonald—have observed that the language of "beaching the ship" (ἐπέκειλαν τὴν ναῦν) in Acts 27:41 reflects language from Homer's *Odyssey* (9.148, 546; 13.113–114). Susan Marie Praeder, "Acts 27:1–28:15: Sea Voyages in Ancient Literature and the Theology of Luke-Acts," *CBQ* 46 (1984): 683–708, here 701; Kenneth L. Cukrowski, "Paul as Odysseus: An Exegetical Note on Luke's Depiction of Paul in Acts 27:1–28:10," *ResQ* 55 (2013): 24–34.

[10] Richard I. Pervo, *Acts: A Commentary*, Hermeneia (Minneapolis: Fortress, 2009), 648.

Emphasizing the third of these factors, Pervo and many others highlight one of the following particular symbolic meanings for the Final Sea Journey: divine providence, death and resurrection, salvation for all peoples, a model for navigating the Roman imperial world, or Paul's vindication.[11] All of these interpretations advance particular insights about the passage, but their emphases tend to avoid the story's most distinctive features: its length, vivid detail, and location in the narrative. As Johnson points out:

> If the author's point was so patently allegorical, we have even less understanding of why the pedestrian elements of the story were retained. Why did Luke distract us with so much detail, if the detail was supposed to be ignored in favor of the overall pattern?[12]

Johnson may exaggerate the nature of allegory, but his point stands: interpretations that emphasize symbolic meaning generally overlook the Sea Journey's most distinctive qualities—its length and position in the narrative. Striving for a worthy goal (discerning symbolic meaning) results in an unfortunate imbalance, which calls for renewed attention to the overlooked factors (the passage's length, detail, and position). The question is this: given the position and length of the Final Sea Journey, how does it impact a reading of Acts on a *literary* level?

The Final Sea Journey makes up 80 percent of the final two chapters of Acts, which Loveday Alexander calls the "narrative epilogue."[13] At this juncture, questions

---

[11] For divine providence, see Charles H. Talbert, *Reading Acts: A Literary and Theological Commentary on the Acts of the Apostles*, Reading the New Testament (New York: Crossroad, 1997), 223–25; Talbert and J. H. Hayes, "A Theology of Sea-Storms in Luke-Acts," *Society of Biblical Literature 1995 Seminar Papers*, SBLSP 34 (Atlanta: Scholars Press, 1995), 321–36; and Bock, *Acts*, 726–47. For death and resurrection, see Pervo, *Acts*, 652–54, 666–67, 677; cf. Talbert and Hayes, "Theology of Sea-Storms," 335–36; and see n. 40 below. For salvation for all peoples, see Floyd V. Filson, "The Journey Motif in Luke-Acts," in *Apostolic History and the Gospel: Biblical and Historical Essays Presented to F. F. Bruce on His 60th Birthday*, ed. W. Ward Gasque and Ralph P. Martin (Grand Rapids: Eerdmans, 1970), 68–77; Praeder, "Sea Voyages," 683–706; and Robert C. Tannehill, *The Narrative Unity of Luke-Acts: A Literary Interpretation*, 2 vols. (Philadelphia: Fortress, 1986, 1990), 2:336–37. For a model for navigating the Roman imperial world, see Warren Carter, "Aquatic Display: Navigating the Roman Imperial World in Acts 27," *NTS* 62 (2016): 79–96. For Paul's vindication, see Garry W. Trompf, "On Why Luke Declined to Recount the Death of Paul: Acts 27–28 and Beyond," in *Luke-Acts: New Perspectives from the Society of Biblical Literature Seminar*, ed. Charles H. Talbert (New York: Crossroad, 1984), 225–39; David Ladouceur, "Hellenistic Preconceptions of Shipwreck and Pollution as a Context for Acts 27–28," *HTR* 73 (1980): 435–49; and John C. Clabeaux, "The Story of the Maltese Viper and Luke's Apology for Paul," *CBQ* 67 (2005): 604–10.

[12] Johnson, *Acts*, 457.

[13] Loveday C. Alexander, "Reading Luke-Acts from Back to Front," in *The Unity of Luke-Acts*, ed. J. Verheyden, BETL 142 (Leuven: Leuven University Press, 1999), 419–46, here 424. So also Daniel Marguerat, "The Enigma of the End of Acts (28.16–31)," in *The First Christian Historian: Writing the 'Acts of the Apostles,'* trans. Ken McKinney, G. J. Laughery, and Richard Bauckham,

about Paul's fate are of paramount importance: his arrival at Rome has been anticipated since chapter 19 (19:21, 23:11, 25:12), and since then threats to his life (21:27–36, 23:12–35, 25:1–12) and omens of his death (20:17–38, 21:1–26) have only increased. Surprisingly, then, the Final Sea Journey slows down the pace of the story dramatically—with nautical details and extensive length—at a point so close to the ending. In this way Acts 27:1–28:15 suspends the story's outcome in ways that generate tension and anticipation. The Final Sea Journey of Acts suspends in order to provoke and, in the process, casts a new vision of hope for apostolic witness and the spaces where it takes place.

I. Defining Suspense

Stated simply, suspense is the act of fostering in an audience (or reader) a prolonged anticipation of what follows.[14] As for what fosters suspense, we take our cue from ancient rhetoricians and authors, who knew well the rhetorical impact of suspense. According to many ancient writers, plots of great stories must generate a sense of organic completion. Aristotle held that "well-constructed plots" must neither begin nor end "arbitrarily" but create the sense that nothing afterward occurs (*Poet.* 1450b30–35; cf. 1452b–1454a).[15] Likewise, Dionysius of Halicarnassus writes that an ending must "draw together the action so that nothing else seems needed" (*Thuc.* 10.830; see also 12.837, 16.847). Referring to history writing, Diodorus Siculus gives one of the fullest descriptions of literary completion:

> In all historical writings it is proper for authors to include in their books occurrences of states or rulers that are complete in themselves from beginning unto the end. For I think history done in this way is most memorable and most intelligible to the readers. Incomplete occurrences, since they have no continuity between the beginning and ending, interrupt the interest of the engaged reader. In contrast, occurrences that have narrative continuity include a full report of events unto its completion [τελευτή]. (16.1.1–2)

This sense of completion, Diodorus suggests, maintains "the interest of the engaged reader" by its focus and unity. In other words, writings that foster a sense of completion best engage readers' interests. In addition, ancient authors indicate that certain forms of writing are associated with particular expectations—like conflict and resolution in tragedy (Aristotle, *Poet.* 1455b) or an end to conflict in a history about

---

SNTSMS 121 (Cambridge: Cambridge University Press, 2002), 216–21, https://doi.org/10.1017/CBO9780511488061.

[14] Cf. Eric S. Rabkin's definition: "An anxious uncertainty about what is going to happen, especially to those characters with whom we have established bonds of sympathy" (*Narrative Suspense: "When Slim Turned Sideways..."* [Ann Arbor: University of Michigan Press, 1973], 60).

[15] All translations of ancient texts in this article are my own unless otherwise noted.

war (Dionysius, *Pomp.* 3.769–771). Sometimes these expectations are fostered not by genre conventions but by the narrative itself. For instance, Dionysius of Halicarnassus criticizes Thucydides because he "promises to set forth all" of the Peloponnesian War but does not—leaving his work flawed and apparently "unfinished" (*Thuc.* 12.837; *Pomp.* 3.711). Whether expectations stem from genre conventions or narrative cues, they foster anticipation of events yet to come that will generate completion. This *anticipation* (or "expectation") of future events is the first and primary component of suspense.

A second primary ingredient to suspense is *deferring* (or "suspension," or "prolonging"). In the *Poetics*, Aristotle names two essential components of the tragic plot: conflict (δέσις) and resolution (λύσις). With conflict he associates events outside of and within the story, "from the beginning to the furthest point before changing to prosperity or adversity" (1455b). His expansive definition of conflict suggests that a story's central conflict is what primarily drives the story, whereas resolution allows for a fitting point of cessation. The art of composing fine tragedy, Aristotle notes, is to balance worthy conflict with an adequate counterpart in resolution, since "many writers handle the conflict well, but the resolution badly" (1456a).[16] Quintilian associates "deferring" in his *Institutes of Oratory* (ca. 95 CE) with the practice of *sustentatio* ("suspension"): to engage one's audience for a time on one trajectory, only to alter the development toward a different end (*Inst.* 9.2.22–23).[17] The practice entails plot reversal, but the core rhetorical effect stems from delaying—or suspending—fulfillment of the audience's expectations. Although Quintilian writes in Latin in the late first century, his ideas build upon Aristotle's ancient concepts of περιπέτεια ("reversal") and ἀναγνώρισις ("recognition").[18] But only with Quintilian do we get the specific language of "suspension" (*sustentatio*) along with its clear description. His notion constitutes an apt definition for "deferring" or "suspension."

A third component that fosters suspense is *uncertainty* (or "raising doubts"). Since a sense of completion was widely expected for virtually all forms of writing in antiquity, uncertainty about whether such completion will happen generates tension. In the earliest surviving composition exercises, the *Progymnasmata* of Aelius Theon (first century CE), the rhetorical practice of "raising doubts" (ἐπαπορεῖν) is named as an engaging way to vary the composition of narrative

---

[16] Aelius Theon also observes the balance between things distressing to hearers and those more pleasing and ultimately encourages favoring the latter (*Prog.* 80).

[17] See also Quintilian's concepts of παράδοξον ("paradox") and *inopinatum* ("surprise") (*Inst.* 9.2.23–24).

[18] That is, altering ("reversing") a long-standing plot trajectory with a sudden illumination ("recognition") of truths that beforehand were obscured (*Poet.* 1452a–b). In Aristotle's mind, the two concepts are linked: "the finest recognition [ἀναγνώρισις] is that which occurs simultaneously with reversal [περιπέτεια]" (*Poet.* 1452a).

(87–88).¹⁹ Quintilian describes a parallel notion in Latin: *dubitatio* ("uncertainty" or "hesitation"): giving the impression that an intended outcome is threatened or uncertain (*Inst.* 9.2.19). He explains that in oral speech *dubitatio* occurs when the speaker conveys uncertainty about how to proceed:

> Uncertainty [is] when we pretend to question ourselves, where to begin, where to end, what may possibly be said, or what is to be said at all. All [speeches] are full of just such examples, but one suffices for now: "moreover, as for myself, I do not know where I might turn. Should I deny that there was a scandalous report that the jury had been corrupted?" (*Inst.* 9.2.19; see also 9.1.35, 9.3.88–89)

Both Aelius Theon and Quintilian describe what seems to have been a well-established rhetorical practice, judging from the number of rhetoricians who refer to it (Rutilius Lupus 2.10; Rhet. Her. 4.40; Apsines, *Ars rhet.* 258.10, 328.15).²⁰ Most of these authors are concerned with the context of oral presentation, but the idea still applies well to written narrative: uncertainty is when a narrative (vs. an orator) gives the impression that an expected outcome will not take place, typically because of insurmountable threats or situations of peril. Such circumstances "raise doubts" about anticipated events in ways that parallel the oratorical practices of ἐπαπορεῖν and *dubitatio* but pertain to the nature of narrative. For example, at the start of the last book of Chariton's novel, the author toys with the idea of more intensified perils:

> So Fortune intended to render something not only paradoxical but moreover cruel: Chaereas, although having Callirhoe in his possession, would not recognize her and would take other wives on board his ship to carry them away but leave his own wife behind ... as spoils of war for his own enemies. (8.1.2)

At this point the author suddenly redirects the novel's course:

> But Aphrodite thought this too harsh.... Aphrodite had mercy upon him, and, after having harassed through land and sea the lovely couple which she at the start had brought together, she again desired to reunite them. And I think that

---

¹⁹Cf. George A. Kennedy, *Progymnasmata: Greek Textbooks of Prose Composition and Rhetoric*, WGRW 10 (Atlanta: Society of Biblical Literature, 2003), 88: "The speaker seems in doubt because, while a questioner seeks an answer, one in doubt does not quite do so but only addresses himself as at a loss."

²⁰The anonymous Rhetorica ad Herennium (first century BCE) discusses *dubitatio* (4.40) using an example that Quintilian later uses (*Inst.* 9.3.88–89), but the Rhetorica does not discuss the topic as extensively as Quintilian. Publius Rutilius Lupus (first century CE) abridges ideas from Gorgias of Athens in discussing the practice of *aporia* (ἀπορία): raising doubts (*On the Figures of Speech* 2.10). The third-century CE *Art of Rhetoric* by Apsines of Gadara names διαπόρησις ("being at a loss") as a worthy rhetorical tactic but without substantial discussion: "Also useful in them are διαπορήσεις: 'What ought I do? Be silent or speak?'" (258.10 [27]; see also 328.15).

> this final chapter will be most pleasurable for my readers, for it is a cleansing of the cruelties earlier on. (8.1.3–4)

The implied author's explicit deliberation (through Aphrodite's feelings) parallels the orator's tactic of "raising doubts," showing both an example of uncertainty in narrative prose and the use of rhetorical practices in various contexts (oral and literary).

A final contributor to suspense is *empathy*. While empathy for narrative characters may transpire by various means, it is essential in order for suspense to be experienced. For instance, Aristotle states that the "superior poet" (ποιητής ἀμείνων) must generate fear and pity in an audience, "so that the one who hears the events transpire experiences trembling and pity at what takes place" (*Poet.* 1453b).[21] Fear and pity are interesting selections, since tragedy might easily generate many other emotions. But G. R. F. Ferrari rightly observes that fear and pity, for Aristotle, are the finest paths to an audience's "sympathetic fear for the hero and his impending fate."[22] For the context of oral speech, Quintilian describes an analogous tactic: *communicatio* ("consultation")—to consult or include one's audience in the thought process of a speech (*Inst.* 9.2.20; cf. 9.1.30; see also Cicero, *De or.* 3.204).[23] Quintilian gives an example from the defense of Cloatilla by Domitius Afer:

> She is in such confusion that she knows neither what is permitted for a woman nor what is becoming for a wife. It may be that chance has brought you into contact with the unhappy woman in her helpless plight. You, her brother, and you, her father's friends: what counsel do you give her?" (*Inst.* 9.2.20–21)

In oral speech, *communicatio* is a form of "codeliberation," which entails addressing the audience directly. But the context of written narrative is different: in most cases the outcome is already written, and direct address is rare. Whereas an orator might "codeliberate" directly with an audience, a literary work achieves the same goal through fostering empathy—whether by fear and pity (so Aristotle) or other narrative techniques.[24] Aristotle readily admits in his discussion of audience empathy that his discoveries have come more from "chance" (τύχη) than by deliberate method (τέχνη) (*Poet.* 1454a). His observation only underscores the fact

---

[21] Aristotle discusses at length what generates this effectively in tragedy, focusing especially on sufferings and sinister acts that occur in family relationships (*Poet.* 1452b–1454a, esp. 1453b–1454a).

[22] G. R. F. Ferrari, "Aristotle's Literary Aesthetics," *Phronesis* 44 (1999): 181–98, here 196.

[23] Quintilian, *Inst.* 9.2.20: "when we take our opponents into consultation."

[24] Ferrari agrees: "After all, the orator's task is to move his audience to action, and to that end he must make them fear for themselves. The dramatist's task is rather to engage his audience in the fiction, to bind them with its spell. The principal means by which he achieves this effect is to make them care enough about the hero to fear for him, that is to say fear on his behalf" ("Literary Aesthetics," 195–96).

that audience empathy may stem from various factors but ultimately yields an emotional engagement with the plight of story characters.[25]

To summarize, the following four components reflect what ancient authors and orators viewed as central contributors to narrative suspense:

1. Anticipation (expectation): the expectation that particular events are yet to come, whether generated by literary conventions or by allusions or forewarnings within the writing itself.
2. Deferring (suspension; cf. *sustentatio*): a delay in fulfilling the audience's expectations, thereby "suspending" them in a state of anticipation.
3. Uncertainty (raising doubts; cf. ἐπαπορεῖν, *dubitatio*): casting doubt on whether an expected outcome will occur—typically by insurmountable obstacles or situations of peril.
4. Empathy (cf. *communicatio*): increased engagement by the audience with the events of the narrative and the plights of its characters.

Where anticipation generates interest, suspension prolongs it, uncertainty intensifies it, and empathy enhances its emotional impact on the audience. According to the discussions among ancient authors, these are the most essential ingredients to narrative suspense.[26]

II. A Tale of Suspense: The Final Sea Journey (Acts 27:1–28:15)

Sea journeys were relatively common in literature of antiquity. Like car-chase scenes in modern action movies, they constituted a conventional type-scene in ancient literature that many readers presumably found engaging. Its origins are at

---

[25] Related to this notion is that of narrative credibility or plausibility, which Aelius Theon discusses at some length (*Prog.* 84–87).

[26] Both Rachelle Gilmour and Ralf Junkerjürgen have similar notions of suspense, but Gilmour includes the concept of a "macrostructure" of shorter episodes, and Junkerjürgen emphasizes narrative positioning to a greater degree as well as the conditioning of the reader (Gilmour, "Suspense and Anticipation in 1 Samuel 9:1–14," *JHebS* 9 [2009]: 5–8; Junkerjürgen, *Spannung: Narrative Verfahrensweisen der Leseraktivierung; Eine Studie am Beispiel der Reiseromane von Jules Verne*, EHS.FS 261 [Frankfurt am Main: Lang, 2002], 62). For more on narrative suspense, see Peter Vorderer, Hans J. Wulff, and Mike Friedrichsen, eds., *Suspense: Conceptualisations, Theoretical Analyses, and Empirical Explorations* (Mahwah, NJ: Lawrence Erlbaum Associates, 1996); Rabkin, *Narrative Suspense*, 7–69. Other studies of suspense in biblical texts are Normand Bonneau, "Suspense in Mark 5:21–43: A Narrative Study of Two Healing Stories," *ThF* 36 (2005): 131–54; Charles H. Cosgrove, "Rhetorical Suspense in Romans 9–11: A Study in Polyvalence and Hermeneutical Election," *JBL* 115 (1996): 271–87, https://doi.org/10.2307/3266856.

least as old as Homer (*Od.* 4.499–511; 5.262–463; 12.402–425).²⁷ In time, the type-scene became prevalent enough to stimulate satire (Juvenal, *Sat.* 12.17–82; Lucian, *Merc. cond.* 1–2) and parody (Lucian, *Ver. hist.* 1.5–6). The ingredients were standard enough to call them conventional.²⁸ Sea-journey stories were entertaining and therefore were especially common in prose fiction, among other genres.²⁹ But they were not simply entertaining; they could also serve as fitting venues for moral lessons on subjects such as pride (Polybius, *Hist.* 1.37), greed (Juvenal, *Sat.* 12.17–82), wealth (Phaedrus, *Fables* 4.23), friendship (Lucian, *Tox.* 19–21), and facing crises (Lucian, *Peregr.* 43–44; T. Naph. 6:1–10).³⁰ In general, sea-journey narratives—more specifically, their outcomes—could serve to indicate those whom divine beings favored. Those who survived the perils of the sea were evidently aided by divine powers—or at least not sufficiently hindered by them.³¹ Likewise, the Final Sea Journey of Acts offers divine testimony of Paul's innocence, just as earlier chapters offered human testimony of his innocence (23:12–26:32).

There is more to Acts 27:1–28:15, however, than simply using a conventional form to make a single theological claim. Pervo observes astutely:

> The keystone to the arch of issues through which all interpreters of Acts 27 must pass is its length. Why did the author devote sixty verses (c. 6 percent of the text) to the story of Paul's transfer to Rome? This is central to the question of meaning, and all discussions of text, source, and form must address it or risk the charge of irrelevance. This is, without doubt, a good story that contributes to the portrait of Paul's character and provides an additional demonstration of divine providence in operation, but those factors do not justify its length.³²

---

²⁷ Homer's sea-journey narratives were imitated in various later works, e.g., Virgil, *Aen.* 1.34–179; Aelius Aristides, *Oration* 48.65–68; Livy 21.58.3–11; Seneca, *Ag.* 465–578; Lucan, *Bel. civ.* 4.48–120. See also n. 9 above.

²⁸ Talbert and Hayes list the following common elements: (1) a warning not to sail, (2) sailing in a bad season, (3) unusually chaotic winds, (4) darkness during the storm, (5) horrendous waves, (6) sailors scurrying about, (7) throwing cargo or tackle overboard, (8) relinquishing control of the ship to the winds and waves, (9) the ship breaking up, (10) abandoning all hope, (11) shipwreck on rocks or shallow beach, (12) drifting ashore on planks, (13) swimming ashore or to another ship, and (14) helpful natives on shore ("Theology of Sea-Storms," 322–23). See also Richard I. Pervo, *Profit with Delight: The Literary Genre of the Acts of the Apostles* (Philadelphia: Fortress, 1979), 50–57, esp. 50–54; Pamela Lee Thimmes, *Studies in the Biblical Sea-Storm Type-Scene: Convention and Invention* (San Francisco: Mellen, 1992).

²⁹ For example: Chariton, *Chaer.* 3.3.9–18; Achilles Tatius, *Leuc. Clit.* 3.1–5; Xenophon of Ephesus, *Ephesiaca* 3.2.11–15; Heliodorus, *Aeth.* 1.22.3–5; 1.5.27; Petronius, *Satyricon* 114. Northrop Frye observes that in the Greek novel "the normal means of transportation is by shipwreck" (*The Secular Scripture: A Study of the Structure of Romance* [Cambridge: Harvard University Press, 1976], 4).

³⁰ These and many other examples are named in Talbert and Hayes, "Theology of Sea-Storms," 323–34.

³¹ On this, see ibid., 324–25; Pervo, *Acts*, 644–54.

³² Pervo, *Acts*, 644.

First of all, many ancient writings show that a sea-journey narrative did not need to be so long. Paul summarizes a shipwreck experience in five words (2 Cor 11:25). Josephus narrates a sea voyage to Rome that entails shipwreck, a night adrift at sea, and rescue by divine initiative (*Vita* 14–16) but uses less than a tenth of the length of Luke's Sea Journey.[33] Certainly there are examples in ancient literature that are comparably long (or longer), but Luke's story is longer than many.[34] From Homer's era to Luke's day and beyond, the general tradition of sea-journey narratives *allows* for the length and detail of Acts 27:1–28:15 but by no means *calls for* it. Homer and many others narrated sea journeys briefly (*Od.* 4.499–511)—why Luke waxed so eloquent at this point is not clear. More interesting, among comparable examples of sea-journey narratives in antiquity, none other occurs so close to the ending of the work. Most often these accounts appear somewhere in the midsection of the narrative, as in Greek novels.[35] That Luke writes a sea-journey narrative of such caliber is not unprecedented; that he places it at this particular juncture is another matter entirely. Collectively, these factors raise the question, what is the significance of Luke's Final Sea Journey, given its length, detail, and location in the narrative?

What the Sea Journey of Acts does at this juncture of the narrative is generate considerable suspense about what is to come—an effect that profoundly influences the reader's experience of the final chapters. First, a central feature of suspense is anticipation, and anticipation riddles the last ten chapters of Acts. From the nineteenth chapter onward, the narrative repeatedly states that Paul will bear witness in Rome. This begins at Acts 19:21 with Paul's explicit resolution: "Now after these things had been fulfilled, Paul resolved by the Spirit to go through Macedonia and Achaia, and then to journey to Jerusalem. He said, 'Afterward it is necessary [δεῖ]

---

[33] Josephus uses sixty-two words for the journey proper (LCL) and Acts 27:1–28:15 uses 746 words, by my count of the Greek texts (NA²⁸).

[34] The following sea-journey narratives, for example, are considerably briefer than the Final Sea Journey of Acts: Homer, *Od.* 4.499–511; Aeschylus, *Ag.* 647–666; Polybius, *Hist.* 1.37.1–10 (chiefly 1–6); Diogenes Laertius, *Lives of Eminent Philosophers* 9.68; Euripides, *Tro.* 77–86; Apollonius of Rhodes, *Argon.* 2.1093–1121; Xenophon of Ephesus, *Ephesiaca* 2.11; 3.2.11–15; Heliodorus, *Aeth.* 1.22.3–5; Lucian, *Ver. hist.* 1.5–6; 2.47; *Merc. cond.* 1–2; *Peregr.* 43–44; Josephus, *J.W.* 1.14.2–3 §§279–280; *Vita* 2–3 §§12–14; Jonah 1:3–17; T. Naph. 6:1–10. Other sea-journey narratives more comparable in length are Homer, *Od.* 5.262–463; 12.402–450; Herodotus 7.188–192; Euripides, *Iph. taur.* 1391–1489; Virgil, *Aen.* 1.34–179; Tacitus, *Ann.* 2.23–24; Seneca, *Ag.* 456–578; Statius, *Theb.* 5.360–421; Lucian, *Tox.* 19–21; Petronius, *Satyricon* 114; Heliodorus, *Aeth.* 5.27; Chariton, *Chaer.* 3.3.9–18; Achilles Tatius, *Leuc. Clit.* 3.1–5. Synesius of Cyrene narrates one of the longest sea-journey narratives in antiquity (longer than Luke's), which takes up most of his *Letter 4*, but it stems from the late fourth century CE at earliest.

[35] E.g., *Chaer.* 3.3.9–18; Achilles Tatius, *Leuc. Clit.* 3.1–5; Xenophon of Ephesus, *Ephesiaca* 3.2.11–15; Heliodorus, *Aeth.* 1.22.3–5; 1.5.27; Petronius, *Satyricon* 114. One sea-journey narrative that occurs just before the end is Lucian's *Peregr.* 43–44, but the author gives an explicit reason for this choice: "I shall add one more thing before I stop, in order that you may be able to have a good laugh" (43). Lucian's sea-journey story also spotlights a specific dishonorable character, which differs from Acts 27:1–28:15.

for me to see Rome'" (Acts 19:21). The language of necessity (δεῖ) and the presence of the Spirit both imply that Paul's travel interests have divine origins.[36] Some translate the phrase "Paul resolved by the Spirit" (ἔθετο ὁ Παῦλος ἐν τῷ πνεύματι) as "Paul resolved in his own spirit,"[37] but this goes against good judgment. Not only does Acts 19:21 use a characteristically Lukan expression for divine providence (δεῖ), but Luke also rarely uses πνεῦμα ("spirit" or "Spirit") elsewhere to refer to a person's state of mind (see Acts 17:16; Luke 1:17, 47). Further, the word πνεῦμα occurs often in Acts without the modifier ἅγιον ("holy") yet clearly refers to the Spirit of God (Acts 6:10; 8:18, 29; 10:19; 11:2; see also 11:28; 20:22; 21:4). Most importantly, Luke regularly draws attention to the role of the Spirit in Paul's ministry, making it odd that he would now assume jurisdiction over his travels (especially in light of 20:22–24 and 16:6–10). Just as Jesus "set his face toward Jerusalem" in Luke 9:51 as part of God's larger purpose, so Paul in Acts 19:21 sets his sights on Rome under divine jurisdiction.

The next scene of significance is Paul's farewell speech to the Ephesian elders (20:17–30), where he foresees ominous threats and no return to Ephesus (vv. 22–25). The speech's genre, tenor, narrative location, and length imply that Paul's next journey will be his last.[38] Furthermore, thirteen verses later Paul expresses a willingness to die: "For I am prepared not only to be bound but also to die in Jerusalem for the name of the Lord Jesus" (21:13). Two chapters later, just after a rescue from violence (23:6–10), the narrative reiterates the importance of Paul's journey to Rome. In a night vision, the Lord stands near Paul and announces, "Take courage, for just as you have testified to the things concerning me in Jerusalem, so is it necessary for you also to testify in Rome" (23:11). As with 19:21, this passage associates Paul's journey to Rome with divine destiny. Like the forewarnings of Jesus's death in Luke's Gospel (9:22, 44–45; 18:31–33), these passages in Acts generate early anticipation about Paul's fate in Rome.

Paul's trial scenes in Acts 22–26 continue to foster anticipation of Paul's fate in two ways. First, various points of conclusion emphasize that Paul will be tried by the emperor (25:10–12, 21, 25; 26:32). It begins with Paul's appeal to Caesar issued to Festus (25:10–11), whose council ratifies the appeal in ominous words:

---

[36] On language of divine necessity in Luke-Acts, see Luke 2:49; 4:43; 9:22; 12:12; 13:14, 33; 17:25; 19:5; 21:9; 22:37; 24:7, 44; Acts 1:16, 21; 3:21; 4:12; 5:29; 9:6, 16; 14:22; 15:5; 16:30; 19:21; 20:35; 23:11; 25:10; 27:24, 26. See also Charles H. Cosgrove, "The Divine ΔΕΙ in Luke-Acts: Investigations into the Lukan Understanding of God's Providence," *NovT* 26 (1984): 168–90.

[37] E.g., Joseph A. Fitzmyer, *The Acts of the Apostles: A New Translation with Introduction and Commentary*, AB 31 (New York: Doubleday, 1997), 652; C. K. Barrett, *A Critical and Exegetical Commentary on the Acts of the Apostles*, 2 vols., ICC (Edinburgh: T&T Clark, 1998), 2:919.

[38] See Jan Lambrecht, "Paul's Farewell-Address at Miletus (Acts 20, 17–38)," in *Les Actes des Apôtres: Traditions, redaction, théologie*, ed. Jacob Kremer, BETL 48 (Leuven: Leuven University Press, 1979), 307–37; Geeske Ballhorn, "Die Miletrede: Ein Literaturbericht," in *Das Ende des Paulus: Historische, theologische und literaturgeschichtliche Aspekte*, ed. Friedrich W. Horn, BZNW 106 (Berlin: de Gruyter, 2001), 37–47, https://doi.org/10.1515/9783110877212.37.

"You have appealed to the emperor; to the emperor you will go" (25:12). The appeal's importance is emphasized again later as Festus brings it up twice (25:21, 25), and Agrippa deems it a binding verdict for Paul (26:32). Second, there are extensive parallels between the journey of Paul to Rome in Acts and that of Jesus to Jerusalem in Luke's Gospel—especially in their trial scenes: both foresee fateful events in Jerusalem (Luke 18:31–33; cf. 9:21–22, 44; Acts 20:22–25; 21:11–13); both are "handed over [παραδίδωμι)] into the hands [εἰς χεῖρας ἀνθρώπων] of others" (Luke 9:44; 18:32; 24:7; Acts 21:11; 28:17); both are condemned with the imperative Αἶρε ("Away with," Luke 23:18; Acts 21:36; 22:22); both are imprisoned in Jerusalem and accused by religious authorities (Luke 22:66–23:25; Acts 22:30–23:10; also 25:1–7; cf. 24:1–9); both appear for trial on four occasions (Luke 22:66–71; 23:1–5, 6–12, 13–25; Acts 22:30–23:10; 24:1–23; 25:6–12; 25:23–26:32; cf. 24:24–25); both are heard by "Herod" (Luke 23:6–12; Acts 25:13–26:32); both are deemed innocent (Luke 23:4, 14–15, 22, 47; Acts 23:29; 25:25–27; 26:31–32); both are evaluated favorably by a centurion (Luke 23:47; Acts 27:3, 43); and the Romans ostensibly wish to set both free (Luke 23:16, 22; see Acts 28:18).[39] These parallels foster anticipation that Paul will meet a fate in Rome similar to Jesus's in Jerusalem.[40]

Building on this anticipation, the Final Sea Journey features a third and final forewarning of Paul's fate in Rome. Like the third of Jesus's three passion predictions in Luke's Gospel (9:22, 44–45; 18:31–33), it occurs much closer to the expected events—little more than a chapter from the end. At a point of despair, Paul shares with fellow seafarers a message he received:

> [23]For last night there stood by me an angel of the God to whom I belong and whom I serve. He said, [24]"Do not fear, Paul; it is necessary [δεῖ] for you to stand before the emperor. And note that God has granted you all those sailing with

---

[39] On the parallels between the journeys and trial scenes of Paul and Jesus, see M. D. Goulder, *Type and History in Acts* (London: SPCK, 1964), 52–64; Talbert, *Literary Patterns*, 15–65, esp. 16–18, 20–22; A. J. Mattill Jr., "The Jesus–Paul Parallels and the Purpose of Luke-Acts: H. H. Evans Reconsidered," *NovT* 17 (1975): 15–46, https://doi.org/10.1163/156853675x00103; Walter Radl, *Paulus und Jesus im lukanischen Doppelwerk: Untersuchungen zu Parallelmotiven im Lukasevangelium und in der Apostelgeschichte*, EHS.T 49 (Frankfurt am Main: Lang, 1975), 103–267; Robert O'Toole, "Parallels between Jesus and His Disciples in Luke-Acts: A Further Study," *BZ* 27 (1983): 195–212.

[40] Based on these parallels, some argue that the Final Sea Journey of Acts parallels Jesus's death and resurrection in Luke's Gospel so much so that Acts 27 becomes Paul's "death" and 28:1–10 his "resurrection" (Glenn R. Jacobson, "Paul in Luke-Acts: The Savior Who Is Present," *Society of Biblical Literature 1983 Seminar Papers*, SBLSP 22 [Chico, CA: Scholars Press, 1983], 131–46; Goulder, *Type and History*, 61; Radl, *Paulus und Jesus*, 222–51; Talbert and Hayes, "Theology of Sea-Storms," 334–35). But this stretches the parallels far beyond viability: reading Acts 27:1–28:15 so simply through the lens of Jesus's passion ignores the passage as its own distinctive narrative.

you." ²⁵Therefore cheer up, men! For I trust God that it will be exactly as I have been told. (27:23–25)

Three features of Paul's words underscore the importance of his arrival at Rome. First, an angel of God conveys the message (vv. 24–25), and there is no reason to think Paul misrepresents it. Second, the angel's promise uses characteristic language for divine necessity in Luke-Acts (δεῖ).⁴¹ Third, Paul verifies the angel's promise with added emphasis: "For I trust God that it will be exactly as I have been told" (v. 25). In many ways this final forewarning—with divine origins, characteristic language, and added emphasis—crystallizes the sense of anticipation mounting since chapter nineteen: Paul must arrive at Rome (19:21; 23:11; 27:24) in order to bear witness (23:11) and be tried by the emperor (23:11; 25:10–12, 21, 25; 26:32; 27:24). Like the last iteration of a building chorus, Paul's word in the Final Sea Journey sounds out a final forewarning of things presumably soon to come.

Yet the Final Sea Journey does not simply build anticipation. It also fosters uncertainty about anticipated outcomes—another ingredient of suspense—through a host of threats. First, the story takes place at sea—a context rife with danger, according to ancient literature. Both Jewish and Greco-Roman literary traditions portray sea travel as perilous, especially during winter.⁴² In Terence's *Hecyra* (second century BCE), the servant Sosia words this sentiment well: "By Heracles, Parmeno, words cannot express how troublesome a thing it is to travel by sea" (416–417).⁴³ Second, more than any other travel narrative in Luke-Acts, the Final Sea Journey features ominous hazards: the risks of winter (27:9, 12), forewarned peril (27:10), loss of direction (27:14–20), prospects of shipwreck (27:27–29, 39–44), potential crew desertion (27:29–32), prisoner execution (27:42–44), and deadly serpents (28:3–6). The sheer length of Acts 27:1–28:15 allows for more extended preoccupation with the perilous. Third, "safety" language pervades the Final Sea Journey narrative (σῴζω, διασῴζω, σωτηρία, 27:20, 31, 34, 43, 44; 28:1, 4) so as to highlight its absence—and its desirability.⁴⁴ These seven "safety" references

---

⁴¹ See n. 36 above.

⁴² In Jewish literature the sea represents the waters of chaos (Gen 1:2, Pss 74:13, 93:3–4, 104:6–9, 107:23–30, Isa 27:1, 51:9–10, Ezek 26:19–20, T. Naph. 6:2–10, y. Ber. 9:1), an association rooted in broader myth traditions of the ancient Near East (cf. Enuma Elish and the Ugaritic Baʻlu Myth). In Greco-Roman literature, sea travel is conventionally dangerous (see Achilles Tatius, *Clit. Leuc.* 5.9.2; Euripides, *Iph. taur.* 1413; Lucan, *Bel. civ.* 5.453–455; 636.37; Ovid, *Trist.* 1.2.23; Apuleius, *Metam.* 7:6; Juvenal, *Sat.* 12.17–82; Lucian, *Ver. hist.* 1.6), and during winters months the Mediterranean was widely deemed a *mare clausum* ("closed sea"; see F. Vegetius Renatus, *De re militari* 4.39; cf. Josephus, *J.W.* 2.10.5 §203; E. de Saint-Denis, "Mare clausum," *REL* 25 [1947]: 196–214). See Talbert and Hayes, "Theology of Sea-Storms"; Pervo, *Acts*, 644–54, esp. 644–45; Praeder, "Sea Voyages," 692–93.

⁴³ Terence, *Hecyra* 416–417: non hercle verbis, Parmeno, dici potest tantum quam re ipsa navigare incommodumst.

⁴⁴ This is not unique to Luke's Final Sea Journey. Since sea travel was widely perceived as threatening, arrival on land was naturally a return to safety. See Diodorus Siculus 3.40.1;

in Acts 27–28 draw attention to the uncertainty of safe haven for the narrative characters involved: "When neither sun nor stars appeared for many days, and no tiny tempest besieged us, then every remaining hope of our being saved dissipated" (27:20). All told, the Final Sea Journey yields a more sustained and intense focus on threats to expected outcomes than any other segment in Acts.

Along with anticipation and uncertainty, the Final Sea Journey enhances empathy with narrative characters in two subtle ways. First, Paul is the human character of greatest interest in Acts from the thirteenth chapter on. The sheer volume of narrative dedicated to his journeys draws the typical reader into a substantial investment in his fate. Second, first-person narration ("we") reappears for the entire Final Sea Journey. Although reasons for this phenomenon are debated, on a literary level the use of an internal persona as narrator has the potential to enhance empathy with the events at hand. In most cases, storytelling through the voice of a narrative participant ("we") can increase not only the narrator's credibility (depicting the narrator as an eyewitness) but also the perceived immediacy of the events.[45] Whatever "Luke's" intentions with first-person narration in Acts 27:1–28:15, its presence can foster the sense of a more immediate representation (mimesis) of events.[46]

While anticipation, uncertainty, and empathy all contribute to narrative suspense, perhaps the most fundamental ingredient is prolonging (or "suspension"), and this is what Luke's Final Sea Journey does best of all. First, the story is remarkably long. Despite the prevalence of Paul's journey narratives earlier in Acts (14:21–28; 16:6–10; 18:18–23; 20:1–6, 13–17; 21:1–6 [cf. 7–16]), all of them combined barely compare in length with this final counterpart.[47] No precedent or convention in Acts or elsewhere demands such length, especially at this juncture. Second, the Final Sea Journey reads at a slow pace. Gérard Genette uses the language of narrative "pace" to describe the ratio between the length of narrative text ("narrative time") and the chronological duration of the story ("story time").[48] For instance, Genette describes four categories of narrative pace (or "speed"):

Herodotus, *Hist.* 8.118–119; Josephus, *Vita* 3 §14; Longus, *Daphn.* 2.24.1; Strabo, *Geogr.* 2.3.4. On this topic, see Praeder, "Sea Voyages," 692–93.

[45] Related to this, Shlomith Rimmon-Kenan highlights the distinctions between "intradiegetic" (within the story) and "homodiegetic" (participating in the events) voices (*Narrative Fiction: Contemporary Poetics*, 2nd ed. [London: Routledge, 1983], 96–97).

[46] Aristotle valued mimesis ("showing, representing") over diegesis ("telling") in literature, since it allows for a more precise contemplation by the audience (*Poet.* 1448b).

[47] In NA[28], the Final Sea Journey is 746 words (59 lines), whereas the other travel narratives of Paul combine for 607 words (36 lines)—or 794 words (46 lines) if including all of 21:7–16. This same comparison also shows that the Final Sea Journey generally uses words that are longer and more complicated, making for an average 12.64 words per line—versus the average 16.86 words (17.26 if including 21:7–16) per line in other travel narratives in Acts.

[48] Gérard Genette, *Narrative Discourse: An Essay in Method*, trans. Jane E. Lewin (Ithaca, NY: Cornell University Press, 1980), 87.

1. *Descriptive Pause*: where narrative text is present but without a progression of story time. Example: an elaborate description of several events happening simultaneously at the moment of the atomic bomb explosion at Hiroshima.
2. *Scene*: where narrative text and story time are conventionally equal (as in dialogue). Example: a dialogue scene from Dostoyevksy's *Brothers Karamazov*.
3. *Summary*: where narrative text swiftly covers a longer period of story time. Example: sections of Jules Verne's *Around the World in Eighty Days* that summarize quickly the travels of Phileas Fogg and Passepartout.
4. *Ellipsis*: where story time progresses but without any corresponding narrative text. Example: a chapter begins with "Two years later" without stating what occurred in those two years. [49]

Over the course of Acts, the travel narratives generally follow a progressive deceleration in pace—with the Final Sea Journey being the "slowest" of all. All of the journey narratives in Acts reflect a "summary" pace, but no other travel narrative is as slow as the Final Sea Journey, in which just a few days of story time correspond to multiple verses of text (27:1–4, 5–8, 9–12, 13–20, 27–32, etc.; cf. 20:13–17; 21:1–6). In fact, the Final Sea Journey approaches the slow pace of "scene" at several points in Paul's interpolated speeches (27:9–12, 21–26, 33–38). Prior journey narratives occasionally approach this pace (14:22–23; 18:19–21; 21:4–6, 8–14) but not in so regular and sustained a fashion. Only during this final journey do both travelers and the reader find themselves "sailing slowly [βραδυπλοοῦντες] and with great difficulty for quite some time" (27:7). The closer Acts comes to its ending, therefore, the slower the narrative progresses.[50]

A third way that the Final Sea Journey "suspends" matters is by its abundant references to time: 27:3, 7–8, 9, 14, 18, 19, 20, 27, 33, 39; 28:11, 12, 13, 14; cf. 27:22, 23. Phrases like "for many days" (27:7), "when substantial time had passed" (27:9), "as it was the fourteenth night" (27:27), and "today is the fourteenth day" (27:33) occur often. The regularity of such references serves to put the passage of story time at the forefront of the reader's mind. In this way, the Final Sea Journey draws attention to how progressively story time ticks away as it uses up the little remaining narrative text of Acts.

The length, slow pace, and abundant time references of Acts 27:1–28:15 all contribute to a feeling of "slow sailing" for the final two chapters. As expectations of Paul's fate in Rome mount with increasing intensity (from 19:21 on) and the perils of sea travel threaten with uncertainty, the Final Sea Journey travels toward

---

[49] Ibid., 93–112. The examples are my own.

[50] For more on "deceleration" and "acceleration" of narrative speed, see Rimmon-Kenan, *Narrative Fiction*, 53–56. Junkerjürgen also emphasizes that typically the closer an episode is to the ending, the more elevated the sense of suspense (*Spannung*, 62).

anticipated outcomes at a plodding pace, placing the reader in suspense in subtle but marvelous ways.

III. Conclusions

If the Final Sea Journey fosters suspense, what is the significance of this for reading Acts?

First, the suspense generated by the Sea Journey gives an experiential dimension to the final two chapters of Acts. Suspense serves primarily to enhance anticipation of final outcomes, which affects the reader on an experiential level. J. R. Morgan gives apt words to this experience:

> We read a novel from a desire to know its ending, for it is only at the end of a novel that its meaning is complete. Yet the pleasure that we derive from following a plot resides in the tensions, uncertainties and thrills that we are made to experience.... And an author can prolong the pleasure of his text by deferring the consummation of his plot.[51]

The earliest readers of Acts were not textual analysts as much as they were hearers of a story. The important question, therefore, about the "slow sailing" of Acts 27:1–28:15 is not simply what the text *says* but what it *does* to the reader. While the story entails theological meaning, the reading of it also generates a distinctive experience of its own. As the narrative heightens anticipation for how and whether the ending will fulfill expected outcomes, the reader is subjected to prolonged tension and uncertainty—which itself constitutes a form of "pleasure," according to Morgan. In contrast to other journey narratives in Acts and in ancient literature, Luke's Final Sea Journey generates a palpable experience of suspense just verses before the ending, and this sets the reader up for experiencing the ending on a more empathetic level. Like Aristotle's "superior poet," who deliberately generates fear and pity in audiences, Luke gives his concluding chapters a heightened experiential dimension "so that the one who hears the events transpire experiences trembling and pity at what takes place" (*Poet.* 1453b). However superficial this experiential quality may be to some readers today, it was hardly lost on the ancients.

The upshot of this experiential dimension is increased engagement with the ending. This leads to a natural follow-up question: what kind of ending is Acts 28:16–31? Many deem the ending inconclusive. Pervo, for instance, writes:

> Luke was not loath to regale his readers with adventure, and he understood the value of retardation, but from this perspective the effort [of the Final Sea Journey]

---

[51] J. R. Morgan, "The Story of Knemon in Heliodoros' *Aithiopika*," *JHS* 109 (1989): 99–113, here 102–3.

was a failure, for the sequel [i.e., Acts 28:16–31] is anticlimactic, repetitious, and disappointing narrative.[52]

Earlier authors had similar experiences. Adolf von Harnack observed, "The place where the narrative now breaks off is as unsuitable as it possibly can be. The readers are kept upon the rack."[53] Much earlier, John Chrysostom famously noted that Luke "leaves the hearer athirst for more" (*Hom. Act.* 55; *NPNF* 1/11:326). Most interpreters find the ending abrupt, as if the larger story of witness to the end of the earth seems unfinished. The two narrative segments of epilogue (Acts 27:1–28:15) and ending (28:16–31) are together partners in the same crime: a deliberately open-ended conclusion. The ending denies decisive closure to particular questions (e.g., regarding Paul's fate), and the Final Sea Journey only accentuates them by its dramatic build-up beforehand. In these ways the entirety of Acts 27–28 functions together to suspend definitive resolution, making the ending of Luke's narrative read less like a final period and more like an unexpected ellipsis.[54]

Acts 27:1–28:15, therefore, does not use ancient rhetorical practices of suspense simply to frustrate; along with the ending (28:16–31), the Final Sea Journey suspends in order to provoke the reader's reflection. After all, as one of the earliest commentators on the ending of Acts points out, "to know everything makes the reader dull and jaded" (John Chrysostom, *Hom. Act.* 55). Whereas neat and tidy closure may satisfy "dull and jaded" human interests, Luke's ending blazes a different trail: it stimulates reflection on how God's activity is in fact present and at work amid uncertainty (threats, obstacles, challenges). Modern literary theorists Frank Kermode and Alice Kuzniar have advocated that, whereas readers generally long for meaningful structure in literature (i.e., closure), actual life experiences often thwart such meaningful resolution.[55] According to Kermode and Kuzniar, lack of closure may reflect reality more accurately than simplified forms of resolution. Lack of closure, however, need not simply convey pessimism about the human experience (à la Kermode); it may also convey hope amid an open-ended future. In the case of Acts, the ending entails frustration (28:17–28) but also glimmers of hope. The work of proclamation and witness continues "in an unhindered manner" despite looming threats (28:31). Whatever particular questions remain about Paul's

---

[52] Pervo, *Acts*, 644.

[53] Adolf von Harnack, "The Conclusion of the Acts of the Apostles and Its Silence concerning the Result of St. Paul's Trial," in *The Date of the Acts and of the Synoptic Gospels*, trans. J. R. Wilkinson, Crown Theological Library 33 (New York: G. P. Putnam, 1911), 97 and n. 2.

[54] For more on the ending of Acts, see Marguerat, "Enigma of the End"; Troy M. Troftgruben, *A Conclusion Unhindered: A Study of the Ending of Acts within Its Literary Environment*, WUNT 2/280 (Tübingen: Mohr Siebeck, 2010).

[55] Frank Kermode, *The Sense of an Ending: Studies in the Theory of Fiction, with a New Epilogue*, new ed. (Oxford: Oxford University Press, 2000); Alice A. Kuzniar, *Delayed Endings: Nonclosure in Novalis and Hölderlin* (Athens: University of Georgia Press, 2008).

fate, the narrative concludes on the note of bold and unhindered witness that presumably persists outside the narrative's end—even "to the end of the earth" (1:8). In this case, the final two chapters of Luke's second volume promise its first hearers no naïve resolutions to earthly troubles, as might please the "dull and jaded" reader. Instead, these chapters acknowledge uncertainty about the future but also profess confidence that the narrative's divine actors are still at work as the book concludes. The message issued to the narrative's earliest hearers is one of qualified but authentic hope: no matter the threats, omens, or uncertainties experienced by Jesus's witnesses, the divine actors of the narrative will not cease their activities of saving, including, redeeming, and proclaiming. On this provocative note, the narrative suddenly ends.[56]

In addition to provocation, the suspense of the Final Sea Journey draws attention to openness and uncertainty as prime places for witness. The passage enhances the reader's overall experience of openness and uncertainty throughout Acts 27–28, which in turn spotlights these characteristics as venues for apostolic witness and God's saving activity. In fact, the slowed pace of Acts 27:1–28:15 draws attention to the journey *itself* (vs. the destination) as a place of significant activity, making the Final Sea Journey more than merely a sideshow to the ending. Like the chapters dedicated to Paul's trials beforehand (Acts 22–26), the plodding pace of the Sea Journey slows down Paul's march to Rome. While narrative cues reiterate the need for Paul to bear witness in Rome (23:11; cf. 19:21; 27:24), the prolonged experience of the journey compels him to bear witness already in various ways and settings. Within the Final Sea Journey narrative, Paul speaks prophetically (27:10, 21–26, 31, 33–34), encourages the dispirited (27:22–25, 33–34), feeds the hungry (27:33–38), heals the sick (28:8–9), and ultimately speaks and acts on behalf of God (27:23–26). He exercises authority and command in the journey, is experienced favorably by many (27:43; 28:7–10; cf. 27:31–32), and is finally vindicated as one favored by God (28:3–6). All this among travelers heavily preoccupied with attaining "safety"— or "salvation" (σωτηρία).[57] In these ways, Paul bears authentic witness to the message of Jesus in word and deed while navigating uncharted waters. Matthew Skinner rightly identifies Paul's settings in custody as places "of possibility, not of restriction," since they counterintuitively offer new locations and audiences for

---

[56] Donald Harrisville Juel has a similar interpretation of the ending to Mark's Gospel, *pace* Frank Kermode, for reasons similarly rooted in the activity of divine actors: "The story gives good reasons to remain hopeful even in the face of disappointment. The possibilities of eventual enlightenment for the reader remain in the hands of the divine actor who will not be shut in—or out" ("A Disquieting Silence: The Matter of the Ending," in *The Ending of Mark and the Ends of God: Essays in Memory of Donald Harrisville Juel*, ed. Beverly Roberts Gaventa and Patrick D. Miller [Louisville: Westminster John Knox, 2005], 1–13, here 11).

[57] Even though "salvation" language (σώζω, διασώζω, σωτηρία) in this context (27:20, 31, 34, 43, 44; 28:1, 4) likely means "safety" from threat, the original audiences would have readily heard other nuances.

witness.[58] The Final Sea Journey is also precisely this—a place of possibility for ongoing witness. The slowed pace of the journey only draws out and draws attention to the potential for uncertain expanses to become venues for proclamation. In this way, the account of the Final Sea Journey says something significant about the nature of witness: it is not limited to sacred moments or particular audiences but instead takes place freely among strangers, at all times, and in the most foreign places. As something inspired and empowered by God, bold witness is neither hindered by human restrictions nor truly threatened by cosmic forces or natural threats. In the Final Sea Journey, Luke's narrative redeems and transforms the significance of a context traditionally associated with threat, hostility, and fear (the sea). The narrative gives the reader the clear impression that, whether on land or at sea, proclaiming the reign of God and the things concerning the Lord Jesus Christ will continue "unhindered" (28:31). Within the story's global movement of witness (Acts 1:8), spaces and places of all shapes and sizes can be venues for God's purposes and activity.

In terms of apostolic witness, then, the extensive nature of Acts 27:1–28:15 draws attention to the journey itself, not the destination. The Final Sea Journey hinders a potential sprint to Rome so that the path of travel will not be overlooked in the process. In this way the slow sailing of Acts 27:1–28:15 would have implied to its original hearers something sacred about traveling "on the way." Here and throughout Acts, those who belong to "the Way" (9:2; 18:25; 19:9, 23; 22:4; 24:14, 22) normally serve as Jesus's witnesses in transit—in motion, going from place to place, en route between one destination and another. In other words, those belonging to "the Way" are most often themselves traveling "on the way" (geographically) in response to divine initiative. In this way, Luke's narrative gave to his early audiences an image of journey as a multifaceted and comprehensive metaphor for what Luke believed the apostolic way of life was truly and most centrally about. As the Final Sea Journey shows, the narrative of Acts recasts and reimagines for the reader the notion of journey itself as sacred space for unhindered witness and God's saving activity.

---

[58] Matthew L. Skinner, *Locating Paul: Places of Custody as Narrative Settings in Acts 21–28*, AcBib 13 (Atlanta: Society of Biblical Literature, 2003), 109; see also 151–89.

Is Every Sin outside the Body except Immoral Sex? Weighing Whether 1 Corinthians 6:18b Is Paul's Statement or a Corinthian Slogan

ANDREW DAVID NASELLI
andy.naselli@bcsmn.edu
Bethlehem College & Seminary, Minneapolis, MN 55415

In 1 Cor 6:18b–c, Paul writes, "Every sin, whatever a person commits, is outside the body, but the sexually immoral person sins against his own body." This essay weighs whether 1 Cor 6:18b is Paul's statement or whether Paul is quoting a Corinthian slogan, and it concludes that the second view is more plausible.

---

[a] Φεύγετε τὴν πορνείαν.
[b] πᾶν ἁμάρτημα ὃ ἐὰν ποιήσῃ ἄνθρωπος ἐκτὸς τοῦ σώματός ἐστιν·
[c] ὁ δὲ πορνεύων εἰς τὸ ἴδιον σῶμα ἁμαρτάνει.
—1 Cor 6:18

[a] Flee from sexual immorality.
[b] Every sin, whatever a person commits, is outside the body,
[c] but the sexually immoral person sins against his own body.
(my form-based translation)

The highlighted words above (1 Cor 6:18b) have puzzled people for centuries. What does Paul mean? His main exhortation to Christians in verses 12–20 is straightforward: *Glorify God with your body by not committing sexual immorality.* And the first and third parts of 6:18 are relatively straightforward: *Flee from sexual immorality.... The sexually immoral person sins against his own body.* But how to interpret the middle part (v. 18b) is not straightforward. Does it prove that immoral sex is uniquely against one's body? Translators have attempted to make sense of verse 18b in one of two ways: (1) Some add the word *other* to smooth it out: "Every *other* sin a person commits is outside the body" (ESV). If this is the correct reading, then Paul divides sin into two categories: nonsexual sins take place outside the

Thanks to friends who examined a draft of this essay and shared helpful feedback, especially Brent Belford, Matt Klem, and Jay Smith.

969

body, and sexual sins are against a person's own body. (2) Some translators attribute these words not to Paul but to the Corinthians: the Corinthians claim, "Every sin a person commits is outside the body," and Paul refutes them. If this is the correct reading, then the Corinthians are using this slogan to justify sex outside of marriage. They are arguing that sin occurs only outside the body—that you cannot sin in or through your body. Paul then refutes that wrong view of the body.

English translations render verse 18b in one of three ways: (1) as Paul's statement without adding the word *other*; (2) as Paul's statement but adding the word *other*; or (3) as a Corinthian slogan. Most render it as Paul's statement, and most of those translations add the word *other* to smooth it out (see table 1). Translations that do not add the word *other* imply it, so there are really just two main views: 6:18b is either (1) Paul's statement or (2) a Corinthian slogan. In this essay, I weigh the arguments for each view and then conclude which is more persuasive.

I. Arguments That 1 Corinthians 6:18b Is Paul's Statement

At least six arguments support the view that verse 18b is Paul's statement.

A. Paul's Argument Implies That He Means "Every Other Sin"

The words πᾶν ἁμάρτημα ("every sin") do not seem to harmonize with the second half of the sentence: ὁ δὲ πορνεύων εἰς τὸ ἴδιον σῶμα ἁμαρτάνει ("but the sexually immoral person sins against his own body"). In other words, πᾶν ἁμάρτημα seems to *include* sexual immorality. But if that is the case, then what Paul says here is incoherent. He must therefore be implying that πᾶν ἁμάρτημα refers to every sin *except* sexual immorality; he must be speaking hyperbolically and then qualifying himself.[1] Paul's argument implies that he means "every *other* sin."

B. Paul Means That Sexual Immorality Is Uniquely against One's Body

Other sins are obviously against one's body such as gluttony or drunkenness or suicide. But Paul argues in verse 18 that sexual immorality is *uniquely* against one's body. How? Many exegetes simply assert that sexual immorality is uniquely against one's body without precisely specifying how it is qualitatively different from other sins such as drunkenness.[2] Exegetes who do specify how sexual immorality is different from other sins suggest at least five ways (which are not necessarily mutually exclusive).

---

[1] Wolfgang Schrage, *Der erste Brief an die Korinther*, 4 vols., EKKNT 7 (Zurich: Benziger, 1991–2001), 2:32–33.

[2] E.g., Johann Albrecht Bengel, "Annotations on Paul's First Epistle to the Corinthians," in *Gnomon of the New Testament*, trans. James Bryce, 5 vols. (Edinburgh: T&T Clark, 1860), 3:242; Will Deming, "The Unity of 1 Corinthians 5–6," *JBL* 115 (1996): 289–312, here 304 n. 55, https://doi.org/10.2307/3266857.

TABLE 1. Three Ways That English Translations Render 1 Cor 6:18b

Paul's Statement: Not Adding *Other*	Paul's Statement: Adding *Other*	Corinthian Slogan
• **NRSV:** Shun fornication! Every sin that a person commits is outside the body; but the fornicator sins against the body itself. • **CEB:** Avoid sexual immorality! Every sin that a person can do is committed outside the body, except those who engage in sexual immorality commit sin against their own bodies.	• **NASB:** Flee immorality. Every *other* sin that a man commits is outside the body, but the immoral man sins against his own body. • **RSV:** Shun immorality. Every other sin which a man commits is outside the body; but the immoral man sins against his own body. • **ESV:** Flee from sexual immorality. Every other sin a person commits is outside the body, but the sexually immoral person sins against his own body. • **NIV:** Flee from sexual immorality. All other sins a person commits are outside the body, but whoever sins sexually, sins against their own body. • **NJB:** Keep away from sexual immorality. All other sins that people may commit are done outside the body; but the sexually immoral person sins against his own body. • **NLT:** Run from sexual sin! No other sin so clearly affects the body as this one does. For sexual immorality is a sin against your own body. • **God's Word:** Stay away from sexual sins. Other sins that people commit don't affect their bodies the same way sexual sins do. People who sin sexually sin against their own bodies.	• **HCSB:** Run from sexual immorality! "Every sin a person can commit is outside the body." On the contrary, the person who is sexually immoral sins against his own body.[3] • **NET:** Flee sexual immorality! "Every sin a person commits is outside of the body"— but the immoral person sins against his own body.

---

[3] The Holman Christian Standard Bible changed its name to the Christian Standard Bible in early 2017, and the CSB updates verse 18 without a translator's note so that it now belongs in the middle column: "Flee sexual immorality! Every other sin a person commits is outside the body, but the person who is sexually immoral sins against his own body."

1. Immoral sex is qualitatively worse than other sins because it creates a one-flesh union that uniquely defiles the body. Some proponents of this view add that immoral sex is not merely physical but has a spiritual component (vv. 15–17). Advocates of this view include Augustine, Marcus Dods, Eckhard J. Schnabel, Roy E. Ciampa and Brian S. Rosner, and Gordon D. Fee.[4] The modern advocate whom recent exegetes most frequently cite for support is Bruce N. Fisk, who concludes:

> The body against which one sins sexually (18c) is the body that has been joined illicitly to another (16a). Sexual sin is uniquely body-defiling because it is inherently body-joining. Again, because Paul believes sexual immorality establishes a "one body" union with the prostitute, he views that act as destructive self-violation.
>
> … For Paul, sexual sin *is* intrinsically different (F. Grosheide, R. Gundry) and more destructive (H. Conzelmann); it *does* have powerful and negative effects on the sinner (C. Hodge, R. Bultmann), and it *does* distort both vertical (G. Fee [1st ed.]) and horizontal relationships (E. Käsemann). But too many of these views import concepts and categories into the argument Paul develops in 1 Cor 6. Given the antecedent Jewish themes and the rhetorical structure we have highlighted, v. 18 should be taken closely with v. 16a; the two are mutually explanatory. In this sense, Paul can declare sexual sin to be fundamentally different. Other sins may be physically destructive (e.g. suicide, gluttony), corporately

---

[4] Augustine, *Serm.* 162.1 (PG 38:885): "It seems that the blessed apostle, through whom Christ was speaking, wished to make the evil of fornication greater than other sins. These others, although they are committed through the body, do not bind and subjugate the human soul to fleshly lust as the overpowering force of sexual desire does. Only the sexual act makes the soul mingle with the body, fastening the one to the other with a kind of glue. The result is that the person engaged in such vice has a mind submerged and drowned in carnal lust and can think of or intend nothing else" (trans. Judith L. Kovacs, in *1 Corinthians: Interpreted by Early Christian Commentators*, Church's Bible [Grand Rapids: Eerdmans, 2005], 100). See also Marcus Dods, *The First Epistle to the Corinthians*, ExpB (London: Hodder & Stoughton, 1889), 156: "This is the only sin in which the present connection of the body with Christ and its future destiny in Him are directly sinned against. This is the only sin, he means, which by its very nature alienates the body from Christ, its proper Partner"; Eckhard J. Schnabel, *Der erste Brief des Paulus an die Korinther*, HTA (Wuppertal: Brockhaus, 2006), 343–44; Roy E. Ciampa and Brian S. Rosner, *The First Letter to the Corinthians*, PilNTC (Grand Rapids: Eerdmans, 2010), 264: "In v. 18b Paul is not saying that only *porneia* damages the body, but rather that only *porneia* establishes a 'one-flesh' union that is 'against the body'"; Gordon D. Fee, *The First Epistle to the Corinthians*, 2nd ed., NICNT (Grand Rapids: Eerdmans, 2014), 290: "In fornicating with a prostitute a man removes his body (which is a temple of the Spirit, purchased by God and destined for resurrection) from union with Christ and makes it a member of her body, thereby putting it under her 'mastery' (v. 12b; cf. 7:4). Every other sin is apart from (i.e., not 'in') the body in this singular sense.… The unique nature of sexual sin is not so much that one sins against one's own self but that one sins against one's own body, as *viewed in terms of its place in redemptive history*."

destructive (e.g. gossip, divisiveness), or spiritually defiling (e.g. idolatry) but for Paul, because sexual sin is uniquely body-joining, it is uniquely body-defiling.[5]

2. Immoral sex is qualitatively worse than other sins because it has more serious effects. It leaves a permanent stain on the body. The best-known advocate of this view is Calvin, and others who hold this view include C. K. Barrett, John H. Armstrong, Craig Blomberg, and F. F. Bruce.[6]

Charles Hodge observes that views 1 and 2 are not mutually exclusive. He argues that number 2 is the *result* of number 1.[7]

3. Immoral sex is qualitatively worse than other sins because it is against one's *entire* body. The most prominent advocate of this view is John Chrysostom.[8]

---

[5] Bruce N. Fisk, "Πορνεύειν as Body Violation: The Unique Nature of Sexual Sin in 1 Corinthians 6.18," *NTS* 42 (1996): 540–58, here 557–58.

[6] John Calvin, *Commentaries on the Epistles of Paul the Apostle to the Corinthians*, trans. John Pringle, 2 vols. (Edinburgh: Calvin Translation Society, 1848–1849), 1:219–20 (italics original): "The body, it is true, is defiled also by theft, and murder, and drunkenness.... I explain it in this way, that he [Paul] does not altogether deny that there are other vices, in like manner, by which our body is dishonoured and disgraced, but that his meaning is simply this—that defilement does not attach itself to our body from other vices in the same way as it does from *fornication*. My hand, it is true, is defiled by theft or murder, my tongue by evil speaking, or perjury, and the whole body by drunkenness; but *fornication* leaves a stain impressed upon the body, such as is not impressed upon it from other sins. According to this comparison, or, in other words, in the sense of less and more, other sins are said to be *without the body*—not, however, as though they do not at all affect the body, viewing each one by itself." Others who cite Calvin in support of this view of 1 Cor 6:18 include C. K. Barrett, *The First Epistle to the Corinthians*, BNTC 7 (Peabody, MA: Hendrickson, 1968), 150–51; John H. Armstrong, *The Stain That Stays: The Church's Response to the Sexual Misconduct of Its Leaders* (Fearn, Scotland: Christian Focus Publications; Reformation and Revival Ministries, 2000), 53–54, 59, 60, 62, 63. See also Craig Blomberg, *1 Corinthians*, NIV Application Commentary (Grand Rapids: Zondervan, 1994), 128: "We dare not lose sight of the unique seriousness of sexual sin that verse 18 upholds. The effects of gluttony are usually reversible by an increase in sweat and a decrease in calories. Some effects of illicit sex can never be undone (though of course they can be forgiven). Memories, emotions, and attachments stay with us for life, although excessive promiscuity can eventually dull or numb our senses in certain ways." Cf. F. F. Bruce, *1 and 2 Corinthians*, NCB (Grand Rapids: Eerdmans, 1971), 65.

[7] Charles Hodge, *An Exposition of the First Epistle to the Corinthians* (New York: Carter, 1860), 105–6: "This does not teach that fornication is greater than any other sin; but it does teach that it is altogether peculiar in its effects upon the body; not so much in its physical as in its moral and spiritual effects. The idea runs through the Bible that there is something mysterious in the commerce of the sexes, and in the effects which flow from it. Every other sin, however degrading and ruinous to the health, even drunkenness, is external to the body, that is, external to its life. But fornication, involving as it does a community of life, is a sin against the body itself, because incompatible, as the Apostle had just taught, with the design of its creation, and with its immortal destiny."

[8] *NPNF* 1/12:101.

4. Immoral sex is qualitatively worse than other sins because it uses only one's body and not any means external to one's body. Advocates of this view include Christian Friedrich Kling, Heinrich August Wilhelm Meyer, Charles J. Ellicott, Leon Morris, Simon J. Kistemaker, and Andreas Lindemann.⁹

5. Immoral sex is qualitatively worse than other sins because the σῶμα in verse 18 is a vehicle of personal self-communication. The most prominent advocate of this view is Brendan Byrne.¹⁰

C. Paul Does Not Clearly Introduce the Statement as a Corinthian Slogan

Elsewhere in 1 Corinthians Paul clearly signals when he is quoting the Corinthians (see esp. 1:12 and 7:1), but in 6:18 he does not clearly introduce a quotation.

> This view [i.e., that v. 18 is a Corinthian slogan] is to be rejected because Paul includes no marker to signal the presence of a quotation. The δέ (*de*), unlike the ἀλλά (*alla*) in 6:12, does not function as a contrastive particle but expresses an exception: "Every sin a man commits is outside his body with the exception of the immoral man who sins against his own body."¹¹

---

⁹ Christian Friedrich Kling, *The First Epistle of Paul to the Corinthians*, trans. Daniel W. Poor (New York: Scribner, 1868), 133–34; Heinrich August Wilhelm Meyer, *Critical and Exegetical Handbook to the Epistles to the Corinthians*, rev. and ed. William P. Dickson, trans. D. Douglas Bannerman, 2 vols., CECNT 5–6 (Edinburgh: T&T Clark, 1877–1879), 1:185–86; Charles J. Ellicott, *St. Paul's First Epistle to the Corinthians: With a Critical and Grammatical Commentary* (London: Longmans, Green, 1887), 106; Leon Morris, *1 Corinthians: An Introduction and Commentary*, TNTC 7 (Downers Grove, IL: InterVarsity Press, 1985), 101; Simon J. Kistemaker, *Exposition of the First Epistle to the Corinthians*, NTC 18 (Grand Rapids: Baker, 1993), 201; Andreas Lindemann, *Der Erste Korintherbrief*, HNT 9.1 (Tübingen: Mohr Siebeck, 2000), 151–52.

¹⁰ This follows Ernst Käsemann's view of σῶμα (see "The Pauline Doctrine of the Lord's Supper," in *Essays on New Testament Themes*, trans. W. J. Montague, SBT 41 [London: SCM, 1964], 108–35). See Brendan Byrne, "Sinning against One's Own Body: Paul's Understanding of the Sexual Relationship in 1 Corinthians 6:18," *CBQ* 45 (1983): 603–16, here 613: "But there is something about fornication that strikes at one's own 'body' in some particularly direct way, in comparison with which other sins are somehow 'outside' the body.... If *sōma* is understood as the physical body particularly under the aspect of personal self-communication and if it carries with it from the argument built up in the preceding verses (15–16) the specific overtones of instrument of personal communication in the sexual act, then the character of fornication as peculiarly a sin 'against one's own body' becomes clear. The immoral person perverts precisely that faculty within himself that is meant to be the instrument of the most intimate bodily communication between persons. He sins against his unique power of bodily communication and in this sense sins in a particular way 'against his own body.' All other sins are in this respect by comparison 'outside' the body."

¹¹ David E. Garland, *1 Corinthians*, BECNT (Grand Rapids: Baker Academic, 2003), 236. Cf. Fisk, "Πορνεύειν as Body Violation," 545 n. 10.

D. Internal Clues Do Not Suggest That the Statement Is a Corinthian Slogan

Verse 18b immediately follows Φεύγετε τὴν πορνείαν (v. 18a). It is unnatural for what follows to be a Corinthian slogan because the transition would be too abrupt.[12]

E. 1 Corinthians 6:18c Does Not Correspond with 6:18b as a Slogan

Verse 18c (ὁ δὲ πορνεύων εἰς τὸ ἴδιον σῶμα ἁμαρτάνει, "but the sexually immoral person sins against his own body") emphasizes one's *own* body. But verse 18b emphasizes that sin occurs outside *the* body; verse 18c, therefore, does not seem to respond to verse 18b as if verse 18b were a slogan.[13]

F. The Grammar Supports Adding the Word Other[14]

At least one other place in the Greek New Testament does not use the word for "other" but necessarily implies it. The grammatical construction in verse 18b parallels Matt 12:31:

πᾶσα ἁμαρτία καὶ βλασφημία ἀφεθήσεται τοῖς ἀνθρώποις,
ἡ δὲ τοῦ πνεύματος βλασφημία οὐκ ἀφεθήσεται.

Every sin and blasphemy will be forgiven people,
but the blasphemy against the Spirit will not be forgiven.

In Matt 12:31, the second clause clarifies the first. The first clause cannot mean "every sin and blasphemy without exception" because the second clause clarifies that there is an exception. So the first clause is a blanket statement, and the second clause is an exception. This parallels 1 Cor 6:18b:

πᾶν ἁμάρτημα ὃ ἐὰν ποιήσῃ ἄνθρωπος ἐκτὸς τοῦ σώματός ἐστιν·
ὁ δὲ πορνεύων εἰς τὸ ἴδιον σῶμα ἁμαρτάνει.

Every [other] sin a person commits is outside the body,
but the sexually immoral person sins against his own body.

Thus, the grammar supports adding the word *other*.

---

[12] Fee, *First Epistle to the Corinthians*, 290.

[13] This is the main argument of Byrne, "Sinning against One's Own Body." Similarly, Schnabel, *Der erste Brief des Paulus an die Korinther*, 343: "Die Formulierung lässt nicht erkennen, dass es sich um ein Zitat handelt, und die Wendung 'gegen seinen *eigenen* Leib' im nächsten Satz wäre keine Entgegnung auf eine solche Parole, die das nicht-leibliche Wesen der Sünde betonen würde."

[14] See Archibald T. Robertson and Alfred Plummer, *A Critical and Exegetical Commentary on the First Epistle of St. Paul to the Corinthians*, 2nd ed., ICC (Edinburgh: T&T Clark, 1914), 127–28; Fisk, "Πορνεύειν as Body Violation," 544; Garland, *1 Corinthians*, 237; Ciampa and Rosner, *First Corinthians*, 263 n. 86.

II. Arguments That 1 Corinthians 6:18b Is a Corinthian Slogan

At least ten arguments support the view that verse 18b is a Corinthian slogan.[15] I am not aware of a proponent of this view who uses all of these arguments to support it. The closest is Jay Smith.[16] The most influential recent proponent of this view is Jerome Murphy-O'Connor.[17]

The question is not whether immoral sex creates a one-flesh union that uniquely defiles the body or whether immoral sex is qualitatively worse than other sins because it has more serious effects. The question, rather, is whether that is what Paul is specifically arguing in verse 18. If verse 18b is a Corinthian slogan, then Paul is not focusing on how immoral sex is qualitatively worse than all other sins but is instead refuting the claim that sin occurs only outside the body.

A. A Slogan Is a More Natural Reading

Taking verse 18b as a Corinthian slogan is a more natural reading because it does not qualify πᾶν ἁμάρτημα ("every sin"). Otherwise, in order for the statement to make sense, one has to supply the word *other*; but "the word *other* is not in the Greek text; this interpretation assumes that Paul has expressed himself imprecisely."[18]

---

[15] This is a cumulative-case argument. The order of the arguments is not crucial.

[16] See the following works by Jay E. Smith: "Can Fallen Leaders Be Restored to Leadership?," *BSac* 151 (1994): 470–78; "The Interpretation of 1 Corinthians 6:12–20 and Its Contribution to Paul's Sexual Ethics" (PhD diss., Trinity Evangelical Divinity School, 1996); "1 Corinthians," in *The Bible Knowledge Word Study: Acts–Ephesians*, ed. Darrell L. Bock (Colorado Springs, CO: Victor, 2006), 250–53; "The Roots of a 'Libertine' Slogan in 1 Corinthians 6:18," *JTS* 58 (2008): 63–95; "Slogans in 1 Corinthians," *BSac* 167 (2010): 68–88; "A Slogan in 1 Corinthians 6:18b: Pressing the Case," in *Studies in the Pauline Epistles: Essays in Honor of Douglas J. Moo*, ed. Matthew S. Harmon and Jay E. Smith (Grand Rapids: Zondervan, 2014), 74–98.

[17] See Jerome Murphy-O'Connor, "Corinthian Slogans in 1 Cor 6:12–20," *CBQ* 40 (1978): 391–96. He reprinted this essay and added an eight-page postscript in Murphy-O'Connor, *Keys to First Corinthians: Revisiting the Major Issues* (Oxford: Oxford University Press, 2009), 20–31. New Testament scholars did not immediately embrace Murphy-O'Connor's argument; many remained undecided while acknowledging that verse 18 is a challenging passage. One author who did embrace Murphy-O'Connor's view is Roger L. Omanson, "Acknowledging Paul's Quotations," *BT* 43 (1992): 201–13, esp. 206–7.

[18] Richard B. Hays, *First Corinthians*, IBC (Louisville: John Knox, 1997), 105. See also Joseph A. Fitzmyer, *First Corinthians: A New Translation with Introduction and Commentary*, AYB 32 (New Haven: Yale University Press, 2008), 268–69; Charles H. Talbert, *Reading Corinthians: A Literary and Theological Commentary*, rev. ed. (Macon, GA: Smyth & Helwys, 2002), 50; Alan F. Johnson, *1 Corinthians*, IVP New Testament Commentary 7 (Downers Grove, IL: InterVarsity Press, 2004), 102–3; Verlyn D. Verbrugge, "1 Corinthians," in *Romans–Galatians*, 2nd ed., EBC

The only problem with this translation [i.e., adding the word *other*] is that there is absolutely no exegetical justification for adding the word "other" except that commentators have difficulty explaining the meaning of the verse without it. Without adding "other" to the translation, the phrase becomes an impenetrable mystery if construed literally as Paul's words.[19]

B. The Other View Is Theologically Incoherent

Reading verse 18b as Paul's statement is theologically incoherent. If verse 18b is Paul's statement, then Paul is confusing and unclear. Why is only immoral sex a sin against your body but not other sins such as suicide or gluttony or drunkenness—a sin he explicitly names in verse 10? Section I.B above explains how those who argue that verse 18b is Paul's statement answer this question: they argue that sexual immorality is *uniquely* against one's body. But the logic that Paul uses in chapter 6 regarding immoral sex is essentially the same argument he uses in Rom 6 regarding any kind of sin: *Christian, you are united to Christ, so don't use the members of your body to sin.* (See table 2.)

TABLE 2. Paul's Similar Arguments in Romans 6 and 1 Corinthians 6

Romans 6	1 Corinthians 6
Christian, you should not sin because you are united to Christ (vv. 1–11). So do not let sin reign in your mortal body (v. 12). Do not sin with the members of your body (vv. 13, 19).	Christian, your body is a member of Christ, so you should not make it a member of a prostitute (v. 15). If you have immoral sex, then you are denying your union with Christ. You become "one flesh" with someone you have sex with, and you should not become one flesh with a prostitute (v. 16).

Paul's argument in 1 Cor 6 specifically applies what he argues broadly in Rom 6 regarding all sin in general. There is a sense in which you can say that any sin is unique—that there is no other sin *exactly* like that sin.[20] But is Paul's point in 1 Cor 6:18 that sexual sin is the *only* sin against the body? If verse 18b is Paul's statement,

---

11 (Grand Rapids: Zondervan, 2008), 312; B. Ward Powers, *First Corinthians: An Exegetical and Explanatory Commentary; A Consideration of Some Views Ancient and Modern in the Light of a Verse-by-Verse Look at What the Text Actually Says; A Somewhat Traditional Interpretation Plus Contemporary Application* (Eugene, OR: Wipf & Stock, 2008), 102–4.

[19] Denny Burk, "Discerning Corinthian Slogans through Paul's Use of the Diatribe in 1 Corinthians 6:12–20," *BBR* 18 (2008): 99–121, here 117. Cf. the NET Bible note on this phrase in 1 Cor 6:18: "This is the most natural understanding of the statement as it is written. To construe it as a statement by Paul requires a substantial clarification in the sense."

[20] See Smith, "Slogans in 1 Corinthians," 68 n. 3; Smith, "Slogan in 1 Corinthians 6:18b," 86 n. 48.

then the answer is yes; but if verse 18b is a Corinthian slogan, then the answer is no. If the answer is yes, then that leaves us guessing precisely how immoral sex is the *only* sin against the body. Exegetes and theologians have been postulating elaborate theories for two thousand years (see section I.B above). "Perhaps it is time to employ Occam's razor to cut this Gordian knot" by recognizing that verse 18b is a Corinthian slogan.[21]

C. The Grammar Does Not Support Adding the Word Other

Contrary to the argument in section I.F above, the grammar does *not* support adding the word *other* but is decisively *against* this. The most authoritative source on this is J. William Johnston's monograph *The Use of Πᾶς in the New Testament*.[22] After meticulously categorizing how the New Testament uses the word πᾶς, Johnston exegetes over a dozen debated passages, one of which is 1 Cor 6:18.[23] Verse 18b is what Johnston classifies as an *E5b* construction: πᾶς + noun + relative clause with ἐάν or ἄν. It occurs only four times in the New Testament: Matt 18:19, Mark 3:28, Acts 15:36, and 1 Cor 6:18.[24] "The sense in 1 Cor 6:18" is this: "every single sin a person commits or might commit."[25] The closest parallel is Deut 19:15 LXX: κατὰ πᾶσαν ἀδικίαν καὶ κατὰ πᾶν ἁμάρτημα καὶ κατὰ πᾶσαν ἁμαρτίαν ἣν ἂν ἁμάρτῃ. That is the closest parallel because the texts share not only similar vocabulary but also similar form: a relative clause intensifies how all-inclusive the statement is.

The grammatical construction in verse 18b–c does not parallel Matt 12:31 in a crucial way (see section I.F above) because Matt 12:31 does not include a relative clause.[26] This is significant because 1 Cor 6:18b includes an indefinite relative clause in an unusual way: πᾶν ἁμάρτημα <u>ὃ ἐὰν ποιήσῃ ἄνθρωπος</u> ἐκτὸς τοῦ σώματός ἐστιν ("Every sin, *whatever a person commits*, is outside the body"). An indefinite relative clause usually functions like a substantive, but here it functions like an adjective by modifying its antecedent, ἁμάρτημα. This unusual construction emphasizes that there are no exceptions to this rule: *absolutely every sin without exception that a person commits is outside the body*. Πᾶς here means *all without exception*.[27]

---

[21] Smith, "Slogan in 1 Corinthians 6:18b," 87. Cf. Preben Vang, *1 Corinthians*, Teach the Text Commentary Series (Grand Rapids: Baker, 2014), 242 n. 7: "Creating qualitative differences between sins proves inherently difficult and significantly coincidental. Furthermore, Paul does not seem to attempt a qualitative distinction between 'bodily sins' and other sins but underscores the spiritual problem in not considering sins against one's own body."

[22] J. William Johnston, *The Use of Πᾶς in the New Testament*, Studies in Biblical Greek 11 (New York: Lang, 2004).

[23] Ibid., 148–57.

[24] Ibid., 98.

[25] Ibid., 99.

[26] Ibid., 149.

[27] Smith, "Slogan in 1 Corinthians 6:18b," 75–87.

Johnston observes that Matt 12:31 and 1 Cor 6:18b–c differ in another significant way:

> Another difference is that in the contrasting clause in 1 Cor 6:18c, ὁ πορνεύων suddenly replaces πορνεία, as though the actor rather than the action is the emphasis.... It is almost as if Paul has changed from speaking about sins in theory and now speaks of the person who is sinning.[28]

Johnston concludes that the grammar does not allow one to add the word *other* to verse 18b. Consequently, the best way to read the passage is as a Corinthian slogan:

> Paul does not single out πορνεία as a particularly heinous example of sin against one's own body, but rather as the particular example of sin against the body; just the kind of sin which the Corinthians want to maintain affects the body but not the spirit.... Paul's objective is not to argue that πορνεία is particularly bad because it is against the body, but that the Corinthian logic allowing πορνεία is patently false. πορνεία is neither one exception to the rule nor a particularly heinous sin; it is one of a number of particular sins that affect the body, and for that reason he shows the Corinthian logic is in error.... The full force of the statement helps to identify it as a Corinthian slogan rather than a statement of the Apostle Paul, enhancing our understanding of the dialog between Paul and the church at Corinth.[29]

D. 1 Corinthians 6:12–20 Is an Ideal Context for Paul to Quote Corinthian Slogans

If one of my students submitted a research paper that cited sources the way Paul does in 1 Corinthians, I would have to give that student a failing grade for commiting plagiarism. Paul, who of course was not following our modern-day standards for research papers, quotes many people in 1 Corinthians without acknowledgment.[30] And that makes it all the more likely that, if he were quoting Corinthian slogans or mottos, he would not explicitly introduce all of them with a formula such as, "As you yourselves say."

What are the criteria, then, for determining whether Paul is quoting a Corinthian slogan? In his 2010 article "Slogans in 1 Corinthians,"[31] Smith explains how interpreters have historically handled Corinthian slogans, and he examines the methodology for identifying those slogans. He suggests nine "specific criteria for

---

[28] Johnston, *Use of Πᾶς in the NT*, 149.

[29] Ibid., 156–57.

[30] See Smith, "Slogans in 1 Corinthians," 72–73, who lists a dozen passages in 1 Corinthians where Paul cites without acknowledgment Old Testament quotations, Old Testament allusions, allusions to sayings of Jesus, the Greek poet Menander, and creedal or hymnic fragments.

[31] Ibid., 68–88. See also Paul Charles Siebenmann, "The Question of Slogans in 1 Corinthians" (PhD diss., Baylor University, 1997), who identifies 1 Cor 6:18b as a Corinthian slogan.

identifying and isolating Corinthian slogans in 1 Corinthians" and then adds "three additional tests":

1. Explicit introductory formulae such as the recitative ὅτι (e.g., 8:1, 4; cf. 7:1).
2. A brief, pithy, and often elliptical statement or generalization in the present tense—that is, a proverb, maxim, catchphrase, or motto (e.g., "all things are lawful," 6:12).
3. Rhetorical features and parallel structures that enhance memorability (e.g., the chiasm in 6:13: food–stomach–stomach–food).
4. Repetition elsewhere in the letter that suggests common currency and/or a formulaic pattern (e.g., "all things are lawful," which occurs four times, twice in 6:12 and twice in 10:23).
5. Diatribal features that suggest "imaginary" dialogue (e.g., 6:12–20).
6. Vocabulary, syntax, or ideas foreign to or inconsistent with Paul (or not normally used for certain concepts) (e.g., 7:1b, which expresses an asceticism foreign to Paul; cf. 9:19–22; 10:25–26, 29b–30; Eph 5:22–33).
7. Contextual or syntactical dislocation (a statement that is inserted abruptly or "point blank," change of addressees, shifts in vocabulary) (e.g., change of addressee from 8:7 to 8:8).
8. A sharp counterattack (including a severe qualification or total rejection) or point–counterpoint argumentation (e.g., 6:13: "Food is for the stomach and the stomach is for food.... Yet the body is not for immorality, but for the Lord, and the Lord is for the body"). [In his n. 59, Smith comments that this is perhaps the most reliable criterion. Paul introduced a statement only to reject it when it held significance for the Corinthians.]
9. Vocabulary or theology that other contexts suggest is exclusively or characteristically Corinthian (e.g., the presence of the Corinthian "buzz word" γνῶσις, "knowledge," in 8:1).

Three additional tests are these:

1. Contextual congruence: Do identifying and isolating a slogan make the best sense of the immediate context?
2. Confirmation by others in the history of exegesis (the mature reflection and collective wisdom of "the interpretive community").
3. Convergence of multiple strands of evidence.[32]

The four slogans in table 3 below fit at least criteria 2, 3, 4, 5, 6, and 8, and they pass tests 1, 2, and 3 with one exception regarding test 2: the interpretive community is split on whether 1 Cor 6:18b is a Corinthian slogan.[33]

---

[32] Smith, "Slogans in 1 Corinthians," 84–86. I changed bullet points to numbers in these two lists.

[33] On the structure of 1 Cor 6:12–20, see David L. Woodall, "The Presence of a Corinthian Slogan in 1 Corinthians 6:18b" (paper presented at the 64th Annual Meeting of the Evangelical Theological Society, Milwaukee, Wisconsin, 14 November 2012). Woodall's primary argument is that the structure of 1 Cor 6:12–20 indicates that verse 18b is a Corinthian slogan.

What may be decisive in confirming that verse 18b is a Corinthian slogan is that verses 12–20 are an ideal context for a Corinthian slogan. C. F. D. Moule popularized this exegetical option in the 1950s when he understatedly suggested that verse 18b makes more sense in light of diatribe and implied dialogue.[34] This passage is a dialogue called diatribe, and diatribe is an ideal genre for quoting and refuting one's opponents (see criterion 5 above).[35] This passage includes four formal features of diatribe:[36]

1. The phrase μὴ γένοιτο appears (v. 15).
2. Paul objects to false conclusions (esp. v. 15).
3. Paul rhetorically asks οὐκ οἴδατε ("Do you not know…?").
4. Paul directly addresses the Corinthians in the second person.

Paul adapts the diatribe form by dialoguing not with an imaginary partner but with a real one.[37]

> In vv. 12, 13, and 18, Paul inserts Corinthian slogans where we would normally expect to see rhetorical questions. Whether Paul uses a rhetorical question (v. 15b) or a Corinthian slogan (vv. 12, 13, and 18), in either case the words function as an *objection* to the argument within the diatribe form. The *objection* is from an imaginary interlocutor in v. 15b but from real ones in vv. 12, 13, and 18.[38]

Paul quotes and refutes the Corinthians three times in 1 Cor 6:12–14, so it is even more plausible that Paul would quote and refute the Corinthians a fourth time in this very same unit (1 Cor 6:12–20).[39] (See table 3.)

The English translation in table 3 tweaks the ESV in three ways: (1) It extends the third slogan by an additional phrase in v. 13 ("and God will destroy both one and the other")—something the parallelism strongly suggests.[40] Contrast the ESV: "'Food is meant for the stomach and the stomach for food'—and God will

---

[34] C. F. D. Moule, *An Idiom Book of New Testament Greek*, 2nd ed. (Cambridge: Cambridge University Press, 1959), 196–97.

[35] Some exegetes who argue that 1 Cor 6:18b is Paul's statement (e.g., Fisk, "Πορνεύειν as Body Violation," 551, 553) affirm that 1 Cor 6:12–20 has features of diatribe.

[36] Burk, "Discerning Corinthian Slogans," 99–121, esp. 103–5.

[37] Ibid., 105–12.

[38] Ibid., 112 (italics original).

[39] Ibid.: "Paul's use of the diatribe form makes the presence of slogans not only likely but expected. Moreover, the diatribe form suggests that the slogans would appear not only in vv. 12 and 13 but also in v. 18. If this text does in fact comprise a special adaptation of the diatribe, then the phrase 'Every sin, whatever a person may do, is outside of the body' appears in precisely the place where we would expect Paul to introduce another objection. Since Paul has used slogans to form an objection in vv. 12 and 13, it is not unlikely that he would do so again in v. 18. Thus, the form of the diatribe in 6:12–20 suggests that v. 18 should also be understood as a Corinthian slogan."

[40] See Hays, *First Corinthians*, 102–3.

destroy both one and the other." (2) It deletes the word "other" in verse 18b. (3) It treats verse 18b as a slogan rather than Paul's statement by adding quotation marks.

Further, in the very next sentence after this unit concludes, Paul again quotes the Corinthians: "Now concerning the matters about which you wrote: 'It is good for a man not to have sexual relations with a woman'" (7:1). Relatively few exegetes debate whether Paul is quoting the Corinthians in 1 Cor 6:12a, 6:12b, 6:13, or 7:1. So it should not be surprising that Paul may be quoting the Corinthians in 6:18b.

TABLE 3. Corinthian Slogans and Paul's Rebuttals in 1 Corinthians 6:12–14, 18

Verses	Corinthian Slogan	Paul's Rebuttal
12a	Πάντα μοι ἔξεστιν "All things are lawful for me."	ἀλλ' οὐ πάντα συμφέρει· But not all things are helpful.
12b	πάντα μοι ἔξεστιν "All things are lawful for me."	ἀλλ' οὐκ ἐγὼ ἐξουσιασθήσομαι ὑπό τινος. But I will not be dominated by anything.
13–14	τὰ βρώματα τῇ κοιλίᾳ "Food is meant for the stomach	τὸ δὲ σῶμα οὐ τῇ πορνείᾳ ἀλλὰ τῷ κυρίῳ, The body is not meant for sexual immorality, but for the Lord,
	καὶ ἡ κοιλία τοῖς βρώμασιν, and the stomach for food,	καὶ ὁ κύριος τῷ σώματι· and the Lord for the body.
	ὁ δὲ θεὸς ... καταργήσει. and God will destroy	ὁ δὲ θεὸς καὶ ... ἤγειρεν And God raised
	καὶ ταύτην both one	τὸν κύριον the Lord
	καὶ ταῦτα and the other."	καὶ ἡμᾶς ἐξεγερεῖ διὰ τῆς δυνάμεως αὐτοῦ. and will also raise us up by his power.
18b–c	πᾶν ἁμάρτημα ὃ ἐὰν ποιήσῃ ἄνθρωπος ἐκτὸς τοῦ σώματός ἐστιν· "Every sin a person commits is outside the body."	ὁ δὲ πορνεύων εἰς τὸ ἴδιον σῶμα ἁμαρτάνει. But the sexually immoral person sins against his own body.

E. Paul Uses ἁμάρτημα Instead of ἁμαρτία[41]

Recall Smith's criterion 6 in section II.D above: "Vocabulary, syntax, or ideas foreign to or inconsistent with Paul (or not normally used for certain concepts)." This is the case with 1 Cor 6:18b: πᾶν ἁμάρτημα ὃ ἐὰν ποιήσῃ ἄνθρωπος ἐκτὸς τοῦ σώματός ἐστιν. Except for Rom 3:25, where Paul likely quotes a formula that did not originate with him, this is the *only* time Paul uses the word ἁμάρτημα.[42] In contrast, Paul refers to sin as ἁμαρτία sixty-four times in his letters.[43] Paul overwhelmingly prefers to use ἁμαρτία over ἁμάρτημα, and in 1 Cor 6:18b ἁμαρτία works just as well as, if not better than, ἁμάρτημα. Secular Greek, on the other hand, preferred ἁμάρτημα over ἁμαρτία.[44] This argument is not decisive, but it is further evidence that verse 18b is a Corinthian slogan rather than Paul's statement.

F. Verses 13–18a and 18b–20 Are Parallel

Verses 18b–20 parallel vv. 13–18a. (I agree with Hays that "a new subsection begins in 6:18b.")[45] This suggests that the back-and-forth between Paul and the Corinthians in vv. 12–14 continues through v. 20.[46] (See table 4.)

As with the two slogans in verse 12 (as well as the slogan in 7:1), Paul introduces the slogans in verses 13 and 18 with asyndeton. The slogans themselves parallel each other by concisely stating a theological maxim, and Paul refutes the slogans by beginning with an adversative conjunction (δέ). The two cycles in verses 13–18a and 18b–20 parallel each other further in the manner of their conclusions: Paul theologically supports his refutations by beginning with the question οὐκ οἴδατε. This suggests that if verses 13–18a begin with a Corinthian slogan then verses 18b–20 begin with a Corinthian slogan as well.

G. Σῶμα in 1 Corinthians 6:13–20 Refers to a Person's Physical Body, Not to the Whole Person[47]

Some argue that σῶμα in verses 13–20 refers to the whole person—not merely that σῶμα is synecdoche for the whole person but that σῶμα itself refers to the whole

---

[41] Smith, "Slogan in 1 Corinthians 6:18b," 87–91.
[42] See Lindemann, *Der Erste Korintherbrief*, 151.
[43] There are fifty-nine occurrences in the undisputed letters (forty-eight in Romans, four in 1 Corinthians, three in 2 Corinthians, three in Galatians, and one in 1 Thessalonians) and five in the disputed letters (one each in Ephesians, Colossians, and 2 Timothy, and two instances in 1 Timothy).
[44] Smith, "Slogan in 1 Corinthians 6:18b," 87–91.
[45] Hays, *First Corinthians*, 105.
[46] Smith, "Slogan in 1 Corinthians 6:18b," 91–95.
[47] See Smith, "1 Corinthians," 250–51.

Table 4. Parallels between the Argument of 1 Corinthians 6:13–18a and 6:18b–20

Argument	6:13–18a	6:18b–20
Corinthian slogan (vv. 13ab, 18b)	τὰ βρώματα τῇ κοιλίᾳ καὶ ἡ κοιλία τοῖς βρώμασιν, ὁ δὲ θεὸς καὶ ταύτην καὶ ταῦτα καταργήσει. "Food is meant for the stomach and the stomach for food, and God will destroy both one and the other."	πᾶν ἁμάρτημα ὃ ἐὰν ποιήσῃ ἄνθρωπος ἐκτὸς τοῦ σώματός ἐστιν· "Every sin a person commits is outside the body."
Refutation (vv. 13c–14, 18c)	τὸ δὲ σῶμα οὐ τῇ πορνείᾳ ἀλλὰ τῷ κυρίῳ, καὶ ὁ κύριος τῷ σώματι· ὁ δὲ θεὸς καὶ τὸν κύριον ἤγειρεν καὶ ἡμᾶς ἐξεγερεῖ διὰ τῆς δυνάμεως αὐτοῦ. The body is not meant for sexual immorality, but for the Lord, and the Lord for the body. And God raised the Lord and will also raise us up by his power.	ὁ δὲ πορνεύων εἰς τὸ ἴδιον σῶμα ἁμαρτάνει. But the sexually immoral person sins against his own body.
Theological support (vv. 15–18a, 19–20)	οὐκ οἴδατε ὅτι τὰ σώματα ὑμῶν μέλη Χριστοῦ ἐστιν; ἄρας οὖν τὰ μέλη τοῦ Χριστοῦ ποιήσω πόρνης μέλη; μὴ γένοιτο. [ἢ] οὐκ οἴδατε ὅτι ὁ κολλώμενος τῇ πόρνῃ ἓν σῶμά ἐστιν; ἔσονται γάρ, φησίν, οἱ δύο εἰς σάρκα μίαν. ὁ δὲ κολλώμενος τῷ κυρίῳ ἓν πνεῦμά ἐστιν. Φεύγετε τὴν πορνείαν. Do you not know that your bodies are members of Christ? Shall I then take the members of Christ and make them members of a prostitute? Never! Or do you not know that he who is joined to a prostitute becomes one body with her? For, as it is written, "The two will become one flesh." But he who is joined to the Lord becomes one spirit with him. Flee from sexual immorality.	ἢ οὐκ οἴδατε ὅτι τὸ σῶμα ὑμῶν ναός τοῦ ἐν ὑμῖν ἁγίου πνεύματός ἐστιν οὗ ἔχετε ἀπὸ θεοῦ, καὶ οὐκ ἐστὲ ἑαυτῶν; ἠγοράσθητε γὰρ τιμῆς· δοξάσατε δὴ τὸν θεὸν ἐν τῷ σώματι ὑμῶν. Or do you not know that your body is a temple of the Holy Spirit within you, whom you have from God? You are not your own, for you were bought with a price. So glorify God in your body.

person.⁴⁸ This may be possible in some passages, but Robert Gundry convincingly argues that it is not possible in verses 13-20.⁴⁹ This is significant because these two views of σῶμα correspond to the two views regarding verse 18b: (1) The view that verse 18b is Paul's statement lines up best with the view that σῶμα refers to the whole person. (2) The view that verse 18b is a Corinthian slogan lines up best with the view that σῶμα refers to a person's physical body.⁵⁰ The issue is not whether it is theologically accurate to say that sexual immorality affects a person's entire being, not just one's body, but whether that is Paul's main argument in verses 12-20. I agree with Smith that "Paul's immediate concern" in vv. 12-20

> is to show that the physical body, because of its relationship with the Lord (vv. 13, 15, 19-20), is of moral and theological significance.... In other words, Paul rejects the Corinthians' view of the body as morally irrelevant and stands opposed to their immorality precisely because it involves the physical body, not because it involves something more than the physical body. Thus, where the Corinthians argued for moral irrelevance because of bodily action, Paul argues for the moral relevance of bodily action.⁵¹

H. The Statement Fits Well with What Paul Says about the Resurrection of the Body in 1 Corinthians 6 and 15

At least some of the Corinthians wrongly thought that God would destroy their bodies in the end. This is especially clear in 6:14 and 15:12, and in both passages Paul argues that God will resurrect the bodies of Christians. A Christian's body matters to God. God cares about a Christian's soul *and* body. The idea that one's soul matters but that one's body does not matter is pagan. That is why Christians affirm in the Apostles' Creed: "I believe ... in the resurrection of the body."

Some of the Corinthians who believed that God would not resurrect their bodies extrapolated that every sin is outside the body. In other words, they argued that what they do with their physical bodies is morally irrelevant.⁵² That logic is exactly what 6:18b captures (if it is a Corinthian slogan), and Paul strongly refutes it in chapters 6 and 15 since it contradicts the gospel.

---

⁴⁸ E.g., John A. T. Robinson, *The Body: A Study in Pauline Theology*, SBT 5 (London: SCM, 1952), 28, 31; Ciampa and Rosner, *First Corinthians*, 263-64.

⁴⁹ Robert H. Gundry, *Sōma in Biblical Theology: With Emphasis on Pauline Anthropology*, SNTSMS 29 (Cambridge: Cambridge University Press, 1976), esp. 79-80.

⁵⁰ Admittedly, in his 1976 monograph Gundry preferred the view that verse 18b refers to Paul's statement (*Sōma in Biblical Theology*, 70-75), but he reversed his position in his 2010 commentary, arguing that verse 18b is a Corinthian slogan; see Robert H. Gundry, *Commentary on the New Testament: Verse-by-Verse Explanations with a Literal Translation* (Peabody, MA: Hendrickson, 2010), 648-49.

⁵¹ Smith, "1 Corinthians," 250.

⁵² Dieter Zeller, *Der erste Brief an die Korinther*, KEK 5 (Göttingen: Vandenhoeck & Ruprecht, 2010), 226.

I. The Statement Plausibly Matches Corinth's Social, Cultural, and Religious Context

Smith attempts to prove that the false proposition "Every sin a person commits is outside the body" (6:18b) plausibly could arise from Christians in Corinth in light of Corinth's social, cultural, and religious context.[53] He notes two major factors that may have given rise to such a slogan: (1) the Corinthian Christians apparently applied philosophy that was popular during the Hellenistic-Roman period, especially Stoicism and incipient Gnosticism; and (2) the Corinthian Christians may have misunderstood what Jesus (Mark 7:14–23) and Paul (1 Cor 8:8) taught about food not defiling a person.

Similarly, Bruce W. Winter demonstrates how elitist secular ethics likely fueled Christian permissiveness in 1 Cor 6:12–20, 10:23, and 15:29–34.[54] In Philo, for example, "the ancient doctrine of hedonism is justified by means of a particular anthropology concerning the mortality of the body but not the soul."[55] The presence of this common philosophy supports the view that 6:18b is a Corinthian slogan rather than Paul's statement.[56]

J. If the Statement Is a Corinthian Slogan, Then It Does Not Matter If It Seems Abrupt to Us

Some argue that Paul does not clearly introduce verse 18b as a Corinthian slogan (see section I.C above). Two counterarguments seem to nullify that argument. First, the three statements in verses 12–13, which most modern translations render as Corinthians slogans, are not introduced as such. Second, speakers or writers can signal that they are quoting someone else in more ways than by explicitly stating "And I quote" or "As you say." One of those ways is by diatribe (see section II.D above).

A related argument is that verse 18b must be Paul's statement because it is simply too abrupt to be a Corinthian slogan (see section I.D above). But if it were a Corinthian slogan, then the Corinthians knew it. It may seem abrupt to us today, but it would not have seemed abrupt to them. It should not surprise us that Paul would use "insider" language in a letter to the Corinthian Christians since he had a close relationship with them. That is a natural way to communicate.[57]

---

[53] Smith, "Roots of a 'Libertine' Slogan," 63–95.

[54] Bruce W. Winter, *After Paul Left Corinth: The Influence of Secular Ethics and Social Change* (Grand Rapids: Eerdmans, 2001), 76–109.

[55] Ibid., 78. See Philo, *Worse* 33–34.

[56] Although Winter does not engage the debate whether 6:18b is Paul's statement or a Corinthian slogan, he does call Bruce Fisk's essay (see section I.B above) "an excellent discussion of Paul's argument on" how πορνεία is a sin against one's body (*After Paul Left Corinth*, 91 n. 51).

[57] See Smith, "Slogans in 1 Corinthians," 77–80.

III. Conclusion

Is verse 18b Paul's statement or a Corinthian slogan? The evidence strongly supports the view that it is a Corinthian slogan. I am not 100 percent certain—more like 90 percent sure. The distance between Paul's historical-cultural context and ours is significant enough to leave some room for doubt, but it is more plausible that verse 18b is a Corinthian slogan. The cumulative force of the arguments has more explanatory power for the view that verse 18b is a Corinthian slogan than for the view that it is Paul's statement.

The following points follow from this conclusion: (1) Verse 18b does not prove that immoral sex is uniquely against one's body. Immoral sex may uniquely defile the body, and it may be qualitatively worse than other sins because it has more serious effects. But that is not Paul's point in verse 18b. (2) Bible translations should add quotation marks to the slogan in verse 18b to cue readers that it is a slogan and not Paul's statement (just as many translations already do for the slogans in verses 13–14). At the very least, translations should indicate in a footnote that reading verse 18b as a slogan is a viable option.

James 3:13–4:10 and the Language of Envy in Proverbs 3

BENJAMIN LAPPENGA
benjamin.lappenga@dordt.edu
Dordt College, Sioux Center, IA 51250

Although a few interpreters have noted in passing the numerous verbal links between Jas 3:13–4:10 and LXX Prov 3:21–35, James's passage is regularly read as a polemic against jealousy that is most at home within Hellenistic moral literature. I argue that the literary and thematic coherence of Jas 3:13–4:10 derives not primarily from the Hellenistic topos of envy (so Luke Timothy Johnson) but from metaleptic interplay with Prov 3:21–35. The explicit appeal to "the Scripture" in Jas 4:5 and the citation of Prov 3:34 in Jas 4:6 indicate that the tropes usually interpreted against the backdrop of Hellenistic moral literature (friendship, violence, etc.) resonate more naturally within the "cave" of Prov 3. Like many passages in sapiential literature (e.g., Prov 14:1, 19; 4Q416 2 II, 11; 4Q418 8, 12; Wis 1:9–12; Sir 9:1–11), Jas 3:13–4:10 foregrounds the language of "jealousy" to expose the tragedy of bad ζῆλος. In trying to locate parallels to James's usage in Hellenistic writings, interpreters have failed to appreciate how the movement from ζῆλος in Jas 3:14, 16 and 4:2 to φθόνος in 4:5 simply resonates with a description found already in Isocrates: an envious person (φθόνος) is one whose good emulation (ζῆλος) has degenerated into jealous imitation because of unfulfilled desires. More significant than the particular semantic choices, then, is that James's usage mimics the way Prov 3:31 links קנאה/ζῆλος with the neglect of the needy, distorted friendship, and emulation of the ways of evil/violent people (Prov 3:27, 29, 31). Using this wisdom motif from Prov 3:21–35 as the interpretive lens for Jas 3:13–4:10 lends further support to a growing consensus about the notorious interpretive crux in Jas 4:5: (1) that the formula in 4:5 does not introduce a citation of an unknown text, and (2) that it is the human spirit (rather than God's) that is characterized by "envy" (φθόνος).

Already in 1983 Luke Timothy Johnson could lament that the interpretive difficulties in Jas 3:13–4:10 have "been dissected so many times that a quiet despair falls over any investigator sufficiently unwary to poke about in the area at all."[1] After

[1] Luke Timothy Johnson, "James 3:13–4:10 and the Topos περὶ φθόνου," NovT 25 (1983): 327–47, here 327. Even ancient and medieval interpreters lamented the difficulties, particularly

another thirty years of labor from undeterred *Neutestamentler*, it is premature to speak of a consensus, but a number of studies have resulted in increased levels of interpretive clarity and confidence. Among what many take to be "givens" are two assumptions. First, interpreters assume that James's[2] citation of Prov 3:34 (like similar citations in 1 Peter, 1 Clement, and the letters of Ignatius) is drawn from a collection of stock Christian texts rather than directly from Proverbs in a form resembling the text available to us today. Second, despite the fact that James is rightly viewed as a wisdom book,[3] Jas 3:13–4:10 is regularly understood as a polemic against jealousy that derives its content and organization primarily from a pattern found in the Hellenistic moralists. Challenging both of these claims, I argue that the language of jealousy foregrounded in Jas 3:13–4:10 is better understood as discourse attuned with Prov 3 (in a manner akin to readings found in early Jewish sapiential literature) than as a riff on envy in the manner of Hellenistic moral literature. After making the case for this reading by examining James, Proverbs, and relevant wisdom texts from the Qumran documents, I will note the implications of this study for an emerging consensus regarding the notorious interpretive crux in Jas 4:5.

I. The Thematic Coherence of James 3:13–4:10 and the Hellenistic Topos of Envy

In his 1983 article and subsequent commentary on James (1995), Johnson offers a comprehensive and much-cited argument for using the Hellenistic topos of envy to explain the cohesiveness of Jas 3:13–4:10.[4] After rejecting the notion that this passage is simply a loose arrangement of independent units joined by linking words,[5] Johnson offers a number of reasons for viewing the passage as a single

---

regarding Jas 4:5, e.g., Calvin: "interpreters toil much, because none such, at least none exactly alike, is found in Scripture" (*Commentaries on the Catholic Epistles*, trans. John Owen [Edinburgh: Calvin Translation Society, 1855], 331).

[2] Throughout this article I use "James" to refer to the author of the epistle, but I make no claims as to the actual identity of the author.

[3] See, e.g., Ulrich Luck, "Der Jakobusbrief und die Theologie des Paulus," *TGl* 61 (1971): 161–79; Richard Bauckham, *James: Wisdom of James, Disciple of Jesus the Sage*, New Testament Readings (London: Routledge, 1999), 29–35.

[4] Johnson, "James 3:13–4:10," 327–47; Johnson, *The Letter of James: A New Translation with Introduction and Commentary*, AB 37A (New York: Doubleday, 1995), 287. The influence of Johnson's reading is clearly seen, for example, in the commentary by Douglas J. Moo: "James depends in this section of his letter on a widespread Hellenistic-Jewish moral *topos* ... that traced social ills back to jealousy (*zēlos*) and envy (*phthonos*)" (*The Letter of James*, PilNTC [Grand Rapids: Eerdmans, 2000], 167; cf. Moo, *James: An Introduction and Commentary*, TNTC 16 [Downers Grove, IL: IVP Academic, 2015], 167).

[5] For the atomistic reading, see Sophie Laws, *The Epistle of James*, BNTC (Peabody, MA:

literary unit. He understands the passage as a sermon, dotted with characteristics of the diatribe (rhetorical questions, contrasts, etc.), in which the *indictment* in 3:13–4:6 is followed by a *response* in 4:7–10 (indicated by the connective οὖν in 4:7). The response mirrors the language of the indictment (e.g., the "heart" in 3:14 and 4:8, the "undivided" and "double-minded" in 3:17 and 4:8, and "lowly" and "humble" in 4:6 and 4:10) and reads as a straightforward "call to conversion."[6] The indictment section (3:13–4:6) is "more complex," but Johnson rightly notes that the three occurrences of ζῆλος/ζηλόω (3:14, 16; 4:2) set up the final rhetorical question concerning φθόνος in 4:5. To this point, few would disagree with Johnson's analysis.

Johnson then offers his rationale for viewing the passage as "a call to conversion which employs the Hellenistic *topos* on envy."[7] After a broad survey of the use of the topos of φθόνος in writers ranging from Hesiod to Plutarch and Dio, Johnson devotes the most attention to the linkage of φθόνος with the terms "murder" (φονεύω), "death" (θάνατος), the "spirit" (πνεῦμα), and the "devil" (διάβολος) in the Testaments of the Twelve Patriarchs. He gives special attention to the Testament of Simeon (titled in Greek περὶ φθόνου),[8] which mentions φθόνος within an explicit framework of *conversion*. Decisive for Johnson are the use of the language of ζῆλος and "the spirit" in T. Sim. 2:6–7 ("in the time of my youth I was jealous [ζηλόω] of Joseph ... [and] the spirit of jealousy [τὸ πνεῦμα τοῦ ζήλου] blinded my mind" [my translation]) and the call to conversion in T. Sim. 2:13 ("I repented and wept; and I prayed to the Lord God that my hand be restored, and that I might refrain from all defilement and envy [φθόνος] and all foolishness"). Johnson finds these features "strikingly similar" to Jas 3:13–4:10.

The movement from multiple occurrences of ζῆλος to an occurrence of φθόνος does indeed resemble the pattern in Jas 3:14–4:5, and Johnson's list of other parallels between James and the Testament of Simeon are worthy of careful consideration.[9] Yet Johnson's insistence that the parallels make James's passage "more

---

Hendrickson, 1980), 158; and esp. Martin Dibelius, *James: A Commentary on the Epistle of James*, trans. Heinrich Greeven, Hermeneia (Philadelphia: Fortress, 1976), 226. Dibelius reads 3:13–17 as dealing with one topic, 3:18 as completely independent in origin and function, and 4:1–6 as taking up another subject altogether.

[6] Johnson, *Letter of James*, 269.

[7] Johnson, "James 3:13–4:10," 332.

[8] For evidence of this title, see R. H. Charles, *The Greek Versions of the Testaments of the Twelve Patriarchs* (Oxford: Clarendon, 1908), xliv–xlvi.

[9] Johnson argues that the Testament of Simeon offers eight separate points of similarity: "(1) the explicit call to conversion; (2) the synonymous use of ζῆλος and φθόνος; (3) the attribution of envy to a πνεῦμα which is a deceiver; (4) the tendency of envy toward murder; (5) the role of envy in generating societal unrest and war; (6) the turning from the evil spirit to God by prayer and mourning; (7) the giving of grace by God to those who turn from envy (or Beliar) and turn to the Lord; (8) the portrayal of envy's opposite as simplicity of soul and goodness of heart" ("James 3:13–4:10," 345).

intelligible"[10] relies on two claims, both of which are tenuous. First, Johnson's contention that "in actual moral discourses, most authors use ζῆλος and φθόνος interchangeably"[11] is misleading. While φθόνος can always be assumed to be negative, the question of whether ζῆλος is to be praised or scorned is provided by the *end to which ζῆλος is directed*.[12] Although the Testament of Simeon uses both terms in close proximity, synonymous use of these terms is not characteristic of the topos of envy (as Johnson states) and thus does not explain the puzzling shift from ζῆλος to φθόνος that occurs in Jas 4:5.

Second, Johnson believes that the linkage of the word ὑπερήφανος ("proud") with φθόνος in the Testaments mirrors James's association of φθόνος in 4:5 with ὑπερήφανος in 4:6. This is taken to explain why James chooses to cite Prov 3:34 LXX.[13] But Johnson's claim that James uses ὑπερηφανία because it is "so frequently associated with that vice [φθόνος]"[14] cannot be sustained, since one of his two citations is misidentified and the other simply does not make use of the term ὑπερηφανία at all.[15] Again, the parallels with the Testaments are not nearly as helpful for accounting for the logic of Jas 3:13–4:10 as Johnson contends.

Johnson concludes that "virtually everything in James 3:13–4:10 could find a comfortable home in Plutarch's *De Invidia et Odio*, and if not there, in the *Testament of Simeon*,"[16] with two exceptions: the moralists would not have spoken of "asking wrongly [κακῶς]" (4:3)[17] nor of "friendship with the world [φίλος εἶναι τοῦ κόσμου]" meaning enmity with God (4:4). For Johnson, these exceptions represent "the

---

[10] Ibid., 332.

[11] Ibid., 335. Johnson cites Plutarch, *Frat. amor.* 485D, E; *De capienda ex inimicis utilitate* 86C, 91B; *Tranq. an.* 470C, 471A; Plato, *Symp.* 213D; *Laws*, 679C; Epictetus, *Diatr.* 3.22.61.

[12] Only special rhetorical circumstances could allow for the possibility of "just envy" (δικαίως φθονήσειεν; Isocrates, *Aeginet.* 23; cf. *Aeginet.* 45; Callim. 51; *Paneg.* 184; *Phil.* 68; *Ep.* 2.21). Suzanne Saïd calls such instances a "surprising use of φθονεῖν" ("Envy and Emulation in Isocrates," in *Envy, Spite, and Jealousy: The Rivalrous Emotions in Ancient Greece*, ed. David Konstan and N. Keith Rutter, Edinburgh Leventis Studies 2 [Edinburgh: Edinburgh University Press, 2003], 217–34, here 225). See further Benjamin J. Lappenga, *Paul's Language of Ζῆλος: Monosemy and the Rhetoric of Identity and Practice*, BibInt 137 (Leiden: Brill, 2016), 72.

[13] Johnson, "James 3:13–4:10," 344.

[14] Ibid., 346.

[15] Johnson cites T. Gad 5:3 but must mean 3:3, and φθόνος does not occur in T. Jos. 10:2–3 as Johnson indicates (though the verses do connect φθόνος and "exalting" [ὑψοῖ]); see "James 3:13–4:10," 344 n. 88.

[16] Ibid., 347.

[17] Johnson links this notion of approaching God with evil motives in 4:3 with James's words about the tongue as a "world of wickedness" (*Letter of James*, 278) but, again, does not indicate the distinctly *sapiential* tone of this language. Compare, for example, James's description of the tongue as an "unstable evil" (ἀκατάστατον κακόν) in Jas 3:8 with Prov 17:4 LXX: "An evil person [κακός] listens to the tongue [γλώσσης] of the lawless, but a righteous person [δίκαιος] does not give heed to false lips."

distinctive touch of James."[18] My contention, on the other hand, is that these so-called exceptions suggest that Johnson's proposed frame is not the most convincing way to apprehend the logic of James's argument. The greatest weakness of prioritizing the Hellenistic topos of envy, and the one that plagues subsequent interpretations of this enigmatic passage, is the failure to account for the specifically *sapiential* nature of James's argument and, in particular, the deep resonances with readings of Prov 3 itself in Jewish wisdom literature.[19]

II. James 3:13–4:10 as a Reading of Proverbs 3

I do not deny Hellenistic influences on James's writing.[20] Yet there are a number of reasons why rehabilitating James as a profoundly *sapiential* writing helps make sense of the passage. In what follows, I show that reading Jas 3:13–4:10 through the lens of Prov 3 not only explains the repeated occurrences of ζῆλος/ φθόνος but also brings into sharp relief a cluster of key emphases that are muted when the topos of envy is foregrounded.

A. James and the Paraenetic Tradition

The citation of Prov 3:34 LXX in Jas 4:6 is widely regarded as a quotation from a collection of decontextualized texts rather than a citation from Prov 3:34 in its literary context. Since James was making a point about grace and humility, the story goes, he turned to one of these collections and found a verse that suited his argument. The evidence offered is that the verse shows up in similar passages in 1 Pet 5:5, in Ignatius's letter to the Ephesians (*Eph.* 5.3), and in 1 Clem. 30.2.[21]

It is possible (though not certain) that such an account fits the evidence in

---

[18] Johnson, "James 3:13–4:10," 347; cf. Johnson, *Letter of James*, 279: "There is no such proverb in the Greco-Roman moral literature, or in Hellenistic Jewish writings…. 'Friendship' language is distinctively James' own and fitted to his thematic concerns."

[19] Although passages such as T. Levi 13:1–9 treat the law as a "virtual synonym for wisdom," the Testaments are hardly on the same plane as sapiential literature; see H. C. Kee, "Testaments of the Twelve Patriarchs," *OTP* 1:775–828, here 780.

[20] For a summary of scholarship on the Hellenistic literary features of James, see Dale C. Allison, *A Critical and Exegetical Commentary on the Epistle of James*, ICC (New York: Bloomsbury T&T Clark, 2013), 81–88.

[21] Decisive for many interpreters is the fact that each of these passages contains θεός ("God") as the subject rather than κύριος ("lord"), as found in the Septuagint manuscripts available to us (see further Dibelius, *James*, 225). Yet our uncertainty about the precise wording of Greek translations available to first-century writers means that there is insufficient warrant for the conclusions that Dibelius and others draw. On Prov 3:34 as part of "stock Christian tradition," see, e.g., M. Eugene Boring, *1 Peter*, ANTC (Nashville: Abingdon, 1999), 174. For the broader discussion regarding James's use of the LXX, see Peter H. Davids, *The Epistle of James: A*

1 Peter, Ignatius, and/or 1 Clement, but a decision regarding these texts is inconsequential for the present study. The assumption that James should be lumped in with these other early Christian writers must be challenged, however, since it has prevented interpreters from giving due consideration to the significance of Prov 3 for understanding Jas 3:14–4:10. Most interpreters who believe "it is clear that they are drawing on common traditions"[22] rely on the work of Martin Dibelius, whose views on James and Scripture were advanced and nuanced in a series of important studies by Wiard Popkes.[23] Popkes denies that James has what we would call "the Bible" available to him ("James can hardly be called an OT exegete").[24] He accounts for the piecemeal nature of James's use of Scripture by positing the existence of an early Christian *Zettelkasten* ("sourcebook"). With respect to Jas 4:5–6, Popkes goes so far as to suggest that James took notes from 1 Peter itself,[25] despite admitting that his hypothesis regarding James's fumbling of source material originates "from sheer despair about these verses."[26]

Clearly, however, Ignatius, 1 Peter, 1 Clement, and James each use Prov 3:34 differently. Whereas James foregrounds grace, 1 Peter focuses on showing humility to one another (5:6),[27] 1 Clement is concerned with "detestable pride" (βδελυκτὴ ὑπερηφανία) as part of a list of unholy behaviors (30.1), and Ignatius condemns the arrogance of opposing the bishop (*Eph.* 5.3). Perhaps a *Zettelkasten* containing Prov 3:34 was the source for one or more of these citations, but each instance must be considered within its own distinct context.

Commentary on the Greek Text, NIGTC (Grand Rapids: Eerdmans, 1982), 10; and Roy B. Ward, "The Communal Concern of the Epistle of James" (PhD diss., Harvard University, 1966), 25–26.

[22] Steve Moyise, *The Later New Testament Writings and Scripture: The Old Testament in Acts, Hebrews, the Catholic Epistles and Revelation* (Grand Rapids: Baker Academic, 2012), 54. Moyise suggests that early Christians were drawn to Prov 3:34 because the LXX rendered the Hebrew word חן ("favor") with the important Christian term χάρις.

[23] Dibelius, *James*, 226. See esp. Wiard Popkes, "The Composition of James and Intertextuality: An Exercise in Methodology," *ST* 51 (1997): 91–112, here 100–101; Popkes, "James and Scripture: An Exercise in Intertextuality," *NTS* 45 (1999): 213–29, here 219–20; and Popkes, *Der Brief des Jakobus*, THKNT 14 (Leipzig: Evangelische Verlagsanstalt, 2001), 28–29, 56–58, 271. Popkes writes: "der bekannte stichworthaft und sprunghaft erscheinende Schreibstil des Jak erklärt sich zum nicht geringen Maß auch aus der Verarbeitung von Traditionssplittern, die er aus verschiedenen 'Quellen' (u.a. Florilegien, Sekundärübernahmen, Notizen) erhielt. Man gewinnt den Eindruck, Jak habe sich eine Art Zettelkasten angelegt, aus dem er sich dann bedient—zuweilen auch mit nicht gerade glücklicher Hand" (28).

[24] Popkes, "James and Scripture," 228.

[25] See esp. Popkes, "Composition of James," 101.

[26] Popkes, "James and Scripture," 227.

[27] First Peter 5:6 echoes the language of "exalting" (ὑψόω) in Prov 3:35 and may indicate an awareness of the wider context of Prov 3:34; see further below for this usage in Jas 4:10. The tendency to assume 1 Peter's use of tradition has been strong, especially since Marie-Émile Boismard's arguments regarding common liturgical material in 1 Peter ("Une liturgie baptismale dans la Prima Petri," *RB* 64 [1957]: 161–83).

The use of biblical material elsewhere in James makes it likely that the author does in fact consider the original literary context of Prov 3:34. Among several passages that might be considered, the citation of Lev 19:18 in Jas 2:8 serves as an example.[28] Popkes acknowledges that "James's text on the whole is rather full of biblical material," but he attributes this solely to James's reliance on extracanonical Jewish writings.[29] Rejecting Johnson's comprehensive (and in this case, convincing) study of the influence of Lev 19 on James's understanding of the law, Popkes wonders why James would not have cited Lev 19:15 (οὐ λήμψῃ πρόσωπον πτωχοῦ, "you shall not be partial to the poor") rather than 19:18 (ἀγαπήσεις τὸν πλησίον σου ὡς σεαυτόν, "you shall love your neighbor as yourself") if he had access to it, since it fits much better with his line of argument in chapter 2.[30] Here Popkes moves in precisely the wrong direction and misses the close verbal and thematic resonances between James and Leviticus. James 2:1 and 2:9 both refer to "partiality" (προσωπολημψία), and the surrounding context of Lev 19 offers at least two specific concerns that feature prominently in Jas 2:1–7 and the letter as a whole: favoring the wealthy (Lev 19:15) and withholding the wages of a laborer (Lev 19:13; explicitly referred to in Jas 5:4). It makes the best sense of the evidence, then, to view the citation of Lev 19:18 as a signal to James's readers about the passage that informs his discourse. As Johnson rightly summarizes, "James assumes among his readers the capacity to catch allusions to the context of the *graphē* he explicitly cites."[31]

B. Intertextuality

If James's citation of Prov 3:34 LXX does indeed signal a sophisticated and attentive reading of the whole of Prov 3 (as I propose) rather than a convenient

---

[28] See Gen 15:6 in Jas 2:24; Gen 1:26 in Jas 3:7–9; Isa 40:6–7 in Jas 1:10–11; and the survey of additional allusions in Moyise, *Later New Testament Writings*, 72–80. Moyise says that this citation "probably derives from the Jesus tradition" (cf. Matt 5:43, 19:19, 22:39) yet rightly comments that "more than any other New Testament writer, [James] has also drawn on [the] surrounding context [in Leviticus]" (73–74).

[29] Popkes, "James and Scripture," 217. See further Peter H. Davids, "The Pseudepigrapha in the Catholic Epistles," in *The Pseudepigrapha and Early Biblical Interpretation*, ed. James H. Charlesworth and Craig A. Evans, JSPSup 14, SSEJC 2 (Sheffield: JSOT Press, 1993), 228–33. Davids notes that James's references to Abraham, Job, Rahab, and Elijah might be indebted to Jubilees, the Testament of Job, 1 Clement, and 4 Ezra, respectively; see also Davids, "Tradition and Citation in the Epistle of James," in *Scripture, Tradition, and Interpretation: Essays Presented to Everett F. Harrison by His Students and Colleagues in Honor of His Seventy-Fifth Birthday*, ed. W. Ward Gasque and William Sanford LaSor (Grand Rapids: Eerdmans, 1978), 113–26, here 115.

[30] Wiard Popkes, "The Use of Leviticus 19 in the Letter of James," *JBL* 101 (1982): 391–401, https://doi.org/10.2307/3260351. See also Popkes, "James and Scripture," 223 n. 38: "[That Lev 19:15 would be the contextually more appropriate quotation] is a surprising fact, speaking against direct access to Leviticus. Warnings against partiality towards the poor are found also elsewhere in Jewish tradition and need not be traced back to Lev 19 by allusion."

[31] Johnson, *Letter of James*, 283.

prooftext plucked from the paraenetic tradition, I must clarify my methodological assumptions regarding "intertextuality."[32] As coined by Julia Kristeva, intertextuality refers to a *theory* about all human communication and not a *method*.[33] Nevertheless, the term has come to describe a wide range of techniques used to explore the relationship between two or more texts, commonly grouped into two approaches: "diachronic" or "temporal," in which historical development and author-oriented questions are explored, and "synchronic" or "spatial," which is reader-oriented and considers possible interrelation when one reads two texts together.[34] In one sense the present study is synchronic, since I am reading James and Prov 3 together and finding significance in the resonances.[35] Yet my desire to correct a trend in the interpretation of this passage inclines me to make some diachronic claims, not about authorial intent (to which we have no access) but about what attentive readers should make of the cues found in the (relatively) fixed text. Put another way, if I must speak of diachronic intertextuality (because the use of Proverbs in a first-century Christian writing is hardly nontemporal or "nonintentional"), I am not making claims about what was "conscious" or "deliberate" but rather about *which is more helpful as the primary lens for understanding Jas 3:13–4:10*: Hellenistic moral literature or sapiential readings of Proverbs. Both are "in the air," but I argue that the text itself nudges readers (ancient and modern) toward the latter.

---

[32] Literary critic William Irwin may be right that "*intertextuality* is a term that should be shaved off by 'Dutton's Razor,' the principle that jargon that does not illuminate or elucidate but rather mystifies and obscures should be stricken from the lexicon of sincere and intelligent humanists" ("Against Intertextuality," *Philosophy and Literature* 28 [2004]: 227–42, here 240).

[33] See, e.g., Julia Kristeva, *Desire in Language: A Semiotic Approach to Literature and Art*, European Perspectives (New York: Columbia University Press, 1980), 36–37. John Barton calls the methodological version "soft" and the theory grounded in poststructuralism and deconstruction "hard" ("*Déjà Lu*: Intertextuality, Method, or Theory?," in *Reading Job Intertextually*, ed. Katharine J. Dell and Will Kynes, LHBOTS 574 [New York: Bloomsbury T&T Clark, 2013], 1–16, here 12). Most important is that biblical scholars using the "soft" version are clear about the extended purposes to which we make use of theories first developed to address broader questions regarding human communication.

[34] For a helpful recent overview, see Barton, "*Déjà Lu*," 1–16. For a recent survey of intertextuality in New Testament studies, see Niall McKay, "Status Update: The Many Faces of Intertextuality in New Testament Study," *R&T* 20 (2013): 84–106. For a number of essays that attempt to bring clarity to the term *intertextuality*, see R. Michael Fox, ed., *Reverberations of the Exodus in Scripture* (Eugene, OR: Pickwick, 2014). See also the helpful taxonomy in R. S. Miola, "Seven Types of Intertextuality," in *Shakespeare, Italy, and Intertextuality*, ed. Michele Marrapodi (Manchester: Manchester University Press, 2004), 13–24.

[35] On the role of the reader in the "act of containment," see, e.g., Timothy K. Beal, "Ideology and Intertextuality: Surplus of Meaning and Controlling the Means of Production," in *Reading between Texts: Intertextuality and the Hebrew Bible*, ed. Danna Nolan Fewell, Literary Currents in Biblical Interpretation (Louisville: Westminster John Knox, 1992), 27–39.

C. Verbal and Thematic Parallels with Proverbs 3 LXX

It is somewhat ironic that, among interpreters, Johnson himself compiles the longest list of verbal resonances between James and Prov 3, and his list is worth citing in full:

> The *context* of Prov 3:34 finds a number of intriguing echoes in James 3:13–4:10: God's wisdom is the basis of reality (Prov 3:19), and following this wisdom is the way to receive God's favor (*charis*; 3:22). This means walking in peace, *en eirēnē* (3:23), not taking away from the needy or saying to them that they will be helped on the morrow (3:27–28; see James 2:15–16); not envying (*zeloun*) the ways of the wicked (3:31...) because their way is "unclean (*akathartos*) before the Lord" (3:32). The curse (*katara*) of God is on the household of the impious, but the dealings of the righteous will be blessed (*eulogein*; 3:33; compare James 3:9). Then there is the present verse, quoted by James (3:34). Finally, "the wise (*sophoi*) will inherit (*klēronomēsousin*) glory (*doxan*; see James 1:12), but the impious will raise up shame" (3:35).[36]

Yet Johnson does not go far enough. Not only does he fail to address the significance of the parallels on his list (some eight shared terms), but his list is far from comprehensive.

At least seven additional resonances are apparent. First, both texts use the unusual phrase "fruit of righteousness" (καρπῶν δικαιοσύνης, Prov 3:9 LXX; καρπός ... δικαιοσύνης, Jas 3:18). Second, in Prov 3, offering such fruit "honors" the Lord (τίμα, Prov 3:9 LXX), "[wisdom] is more honorable [τιμιωτέρα] than precious stones ... nothing honorable [τίμιον] is worthy of her" (Prov 3:15 LXX), and "the wise will inherit glory, but the impious have exalted dishonor [ἀτιμίαν]" (Prov 3:35 LXX). Likewise, just prior to Jas 3:13–4:10, James sets the frame for the whole passage by warning against "dishonoring" (ἀτιμάζω) the poor and needy (Jas 2:6). This emphasis is reinforced in both Jas 3:13–4:10 and Prov 3 with the language of "exalting" (ὑψόω, Prov 3:35 LXX; Jas 4:10) and "humbling" (ταπεινός/ταπεινόω, Prov 3:34 LXX; Jas 4:6, 10). Third, both texts feature the language of showing "mercy" (ἔλεος, Prov 3:16; Jas 3:17) and doing "good" (καλός/εὖ/ἀγαθός, Prov 3:17, 27, 28 LXX; Jas 3:13, 17). Fourth, both texts assert that warring "cravings" (ἡδονή, Jas 4:1; cf. Prov 17:1 LXX) within the community and the human body (μέλος/σάρξ/ὀστέον, Jas 4:1; Prov 3:22 LXX) are healed through the "peace" (εἰρήνη, Prov 3:17, 23; 17:1 LXX; Jas 2:16; 3:17–18) that attends true wisdom. Fifth, both texts are punctuated by the language of "quarreling" (μάχη/μάχομαι) and "enmity" (ἔχθρα/φιλεχθρέω) as the cause of evil (Jas 4:1, 2, 4; Prov 3:30; 17:1 LXX).

Two final resonances are particularly telling in light of Johnson's analysis of the passage. As noted above, Johnson finds two elements of James's passage at odds

---

[36] Johnson, *Letter of James*, 283 (my underlining). Given Johnson's assertion that "the parallels are sufficiently dense and striking to suggest that James had more of this passage from Proverbs than simply 3:34 in mind," it is peculiar that he pursues the parallels no further.

with the Hellenistic topos of envy and calls them "the distinctive touch of James": the moralists would not have spoken of "asking wrongly [κακῶς]" (4:3) or of "friendship with the world [φίλος εἶναι τοῦ κόσμου]" meaning enmity with God (4:4).[37] Both of these elements are apparent in Prov 3. In Prov 3:29–32 LXX, the writer warns against planning "evil" (κακός) against one's "friend" (φίλος). People who work "evil" (κακός) against you are called "evil men" (κακοὶ ἄνδρες), are not counted among the "righteous" (δίκαιος), and are the kind who would be "friendly with hatred" (φιλεχθρέω). This is precisely the language found in Jas 4:4: "Adulterers, do you not know that friendship [φιλία] with the world is enmity [ἔχθρα] with God? Therefore whoever wishes to be a friend [φιλία] of the world makes himself an enemy [ἐχθρός] of God."

Importantly, this cluster of themes in Prov 3:30–32 is wrapped around the very language of ζῆλος (ζηλόω in 3:31) that prompted Johnson to look elsewhere to explain the wording and organization of Jas 3:13–4:10. Like the writer of Prov 3, James uses the language of ζῆλος to caution against strife and murderous desire (Jas 3:14, 16; 4:2). Already it becomes clear that James's usage mimics the way Prov 3:31 links ζῆλος with the neglect of the needy (Jas 3:17; Prov 3:27), distorted friendship (Jas 4:4; Prov 3:29), and emulation of the ways of evil and violent people (Jas 4:2; Prov 3:31).

III. Readings of Proverbs in Jewish Sapiential Literature

The verbal connections between Prov 3 and James may be enough to explain why ζῆλος is repeated three times in James's passage, but a more convincing case can be made by examining how the language of "zeal" was frequently foregrounded in sapiential literature, including literature specifically attending to Prov 3. An analysis of the use of ζῆλος and קנאה (the Hebrew term nearly always translated using ζῆλος in the LXX) in Jewish sapiential writing, especially in the Qumran literature, reveals that writings influenced by Proverbs readily turned to the language of "zeal" in ways that resemble James's usage.

Johnson gives brief attention to the evidence in Sirach; however, Johnson does not consider the sapiential texts that speak of φθόνος and ζῆλος in their own right, apart from wisdom writings that exhibit a much higher degree of Greek influence (e.g., Wisdom and Pseudo-Phocylides's *Sentences*), or even apart from narrative and historical works like Tobit, 1 Maccabees, Philo, and Josephus. In what follows, I will survey the relevant literature to hear the distinctive voice of the sapiential literature and thereby substantiate my argument that the language of ζῆλος in Jas 3:13–4:10 is best viewed using the lens of Prov 3.

---

[37] Johnson, "James 3:13–4:10," 347.

A. Wisdom of Solomon, the Sentences of Pseudo-Phocylides, and Sirach

Wisdom 1:1-15 is punctuated by occurrences of the terms "spirit" (πνεῦμα, 1:5, 6, 7) and "zeal/envy" (ζήλωσις/ζηλόω, 1:10, 12; cf. φθόνος in 2:24 and 6:23), which seem to indicate the presence of the topos of envy. Yet despite its Hellenistic flavor, Wisdom of Solomon remains deeply indebted to Proverbs. Wisdom 1:1-15 in particular can be seen to draw heavily from Proverbs (cf. Prov 8:15-16; 16:10-15; 20:26-28; 25:1-7; 29:4, 12-14). At the very least, then, the author of Wisdom of Solomon is an example of a sapiential writer who finds the language of ζῆλος/φθόνος compatible with a close interaction with Proverbs, despite the relative scarcity of references to "zeal" in Proverbs itself.[38]

Similarly, Johnson attributes the intriguing parallels between Jas 3:13-4:10 and the didactic wisdom poem known as the *Sentences* of Pseudo-Phocylides to the common influence of non-Jewish Hellenistic moralistic literature.[39] Although the *Sentences* clearly mix pagan precepts with ethical commandments from the Greek Pentateuch, Pseudo-Phocylides's foregrounding of the language of "jealousy" betrays the influence of Proverbs. For example, warnings against the love of money (Ps.-Phoc. 42) and priding oneself on wisdom, strength, or wealth (Ps.-Phoc. 53) resonate with Proverbs (cf. Prov 11:28; 17:16), and even the section widely regarded as addressing the "topos of envy" (Ps.-Phoc. 70-75) shares a number of terms and concerns with Prov 3.[40] The notion of ἀφθονία as a quality of divine generosity (Ps.-Phoc. 71) is similar to Jas 4:6 and may derive from pagan usage, but the focus on God's generosity fits with the portrayal of grace in the context of Prov 3, quite apart from Hellenistic concerns.[41]

---

[38] Johnson notes the significance of the association of φθόνος with the devil in Wis 2:24: "Envy has been seen to play a role in the stories of Adam and Eve, Cain and Abel, Joseph and his brothers, Jesus and the Jewish leaders, and the Apostles and Jewish leaders. The connection between envy and murder could not be more explicitly drawn in this Hellenistic-Jewish literature. The 'devil,' however, has been found explicitly in only one text, Wisdom 2:24" ("James 3:13-4:10," 341).

[39] For a concise summary of the issues and influences, see Pieter W. van der Horst, "Pseudo-Phocylides, *Sentences*," in *Outside the Bible: Ancient Jewish Writings Related to Scripture*, ed. Louis H. Feldman, James L. Kugel, and Lawrence H. Schiffman (Philadelphia: Jewish Publication Society, 2013), 2353-61. See also Walter T. Wilson, *The Sentences of Pseudo-Phocylides*, CEJL (Berlin: de Gruyter, 2005); and John J. Collins, who speaks of the work as "Jewish ethics in Hellenistic dress" (*Jewish Wisdom in the Hellenistic Age*, OTL [Louisville: Westminster John Knox, 1997], 158-77).

[40] E.g., compare Ps.-Phoc. 70-75 ("Do not envy others for their goods [μὴ φθονέοις ἀγαθῶν ἑτάροις].... For if there were strife [ἔρις] among the blessed, the city would not stand") with Prov 3:27-31 LXX ("Do not withhold doing good [εὖ ποιεῖν] to the needy.... Do not quarrel [φιλεχθρήσῃς] with anyone ... and do not envy [ζηλώσῃς] their ways").

[41] Van der Horst sees two elements at work in the text: envy as a human vice and ἀφθονία as a divine attribute (*The Sentences of Pseudo-Phocylides, with Introduction and Commentary*, SVTP

In Sirach, which was originally composed in Hebrew, the influence of Proverbs becomes clearer. Although a phrase like "ζῆλος for the good" in Sir 51:18 resonates with language found in Hellenistic moral literature,[42] it is clear that Sirach echoes the book of Proverbs far more than it does non-Jewish moralistic literature. Of particular interest to our study of James is that the passages in Sirach that owe the most to Proverbs are punctuated by references to ζῆλος/φθόνος. Among these are the description of one who is "envious" (φθονερός) of bread in Sir 14:10, the proverb about the hastening of old age because of anxiousness and rivalry (ζῆλος) in Sir 30:24, and the warnings against dealing with the envious in Sir 37:11. Sirach 9 echoes Proverbs extensively. For example, the warning against ζῆλος toward one's wife in Sir 9:1 is closely reminiscent of Prov 6:34 ("for filled with envy [ζῆλος] is the anger of her husband"), and, importantly, the warnings against the fame of sinners in Sir 9:11 echo the language of Prov 3:31 (cf. Prov 23:17; 24:1, 19; Pss 37:1; 73:3):

> Do not envy [μὴ ζήλου] the wife of your bosom, nor teach an evil lesson against yourself.... Do not envy [μὴ ζηλώσῃς] a sinner's fame, for you do not know what his ruin will be. (Sir 9:1, 11)

> Do not acquire the disgrace of evil men, and do not envy [μηδὲ ζηλώσῃς] their ways. (Prov 3:31 LXX)

When combined with other references to Prov 3 such as the citation of Prov 3:35 in Sir 37:26 (MSS C, D), Sirach (esp. ch. 9) can certainly be seen to use the language of ζῆλος/φθόνος in a way that reflects from the logic found in Proverbs.[43]

B. Sapiential Texts from Qumran and the Language of Zeal (קנאה)

The Jewish sapiential writings of the Dead Sea Scrolls are the least influenced by Hellenism. As George J. Brooke notes, most scholars read the wisdom compositions found at Qumran "in light of scriptural antecedents, since there seems to be little that matches explicitly the philosophical and ethical concerns of the broader hellenistic world view which we know was available even in Palestine from the fourth century BCE or even earlier."[44] Among the many passages that use the term

---

4 [Leiden: Brill, 1978], 161–65). Likewise, W. C. van Unnik observes that ἀφθονία comes to be seen as a quality of generosity, or liberality, which is reminiscent of Jas 4:6 (*De ἀφθονία van God in de Oudchristelijke Literatuur*, MNAW.L [Amsterdam: North-Holland, 1973], 24–29).

[42] See further Lappenga, *Paul's Language*, 89–92.

[43] The ζηλ- word group occurs in LXX Prov 3:31; 4:14; 6:6, 34; 23:17; 24:1, 19; 27:4; cf. קנאה in Prov 3:31; 6:34; 14:30; 23:17; 24:1, 19; 27:4.

[44] George J. Brooke, "Biblical Interpretation in the Wisdom Texts from Qumran," in *The Wisdom Texts from Qumran and the Development of Sapiential Thought*, ed. Charlotte Hempel, Armin Lange, and Hermann Lichtenberger, BETL 159 (Leuven: Peeters, 2002), 201–20, here 204. Brooke notes that the copies of Sirach found at Qumran are as close as the Qumran material comes to the cosmopolitan traditions even of Palestine, much less literature from the diaspora. The contrast with the kind of topos that Johnson identifies in the Testaments of the Twelve Patriarchs

קנאת and could be explored profitably here,[45] four texts will be particularly helpful for our reading of James: 4QInstruction (1Q26, 4Q415–418, 423), 4QInstruction-like Composition B (4Q424), the wisdom passage known as the Treatise on the Two Spirits in the Community Rule (1QS III, 13–IV, 26), and, most important, 4QBeatitudes (4Q525).

The writer of 4QInstruction warns against exchanging one's "holy spirit" (רוח קודשכה) for any amount of money (4Q416 2 II, 6; 4Q418 8, 6), ending with the declaration, "how powerful is human jealousy" (רבה קנאה אנוש; 4Q416 2 II, 11; 4Q418 8, 12). In 4QInstruction-like Composition B (4Q424), we read of a man of understanding who humbly "recognizes wisdom" (יפיק חכמה) and has "zeal" (יקנא)[46] in his concern for those who lack money and in doing "justice to the needy" (צדקה לאביון; 4Q424 3, 8–10).

The Treatise on the Two Spirits (1QS III, 13–IV, 26), which shares a number of resemblances with 4QInstruction and the Book of Mysteries,[47] contains a passage that compares the "spirit" of wisdom in a man that "makes straight before him all the paths of true righteousness" (לישר לפניו כול דרכי צדק אמת) with the spirit of falsehood (1QS IV, 2). The language of "paths of righteousness" permeates Proverbs (e.g., דרכי צדק/ὁδός δικαιοσύνης in Prov 2:8, 16; 11:5; 12:28; 13:6; 15:9; 16:31). 1QS continues:

---

is stark. James L. Kugel notes that, even if a Hebrew precursor existed, when it was translated into Greek, "those parts most resonant with Hellenistic thought may well have moved the Greek translator to embellish upon them" ("Testaments of the Twelve Patriarchs," in Feldman, Kugel, and Schiffman, *Outside the Bible*, 1697–1855, here 1701).

[45] For example, the acrostic version of Sir 51:13–30 found in the Psalms Scroll from Qumran (11QPs[a] XXI, 11–17 and XXII, 1) uses the language of envy and draws on the imagery of Proverbs' Lady Wisdom (11QPs[a] XXI, 15: "I was zealous for goodness and I did not turn back" [קנאתי בטוב ולוא אשוב]). For a discussion of the echoes of Proverbs' Lady Wisdom in the erotic reading of Sir 51:13–30 found in this scroll, see Matthew J. Goff, *Discerning Wisdom: The Sapiential Literature of the Dead Sea Scrolls*, VTSup 116 (Leiden: Brill, 2007), 247–57. In addition, the Book of Mysteries (1Q27, 4Q299–301), a scroll widely regarded as sapiential (see, e.g., John J. Collins, "Wisdom Reconsidered, in Light of the Scrolls," *DSD* 4 [1997]: 265–81, here 276), likewise echoes Proverbs and features the language of jealousy: "What fear [for a person] … he shall abandon the jealous strife [יעזוב קנאת מדנים] … his transgression which he committed … evil, except for him, the beloved" (trans. Goff, *Discerning Wisdom*, 94–95). Goff lists 4Q300 2 II among the material in Mysteries that "echoes Proverbs" (95). In addition to the overtly sapiential texts from Qumran, a number of other texts speak of a zeal that regularly refers to "spirit," "anger/contention," or both (4Q286 20, 9; 4Q288 1, 6; 4Q434 1 I, 6). For a helpful survey of all occurrences, see Dane C. Ortlund, *Zeal without Knowledge: The Concept of Zeal in Romans 10, Galatians 1, and Philippians 3*, LNTS 472 (London: T&T Clark, 2012), 91–103.

[46] The object of zeal is missing in this fragmented text.

[47] The terminological links between 4QInstruction, the Book of Mysteries, and the Treatise of the Two Spirits are examined in Eibert J. C. Tigchelaar, *To Increase Learning for the Understanding Ones: Reading and Reconstructing the Fragmentary Early Jewish Sapiential Text 4QInstruction*, STDJ 44 (Leiden: Brill, 2001), 194–203.

> And this is a spirit of humility [ענוה], patience, great compassion [רחמים], everlasting goodness [טוב], insight, understanding, and mighty wisdom entrusting to each of God's deeds, sustained by his abundant mercy. A spirit of knowledge of every plan of action, and of *zeal for the laws of righteousness* [קנאת משפטי צדק], holy in thought, and firm in inclination. And great mercy upon all the sons of truth, and glorious purity with visceral abhorrence of impurities. (1QS IV, 3–5; my translation)

The passage goes on to contrast this zeal for righteousness with the "zeal for arrogance" (קנאת זדון) that is attended by (among other vices) "neglect of righteous deeds" (שפול ידים בעבודת צדק), "wickedness" (רשע), and "pride" (זדון) in IV, 9–10. After declaring that the destinies of all humans are under the power of these spirits until the last age (IV, 15–17), in lines 17–18 we read that "zeal attends every point of decision" (וקנאת ריב על כול משפטיהן) between these spirits. The passage concludes in line 23: "Until now the spirits of truth and perversity have contended within the human heart" (עד הנה יריבו רוחי אמת ועול בלבב גבר). Thus, within a short passage, the term קנאת is used to describe positive zeal, negative zeal, and conflict itself. In short, the writer has foregrounded the language of "zeal" to draw out the bitter conflict between the spirit of the righteous and the spirit of the wicked.

Already we see a number of similarities to the injunction not to have zeal for the "ways" of evil men in Prov 3:31–32: "Do not acquire the disgrace of evil [κακός] men, and do not have zeal [ζηλόω] for their ways [ὁδοί], for every transgressor is impure [ἀκάθαρτος] before the Lord, and he does not sit in council among the righteous [δίκαιοι]." This is especially so in light of the many references to the "righteous" (δίκαιος, Prov 3:9, 32) and "good ways" (ὁδοὶ καλαί, Prov 3:17) in Prov 3, as well as the importance of the *object* of zeal for determining whether to endorse or condemn it (e.g., Prov 23:17, 24:1, 1 Kgs 19:10, Ps 69:9).

For this reason, we consider one final passage from the Qumran literature, 4QBeatitudes (4Q525). Although the text is fragmentary, two things are clear. First, the document contains a citation of Prov 3:13 in 4Q525 2 II + 3, 3: "Blessed is the man who attains wisdom and walks in the law of the Most High" (אשרי אדם השיג חוכמה ויתהלך בתורת עליון; cf. Prov 3:13 MT: "Blessed is the man who finds wisdom, and the man who obtains understanding" [אשרי אדם מצא חכמה ואדם יפיק תבונה]). Then a bit later in the document, we find the same correlation of "spirit" and "zeal" that emerges in the Treatise of the Two Spirits, all in a context of extolling the benefits of humility in the ways of the righteous over the pride of the wicked:

> Those who love God walk humbly in it and in [the] wa[ys of…] […without] answer and having zeal [ומקנאת] without […] that he might not understand because of an erra[nt] spirit [… that he might not] know because of a perverted spirit […] with weakness and causes stumbling witho[ut …] certainty and sends away without … pride and exalts [גאוה ומרימת] without [… and]honor[s without

...] because of the inclination of [...] thoughts [...] because of a troubl[ed] spirit. (4Q525 5, 13–7, 5; my translation)⁴⁸

The foregoing analysis demonstrates that Jewish writers could and did foreground the language of zeal, quite apart from the Hellenistic topos of envy. This evidence suggests that sapiential writers who read Prov 3 would find the explicit warning against having קנאה/ζῆλος toward evildoers (cf. Prov 23:17; 24:1, 19) wholly compatible with the matters they address in their own writing, perhaps enough so that the concept of קנאה/ζῆλος would be used to organize and punctuate a given passage. James is such a writer.

IV. The Progression from ζῆλος to φθόνος in James 3:13–4:10

What remains is to explain why James would refer to Prov 3 as a passage "concerning φθόνος" when in fact Prov 3:31 LXX uses the verb ζηλόω. Here we may recall that Johnson sees in James's use of φθόνος a parallel with the Testament of Simeon, where both φθόνος and ζῆλος are used. Although the terms are not synonymous, as Johnson claims, and although no appeal to a Hellenistic topos is necessary, James's use of φθόνος is helpfully illuminated by comparing the two texts.

In the Testament of Simeon, the ζηλ- word group is used only three times, and each instance demonstrates that the negative evaluation of the term must be provided by context. Testament of Simeon 2:6 directly alludes to the anecdote in Gen 37:11, where ζηλόω expresses the brothers' "jealousy" toward Joseph.⁴⁹ In T. Sim. 4:9 the object of zeal reveals the negative character of the term: a "zeal for evil" (ζῆλος κακίας). Likewise, in T. Sim. 4:5, ζῆλος is determined to be negative by its pairing with φθόνος, a word that is evaluated negatively. This is similar to what James has done with the movement from ζῆλος in 3:14, 16 and 4:2 to φθόνος in 4:5 and can be explained without recourse to a Hellenistic topos. The usage in both James and the Testament of Simeon resonates with a description found already in Isocrates: an envious person (φθόνος) is one whose good emulation (ζῆλος) has degenerated into jealous imitation because of unfulfilled desires.⁵⁰

---

⁴⁸ Adapted from Florentino García Martínez and Eibert J. C. Tigchelaar, *The Dead Sea Scrolls Study Edition*, 2 vols. (Leiden: Brill, 1997–1998), 2:1055. So also Ortlund: "[the] context is the blessings of humility instead of pride" (*Zeal without Knowledge*, 94).

⁴⁹ Some manuscripts also include the phrase τὸ πνεῦμα τοῦ ζήλου in 2:7; even if original the reference is still to Gen 37:11.

⁵⁰ E.g., Isocrates writes, "I am of the opinion that ... all those who are envious of my success covet the ability to think and speak well.... [T]hey grow irritated, jealous [ζηλοτυπεῖν], perturbed in spirit.... They envy [ζηλοῦσι] the good fortune of [others].... I do not want to descend to the level of men whom envy [φθόνος] has made blind" (*Antid.* 244–259; cf. *Phil.* 11). Saïd characterizes Isocrates's description of one who is envious as a sort of "ζηλωτής manqué" ("Envy and Emulation," 221).

James's text displays something here that is less apparent in the Testament of Simeon but resonates nicely with Prov 3, as well as with the sequence of occurrences of קנאה in the Treatise on the Two Spirits discussed above. In Prov 3:31 (as in much of Proverbs), the listener is encouraged to seek, strive toward, and pursue what is good (3:17, 27–28) and peaceful (3:17, 23) as opposed to what is evil (3:29–31). James, asking about "who is wise and understanding" (3:13), encourages his readers to see in Prov 3 a firm rebuke of those who should be zealous for what is "good" (Jas 3:13, 17) and brings "peace" (Jas 3:17–18) but whose zeal is "bitter" (Jas 3:13), paired with "strife" (ἐριθεία, Jas 3:16), and directed toward murder (Jas 4:2). This is the key for grasping the logic of the passage: James uses a play on language found in writers such as Isocrates to make the point that the ζῆλος described in Prov 3 is no ζῆλος at all but has degenerated into φθόνος.

V. Implications for the Interpretive Crux in James 4:5–6

In the reading presented here, the paraenetic usefulness of the pattern of ζῆλος/φθόνος derives from Prov 3 itself, regardless of whether the Hellenistic topos also influenced James's writing. Importantly, such a reading sits comfortably with recent interpretive trends regarding the notorious crux in Jas 4:5: the ideas that (1) the formula in 4:5 does not introduce a citation of an unknown text, and (2) it is the human spirit (rather than God's) that "envies."[51] Commentators have long battled over the many options, and no panacea is proffered here. Yet Friedrich Spitta's contention some 120 years ago that πρὸς φθόνον should be taken with λέγει rather than with ἐπιποθεῖ has never been sufficiently refuted, and a recent study by William J. Johnston has advanced Spitta's reading with considerable force.[52] Interpreters usually insist that πρὸς φθόνον must be taken with ἐπιποθεῖ because ἐπιποθεῖ would otherwise indicate a positive "desire" (cf. Rom 1:11, 2 Cor 5:2, Phil 1:8, 2:26, 1 Pet 2:2). Yet to take πρὸς φθόνον in the adverbial sense of "jealously" is somewhat

---

[51] Surveys of the interpretive options are readily available; see, e.g., Craig B. Carpenter, "James 4.5 Reconsidered," *NTS* 46 (2000): 189–205; and Sophie Laws, "Does Scripture Speak in Vain? A Reconsideration of James IV.5," *NTS* 20 (1974): 210–15. For a compelling argument that the reference cannot be to God's φθόνος, see Joel Marcus, "The Evil Inclination in the Epistle of James," *CBQ* 44 (1982): 606–21, here 608–9 n. 7; Richard Bauckham, "The Spirit of God in Us Loathes Envy: James 4:5," in *The Holy Spirit and Christian Origins: Essays in Honor of James D. G. Dunn*, ed. Graham N. Stanton, Bruce W. Longenecker, and Stephen C. Barton (Grand Rapids: Eerdmans, 2004), 270–81, here 273. Ralph P. Martin's claim that both ζῆλος and φθόνος "are often used for the 'jealousy' of God" is patently false, since the examples he cites (1 Macc 8:16; T. Sim. 4:5; T. Gad 7:2; 1 Clem. 3.2; 4.7; 5.2) all refer to *people*, not God (*James*, WBC 48 [Waco, TX: Word, 1988], 150).

[52] Friedrich Spitta, *Der Brief des Jakobus* (Göttingen: Vandenhoeck & Ruprecht, 1896), 118; J. William Johnston, "James 4:5 and the Jealous Spirit," *BSac* 170 (2013): 344–60.

forced, and Johnston is correct that the context already makes clear that "desire" here is negative (as it does, e.g., in Sir 25:21). From a grammatical perspective, the phrase πρὸς φθόνον can naturally be seen to express opposition ("against jealousy") or reference ("with reference to jealousy").[53] Against Franz Mussner's complaint that περί would be more fitting than πρός, Johnston points to numerous examples that show that reference is regularly expressed when πρός is used with a verb of saying, for example, Rom 8:31 (τί οὖν ἐροῦμεν πρὸς ταῦτα).[54]

There is little space here to address the debate about whether James's reference is to God's spirit or the human spirit, apart from stating that the context of Prov 3 strongly favors the latter. If it is true (as I suggested above) that James's text prompts readers to consider the question of the proper ends to which zeal must be directed, the ambiguity of the word ἐπιποθέω ("desire") is rhetorically effective: "The spirit that he has made to dwell in us desires [ἐπιποθεῖ]"—so, reader, what kinds of things will the human spirit desire? Will it demonstrate rightly directed ζῆλος, or will it degenerate into φθόνος?

Although this reading fits the context nicely, one may object that the term "spirit" does not seem to derive from Proverbs. If the term does not occur in Prov 3 (and in fact appears only once in Proverbs [15:4]), how does the phrase regarding "the spirit he has made to dwell in us" fit as part of what the Scripture says "concerning jealousy" (πρὸς φθόνον, Jas 4:5)? Decisive here is our examination of sapiential literature, which determined that early Jewish texts that interact meaningfully with Proverbs regularly speak of the "spirit." In addition, in passages ranging from Genesis and Exodus (e.g., Gen 41:38–39, Exod 31:3) to Isaiah (e.g., Isa 11:2), the spirit is linked with *wisdom*, and wisdom is highly personified (e.g., Prov 8:22–31).[55] Thus, concern about the misplaced desire of the spirit that God "has made to dwell in us" (Jas 4:5) is fitting, particularly since the pursuit of true wisdom (as presented in Prov 3) and the manifestation of misdirected zeal in the actions of evil men (Prov 3:31) are prominent concerns in Jas 3:13–4:10.

---

[53] Martin notes that there would be no difficulty in repunctuating the Greek ("the same sense would be obtained [so that it reads] 'that the scripture speaks in vain against envy,' making φθόνον the object of the verb") and notes that interpreters dismiss this "for no real reason" (*James*, 141). Dibelius notes Spitta's reading of πρὸς φθόνον ("with regard to jealousy") and points to two Greek variants (241 and 489) and the Latin of *ff* (aut pu tatis quoniam dicit scriptura ad invidiam convalescit spiritus qui habitat in vobis) that seem to read πρὸς φθόνον the same way, but Dibelius still concludes that the usage is adverbial (*James*, 222 n. 80).

[54] Franz Mussner, *Der Jakobusbrief: Auslegung*, HThKNT 13 (Freiburg im Breisgau: Herder, 1964), 181; Johnston, "James 4:5," 357. See, e.g., Matt 19:8, 27:14, Mark 10:5, Luke 14:6, Acts 24:16, and Heb 1:7–9. See also Daniel B. Wallace, *Greek Grammar beyond the Basics* (Grand Rapids: Zondervan, 1996), 380; BDAG, s.v. "πρός," 3.d.α; BDF §239.5, 6.

[55] See further, e.g., Davids, *Epistle of James*, 52.

VI. Conclusion

The repeated references to "zeal" in Jas 3:13–4:10 are best accounted for not by reference to the Hellenistic topos of envy but by close attention to the influence of Prov 3 on the logic of James's passage. The Letter of James is a Hellenistic document, to be sure, but comparison with early Jewish wisdom literature shows the profoundly *sapiential* nature of the letter. By attending closely to Prov 3, James highlights for his readers the way that misdirected zeal manifests itself in the neglect of the needy, distorted friendship, and emulation of the ways of evil/violent people (Prov 3:27, 29, 31). Since it is precisely these concerns that are woven throughout James, the present study validates our continuing efforts to "poke about" in such a highly contested section of the epistle.

Annual Index
Volume 136 (2017)

Abernethy, Diana, "Translation of Horse Colors in Zechariah 1:8; 6:2–3, 6 Based on Textual and Material Evidence," 593–607

Albrecht, Felix. *See* Suciu, Alin

Aster, Shawn Zelig, "Isaiah 31 as a Response to Rebellions against Assyria in Philistia," 347–61

Balch, David L., "Mary's Magnificat (Luke 1:46b–55) and the Price of Corn in Mexico," 651–65

Baum, Armin D., "Content and Form: Authorship Attribution and Pseudonymity in Ancient Speeches, Letters, Lectures, and Translations—A Rejoinder to Bart Ehrman," 381–403

Ben-Dov, Jonathan. See Ratzon, Eshbal

Botner, Max, "The Messiah Is 'the Holy One': ὁ ἅγιος τοῦ θεοῦ as a Messianic Title in Mark 1:24," 417–33

Brooten, Bernadette J., "Research on the New Testament and Early Christian Literature May Assist the Churches in Setting Ethical Priorities," 229–36

Cho, Paul K.-K., "Job 2 and 42:7–10 as Narrative Bridge and Theological Pivot," 857–77

Cook, Gregory D., "Naqia and Nineveh in Nahum: Ambiguity and the Prostitute Queen," 895–904

Dinkler, Michal Beth, "Building Character on the Road to Emmaus: Lukan Characterization in Contemporary Literary Perspective," 687–706

Evans, Paul S., "Creating a New 'Great Divide': The Exoticization of Ancient Culture in Some Recent Applications of Orality Studies to the Bible," 749–64

Gafney, Wil, "A Reflection on the Black Lives Matter Movement and Its Impact on My Scholarship," 204–7

Gaventa, Beverly Roberts, "Reading Romans 13 with Simone Weil: Toward a More Generous Hermeneutic," 7–22

Geobey, Ronald A., "Joseph the Infiltrator, Jacob the Conqueror? Reexamining the Hyksos–Hebrew Correlation, 23–37

Goldstone, Matthew, "Rebuke, Lending, and Love: An Early Exegetical Tradition on Leviticus 19:17–18," 307–21

Greene, Nathaniel E., "Creation, Destruction, and a Psalmist's Plea: Rethinking the Poetic Structure of Psalm 74," 85–101

Grillo, Jennie, "'From a Far Country': Daniel in Isaiah's Babylon," 363–80

Grindheim, Sigurd, "A Theology of Glory: Paul's Use of Δόξα-Terminology in Romans," 451–65

Hollenback, George M., "Who Is Doing What to Whom Revisited: Another Look at Leviticus 18:22 and 20:13," 529–37

Janzen, David, "Yahwistic Appropriation of Achaemenid Ideology and the Function of Nehemiah 9 in Ezra-Nehemiah," 839–56

Gafney, Wil, Nyasha Junior, Kenneth Ngwa, Richard Newton, Bernadette J. Brooten, and Tat-siong Benny Liew, *JBL* Forum: "Black Lives Matter for Critical Biblical Scholarship," 203–44

Jeon, Jaeyoung, "The Visit of Jethro (Exodus 18): Its Composition and Levitical Reworking," 289–306

Johnson, Nathan C., "Romans 1:3–4: Beyond Antithetical Parallelism," 467–90

Junior, Nyasha, "The Scholarly Network," 208–12

Jurgens, Blake A., "Is It Pesher? Readdressing the Relationship between the Epistle of Jude and the Qumran Pesharim," 491–510

Keefer, Arthur, "A Shift in Perspective: The Intended Audience and a Coherent Reading of Proverbs 1:1–7," 103–16

Kiel, Micah D., "The Open Horizon of Mark 13," 145–62

Kiel, Yishai, "Reinventing Mosaic Torah in Ezra-Nehemiah in the Light of the Law (*dāta*) of Ahura Mazda and Zarathustra," 323–45

Kislev, Itamar, "Joshua (and Caleb) in the Priestly Spies Story and Joshua's Initial Appearance in the Priestly Source: A Contribution to an Assessment of the Pentateuchal Priestly Material," 39–55

Kochenash, Michael, "You Can't Hear 'Aeneas' without Thinking of Rome," 667–85

Kraus, Matthew, "Rabbinic Traditions in Jerome's Translation of the Book of Numbers," 539–63

Kujanpää, Katja, "From Eloquence to Evading Responsibility: The Rhetorical Functions of Quotations in Paul's Argumentation," 185–202

Lappenga, Benjamin, "James 3:13–4:10 and the Language of Envy in Proverbs 3," 989–1006

Lee-Sak, Yitzhak, "The Lists of Levitical Cities (Joshua 21, 1 Chronicles 6) and the Propagandistic Map for the Hasmonean Territorial Expansion," 783–800

Leuchter, Mark, "The Aramaic Transition and the Redaction of the Pentateuch," 249–68

Liew, Tat-siong Benny, "Black Scholarship Matters," 237–44

Litwa, M. David, "Paul the 'god' in Acts 28: A Comparison with Philoctetes," 707–26

MacDonald, Nathan, "The Date of the Shema (Deuteronomy 6:4–5)," 765–82

Matthews, Shelly, "Fleshly Resurrection, Authority Claims, and the Scriptural Practices of Lukan Christianity," 163–83

Naselli, Andrew David, "Is Every Sin outside the Body except Immoral Sex? Weighing Whether 1 Corinthians 6:18b Is Paul's Statement or a Corinthian Slogan," 969–87

Newton, Richard, "The African American Bible: Bound in a Christian Nation," 221–28

Ngwa, Kenneth, "At Exodus as the Door of (No) Return," 213–20

Pajunen, Mika S., "The Saga of Judah's Kings Continues: The Reception of Chronicles in the Late Second Temple Period," 565–84

Park, Wongi, "Her Memorial: An Alternative Reading of Matthew 26:13," 131–44

Ratzon, Eshbal, and Jonathan Ben-Dov, "A Newly Reconstructed Calendrical Scroll from Qumran in Cryptic Script," 905–36

Rogland, Max, "A 'Cryptic Phrase' in Haggai 2:6," 585–92

Schlimm, Matthew Richard, "Jealousy or Furnace Remelting? A Response to Nissim Amzallag," 513–28

Schwiebert, Jonathan, "Jesus's Question to Pilate in Mark 15:2," 937–47

Shuali, Eran, "Did Peter Speak Hebrew to the Servant? A Linguistic Examination of the Expression 'I Do Not Know What You Are Saying' (Matt 26:70, Mark 14:68, Luke 22:60)," 405–16

Sneed, Mark, "הבל as 'Worthless' in Qoheleth: A Critique of Michael V. Fox's 'Absurd' Thesis," 879–94

Strait, Drew J., "The Wisdom of Solomon, Ruler Cults, and Paul's Polemic against Idols in the Areopagus Speech," 609–32

Suciu, Alin, and Felix Albrecht, "Remarks on a Coptic Sahidic Fragment of 3 Kingdoms, Previously Described as an Apocryphon of Solomon," 57–62

Toorn, Karel van der, "Celebrating the New Year with the Israelites: Three Extrabiblical Psalms from Papyrus Amherst 63," 633–49

Troftgruben, Troy M., "Slow Sailing in Acts: Suspense in the Final Sea Journey (Acts 27:1–28:15)," 949–68

Trotter, Jonathan R., "2 Maccabees 10:1–8: Who Wrote It and Where Does It Belong?," 117–30

Vermeulen, Karolien, "Hands, Heads, and Feet: Body Parts as Poetic Device in Judges 4–5," 801–19

Warner, Megan, "'Therefore a Man Leaves His Father and His Mother and Clings to His Wife': Marriage and Intermarriage in Genesis 2:24," 269–88

Wasserman, Emma, "Gentile Gods at the Eschaton: A Reconsideration of Paul's 'Principalities and Powers' in 1 Corinthians 15," 727–46

Whitters, Mark, "The Persianized Liturgy of Nehemiah 8:1–8*," 63–84

Wilson, Benjamin, "Directly Addressing 'Jesus': The Vocative Ἰησοῦ in Luke 23:42," 435–49

Yee, Gale A., "'He Will Take the Best of Your Fields': Royal Feasts and Rural Extraction," 821–38

New and Recent Titles

Biblical Archaeology Society 2017 Publication Award Winner
A POLITICAL HISTORY OF THE ARAMEANS
From Their Origins to the End of Their Polities
K. Lawson Younger Jr.
Paperback $97.95, 978-1-58983-128-5   886 pages, 2016   Code: 061713
Hardcover $117.95, 978-1-62837-080-5   E-book $97.95, 978-1-62837-084-3
Archaeology and Biblical Studies 13

FIGHTING FOR THE KING AND THE GODS
A Survey of Warfare in the Ancient Near East
Charlie Trimm
Paperback $89.95, 978-1-62837-184-0   748 pages, 2017   Code 060394
Hardcover $109.95, 978-0-88414-238-6   E-book $89.95, 978-0-88414-237-9
Resources for Biblical Study 88

SARGON II, KING OF ASSYRIA
Josette Elayi
Paperback $41.95, 978-1-62837-177-2   310 pages, 2017   Code: 061722
Hardcover $56.95, 978-0-88414-224-9   E-book $41.95, 978-0-88414-223-2
Archaeology and Biblical Studies 22

UNCOVERING ANCIENT FOOTPRINTS
Armenian Inscriptions and the
Pilgrimage Routes of the Sinai
Michael E. Stone
Paperback $34.95, 978-1-62837-173-4   202 pages, 2017   Code: 069024
Hardcover $49.95, 978-0-88414-216-4   E-book $34.95, 978-0-88414-215-7

LIFE IN KINGS
Reshaping the Royal Story in the Hebrew Bible
A. Graeme Auld
Paperback $39.95, 978-1-62837-171-0   330 pages, 2017   Code 062632
Hardcover $54.95, 978-0-88414-212-6   E-book $39.95, 978-0-88414-211-9
Ancient Israel and Its Literature 30

SENSING WORLD, SENSING WISDOM
The Cognitive Foundation of Biblical Metaphors
Nicole L. Tilford
Paperback $34.95, 978-1-62837-175-8   258 pages, 2017   Code 062634
Hardcover $49.95, 978-0-88414-220-1   E-book $34.95, 978-0-88414-219-5
Ancient Israel and Its Literature 31

SBL Press • P.O. Box 2243 • Williston, VT 05495-2243
Phone: 877-725-3334 (toll-free) or 802-864-6185 • Fax: 802-864-7626
Order online at www.sbl-site.org/publications

SBL PRESS

New and Recent Titles

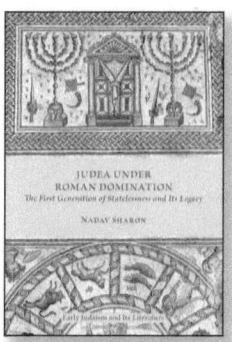

JUDEA UNDER ROMAN DOMINATION
The First Generation of Statelessness and Its Legacy
Nadav Sharon
Paperback $79.95, 978-1-62837-176-5   552 pages, 2017   Code 063547
Hardcover $99.95, 978-0-88414-222-5 E-book $79.95, 978-0-88414-221-8
Early Judaism and Its Literature 46

REFLECTIONS OF EMPIRE IN ISAIAH 1–39
Responses to Assyrian Ideology
Shawn Zelig Aster
Digital open access, 978-0-88414-272-0
https://www.sbl-site.org/publications/Books_ANEmonographs.aspx
Paperback $54.95, 978-1-62837-201-4   382 pages, 2017   Code: 062823
Hardcover $74.95, 978-0-88414-273-7 Ancient Near East Monographs 19

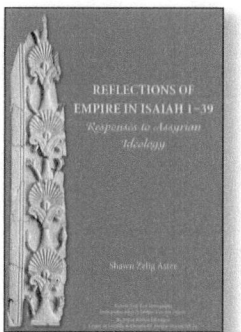

THE SBL COMMENTARY ON THE SEPTUAGINT
An Introduction
Dirk Büchner, editor
Paperback $37.95, 978-1-62837-187-1   280 pages, 2017   Code 060466
Hardcover $52.95, 978-0-88414-244-7 E-book $37.95, 978-0-88414-243-0
Septuagint and Cognate Studies 66

READING THE BIBLE IN ANCIENT TRADITIONS AND MODERN EDITIONS
Studies in Memory of Peter W. Flint
Andrew B. Perrin, Kyung S. Baek, and Daniel K. Falk, editors
Paperback $82.95, 978-1-62837-191-8   746 pages, 2017   Code: 063546
Hardcover $102.95, 978-0-88414-254-6 E-book $82.95, 978-0-88414-253-9
Early Judaism and Its Literature 47

PEDAGOGY IN ANCIENT JUDAISM AND EARLY CHRISTIANITY
Karina Martin Hogan, Matthew Goff, and Emma Wasserman, editors
Paperback $49.95, 978-1-62837-165-9   424 pages, 2017   Code 063548
Hardcover $64.95, 978-0-88414-208-9 E-book $49.95, 978-0-88414-207-2
Early Judaism and Its Literature 41

SBL Press • P.O. Box 2243 • Williston, VT 05495-2243
Phone: 877-725-3334 (toll-free) or 802-864-6185 • Fax: 802-864-7626
Order online at www.sbl-site.org/publications

www.ingramcontent.com/pod-product-compliance
Lightning Source LLC
Chambersburg PA
CBHW021823300426
44114CB00009BA/291